The Holy Axis

A Modern Grail Pilgrimage Across the Neck of Britain
Exploring Sacred Sites and the Earth's Hidden Energies

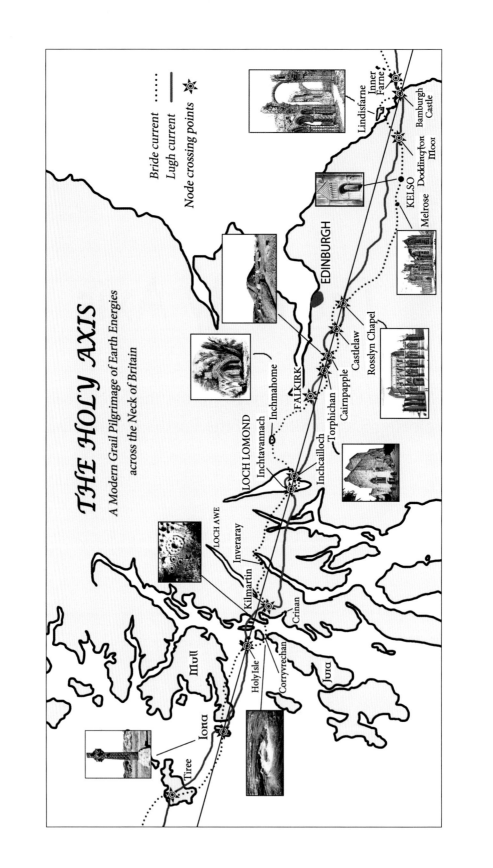

THE HOLY AXIS

*A Modern Grail Pilgrimage of Earth Energies
across the Neck of Britain*

Bride current ·······
Lugh current ────
Node crossing points ✦

Inner Farne
Lindisfarne
Bamburgh Castle
Doddington Moor
KELSO
Melrose
EDINBURGH
Castlelaw
Cairnpapple
Rosslyn Chapel
Torphichan
FALKIRK
Inchmahome
Inchtavannach
LOCH LOMOND
Inchcailloch
LOCH AWE
Inveraray
Kilmartin
Crinan
Mull
Holy Isle
Corryvrechan
Jura
Iona
Tiree

The Holy Axis

A Modern Grail Pilgrimage Across the Neck of Britain
Exploring Sacred Sites and the Earth's Hidden Energies

Gary Biltcliffe
Caroline Hoare

Thus saith the Lord

Stand ye in the ways and see

And ask for the old paths

Where is the good ways

And walk therein

And ye shall find rest for your souls

(Jeremiah VI 16)

Sacred Lands Publishing

© 2023 Gary Biltcliffe and Caroline Hoare

Published by
Sacred Lands Publishing
www.belinusline.com

First published 2023 by Sacred Lands Publishing

ISBN: 978-0-9572382-2-0

British Library Cataloguing in Publication Data
A catalogue record for this book is available from the British Library

All photographs, line drawings and maps are by Gary Biltcliffe and Caroline Hoare unless otherwise stated
Front cover artwork by Yuri Leitch designed by Yuri Leitch and Gary Biltcliffe
Back cover photos by Caroline Hoare and Gary Biltcliffe

Set in 11/12.5 pt by Beamreach
Printed and bound by Beamreach (www.beamreachuk.co.uk)

This book is dedicated to those who walk the trails with love in their hearts, tread the paths of truth, and seek the timeless wisdom of the grail.

Contents

Acknowledgements

Over the past ten years, many people have kindly helped us with our Holy Axis quest. Special thanks go to Grahame Gardner for his help and guidance at different sites along the line and Sue Turnbull for hosting our research in Northumberland and providing insight. Also, our friends Bill Holding and Nigel Twinn for helping to organise that unforgettable weekend dowse on Lindisfarne, and of course Ronnie and Rebecca Neilson for accompanying us on some magical adventures risking life and limb to get to the Garvellachs. Thanks also go to the help we have received from the higher planes with the aid of various individuals, including our friends Marie Field and Alphedia Arara Kenchington.

We are again indebted to Yuri Leitch, whose insightful artwork for the front cover is all part of the Holy Axis adventure, and to Rob Wildwood for his amazing photos and for accompanying us to the lost city of Roxburgh and its enchanted castle. We are also grateful to Paul Broadhurst for allowing us to reproduce the St Michael Line map and preserve the legacy of Hamish Miller and his dowsing discoveries.

We would also like to thank Hugh McArthur, the late Philip Coppens, Bamburgh Research Project and The Heritage Centre in Kilmartin for their valuable insights and research, and the staff at Bamburgh Castle for their fascinating stories and permission to use our photos. Also, the staff and trustees of Rosslyn Chapel for preserving a temple of wisdom.

Finally, special thanks goes to Marian Cavin for her invaluable support, which has helped make this book possible.

Picture Credits

Engraving of Badminton Estate in the County of Gloucester by Johannes Kip c.1712. Published by Leiden, 1707. Public Domain.

Nazca Lines, courtesy of Wojciech Kocot, CC BY-SA 4.0, Wikimedia Commons.

Arch Angel Michael in Monte Gargano by Cesare Nebbia. CC0 1.0 Universal (CC0 1.0), Wikimedia Commons.

17th century Woodcut of the Widecombe Storm and ball lightening, artist unknown. Public Domain, Wikimedia Commons.

Twin-jet nebula showing the classic features of a plasma z-pinch, courtesy of ESA/ Hubble].

Lindisfarne Priory with view of the castle, courtesy of Stephen Brown. CC BY 4.0, Wikimedia Commons.

Map of Lindisfarne, Holy Island (1866) by Capt. E.R. James (Contours), Colonel Cameron (Engraving). Nilfanion (SVG) Derivative work MagentaGreen - Own work under the use of the file Northumberland_UK_constituency_map_(blank). svg based on the following document: Northumberland XII (includes: Elwick; Holy Island; Kyloe; Ross.) National Library of Scotland, CC BY-SA 3.0, Wikimedia Commons.

Ardagh Chalice. Collections of the National Museum of Ireland, Kildare Street. By Sailko, CC BY 3.0, Wikimedia Commons.

St Mary's Church, Lindisfarne, courtesy of David Smith. Flickr: CC BY 2.0, Wikimedia Commons.

Dragon carving inside Bamburgh Castle, by kind permission of Bamburgh Castle Estate.

Green Man carving inside Bamburgh Castle, by kind permission of Bamburgh Castle Estate.

Well inside the Keep at Bamburgh Castle, by kind permission of Bamburgh Castle Estate.

Sir Lancelot at the Chapel of the Holy Grail from The Earthly Paradise by Edward Burne-Jones 1890s. Public Domain. Wikimedia Commons.

Engraving of Lancelot on the Road to Shalott by Gustave Doré 1867. Public Domain. Wikimedia Commons.

Lancelot on the road to Shalott in Gustave Doré's 1867 illustration for Tennyson. Public Domain. Wikimedia Commons.

Lancelot and the dragon By Arthur Rackham. Public Domain, Wikimedia Commons.

Etching of the knight's tomb in Bamburgh Church, unknown author. Northumberland County Archives.

The Laidly Worm of Spindleston Heugh by Walter Crane 1881. Public Domain, Wikimedia Commons.

Illuminated manuscript from Bede's Life of St Cuthbert, showing the discovery of the saint's Incorrupt Body. Body of Cuthbert. British Library MS 39943 By unknown monk. Public Domain, Wikimedia Commons.

Dechmont Law, courtesy of Taras Young. CC BY-SA 3.0, Wikimedia Commons.

View of Falkirk, engraving by John Heaviside Clark 1824. Public Domain. Wikimedia Commons.

Map of Falkirk from 1645 Joan Blaeu Antique Map of The County of Stirling, Scotland. Public Domain. Wikimedia Commons.

Arthur's Oven or Oon by Alexander Gordon 1726. Public Domain. Wikimedia Commons.

Mousa Broch, Shetland, Scotland by Otter, CC BY-SA 3.0, Wikimedia Commons.

Aerial view of Inchmahome Priory, Lake of Menteith, courtesy of Andrew Shiva / Wikipedia / CC BY-SA 4.0, Wikipedia Commons.

Aberfoyle Old Parish Kirk with Doon Hill in the background, courtesy of Creagmhor. CC BY-SA 4.0, Wikimedia Commons.

Will-o'-the-wisp and snake, col lithograph by Hermann Hendrich 1931. Public Domain. Wikimedia Commons.

View of Loch Lomond from the summit of Conic Hill courtesy of Yvesdebxl CC BY-SA 4.0, Wikimedia Commons.

Reconstruction of Roman Vindobala by unknown author. Schautafel am Kastellgelände. CC0 1.0, Wikimedia Commons.

The Hills of Dunipace, courtesy of Nigel J C Turnbull. CC BY-SA 2.0, geograph.org.uk.

UFO incident at Rendlesham, courtesy of Dimìtar Nàydenov. CC BY-SA 3.0, Wikimedia Commons.

Kilmalieu, old town of Inveraray with Dun na Cuaiche in the background, drawing by Paul and Thomas Sandby. Postcard illustration based on the drawings of Paul and Thomas Sandby while in the 3rd Duke's employ. Public Domain. Wikimedia Commons.

Devils' handprint Kilneuair Church © *Ronald Morris 1977.* BRAC website.

Plan of fort on summit of Dunadd © Crown Copyright: Historic Environment Scotland (Society of Antiquaries of Scotland Collection).

The Corryvreckan Whirlpool, courtesy of Walter Baxter. CC BY-SA 2.0, Wikimedia Commons.

Cailleach and her hammer, illustrated by John Duncan in Wonder Tales from Scottish Myth and Legend (1917) by Donald Alexander Mackenzie. Public Domain. Wikimedia Commons.

Cornacopia drawing by Yves, CC BY-SA 3.0, Wikimedia Commons.

Engraving of Orion the Hunter by Elijah H. Burritt 1835. Pl. III. "The Constellations (January, February, March)". From *Atlas, Designed to Illustrate the Geography of the Heavens.* Hartford: F.J. Huntington. Public Domain. Wikimedia Commons.

Loch Buie, Isle of Mull, courtesy of W. L. Tarbert. CC BY 3.0, Wikimedia Commons.

Carsaig Arches by Hopgrove James. Public Domain, Wikimedia Commons.

The Holy Isle of Iona. By PaulT (Gunther Tschuch) CC BY-SA 4.0, Wikimedia Commons.

Map of Iona 1879 shaped like a fish or dove. By John Bartholomew - http://www.eccentricbliss.com/tag/john-bartholomew/, Public Domain. Wikimedia Commons.

About the Authors

Gary Biltcliffe was born in 1960 and brought up in Lancashire. He has dedicated the last 30 years to historical research and investigation of earth mysteries, dowsing ancient sites, uncovering lost knowledge and early folklore. He has appeared on radio and television and has lectured widely in the UK and North America. Gary has also led International groups around Britain's sacred sites and written articles for journals and magazines. He moved to Dorset in 1993 and researched much of its ancient history culminating in his first publication *The Spirit of Portland, Revelations of a Sacred Isle* in 2009, republished as a revised edition in 2022 entitled *Mysterious Portland*. In 2012 he co-authored *The Spine of Albion* and *The Power of Centre* in 2018 with his partner Caroline Hoare.

Caroline Hoare was born in 1958 and brought up on a farm in the heart of the Dart Valley in South Devon. She started her working life in a Fine Art auction house and later transferred to the world of publishing and book selling. Caroline moved from London to Dorset in 2003 and trained as a Geomancer, Feng Shui Consultant and Holistic Interior Designer. She has also spent the last thirteen years alongside Gary travelling to lost cities around the world, researching history and ancient civilisations and has a keen interest in the mythology and folklore of Britain. Caroline continues to research and write alongside Gary and co-authored *The Spine of Albion* and *The Power of Centre*.

'Cadmus and the Dragon' from a 6th century BCE Laconian black-figure pottery kylix depicting an archetype of the warrior god Lugh/Orion, a bird (raven), a hare (Lepus constellation below Orion), a serpent and the world pillar (Apprentice Pillar at Rosslyn Chapel), all features of The Holy Axis.

The Salisbury Ley

Introduction

Leys and Linear Features

Since the 1920s, *leys* or ley lines have been scrutinised, explored, debunked, demystified and resurrected, but in these unpredictable times, the concept has found its way back into our consciousness. Today it is once more enticing people to explore Britain's landscape and discover its magical places. Modern ley hunters have rekindled a desire to understand their heritage with an added sense of adventure, mystery and imagination never seen before.

But what is the real truth about this influential network of invisible straight lines crisscrossing our countryside? Are they natural telluric energy beams of etheric power linking sacred sites – if so, what purpose do they serve? Are the ancient linear features in our landscape somehow marking or recording the old hidden paths that are now beyond our perception?

Secreted beneath our feet is evidence of a man-made network of straight paths connecting Britain's sacred sites, although their true purpose is yet to be understood by academia.

Between 4000 BCE and 2000 BCE, the Neolithic peoples built a series of parallel earthen banks around the country, some stretching for several miles. 18th-century antiquarian William Stukeley referred to these linear features in 1723 when remarking about the 'noble' earthwork about half a mile north of Stonehenge in Wiltshire. He believed it was a racecourse and called it by its Latin name – *cursus*. In their book *Lines on the Landscape: Leys and Other Linear Enigmas*, Paul Devereux and Nigel Pennick assembled the site names and grid references of over fifty-one cursuses collated from fragmented archaeological records and aerial photography.[1]

Many of these features are no longer visible on the ground except for small surviving sections, and the remainder are only revealed from the air through crop marks or dark patches in fields after ploughing. However, some lines cluster in areas such as Barford in the Avon Valley near Warwick, where three linear earthworks of differing orientations point towards pre-Reformation churches. Perhaps they mirrored the linear beams of energy that our ancient ancestors could perceive, and the religious houses were deliberately erected on these lines to absorb their power. Many churches stand over former Neolithic burial sites, such as a barrow or tumulus to which the ancient feature initially aligned. Moreover, the Stonehenge Cursus has barrows at either end and can be extended with a map and ruler to include a fallen megalith called the Cuckoo Stone and Woodhenge at Durrington. It seems evident that the Neolithic culture built cursuses on these etheric energy beams to connect the living world with the realms of the dead.

Other straight-line features exist in many areas of the UK in the form of boundary markers or grouped parallel coaxial field systems, such as those on Dartmoor in Devon called *reaves*. Many Dartmoor Iron Age field systems consist of low stone banks less than 2 ft (0.5 m) high and 5 ft (1.5 m) wide, with some stretching for miles across the moor.[2] Visible from the air are straight courses in the landscape formed by

Roman roads, like the Fosse Way, Ermine Steet, Watling Street and the Icknield Way. Undoubtedly the Romans constructed these major highways, but there is evidence of an earlier system of Iron Age and Bronze Age rifle-straight ditched tracks of compacted earth that the Romans paved over for their marching armies.

From the 18th century, with the advancement of maps and surveying equipment, people began to notice that out in the open countryside, many church spires and towers aligned with others over many miles. These alignments also included mounds, crossroads, and distant hilltop features. Researchers believed this was evidence of prehistoric straight tracks that had disappeared under the plough and land development. Alfred Watkins (1855-1935) researched and catalogued these alignments and wrote *The Old Straight Track* in 1925. He was the first to use the word *ley,* which he interpreted as meaning strip-clearances along forest stretches of the old straight tracks.[3]

Many of the great estates of Europe laid out their garden landscapes using straight lines or parallel rows of trees. The designers of the Badminton estate gardens in Gloucestershire sited the landscaped avenues to align with distant church towers and burial grounds as if the knowledge and benefits of leys were known to a select few.

Devereux refers to the work of Alan Wharam, who found that the word '*laia was used in legal English, at least until the seventeenth century, as meaning a roadway in a wood*', and in French, the word still relates to such features. In a personal communication with Belgian researcher Francois Geysen, Devereux writes that the word *lei* was well-known around Antwerp and on old maps it referred to straight roads leading to a

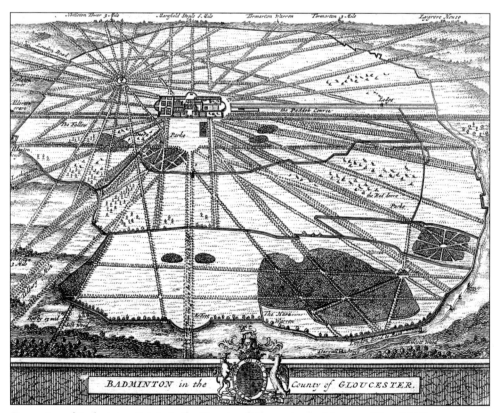

Engraving of Badminton Estate in the County of Gloucester by Johannes Kip c.1712]

church or chapel.[4] Paul Screeton, in his excellent book *Quicksilver Heritage*, explores the Sanskrit word *lelay* meaning 'to shine', perhaps taken from the root *lila* or cosmic creation, suggesting an energy linked to the cosmos. [5]

Whilst researching these straight tracks over his home county of Herefordshire, Watkins noted that natural features, including boulders, springs, fording places and hilltops, combine with artificial features such as pre-Reformation churches, castles, crossroads, hillfort camps and crosses. Moreover, they inevitably stood on much earlier prehistoric sites determined by ancient surveyors with knowledge of the geomancy that has now been either forgotten or suppressed. Perhaps the early geomancers were somehow divinely guided by a higher consciousness. It was common practice to build churches on the sites of earlier temples and gathering places, and so, whether it be a conscious or unconscious act, the stonemasons have managed to preserve the ancient ley systems.

Watkin's book inspired the formation of The Straight Track Club, its members practising a new outdoor pursuit called' ley hunting', which involved picnicking on the best viewing point of the leys. After the death of Watkins in 1935, his followers continued to record leys across the country until the 1940s. However, his theories found many critics, including archaeologists, who pointed out that given the high density of prehistoric monuments in Britain, a line drawn through any part of the country would inevitably clip several sites, including vast earthworks such as hillforts, henges and sculptured hills. As a result, his work was unrecognised by the academic world. But Watkin's research was not confined solely to observing maps, for he mentions, *'Experience and practice brings an insight, which quickly spots a ley. Often one can be first seen on the map, but I more often see it out of doors in "the lay of the land" itself, and this before the mark points are found.'*[6]

Watkins' leys were more than just tracks because they went over hills instead of going around them, and this curious behaviour is seen in the landscapes of many ancient cultures worldwide. For example, there is a massive complex of lines on the landscape at Nazca, near Cusco in Peru. Commercial air flights discovered them across the high desert plains or tablelands called *pampa*. These straight lines are a complex arrangement of crisscrossing radiating lines of various widths from 11 ins (30 cm) to 6 ft (1.8 m). Some are extremely wide, like the Stonehenge Cursus, and run parallel to one another, starting and finishing at different parts of the pampa. Most lines are formed on the ground by a 4–6 in (10–15 cm) shallow trench of light-coloured clay exposed by removing the reddish-brown, iron oxide-coated pebbles that cover the surface of the Nazca Desert.

Connected to the lines are geoglyphs in the shape of various animals created by one continuous line. Their longevity is due to the arid rainless conditions and lack of winds that would disturb its soil, and as a result, furrows dug thousands of years ago have remained virtually untouched. Various theories attempted to explain the lines and glyphs, including an astronomical device that points towards the sun, moon, planets or stars, like a gigantic calendar or map of the heavens, and runways for ancient astronauts. However, most of these ideas are unsubstantiated, so perhaps these lines had a more spiritual purpose.

Devereux noted that there was 'ritual walking' at Cuzco along straight predetermined routes during certain pilgrimages, a practice seen in other early cultures in the Americas.[7] Helaine Silverman found that many lines point to the Cahuachi burial

Nazca Lines (courtesy of Wojciech Kocot)

mounds, the ceremonial centre or axis mundi of the Nazca culture. She believes the Nazca priests observed the natural and supernatural world from there and the pampa. However, Silverman also discovered that they ritually swept the lines to maintain visibility. This link to sacred burial mounds is reminiscent of the British cursuses, also known as 'roads of the dead'. But why did these ancient cultures construct these symbolic roads connected to the dead? The answer perhaps lies in the profound spiritual practice of shamanism.

Spirit Paths and the UFO Enigma

In *Shamanism and the Mystery Lines,* Devereux states that a vital element of shamanism is the ability to use the power of the mind to astral travel through the environment and observe distant events. The shaman accomplished this by assuming the form of an animal or bird or directly through an out-of-body experience. Only with psychic ability could a man or woman practice as a shaman – perhaps a gift obtained naturally or from a near-death experience where the spirit world revealed itself. Spirit travel is fast and direct, for straight flight is the quickest way between two points – while in his spirit body, the shaman was able to project his thoughts to a place and instantly arrive there, travelling in a dead straight line like a beam of light.

Having researched hundreds of leys across Britain, there is no doubt that they connect with places of the dead as they travel through burial grounds of the earlier Neolithic, Bronze and Iron Age cultures, later usurped by the Christians and their churches and graveyards. Devereux cites European traditions that forbid the carriage of corpses to the burial ground by means other than straight roads. Furthermore, many avoided them for fear of attracting spirits. The Dutch landscape has many direct roads leading to burial places known as Doodwegan or 'death roads', many of which pass megalithic tombs of the Neolithic peoples, continuing the old traditions.[8]

However, were these spirit paths continually maintained by the various ancient cultures to specifically aid the spirit of the dead as they journeyed to the afterlife, or was it to honour the spirit flight of the shaman? Did the shamans use the discovery of these spirit lines to advise their people where to bury the dead? Interestingly, the shamans not only astral travelled along these paths of existing energy but were able to journey to the 'spirit world' to obtain knowledge for the welfare of their people. Perhaps the answer to unravelling the mystery of these straight lines lies in whether they were attracting or drawing 'spirit energy' from a divine cosmic source.

An old straight track on the Isle of Wight

Many individuals and groups worldwide have seen balls of light travelling in straight lines across the land, believing them to be spirits, elementals or intelligent alien craft from another universe using the energy of the ley to power their machines. Devereux found ethnological records of shamans deriving their powers from encounters with earth lights seen on many leys.[9] Devereux's research on the mystery lights associates the phenomena with the geological pressures of crystalline rocks in fault lines. Many believe the lights are extraterrestrial because they manoeuvre and dart around, displaying some form of inquisitive intelligence – indeed, a correlation exists between earth lights, the UFO phenomena, and straight paths and leys.

My experience of encountering a ball of light with a group of school friends near the Forest of Dean in Herefordshire changed my life. As we gazed at the stars, one of the group members suddenly spotted a slow-moving light in the clear night sky. We followed the luminous ball with our eyes as it travelled south to north, but to our surprise, it stopped dead. I mentioned that I had never seen a shooting star stop before. Then, to our amazement, it started rapidly moving towards us, growing larger and larger until it hovered about 30 ft (9 m) above us. It appeared to resemble a miniature gaseous sun. After a few seconds, it accelerated away in a straight line at an unbelievable speed. Many years later, I discovered its departure route was a well-known ley. Thousands of confirmed UFO sightings, or seemingly intelligent balls of light, are connected to leys and alignments. Many believe that the earth's natural lines of electromagnetic energy hold a power that attracts these luminous objects and aids their navigation and manifestation. Ufologists suggest that extraterrestrial UFOs use this energy and gyroscopes to power the ships and navigate.

The 1960s revival of ley research stems from Philip Heselton and Jimmy Goddard, who formed a ley hunter's club in 1962. They were initially interested in Tony Wedd's theory that UFOs followed the leys in the landscape. Wedd discovered a network of lines radiating from a crossing point near his home, connecting tree clumps and healing wells. Later, he found mysterious lights were attracted to the tree clumps leading him to believe that they were extraterrestrial astronauts who were using these earthly lines as flightpaths. In addition, Wedd was impressed by French author Aimé Michel's *Flying Saucers and the Straight Line Mystery* (1958), which mentions the 1954 French UFO 'flap', where landing sites or places where the UFOs hovered near the ground fell into straight lines, which Michel called 'orthotenies'.[10]

Paul Screeton made a profound statement when he assimilated all the various suggestions as to why UFOs are attracted to leys and concluded that unless we fully understood the nature of the UFO phenomenon, no answers would be forthcoming.[11]

Jimmy Goddard organised a London meeting in 1966 to put forward their ideas of leys and orthotenies, which John Michell and Devereux attended. Also, during that enlightening era, Professor Alexander Thom, in his book *Megalithic Sites in Britain*, introduced to the world astronomical observations of many megalithic sites, including Stonehenge and Avebury. He proposed that precise units of an ancient measure were used in constructing the monuments, leading researchers to believe that a sophisticated society must have built the standing stones on alignments orientated towards specific sun and moon risings and settings.[12]

Michell went on to write the seminal book *The View over Atlantis* in 1969, introducing a broader spectrum of the ley enigma under the umbrella term 'Earth Mysteries.' Here he refers to longer leys, particularly the St Michael Line, which seemed to follow an ancient route from Land's End to the Norfolk coast and included many hilltop churches dedicated to St Michael.

The St Michael Line became Britain's most famous long-distance ley, linking holy hills such as St Michael's Mount in Cornwall, Burrow Mump and Glastonbury Tor in Somerset. This 350-mile-long energy corridor also connects with prehistoric centres, such as the largest stone circle in the world at Avebury in Wiltshire, the Hurlers Stone Circles in Cornwall and the spiritual centres of Glastonbury Abbey in Somerset and Bury St Edmunds in Norfolk.[13]

Dragon lines and orgone energy

After publishing *The New View over Atlantis* in 1986, Michell introduced the Chinese concept of *feng shui* to explain leys and Earth's hidden energies. For example, the universal life force that flows across the land is called *chi*, meaning 'two breaths'. These vital lines of force flow along winding paths known as *lung-mei* or 'dragon veins'. The Chinese geomancers were masters of the dragon lines and trained gifted individuals called geomancers to control and manipulate these forces taking great care in constructing their towns and dwellings to regulate the chi to promote harmony and balance in the land. Some of the significant leys, such as the St Michael Line, are said to be the invisible magnetic veins of the Earth, like the meridians around the human body, as seen in Chinese acupuncture.

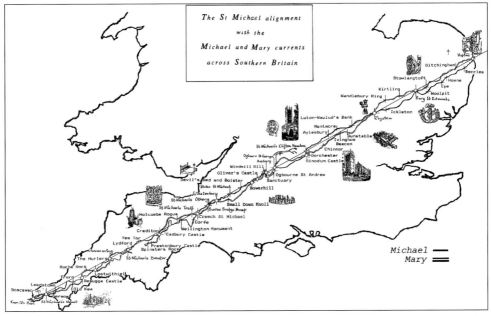

The St Michael Alignment adapted from 'The Sun and the Serpent' by Hamish Miller and Paul Broadhurst

The Chinese geomancers would influence the dragon paths to visit the emperor's palaces, tombs and holy cities to enhance their power in life and death and the success of their future lineage. Like the early kings of Britain, the emperors were ritually married to the land and controlled the energies by performing ceremonies at crucial times of the year. However, many aboriginal tribes believe it is man's task to balance the dragon force as it could destroy our health and well-being.

The feng shui masters may have recognised the Earth's energy matrix as the manifestation of primary forces such as electromagnetism, gravity and light, which quantum physicists today would see in terms of a fifth force, namely chi, orgone or plasma. Long ago, geomancers and their kings became corrupted by the power of these terrestrial forces and sought to control them instead of working positively with the land's natural energies. Even today, certain groups deliberately manipulate the darker or negative aspect of the dragon or serpent energy to amplify their darker version of the God/Goddess, thereby disconnecting humankind from the pure source or universal consciousness and imprisoning humans in a world of fear and greed. In other words, they created an independent artificial matrix or dark web to influence others to fulfil a specific negative agenda.

John Michell cites *The Chinese Dragon* by Newton Hayes, '*The Chinese recognise certain straight lines stretching out over the globe corresponding to the lines along which fiery dragons fly between their hilltop homes.*'[14] The St Michael Line links many hilltop shrines dedicated to St Michael, whose apparition began with a ball of light or fire descending from the sky. For instance, St Michael's Mount takes its name from the many appearances of St Michael warning fishermen of imminent danger. St Aubert, Bishop of Avranches in France, also saw an apparition of St Michael, which led to the construction of Mont-Saint-Michel off the coast of Northern France. The famous catholic shrine on

7

Monte Gargano also marks where a bishop in Italy had a vision of the same saint. Both Mont-San-Michel and Monte Gargano lie upon another long-distance ley researched by Miller and Broadhurst called *The Apollo and St Michael Axis*.[15]

Archangel Michael in Monte Gargano by Cesare Nebbia

Michell introduced the concept of orgone energy into the mix, first discovered by the exiled Austrian scientist Wilhelm Reich in the late 1930s in America. Orgone energy is a form of subtle radiation or wave emission produced by a particle known as *bion*, which is biological ether, created through the interaction of sunlight with all living organisms. Orgone becomes concentrated when caught by large electromagnetic bands in the upper atmosphere and geomagnetic fields on the earth's surface. Reich believed that orgone allies the concept of the cosmological ether of space and the hidden life force that regulates the planet and its weather system. Researchers have since associated orgone with the life force chi, the Japanese *ki* and the Asian Indian *prana*.[16]

Reich's discovery that straight tubes attract and focus orgone led to the discovery of the 'cloudbuster', a device consisting of long hollow tubes connected to underground water that, when pointed to a cloud, would remove its orgone potential and shrink it to become non-existent. However, he found that if he aimed the device at the edge of the cloud, orgone from underground water would increase the cloud's mass to produce rain. So, it seems that orgone and chi are the same energy, and interestingly, drawing orgone from water might be why so many leys begin or end at lakes, rivers and the sea coast. If straight lines attract orgone or chi, then perhaps the ceremonial monuments laid upon them were placed there to benefit from the healing aspects of orgone.

Reich eventually developed a device that stored this energy called an 'orgone accumulator', a chamber lined with alternating layers of organic and inorganic material to attract and focus this chi 'life force'. He built accumulators large enough to contain a person and claimed noticeable healing results when curing mental disorders and cancer. However, in experiments with orgone, Reich stumbled on 'DOR' or 'deadly orgone radiation', which has the potential to create disharmony and sickness. In feng shui, *sha* is the name of the opposite force that stops the flow of chi and interrupts and destroys the natural energy cycle. Dowsers have encountered this dark energy called 'black streams', especially where there are accident black spots or areas of earth disturbance through quarrying, new road systems or significant building developments.

Despite the positive results, investigations by the government claimed Reich's accumulators were a sham and orgone energy non-existent. As a result, a judge ordered an injunction to destroy all accumulators and cease research on orgone energy. Two years later, Reich died in prison just before his release, having served a sentence for contempt of court.

Michell writes that *'there can be no doubt that the dragon current refers to some natural flow of force, related to the earth's magnetic field and only discovered in modern times by the late Wilhelm Reich who called it orgone.'*[17]

What confuses many newcomers to ley hunting is the two types of energy associated with leys – the straight band of energy marked by the ancients in the landscape that later became the old straight tracks and the other that meanders like a serpent along the whole length of its course. This serpent or dragon-like energy is a dowsable electromagnetic current of dual polarity that accompanies and interacts with the ley, one male and one female, which cross at significant points in the landscape, creating vortexes called *nodes*. The late Hamish Miller, to whom we are greatly indebted for his pioneering dowsing of energy lines, detected these dragon paths along the St Michael

Winged Caduceus

Line and named the male energy line Michael and the female Mary. Their behaviour of entwining around the straight ley appears to mirror the ancient caduceus symbol.

Author and researcher Paul Broadhurst originally initiated Miller's quest to detect if the St Michael Line had a dowsable energy. But soon after they began following the line from Land's End, they realised its journey was not straight but a sinuous one, which weaved across the landscape visiting prehistoric sites and Christian sanctuaries on either side of the straight track alignment. Hamish's remarkable dowsing ability was due to a near-death experience that gave him the psychic ability to connect with these higher vibrational lines in the landscape. Also, his meticulous work gave the dowsing community a better understanding of earth energy currents and their behaviour. Miller

and Broadhurst's research was published in *The Sun and the Serpent* in 1989. Their discoveries continue to inspire and motivate generations of Earth Mystery enthusiasts worldwide to rediscover and re-examine their local sacred sites.[18]

The Michael and Mary lines equate to the two breaths of the chi, one male (*yang*), or white tiger, and the other female (*yin*), the blue dragon. The two breaths travel along 'secret arrows', the name given to straight courses or leys, in this case, the St Michael Line.

In the late 1970s, Devereux became editor of the popular magazine *The Ley Hunter*, first initiated in April 1965 by Philip Heselton and Jimmy Goddard. By now, exploration at sacred sites had uncovered various types of earth energy, including vortexes detected by psychic impressions and dowsing. Later, Devereux set up 'The Dragon Project' using sophisticated sensing equipment in an attempt to provide a scientific explanation for these energies at specific sites. After several years of experiments around the country, but mainly at the Rollright Stone Circle in Oxfordshire, Devereux recorded anomalies detected by ultrasound, infrasound, background radiation and magnetism, but not chi or energy lines. Devereux discovered that many sites, including stone circles, were somehow enhancing natural energy. The findings were published in *Places of Power, Secret Energies at Ancient Sites*, although they proved inconclusive and controversial.[19] This disappointed many dowsers and sensitives who continued to detect lines of chi energy at sacred sites worldwide. I believe those with a natural psychic ability and a strong connection with the landscape find it easier than most to identify these lines of chi, seeing them occasionally as glowing beams or tubes of terrestrial power. But alas, leys appear to exist on a vibrational level beyond our ordinary senses and are difficult to detect with scientific equipment.

The Superspectrum and Non-Locality

Manifestations of strange lights, often in the form of angels, gods and demons, have haunted humankind for thousands of years. Their appearances have helped manipulate people's ordinary lives and, on occasion, inspired them to do extraordinary things.

Scores of scientists working in widely separated unrelated disciplines are crossing the threshold into the world of the esoteric and getting closer to revealing that other realities exist around us on a higher vibrational level that occasionally intrude upon our reality from the multiverse. One of the most remarkable investigators of the paranormal and the UFO phenomena was John A Keel (1930–2009). He introduced the concept of an extradimensional 'superspectrum' that overshadows the Earth's electromagnetic spectrum. Superspectrum energies include gravity, kinesiology, leys, astrology and extrasensory perception. These energies cannot be measured with present-day scientific devices because the superspectrum is beyond the realm of our normal senses, and yet it influences everything within our reality. Humans can only perceive a narrow band in the electromagnetic spectrum as visible light, but some animals see way beyond our visual scope. Those with psychic abilities can tap into the superspectrum, which some eminent researchers, such as Alice Bailey and Rudolf Steiner, call the etheric or hyperplane.[20]

Keel's lifelong research using thousands of case studies led him to believe that ancient knowledge of the Earth's electromagnetic fields of force and the superspectrum were universal and considered so important to the human condition that leaders of civilisations secretly strived over millennia to explore them.

Because higher intelligent forms from other planes of existence need a source of energy to communicate and interact with us in our world of dense energy, our ancient ancestors discovered a way to prolong their sojourn by tapping into the natural force emitted from geomagnetic anomalies in the land. They built temples, mounds and pyramids to amplify these energies to allow entities from the superspectrum to manifest. But the priests failed to balance the force and tend to the portals and, in their greed, sought power over others, attracting darker entities to our Universe.

Keel inspired many sci-fi detectives such as Mulder in the *X-Files*, and his research of 'Big Hairy Monsters' and UFOs is legendary. However, his book *The Eighth Tower* concludes that higher intelligent forms are both malevolent and benevolent and generally appear out of nowhere and then promptly disappear as if they could step in and out of our world through an etheric doorway or window.

Many of the world's spiritual traditions maintain that the consciousness of humanity is at one with the 'universal mind', an all-knowing, all-powerful, all-creative entity, a present, intelligent consciousness likened to God. Consciousness defies scientific analysis and cannot be isolated or manipulated because it is part of everything. In quantum physics, the behaviour of subatomic particles is crucial to understanding the mystery of interconnectedness. Scientific research has shown that when one subatomic particle splits from another, it becomes separate and independent of the other but continues to communicate instantaneously, even though they may be at opposite ends of the galaxy.

The idea of non-locality, which Albert Einstein termed 'spooky actions at a distance', is 'the apparent ability of objects to instantaneously know about each other's state, even when separated by large distances'. It seems that the phenomenon of particle entanglement potentially connects separate parts of the Universe intimately and immediately. Therefore, the builders of spiritual shrines, such as churches, temples, stone monuments or earthworks, may, through particle entanglement, unconsciously align them with other sacred places and natural shrines, such as holy hills, wells and springs. These revered structures will also be influenced and empowered by the subtle energies emitted by the active geology, earth energy lines and underground water prevalent at these natural places of power.

I have known psychics who see the ley system as a glowing grid of lines. Often they can only be glimpsed in a heightened or relaxed state because the lines exist on a superspectrum level barely perceived in our atomic world. For example, in the 1940s, gifted psychic Iris Campbell observed leys on the downs near Brighton as glowing lines of light spreading out before her, which she sensed had great spiritual significance. However, she was embarrassed to discuss it and only pursued the matter after reading about leys in John Michell's book *The View over Atlantis*.[21]

The Earth holds memory within its sacred rocks and waters, and sensitive people can see, hear, or feel the information at these places. Those with a deep affinity with the natural environment sense the spirit of a place called a *genius loci*. In Etruscan mythology, the local landscape's protective intelligence or elemental essence was seen as a serpent. On an unconscious level, the genius loci may be the creative force that inspires psychics, artists and poets when visiting such places as woodlands, rivers or mountains. The spirit may also guide them consciously or unconsciously to create an image of the local god or goddess as a physical representation in the landscape, such as a rock carving or landscape figure formed from roads, footpaths and rivers. In addition, they may urge you to uncover something of importance locally to help heal the land, like an artefact previously buried or hidden to control the energy matrix.

In American Indian philosophy, spirit energy embodies all matter – rock is spirit solidified, water is spirit flowing, fire is spirit released, and crystals are dense purified spirit. Their culture also shaped the landscape to embody the elements into sacred enclosures so they could commune with them. Thus, an enclosed circle of stones with a surrounding ditch of water makes the perfect sanctuary for the spirits to emerge and communicate with us.

While exploring the Spine of Albion, we realised that alignments and serpent/dragon lines are spiritual paths of connection. Walking their routes through the landscape with pious thoughts and heart-felt intentions will inevitably create a positive energy within the flow. When spending time on these lines and connecting with them on a positive heart level, a spirit or elemental consciousness will emerge. This subtle intelligence wants to communicate with us and give guidance as to how to heal certain places along the lines to help restore balance and harmony in the land. We have met many people who are naturally drawn to do this work along energy lines and leys worldwide.

Collective Consciousness and Unconsciousness

The renowned analytical psychologist Carl Jung (1877–1961) taught us that collective consciousness is common to all human beings and responsible for many deep-seated beliefs and instincts. For example, it influences our perspective of life and death, spirituality and sexual behaviour as part of human programming. However, collective unconsciousness is inherited from the shared experience of humanity, like a thought cloud absorbing and storing past experiences and events, both globally and locally. Some religions call this recorder the Akashic Records, which acts like some giant quantum computer absorbing all information.

In 1996, I began to understand that 'collective unconsciousness' manifests within alignments and leys, particularly during my research of the mysteries on the Isle of Portland in Dorset, culminating in the book *The Spirit of Portland* and recently updated as *Mysterious Portland*.[22] I believe humanity had an unconscious aptitude for constructing their sacred places in alignment with each other as if having an inner awareness of the invisible electromagnetic lines or chi linked to a grid that surrounds the world used by ancient builders in the distant past.

Under the principle of quantum entanglement, the power of a natural site in the landscape, such as a dome-shaped hill, may respond to the energetic quality of an artificial structure, such as a stone shrine, stone avenue or circle and establish some form of connection if aligned with it. Many temples of the ancient world are orientated to a sacred mountain or mound to draw upon its spiritual potential and perhaps even embody its divine life-force.

Energy such as light generally travels in straight lines, as does astral energy and thought transference. Therefore, building a church or temple in alignment with other natural and artificial places of power will draw chi to it. If an energy line is detected passing through a church or temple, sensitive people who stand in its path for more than a moment may find themselves communicating with the consciousness of that line. I have often experienced this whilst meditating on a ley at a particular place and gaining impressions of its other locations. An example of this occurred while I sat next to a node of the Belinus Line at Castle Ring in Cannock Chase. Here, Caroline and I faced the daunting task of dowsing a serpent current through dense forest and large stretches of private land. During our meditation, we asked the spirits of the line to show us a mental picture of the next node point. Quite by surprise, we both received the same image of a distinctive hill with large golden rocks on its summit, half hidden within the forest. After a search, we discovered it to be Etching Hill, with a sandstone cap surrounded by trees.

The concept of 'collective unconsciousness', first developed by Émile Durkheim in the late 19th century,[23] may help to explain why geomancers of the past could intuitively 'site' their sacred shrines on these alignments without the need of a surveyor. I believe that when certain individuals tap into this universal mind, they get a sense of whether a specific place 'feels right' when creating sites of sanctity in the landscape.

The straight alignment and its entwining serpentine male and female dragon lines create a tripart stream or trinity of energy with male–female and neutral or earth components similar to electricity wires.

The science of yoga has a basis in the functions of the three main energy channels – *ida, pingala,* and *sushumna.* Ida (lunar, feminine) corresponds to the left nostril and the left side of the body, pingala (solar, masculine) to the right nostril and the right side of the body and sushumna to the central axis of the body. The flow of energy in these three channels influences the functioning of our nervous system and affects our outlook, mood, and emotional stability. Therefore, we could equate leys and serpent lines with the nervous system of our planet Earth, and nurturing them is essential to its well-being.

Earth Energy Currents around the Belinus Line

We have demonstrated that energy lines contain a dynamic life force and consciousness, which reacts and responds to human consciousness and the environment. Many ancient cultures associate the Earth's natural energies with the serpent or dragon archetype. Likewise, dragon-slaying or taming is an allegory for man's control of the natural force within the land. When detecting earth energy lines, dowsers have determined that their widths vary at certain times of the year and, under certain conditions, their strength waxing and waning like the moon. Residual energies from positive or negative environmental experiences and events also affect the width and vitality of the serpent lines.

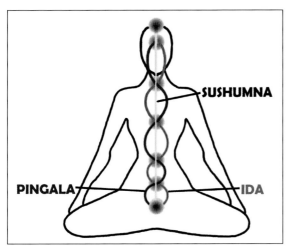

sushumna, ida and pingala, the body's three main energy channels

Plasma and Ether Tubes

The Earth Mystery debate continues to supply us with new insights, such as the recent scientific discoveries regarding particle entanglement and intelligent plasma. In 1991, Terence Meaden and Dr Yoshi-Hiko Ohtsuki of the Waseda University in Tokyo made a dramatic breakthrough by establishing their 'plasma vortex' theory to explain the crop circle phenomenon. Dr Ohtsuki was the first to create spinning plasma vortices in a laboratory that formed circles in a tray of aluminium powder. Meaden stated that the high-strength electromagnetic fields of plasma were responsible for certain anomalies, including magnetic variations and electrical interferences, which explains why some people were experiencing dizziness and nausea while visiting crop circles.[24] Although the complexity of the circles cannot be fully explained by spinning vortices, plasma intelligence may have been behind the making of some of the larger and more sophisticated crop formations, and perhaps collective unconsciousness could explain the guidance behind many of the artificial constructions.

Earth-born plasma, called geoplasma, has been witnessed worldwide in the form of strange clouds during the day and high luminosity balls of light at night, often called earth lights. Plasma is the fourth of the fundamental states of matter after solids, liquids and gasses and is an ionised or electrically charged gas with peculiar properties. When you apply heat or energy to gas, the atoms lose their electrons and become a soup of positively charged particles (ions) and negatively charged particles (electrons). The lost electrons are then able to float freely. This process is called 'ionisation'. Plasma is the most abundant form of matter in the Universe and is the substance of the stars and our sun, including the gaseous planets of Jupiter and Saturn. Because this substance is highly conductive, electromagnetic fields dominate its behaviour, possibly explaining why electromagnetic emissions from local faulting and high-water pressure under rocks or chalk aid the manifestation of plasma balls.

Plasma's highly excited electrons can also take the form of energetic light emissions such as lightning, the aurora borealis and sunlight. Scientists now understand that plasma is one of the fundamental and dynamic components of everything that exists and that our physical Earth, which is atomic matter, is a lower state of plasma, a rarity in a Universe teeming with high-frequency plasma. The spirit or soul is also plasma in an atomic environment, and therefore when we die, we return to our original plasma state.

Vinod Krishnan, a senior Professor and Dean of Sciences at the Indian Institute of Astrophysics in India says that:

> 'Nature began with plasma. Cooling of the plasma converted it into gas. Cooling of the gas converted it into liquid. Cooling of the liquid converted it into solid matter. That plasmas are the first state of matter, out of which arose the other three states of matter has been demonstrated. The ubiquity of plasmas in the Universe needs no demonstration. The phenomenal diversity of plasmas is there all over the Universe for all to see.' [25]

Ball Lightning, a natural occurrence of plasma in our physical world, is seen as a spherical ball of bright light, witnessed throughout history entering buildings, ships and planes causing mayhem and even fires. However, many reports and documented cases say that plasma has consciousness and behaves with intelligence akin to a curious animal. Moreover, because it exists in a high vibrational state of matter and, therefore, slightly out of our 3-dimensional world, it can pass through walls and manoeuvre at impossible speeds.

Examples of recorded plasma ball incidents derive from many parts of the world. One includes a sighting on the night of 21 October 1638, when a great storm hit the Dartmoor village of Widecombe-in-the-Moor in Devon. Witnesses described an 8-ft (2.4 m) ball of fire entering the church and causing severe damage. The fiery globe then divided into two, one exiting through a window by smashing the glass, and the other imploded, leaving the church with a foul sulphurous odour and dark, thick smoke. Because of the smell of sulphur, superstitious locals believed the 'devil' had entered the church – this was later blamed on two people playing cards in the pews during the sermon.[26]

17th-century Woodcut of the Widecombe Storm and ball lightening

Several people observed a similar plasma ball entering the famous Golden Temple at Amritsar in Punjab, India, in 1877. The ball entered through the main door and exited through a side door. An inscription records the incident on the front wall of the main entrance. In the ancient world of the Greeks and Phoenicians, they were called thunderbolts, supposedly sent by Zeus. St Elmo's Fire is a mysterious plasma ball of light that often appears on ship masts or aircraft wings before a storm. Sometimes they perform intelligent manoeuvres like the mysterious earth lights seen on tops of mountains and hills, which many believe to be gods or alien spaceships.

In his seminal works *Earth Lights* and *Earth Lights Revelation*, Paul Devereux records that in modern times, witnesses who had close encounters with earth lights reported hallucinatory episodes. This mind-altering state suggests that magnetic fields can affect parts of the brain, such as the temporal lobe, and stimulate psychic or 'out-of-body' experiences identical to many UFO abduction cases reported worldwide. Earth lights are also known to behave as if they have a rudimentary intelligence, as they can pass through solid walls unaffected by the wind.[27]

Because plasma consists of a higher vibrational non-atomic energy, it can easily pass through solid matter of a lower vibration. David Bohm, who established the foundations of plasma physics, observed that '*once electrons were in a plasma state, they stopped behaving like individuals and started acting as if they were part of a larger and interconnected whole*.' He also remarked that he frequently thought the sea of electrons was '*in some sense alive*' or representative of the collective.[28]

Geoplasma or earth-born plasma can appear worldwide, especially in seismic areas such as mountains, lakes and around geological faults where certain rocks rub together, causing piezoelectricity and ionisation of the air above. In addition, this phenomenon appears in certain areas in waves called 'hotspots', sometimes after heavy rainfall or solar storms. Author and researcher Andrew Collins has delved deeply into the plasma light ball mystery in his book *Lightquest* in an attempt to interpret many of these mysterious hotspots around the world.[29]

Researchers at the Federal University of Pernambuco in Brazil used electricity to vaporise tiny silicon wafers, artificially creating small plasma spheres the size of ping-pong balls that hovered around for as long as eight seconds. During the 1980s, Dr Brian Brady, a US specialist in rock mechanics, conducted experiments compressing quartz-bearing rock in a darkened room and filmed it in slow motion. These experiments created tiny balls of light, which behaved similarly to the larger plasma balls often mistaken for alien craft. Canadian neuropsychologist Dr Michael Persinger discovered that light ball phenomena, UFO encounters, and abduction scenarios have a link to geologically active zones across America.[30]

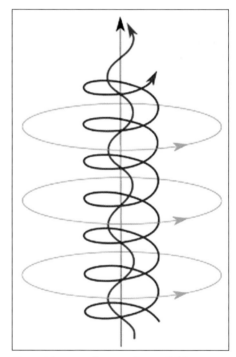

Fig. 1 Magnetic lines within a field-aligned Birkeland current, by NASA

In *A New Science of Heaven*, Robert Temple reveals how the science of plasma will transform humanity's understanding of its place in the Universe. Temple cites the work of Hannes Alfvén (1908–1995), who discovered that plasma was the medium by which electrical currents could travel through space. Temple reveals that the Universe is a 'cosmic web' and space as we know it is not a void but teeming with electromagnetic energy channelled as connective lines called filaments or Birkeland currents.[31] The currents have twisted rope-like magnetic structures, also known as field-aligned currents, magnetic ropes, magnetic cables, or tubes. Filamentary structures are common in plasma because they contain free electrons, making them highly electrically conductive – even more than metals. As charged particles readily move in plasma, a magnetic field forms around the current like a ring that can squeeze it into filamentary strands, known as 'pinched filaments' (See Fig. 1).

The plasma filaments are possibly what dowsers and sensitives detect when finding positive and negative bands within earth energy lines like wires in an electric cable. So if the cosmos is a jungle of plasma lines on a subatomic level, then on a microcosmic level, they could relate to energy lines on Earth.

Temple explains the 'double-helix' phenomenon of the Birkeland currents, '*magnetic currents applied at right angles to Birkeland currents have the result that two currents running parallel to each other start wrapping themselves around each other in a kind of 'lovers embrace.'* The two surrounding magnetic fields join and become stronger as a result. The magnetic fields further constrict and compress the plasma of the double helix, and at specific points, the inward pressure forms nodes called Z-pinches.[32]

Hamish Miller was the first dowser to notice the Michael and Mary serpent energy lines shrinking to a point in the ground and then expanding out again as if some unseen force was 'pinching' them together, which he called nodes (*See Fig. 2*).[33]

When comparing serpent energy lines with Birkeland currents, both have a straight core with two entwined energies of different polarities that occasionally come together to form nodes. Furthermore, Robert Temple says there is a distinct similarity between the structure of DNA molecules and the Birkeland currents, which can contain filaments in a double helix and carry information. Therefore, we can conclude from this scientific understanding of plasma that the Universe, the Earth, humanity and the Earth's energy lines are all connected by Birkeland currents. Unfortunately, most of society has lost its connection to the land and spirit due to the dominance of negative influences and modern communication networks that perpetually swamp the senses and lower our vibrations and effect our ability to be fully enlightened. Despite this, many more of us are feeling and responding to the Earth's potent energies and are able to commune with the spirit world and connect with the Universal Consciousness.

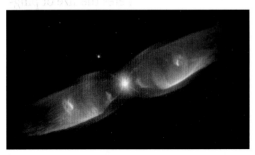

Twin-jet nebula showing the classic features of a plasma z-pinch by ESA/Hubble

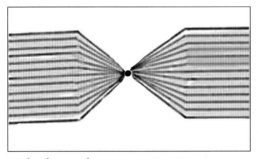

Node of an earth energy current

The Belinus Line

In 2012, Caroline and I self-published *The Spine of Albion,* which detailed our 15-year research and exploration of the Belinus Line, the north–south equivalent of the St Michael Line and considered Britain's longest ley. The line starts at the Isle of Wight on the south coast and leaves through Durness at the northern tip of Scotland. This 'spine' of Britain or Albion also connects six cities, including Winchester and Dunfermline, the former capitals of England and Scotland and Carlisle, the old capital of the north. Also associated with this line are geographical centres, including Stratford-upon-Avon, Whalley in Lancashire, Pitlochry and Lairg in Scotland, and many famous prehistoric complexes such as the Uffington White Horse, the Rollright Stones, the Shap Avenue or 'serpent temple' and Long Meg and her Daughters stone circle in Cumbria.[34]

Like the St Michael Line, the Belinus Line has accompanying male and female serpent energy lines, which we named Belinus and Elen. Belinus and Elen are drawn to particular places of power along their course – the solar male preferring the high places such as mountaintops and prominent rocks and the lunar female caves, lakes, wells and springs deep in the valleys. Having a natural ability to detect these lines of power, Caroline and I set out to follow their route through the English and Scottish countryside, discovering powerful nodes at key places of power already marked as revered sites of sanctity by our ancient ancestors. Naming the serpent lines gave us a more intimate association with them and helped establish a conscious and unconscious connection with their subtle energies.

The straight alignments of the St Michael and Belinus Lines cross each other close to the Uffington prehistoric complex and the Bronze Age turf cut image of the White Horse. The Elen and Belinus energy lines flow north–south through the centre of the complex, forming two nodes or 'plasma pinches', one at the hillfort and the other on Dragon Hill. In contrast, the east–west Michael and Mary energy lines encircle the complex as if to protect this sacred area. The Michael and Belinus serpent lines cross south of Uffington at Lambourn's St Michael and All Angels Church. Mary and Elen meet at Uffington's St Mary's Church to the north. The old tribes of the area may well have created the landscape figure to represent the powerful fusion between these two sets of dragon lines to empower this ancient gathering place and beacon site.

We discovered node points at many other beacon sites along the Belinus alignment, including Beacon Hill in Hampshire, Barr Beacon on the outskirts of Birmingham and Alderley Edge near Manchester. Uffington was also on a sighting line towards the setting of Deneb in the constellation of Cygnus, the brightest of the northern stars in prehistoric and Iron Age Britain.

Many ancient cultures worldwide regard the stars of Cygnus as a gateway to the afterlife or the spiritual realm. The very moment Deneb touched the horizon was considered sacred by the ancients, when heaven and earth combined forces and were in perfect harmony. The constellation of Cygnus, also known as the Northern Cross, lies near the centre of our galaxy within a split in the Milky Way called the Great Rift. Interestingly, Britain is orientated toward these stars as they set in the north. It is possible that civilisations of the ancient world knew of this and regarded Britain's islands as realms of the dead. However, North American tribes such as the Blackfoot believed that Cygnus was not just a destination for the soul to pass into the afterlife but also inhabited by sentient beings, which could travel to Earth through a portal in the Milky Way or the sky pole. Furthermore, the shamans believed that these sky beings provided them with spiritual knowledge from their ancestors.

We discovered that the celestial influences of Cygnus and its brightest star, Deneb feature at many node points along the Belinus Line, such as St Catherine's Hill in Winchester, the Rollright Stones and Stratford-upon-Avon. Most of these sites have views of the northern horizon, which seemed integral to their ritual function. In addition, particular structures within these sites, such as standing stones, were deliberately orientated to mark the setting or rising of Deneb. Likewise, the modern industrial capitals of Manchester and Birmingham may have prospered because they align with the old spiritual centres of Winchester and Dunfermline towards the centre of our galaxy. Alternatively, the collective unconsciousness may have influenced our forebears to build and site these important centres in harmony with the land and the cosmos. A pilgrimage along the Spine of Albion is akin to a journey through British history, with its prehistoric spiritual places, Christian shrines, New Age centres and Arthurian Grail sites, many of them long forgotten.

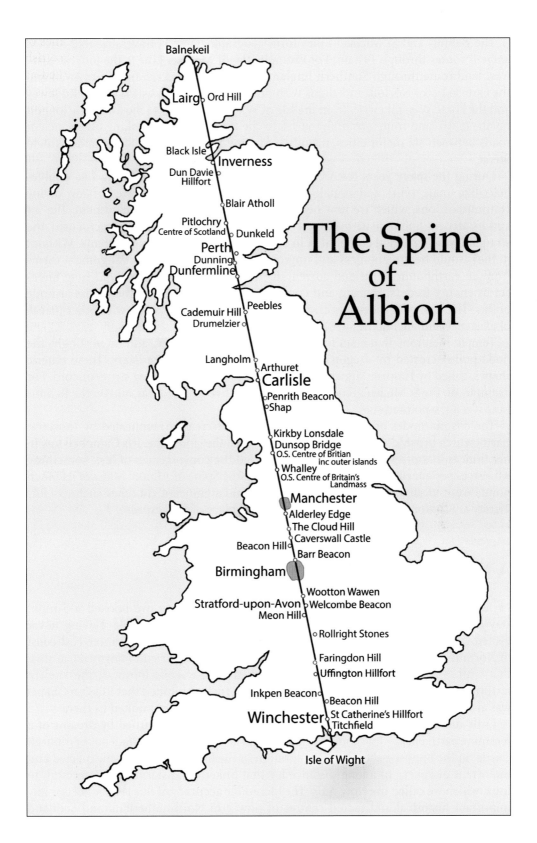

The Spine of Albion

- Balnekeil
- Lairg
- Ord Hill
- Black Isle
- Inverness
- Dun Davie Hillfort
- Blair Atholl
- Pitlochry
- Centre of Scotland
- Dunkeld
- Perth
- Dunning
- Dunfermline
- Peebles
- Cademuir Hill
- Drumelzier
- Langholm
- Arthuret
- Carlisle
- Penrith Beacon
- Shap
- Kirkby Lonsdale
- Dunsop Bridge
- O.S. Centre of Britian inc outer islands
- Whalley
- O.S. Centre of Britain's Landmass
- Manchester
- Alderley Edge
- The Cloud Hill
- Caverswall Castle
- Beacon Hill
- Barr Beacon
- Birmingham
- Wootton Wawen
- Stratford-upon-Avon
- Welcombe Beacon
- Meon Hill
- Rollright Stones
- Faringdon Hill
- Uffington Hillfort
- Inkpen Beacon
- Beacon Hill
- Winchester
- St Catherine's Hillfort
- Titchfield
- Isle of Wight

The Belinus and St Michael Lines form geographical axes, traversing well-known ancient routes through Britain. For example, the St Michael Line is the longest east–west land route through Southern England between the western tip of Cornwall and the eastern tip of Norfolk and aligns with prehistoric trackways such as the Ridgeway and the Fosse Way. Likewise, from the Isle of Wight, the Belinus Line forms the longest north–south land route avoiding the sea to the tip of Scotland, linking other ancient roads between six major cities, including Ermine Street, Watling Street and Icknield Street,

During the many years researching and walking the Belinus Line and its double-helix-like male (yin) and female (yang) energy lines, we received many divine communications, which we now believe was through plasma consciousness. The ley and its serpent lines equate to Robert Temple's Birkeland currents in microcosm, the straight ley being a vital component in controlling the meandering currents. Without it, they would be directionless and ungrounded. When a significant alignment forms from an earthbound Birkeland current, its double-helix lines of *yin and yang* forces act as energy feeders, sharing and combining their power when they cross at node points. The energy at the nodes creates a vortex that communicates with other planes of existence, enhancing the site's life force.

Temple mentions that stars form at Z-pinches out in space, and interestingly, the node points created by dragon earth energy lines also develop stars. These etheric shapes, called by Hamish 'signatures', can be dowsed at nodes using string or cord. For example, on the St Michael Line, the signature is a five-pointed star, and on the Belinus Line it is a six-pointed star.

The cosmic nodes are, therefore, vital points of creation, replicated by those on Earth, which provide significant places of power in the landscape. Iris Campbell saw in her trances that priests and occultists controlled the convergences of leys, something we also experienced in modern times following the Spine of Albion. Many of its pinch points were located inside cathedrals, abbeys and significant churches such as Holy Trinity at Stratford-upon-Avon, the final resting place of Shakespeare.

A New Discovery

In June 2013, during one of the best summers in a decade, we booked a 5-night stay in a rented cottage on Lindisfarne, Northumberland's Holy Isle. Having never visited this area before, we were looking forward to exploring this remote east coast of Northumberland. A week before our departure, a psychic friend informed Caroline that while there, we needed to connect with the Bride consciousness, the ancient fertility goddess, also known as Brigid. Our friend further intuited that Rosslyn Chapel was also a vital place to visit, as something of great importance awaited us there.

Little did we know that our peaceful sojourn would be disturbed by dreams of a feminine earth energy line connecting Lindisfarne with the great citadel of Bamburgh Castle on the opposite shore. The exploration of the line led us to the unexpected and important discovery of a long-distance ley that linked Lindisfarne and Bamburgh to Iona, which we called the Holy Axis. The incredible accuracy of this ley connects many important historical and sacred centres of power in Northumberland and Scotland with Celtic saints, the old kings of the north, and renowned legendary and real-life characters. Moreover, the recurring spiritual themes of an esoteric nature that the journey revealed suggested that this holy alignment is an essential path for the modern pilgrim.

After ten years of researching its many fascinating sites, the spiritual and cultural importance of the Holy Axis has become even more apparent. At 107 degrees, the ley points towards the stars of Orion as they rise in the east, particularly the star Regal on his foot. However, in the Bronze Age, all three of the main stars of Orion's Belt rose at this location. Orion is the mythical warrior god and hunter characterised as Lugh Lamhfada or Lugh of the Long Arm in Irish Legends.

We also discovered that rising at 107 degrees is the constellation of Virgo carrying the star Spica in her wheatsheaf. In ancient Greek mythology, she is the goddess of purity, innocence and fertility. At 287 degrees, the ley orientates to the setting of the heads of Orion and Virgo, marked by Iona in the west. Interestingly, many characters linked with these cosmic deities seem to be associated with this east–west line of power.

At present and for another decade a least, Orion, the anthropomorphic warrior/god/hunter constellation, carries the sun across the sky in his upraised arm, or sword, at the summer solstice. Here Orion symbolically represents the Celtic warrior/god/hunter Lugh of the Long Arm, who throws the sun across the sky. Interestingly, Lugh/Orion is an archetypal warrior and appears in the mythology and folklore of many sites associated with the Holy Axis.

Accompanying the Holy Axis are two dragon lines, one male and the other female, that begin their journey at Inner Farne in the North Sea, the largest of the Farne Islands located 3.6 miles (5.8 km) off the east coast of Northumberland. Next, they meet on the mainland at the site of the imposing Bamburgh Castle, where in legend, an Arthurian knight sets out on a quest for the Holy Grail. From Bamburgh, this path of tripart energies continues westwards along the 'Neck of Britain', where we encounter many places associated with the mythos of Arthur and Merlin. We also visit holy islands on a legendary lake linked with the Nine Maidens and a Neolithic 'valley of kings' in Argyll, ending at the Iona – Scotland's Avalon.

We named the male dragon Lugh, symbolic of Orion, and the female, Bride, the goddess archetype of Virgo. This pre-Celtic female deity, known variously as Brid, Brig or Brigid and later Christianised as St Bridget, derives from a more ancient indigenous version of the goddess from Scottish prehistory.

The Holy Axis also connects many important regional landscapes of Scottish history on the isthmus or Neck of Albion, including the old territory of the ancient kingdom of Lothian and Manau south of the Firth of Forth and Aberfoyle, an area once known as 'The Moat of Britain'. It also passes through the enchanted lands of the Dal Riata and the great Lochs of Argyll and the Western Isles, where we encounter characters from Arthurian Romances.

Throughout the Holy Axis quest, we have visited sacred sites, both natural and artificial, located on geological faults and magnetic rocks as if to draw upon the power of the earth to create a conduit for communication with ancestral spirits or beings from the multiverse. These places have incredible folklore linked to elemental, UFO and otherworldly encounters and more recent experiences where ordinary folk have found themselves beyond the space–time continuum.

While researching the Spine of Albion, we developed the ability to communicate with the plasma consciousness of the Elen and Belinus serpent lines. Through meditation, we could sense their wisdom and their hurt or imbalance. We discovered that many of the sites on the Belinus line had suffered through the effects of deliberate, wanton abuse, neglect, quarrying, battles, geological disruption and fear. As a result, the alignment and currents were like a broken and blocked electrical circuit that could no longer produce the power to fertilise and animate the land. The dragon lines guided us to heal their wounds and rejuvenate the sites they visited to mend the broken circuit and reconnect them to the grid system of the earth. This practice helped us understand what it meant to feel fully connected to everything on Earth's plane of existence, the Universal realms and the superspectrum.

Walking these lines of power with conscious heart-felt intentions can have a curative and inspirational effect on the land. Since the publication of *The Spine of Albion*, people have been sharing their experiences of healing the Belinus Line and its dragon energies in their local area with positive effects. Many readers have informed us of their karmic or personal connection to the line, eventually leading them to establish healing and creativity centres of learning at certain places on the currents.[35]

This experience prepared the way for re-establishing the Holy Axis by providing the required healing to make it a fully functioning key component of the Earth's energy grid, which included rejuvenating and reanimating the serpent lines and many of the places of power along its route.

The research of this line, and the accompanying male and female energies, has all the ingredients for a modern Grail quest. It is a path that guides the traveller to rich and evocative sites linked to the 'Matter of Britain', a collection of medieval literature and legendary writings associated with Britain and Brittany and its legendary kings and heroes, particularly King Arthur.

The Holy Axis will guide you through mystical, ethereal landscapes where distant voices from the past reach out to open-minded and sensitive people. The spirit of the alignment and the Lugh and Bride serpent energies and those of the upper worlds are eager to share their knowledge with you during these times of transition when the planet's consciousness desires us to grow spiritually.

Walking the ancient trails of Albion with a pure heart and good intentions unconsciously creates positive changes around us, contributing to the healing of the land and nature. Restoring balance and harmony to the Holy Axis along the 'Neck of Britain' will help the land function as a place of spiritual illumination and empowerment.

---

1. 2. 4. Devereux, P. Pennick, N. 1989. *Lines on the Landscape: Leys and Other Linear Enigmas*. Robert Hale Ltd, London.

3. 6. Watkins, A. 1925. *The Old Straight Track*. Methuen Publishing, London.

5. 11. Screeton, P. 1974. *Quicksilver Heritage. The Mystic Leys: Their Legacy of Ancient Wisdom*. Thorsons, London.

7. 8. 9. Devereux, Paul. 1992. *Shamanism and the Mystery Lines: Ley Lines, Spirit Paths, Shape-Shifting and out-of-Body*. Quantum, Slough.

10. Michel, A. 1958. *Flying Saucers and the Straight Line Mystery*. S G Phillips

12. Thom, A. 1967. *Megalithic Sites in Britain*. Oxford University Press, Oxford.

13. 19. Michell, J. 1975. *The View Over Atlantis*. Abacus Books, London.

14. Hayes, N. L. 1922. *The Chinese Dragon*. Commercial Press, Ltd, Shanghai, China.

15. Miller, H. Broadhurst, P. 2000. *The Dance of the Dragon*. Pendragon Press, Launceston.

16. 17. Michell, J. 1983. *The New View Over Atlantis*. Thames & Hudson, London.

18. 33. Miller, H. & Broadhurst, P. 1989. *The Sun and the Serpent*. Pendragon Press, Launceston.

19. Devereux, P. 1990. *Places of Power, Secret Energies at Ancient Sites: A Guide to Observed or Measured Phenomena*. Blandford Press, London.

20. Keel, John. 2013. *The Eighth Tower: On Ultraterrestrials and the Superspectrum* Anomalist Books, San Antonio, USA.

21. Foster Forbes, J. 1945. *Giants of Britain, Being a Short Treatise Dealing with the Story of Giants of All Ages*. Thomas's Publications.

22. Biltcliffe, G. 2022 *Mysterious Portland: Revealing the Sacred Landscape and Legacy of Britain's Masonic Isle*. Sacred Lands Publishing, Weymouth.

23. Smith, K. 2014. *Émile Durkheim and the Collective Consciousness of Society A Study in Criminology*. Anthem Press, London.

24. Meaden, T. 1989. *The Circles Effects and its Mysteries*. Artetech Publishing Co, Bradford-on-Avon.

25. Krishan, Vinod. 2014. *Plasmas: The First State of Matter*. Cambridge University Press, Cambridge.

26. Warden, J. L. 1895. *An Exploration of Dartmoor and its Antiquities* (4th ed.). Seeley & Co Ltd, London.

27. Devereux, Paul. 1989. *Earth Lights Revelation: UFOs and Mystery Lightform Phenomena: the Earth's Secret Energy Force*. Blandford Press, London.

28. Bohm, D. 1980. *Wholeness and the Implicate Order*. Routledge, London.

29. Collins, C. 2012. *Lightquest*. Eagle Wing Books, Memphis, USA.

30. Persinger, M. A. & Lafrenière, G. F. 1977. *Space-Time Transients and Unusual Events*. Nelson-Hall, Chicago, USA.

31. 32. Temple, R. 2021. *A New Science of Heaven*. Hodder & Stoughton Ltd, London.

34. 35. Biltcliffe, G. Hoare, C. 2012. *The Spine of Albion*. Sacred Lands Publishing, Weymouth.

Chapter 1

Lindisfarne, England's Holiest Isle

Lindisfarne, also known as Holy Island, is a liminal place where the raw elements of nature blend with enchanted stories of miracles and apparitions. The little island lies on Britain's remote northeastern shoulder, 9 miles southeast of Berwick-upon-Tweed in Northumberland and 5 miles (8 km) north of Bamburgh's formidable yet imposing turreted castle. Earlier names for the island include *Lindisfarena* in *The Anglo-Saxon Chronicle* for 793 CE and *Innis Medcaut* in the *Historia Brittonum,* written in the 9th century by the Welsh monk Nennius. This early British name may derive from the Latin *Medicata,* meaning 'Isle of Healing', perhaps alluding to the healing plants or herbs that still grow naturally on the island. Alternatively, it may derive from the island's ozone-rich air quality.

The causeway joining the island to the mainland floods for several hours twice a day, depending on the time of year, by the fast-moving tides of the North Sea. When the waters recede, modern pilgrims fulfil their journey to the island across the sandy

Lindisfarne Priory with Lindisfarne Castle beyond (courtesy of Stephen Brown)

expanse using wooden marker poles, which follow the final stretch of the St Cuthbert's and St Oswald's Way. In 1954, the construction of a metalled road across the causeway allowed vehicles onto the island.

From above, the island's shape resembles an 'axe' complete with its handle, whereas others see it as a tadpole. David Adam, a former rector of Lindisfarne, refers to a local legend that states: *'when Satan made war in heaven, his battle axe was struck from his hand, fell to earth and landed in the sea, becoming the island of Lindisfarne.'* The axe is

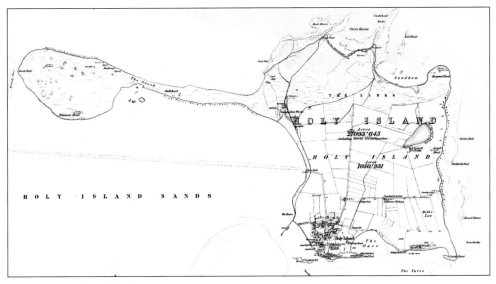

Map of Lindisfarne dated 1866

one of humanity's oldest tools, dating back to the Neolithic age. Many ancient traditions associate it with lightning, water, fertility and the power to manipulate rainfall. The axe also symbolises creation and destruction, war and justice, and defence and attack. The central figures in mythology, such as gods and warrior heroes, wield an axe, and this, as we were to discover, was indicative of the legends and history of Lindisfarne.

The island measures about a mile and a half (2.4 km) north to south and a mile (1.6 km) east to west, though the handle of the axe or the tail of the tadpole extends another two miles (3.2 km) to the west, making its length three miles (4.82 km) in total. The island's population, around 180 people, live in the village at the southeast corner of the island and make their living from farming, fishing and tourism, which attracts thousands of holidaymakers and pilgrims each year.

When visiting Lindisfarne for the first time during the summer of 2013, we were fortunate that the weather provided us with blue skies and warm temperatures for the few days we were there. We rented a small self-catering cottage in the village, which stands within the ancient monastic boundary. As soon as we arrived, we were keen to explore the island's pathways and visit the ruins of the priory, the castle and the dunes on the north coast. We heard an eerie wailing noise as we headed towards the coast and later discovered its source, a large colony of grey seals and their pups in the far estuary – their sounds and the haunting cries of the sandpiper heightening the island's potent atmosphere.

Contact

That night, I dreamt of being led by a lady dressed in white across the island, showing me a line of black rocks. When I awoke the following day, I discovered that Caroline had almost the same dream. I have had dreams at sacred places on many occasions, and often they contain information about the underlying history of the site. I believe that sensitive people can communicate directly or indirectly with nature's consciousness or *genius loci* of the land to help connect us with the local energy field, whether for healing purposes or to receive specific messages. Our first reaction was to ignore the dreams as we were on holiday and needed a rest, but the same vision occurred the following night, so we felt compelled to investigate.

We soon realised that the consciousness of Lindisfarne, or its genius loci, was calling us to walk a fault line, which we discovered was a unique geological upthrust of black volcanic basalt running east–west through the southern part of the island. The fault included the hill upon which the iconic castle stands and the long ridge that overlooks the monastery complex called The Heugh.

Basalt, locally called *whin sill*, was formed about 295 million years ago when a spectacular cataclysm caused the dramatic movement of the Earth's tectonic plates forcing to the surface millions of tons of magma or molten rock from deep within the Earth's crust, which eventually cooled. Also called dolerite, these volcanic upthrusts appear across Northern England as elongated geological bands interspersed across southern Scotland to the Isle of Mull near Iona. Stretches of the world-famous Hadrian's Wall, built in Roman times, were constructed upon these basalt faults. Basalt has iron ore mineral magnetite within its composition, giving the rock subtle magnetic

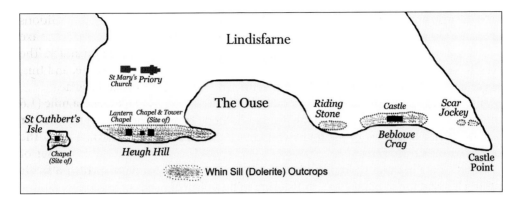

qualities. Quarrymen of Northern England used the term 'sill' to describe a more or less horizontal body of rock – the word 'whin' applies to dark, hard stones. Perhaps sleeping near this fault line and its energy affected our dreams.

According to a geological map of the island, at the western tip of the basalt seam is a protrusion forming the tiny islet named after St Cuthbert, just south of the monastic ruins. Formerly known as Thrush or Hobthrush Island, the saint built a cell here, where he spent much of his time in seclusion. Many believe it was originally the retreat of Aidan, the island's first bishop, and acquired the name St Cuthbert's or Cuddie's Isle much later, possibly around the time of the Reformation. During excavations in the 1880s, Major-General Sir William Crossman, lord of the manor and owner of Lindisfarne at the time, unearthed the remains of a small chapel there, including a south-facing door with a stone lintel and well-cut stone steps leading to it. Also found were the footings of a two-roomed structure consisting of a kitchen with a hearth and, near it, much older remains, which he believed to be the site of Cuthbert's cell. There is little left of these ruins, as time and vegetation have reclaimed any remnants of this tiny island's illustrious history.[1]

Life of St Cuthbert

St Cuthbert (634–687 CE) is renowned in Northern Britain with many churches, holy wells and a pilgrimage route dedicated to him. He was a Celtic Christian monk, bishop and hermit whose birthplace was Kells in Ireland. According to *The Book of the Nativity of St Cuthbert*, taken and translated from the Irish and adopted by Reginald of Durham, Cuthbert was the son of an Irish princess called Saba or Sabina, who was abducted and violated by a neighbouring king. She gives birth to Cuthbert, then escapes with him to Scotland on a stone which miraculously floated on water.[2] After various adventures, they arrive at the Leader Valley near Melrose, where Cuthbert is left in the care of a holy man while Saba departs on a pilgrimage to Rome, never to return. A church was built here for the saint, later named Childeschirche (Child's Church), now Channelkirk. In *The Anonymous Life of St Cuthbert*, written by an unnamed monk at Lindisfarne Priory, a tale reveals that as a sturdy fair-haired youth, he tended sheep in the Lammermuir Hills near the River Leader. One night, while holding vigil over the flock, he observes the vision of a soul being taken up to heaven by an angel. A few days later, he hears of the death of Bishop Aidan of Lindisfarne and vows then and there to enter the church.[3]

According to Bede, the young monk came under the tutelage of Eata, one of twelve Anglo-Saxon boys trained by St Aidan at the Iona school of Celtic Christianity. Cuthbert began his missionary work at Ripon but returned with Eata to Aidan's Monastery at Mailros or Old Melrose by the River Tweed in protest after Ripon's monastery came under the auspices of Wilfred and the Roman Catholic religious doctrine. Old Melrose was the furthest outpost of the many churches founded by Celtic Christian followers of St Columba from Iona.[4]

In 665, Eata became Bishop of Lindisfarne, and Cuthbert accompanied him as his prior. He spent much of his time ministering to the spiritual needs of his congregations and travelled widely to preach. His charm and generosity to people experiencing poverty and his reputation as an insightful and gifted healer led to Cuthbert being called 'The Wonder Worker of Britain'.[5] In 676, Cuthbert retired to the little islet attached to Lindisfarne called Hobthrush. However, the many pilgrims crossing at low tide to visit him disturbed his solitude, so he retreated to Aidan's old cell on Inner Farne, the largest of the Farne Islands that sits out to sea opposite Bamburgh Castle.

Cuthbert became Bishop of Hexham during his retirement, a position he refused at first until a visit from King Ecgfrith persuaded him to take up the post. He eventually returned to Lindisfarne Priory, but after two years of being its bishop, he sought sanctuary again on Inner Farne, but died a few weeks later. His body was interred on the right side of the high altar of Lindisfarne's priory church until attacks by the Danes forced the monks to take his relics on a journey that ended in his eventual entombment at Durham Cathedral.

From the opposite shore, we waited for the tide to recede before crossing over the slippery rocks to St Cuthbert's Isle, for like Lindisfarne, the sea surrounds the tiny islet twice a day. We sensed that the action of the tide and the seal's wraithlike calls seemed stronger here, adding to its charm. We also wondered whether St Cuthbert was psychic and recognised this islet's ethereal atmosphere, especially in light of his vision of Aidan's spirit. Perhaps he had the ability or gift to communicate with otherworldly spirits at this 'thin veil' place.

We headed for the highest part of the tiny island, where we noticed the foundation stones of a cell or chapel that held an impressive wooden cross. Its size and appearance reminded us of the small Celtic chapels called *keeills* found all over the Isle of Man.

As we admired the view from the top of Cuthbert's Isle, we noticed a large group of seals and their pups swimming across the estuary to their daytime basking area at Guile Point. Here, two tall obelisks called 'The Beacons' stand as navigational towers to guide boats to Holy Island's harbour. As the seals propelled themselves through the water, we sensed a timeless moment, for seals have probably been swimming across this bay for thousands of years, and Cuthbert must have observed this same scene during his sojourn here.

The tall white obelisks standing like sentinel pillars guarding the southern entrance to Holy Island seem out of place in this picturesque landscape. Yet, they reminded me of an important historical event that took place here during the Dark Ages.

The Fate of Urien, the Raven King

The Angles arrived on the Northumbrian shores in the 6th century sailing up the coast from Norfolk. However, initially, they came from Denmark, and although historians insist they were Germanic peoples, most in-depth researchers have discovered their true ancestry to be a mystery. Under Ida's leadership, they secured a territory stretching from the Rivers Forth to the Tees, a kingdom later known as Bernicia. The Angles fought many battles to secure their domain, culminating in their most crucial fight against the combined forces of the Northern Britons.

At the time, Rheged was the most influential Northern kingdom of the post-Roman Britons, ruled by a legendary warrior called Urien, the great-great-great-grandson of Coel Hen (Old King Cole). According to the Welsh Triads, Urien was one of the '*three great battle-leaders of Britain*',[6] who united the British tribes, '*like Arthur before him*', and fought a series of successful campaigns against Ida's son Theodoric. In *c.* 590 CE, these successful battles culminated in Urien's army driving the Angles out of their stronghold at Bamburgh and onto the island of Lindisfarne, where they held them under siege. Unfortunately, during the siege, Urien was assassinated by his cousin, which would change the course of English history. Nennius in *Historia Brittonum* recorded the fame of this last stand, called the siege of *Ynys Metcaut*:

> 'Against him [Thodoric] fought four kings; Urien, and Rhydderch the Old, and Gwallawg, and Morcant. [Morgant]. Theodoric fought vigorously against Urien and his sons. During that time, sometimes the enemy, sometimes the Cymry [Britons] were victorious, and Urien blockaded them for three days and three nights in the island of Lindisfarne. But, while he was on campaign, Urien was killed on the instigation of Morcant, from jealousy, because his military skill and generalship surpassed that of all the other kings.'[7]

For the Britons, the battle's success relied upon an alliance between the Kings of Strathclyde, Ulster, Gododdin and Urien's British cousin King Morgant (Morcant) Bwlch (Bulc) of Bryneich, High Chief of the Gododdin, whose territory included this area of northeast Britain. Like in most epics, the traitor seeks to seize power and glory away from the heroic warrior. In this case, Morcant coveted the position of overall leader of the British tribes.

While camped at night amongst Lindisfarne's dunes, Morcant had Urien assassinated by a foreign mercenary called Llofan Llaf Difo, who cut off his head with an axe. His body was said to lie beneath a cairn of blue stones at Aber Lleu (Ross Low) somewhere in the region of the two white obelisks. The colour of these stones matches the description of the native whin sill rocks found locally in abundance. So, ironically, Urien met his fate with an axe on an island shaped like an axe.

Before the assassination, the British were in a solid position to utterly defeat the Angles, having secured the lands taken from them. However, Morcant's treacherous act caused Urien's army to fall into disarray, forcing the alliance to crumble and the siege to fall. The Angles took this opportunity to re-assert themselves in the region once more. For decades afterwards, the warriors of Rheged continued to battle with the Angles until Urien's great-granddaughter Rieinmelth married the Anglian king Oswiu of Northumbria, and Rheged merged with his kingdom.

Interestingly, Urien led an unsuccessful rebellion against Arthur's accession to the throne after the death of Uther Pendragon. According to many authorities, Urien married Arthur's sister Morgaine, Morgana or Morgan le Fay. However, in the Arthurian Romances, Morgaine plots to kill Urien and Arthur and take the sword Excalibur, placing herself on the throne alongside her lover Accolon.

The story of Morcant's betrayal of Urien on Lindisfarne seems reminiscent of the many legends of King Arthur and his illegitimate son, Mordred. In Malory's *Morte d'Arthur*, Mordred battles with Arthur using a spear. However, just before Mordred dies, he inflicts a fatal wound on Arthur's head.[8] Moreover, the grave of Urien lies between two obelisks, like Arthur's supposed grave in Glastonbury and Urien's son Owain, who is buried between two great standing pillars in Penrith on the male current of the Spine of Albion.

Site of Urien's grave, Guile Point

Over the centuries, the many feats of Urien of Rheged and his son Owain remained in the hearts and minds of the Northern Britons, which filtered into Welsh history and later merged into some of the Arthurian legends as they spread from Britain to mainland Europe. Geoffrey of Monmouth, who wrote *History of the Kings of Britain* in the 12th century, places Arthur's death *c.* 542 [9] and Gildas in *On the Ruin of Britain* *c.* 539,[10] fifty years before the death of Urien at the siege of Ynys Metcaut. However, unlike Arthur, the life and exploits of Urien of Rheged are well documented and proven historically.

Gazing across the estuary towards the white obelisks shimmering in the warm summer sun, the grey seals and their pups had now gathered on the blue rocks of Urien's grave to bask for the day. Their wails seemed louder and more intense here as if lamenting the loss of this once great warrior king of the Britons.

On reflection, Lindisfarne's axe-shaped outline, seen from the air, appears more like Urien's crowned head and neck, with the lake called the Lough at the northeast of the island marking his eye. The bay called The Ouse forms his mouth, a group of rocks on the southeast tip of the island called Castle Point creates his long nose, and Bride's Hole on its eastern shores opposite The Lough represents his third eye.

Whin Sill and the Bamburgh Dragon

From St Cuthbert's Isle, we followed the basalt fault line across a long high ridge that overlooks the ruins of Lindisfarne Priory called the Heugh. On the highest point of this ridge is the old coastguard lookout tower built in the 1940s, now the National Nature Reserve information centre. Nearby are medieval foundations believed to be a small lighthouse chapel belonging to the priory. However, archaeologists recently found the foundations of a much earlier chapel a few meters away to the east.

A bay called The Ouse interrupts the basalt fault for a short distance as it continues east to rise dramatically to form Beblowe Crag, on which stands Lindisfarne Castle. This picturesque citadel is one of the most famous visual landmarks of the northeast. Its fairy-tale appearance makes it one of Northumberland's most photographed historic buildings and has attracted tourists for centuries, including artists and poets.

However, the first stone fortification on the crag was during Henry VIII's time, who constructed a fort using the demolished priory's stone as building material after its Dissolution. Further construction took place during the reign of Elizabeth I, although later monarchs considered it of little use, and by the 18th century, it was a lookout tower for the coastguard. In 1901 the publishing magnate Edward Hudson, owner of *Country Life* magazine, refurbished it in the Arts and Crafts style with the help of Sir Edwin Lutyens.

Beblowe Crag is the highest up-thrust of the basalt fault and naturally forms the best defensive position on the island, which suggests that it may have been the site of an Iron Age or Saxon fort. 'Lowe' is a British word for 'hill', and some believe Beb may refer to Bebba, the Anglian queen of Aethelfrith. The nearby hillfort settlement of Bebbanburgh, now known as Bamburgh Castle, may also be attributed to her. Unfortunately, the erection of the Norman Castle destroyed any archaeology from the period of the Angles.

Bamburgh Castle sits on an outcrop formed from the same magnetic whin sill as Beblowe Crag, giving the two sites an energetic connection. We have often found that powerful geology has been the focus of numerous reports of paranormal activity, especially where several fault lines merge. While researching the Belinus Line, we investigated this phenomenon, discovering that geology is also important when explaining the power of significant ancient places such as standing stones, long barrows and earthen mounds.

In our book *The Spine of Albion*, we mention the mystical Isle of Wight and its long history of paranormal events, which include ghostly encounters, time-slips and sightings of strange lights that we believe are due to its unusual tilted geology. The Isle of Wight marks the southernmost point on the Belinus Line and has a unique layer of Upper Greensand, forming a serpent-shaped ridge across the island's spine, stretching from Bembridge Down in the east to the Needles in the west. Like whin sill, which contains layers of limestone, shale and sandstone, Upper Greensand consists of hard crystalline iron-bearing sandstone, otherwise known as Firestone, because of its fiery colour. Local author Gaynor Baldwin writes that the Isle of Wight has many unexplained paranormal phenomena that have taken place all over the island but especially along the serpent ridge, observed by both locals and visitors alike. For example, people have witnessed phantom Roman soldiers marching across Brading Down, marauding Vikings carrying flaming torches and ghostly houses.[11]

Lindisfarne Castle also has its fair share of supernatural 'goings-on', including the apparition of a soldier from the time of the English Civil War when Parliamentarian forces attacked a royalist garrison there. Others have seen a phantom monk, who disappears through a wall, and St Cuthbert himself haunts this area but only becomes visible at night when the moon is full and the tide is high. In his book *The Haunted Isle*, Peter Underwood writes:

> 'Perhaps the most famous appearance of this ghost, if not the best authenticated, is the occasion when it was seen by Alfred the Great, who was a fugitive at the time. Cuthbert's ghost indicated that all would be well and that Alfred would one day sit on the throne of England, and so it came to pass.'[12]

This story is a typical example of the interaction of supernatural beings from the upper worlds or higher planes of existence who can enter our world at magnetic places of unusual geology called thin veil areas and appear as gods or angels to those who encounter them. Likewise, plasma is able to rearrange its own molecular structure for a short time to interact with us here in this dense atomic world.

Lindisfarne Castle from across The Ouse

Basalt rock provides the power to manifest similar mystical occurrences in other parts of the world, including Sedona in Arizona, USA, where it forms the central core of several sacred hills surrounding the town. The Sedona locals call these hills 'vortexes' because of the upward-spiralling behaviour of the energy emitted from them. Furthermore, many psychics are drawn to the Sedona vortexes from across America, unaware of why.

We walked around the steep-sided base of the castle heading east to another smaller flat-topped hillock called Little Beblowe formed of basalt, which reminded us of a miniature version of Uffington's Dragon Hill. From its summit, we had a fantastic panoramic view of the vast expanse of the North Sea, with its dramatic sky and the enigmatic Bamburgh Castle in the distance. We then made our way across the marshes to the end of the whin sill seam on the southeast edge of the island, marked by Castle Point.

Satisfied that we had walked the line of rocks as requested by the insistent dreams and doing our bit to heal the fault line with positive and healing thoughts, crystals and stones along the way, we walked up to the lake called the Lough and Bride's Hole, the remains of a sea cave. On our way back to the village, we visited the Bridge Well, recorded on earlier maps as Brig Well, another name for Bride or Brigid.

That night we had more vivid dreams, and the following day, over breakfast, we realised that yet again they followed the same theme. This time, we were dowsing the line of whin sill with angle rods. We initially ignored the implications of this revelation and decided instead to appease our overwhelming urge to visit Bamburgh Castle.

The castle, standing high on its basalt outcrop, is clearly visible from Lindisfarne and its timeless grandeur is awe-inspiring. The dramatic medieval walls and turrets seem almost sculptured as they stand guard over the North Sea. Its setting is breathtaking, surrounded by sand dunes and one of the UK's most beautiful unspoilt stretches of white sandy beach.

Bamburgh has a fascinating and illustrious history as the Dark Ages royal seat of the Anglian Kings of Northumbria, who were at one time overlords of Britain called Bretwalda's. It seems unlikely but true that this incredible castle was once considered the royal capital of a significant part of Britain for perhaps four hundred years.

Along with crowds of tourists and school children that flock to the castle daily, we wandered around the interior and approached a local guide. He told us about a rather curious dragon myth portrayed in many of the rooms called the 'The Ballad of the Laidly Wyrme' – *wyrme,* or worm, derives from Old Norse meaning serpent or dragon. The tale concerns the daughter of a king, who is turned into a dragon by her jealous stepmother, who terrorises the area until a hero knight sets the princess free. The wicked stepmother's spell rebounds on her and is turned into a toad, which continues to haunt a cave beneath a well under the castle.

Such allegorical tales often refer to the local earth energies and their connection with the site. However, Caroline sensed that the myth might symbolise a feminine dragon energy current, ritually bound within this dramatic magnetic outcrop to harness her flow.

As we made our way to the castle's Keep, we came to the Guard's Chamber and the location of the well mentioned in the legend. The well is said to date from the time of the Anglian kings and has a deep shaft smoothly cut through 140 ft (42 m) of tough whin sill quartz. How in the 6th century they achieved this level of engineering intrigued us, as the only tool capable of carving such a smooth shaft through this type of stone today would be a diamond-tipped drill. Many historians have put forward various theories concerning its construction, including using a combination of fire and water. However, why go to all that trouble to create such perfectly smooth sides unless they could do it effortlessly? This incredible feat reminded us of the expertise of the ancient Egyptians, Phoenicians and Etruscans, who could skilfully cut and smooth the hardest of rocks.

The castle is a hot spot for psychic activity, and an elderly guide entertained us with many of its ghost stories. One included the dramatic spectral leap of a white lady from the castle walls, which only happens at certain times of the year, as if the tragic incident was recorded and constantly replayed. I believe the castle's position on this volcanic plug, the tidal movements of the sea, and the emotionally charged events over the centuries of its long and fraught history have created a 'loop recording' or rip in time, which only psychic people can see. We discovered this to be the case on the world's most paranormal island – the Isle of Wight. Scottish historian Archie McKerracher of the Society of Antiquaries of Scotland claims the Earth's magnetic field can retain the memory of an 'emotional or violent event' that recurs and haunts an area, with generated wavelengths of electromagnetic energy bearing the resemblance of a persistent bad dream.[13]

Although we had plans to visit other areas of Northumbria for our two remaining days, we sensed that the unrelenting dreams were a message from spirit alerting us to either help or recognise this area as unique.

After hearing the story of the dragon princess and her maltreatment at the hands of the evil stepmother at Bamburgh, we felt sure that a feminine dragon or serpent line similar to Elen of the Belinus Line was attached to its castle and needed healing. We also felt strongly that this same feminine energy was present on Lindisfarne and somehow linked to the dowsing of the whin sill ridge we had dreamt about the previous night. Therefore, we decided to spend another day investigating Lindisfarne but this time with our dowsing rods.

Dowsing the Serpent

There was barely a cloud in the sky when we set off from our holiday cottage the following morning, excited about what we might discover on the island after our revelations at Bamburgh. Returning to St Cuthbert's Isle at the western end of the whin sill upthrust, we took out our copper dowsing rods and began dowsing around the shore while waiting for the tides to recede. The ebb and flow of the tides reflect Lindisfarne's history, where periods of significant spiritual importance combine with some of the island's bloodiest and most traumatic events, notably Urien's assassination and the Vikings raids leading up to the destruction of the monastic buildings and shrines. The tide's movements also remind me of the two forces that rule our plane of existence – balance and chaos, where 'entropy' is ever present to upset the natural balance of our world on this vibrational level or school of existence.

The Venerable Bede (672–735 CE), who wrote *Ecclesiastical History of the English People* [14] and *Life of St Cuthbert*,[15] was also fascinated with the tides on Lindisfarne and their relationship to the different phases of the moon. Interestingly, many have witnessed the ghostly apparition of St Cuthbert walking around the little islet on moonlit nights. Many paranormal researchers believe this phenomenon relates to anomalies in the Earth's local magnetic field, causing a ripple in time and allowing us to see the past. St Cuthbert's Isle marks the western tip of the basalt seam, which energetically links it with the castle on Beblowe Crag and Bamburgh Castle across the bay. This unique tidal action severs Lindisfarne's physical and spiritual attachment to

St Cuthbert's Isle, Lindisfarne

the mainland twice a day, creating a change in the ethereal atmosphere perceived by those left on the island – its holy essence and enchanting spirit becoming real and tangible.

From the tales told throughout history about the many miracles associated with Celtic monks such as Columba and Cuthbert, it seems they had great psychic ability and knew how and where to meditate to communicate with spirits and angels, further enhanced through near starvation and sensory deprivation.

Around the shore of St Cuthbert's Isle, visitors collect the tiny bead-like fossils called St Cuthbert's or Cuddy's beads during low tide. These 'beads' come from the stems of carboniferous crinoids, a form of marine echinoderm or 'sea lily'. The holed fossils were then strung together as necklaces or rosaries, hence their association with St Cuthbert and seen as 'fairy money' or good luck charms worn for protection against downing.

The hammering sound on an anvil often accompanied sightings of Cuthbert's ghost, many believing the saint was forging holes in the beads, which he left on the nearby beach for others to find the following day. As we clambered over the rocks, we soon picked up a female serpent or dragon line about 5 ft (1.5 m) wide entering the isle from the west through the foundations of a stone chapel marked by a wooden cross. The energy line continues to a rock on the highest part of the little islet, the possible site of Cuthbert's cell. We felt drawn to meditate on the flow of the feminine dragon energy holding one of our sacred healing stones to help balance and harmonise its flow.

Three years later, Cornish author and dowser Nigel Twinn accompanied us during a weekend trip guiding members of the Ridings Dowsers around the island and found other energy lines here. He wrote of his experiences:

'Three energy currents cross the island [St Cuthbert's Isle], including a particularly strong long-distance female line discovered and described by earth energy specialists Caroline Hoare and Gary Biltcliffe. Some dowsers have said that energy lines begin here, adding yet another level of mystery to the site. I feel they may have interpreted differently the lines that are not 'energy' or 'force', which do indeed start at the chapel on the mound, but which I find to be those of 'consciousness'. There are at least four of them, dating from the Bronze Age or earlier, each aligned to a local or a distant hill, to an island or to a notch on the horizon. While these certainly emanate from the isle, they predate Cuthbert by several generations.'[16]

To our surprise, rather than continuing to follow the whin sill fault across The Heugh, the female energy veered off to the northwest across a little beach towards the Parish Church. On the way, the current passes close to Jenny Bell's Well. Its name and significance are long forgotten but recorded in the late 18th century. The well, now dry, lies at the foot of a stone wall and has steps leading down to allow access to the spring water before it became a midden, cleared by archaeologists in the 1990s.

St Aidan, first Bishop of Lindisfarne

The female current enters the west wall of St Mary the Virgin Parish Church, marked by a stone arch that appears just above ground level. We later discovered that this curious feature was the remains of a doorway belonging to a chantry built in 1304 dedicated to St Mary and St Margaret when the original church floor was two feet lower. The current continues along the church's central aisle to the high altar and through the east window towards the priory ruins. Under the chancel arch, she intersects with a north–south flowing male energy line without forming a node, as if operating on a different frequency.

The old parish church lies at the centre of the small Island community and serves an all-year-round focus for thousands of visitors and pilgrims of different faiths. The building stands on the original site of St Aidan's monastery and wooden church founded in 635 CE, dedicated to St Mary the Virgin, all contained within an earthen boundary ditch and bank. Another church dedicated to St Peter, built during the time of Finan, Bishop of Lindisfarne (651–661), was located a short distance to the east where the priory church now stands, on the same east–west axis as Aidan's monastery. St Peter's was adorned with elaborate carvings in the 'Irish style' and served the monks, whereas St Mary's catered for the wider community. In the early 700s, various Viking raids devastated the island's monastic settlement, which led to its complete abandonment in 875, the surviving monks having fled with the relics of St Cuthbert.

St Mary's Church, Lindisfarne (courtesy of David Smith)

The Celtic Church differed from the doctrines of the Roman Church in several respects, particularly regarding their different methods of calculating the date of Easter, which over many years became 28 days apart. King Oswiu surrendered the Celtic Church of Northumbria to the Church of Rome during the Synod of Whitby in 664 CE, resulting in a split between Lindisfarne and Iona. Many Lindisfarne monks would not accept the decision and departed for Iona, each island becoming the focal point of two separate and distinct Christian traditions. Cuthbert further implemented the principles of the Church of Rome when he arrived as Lindisfarne's new prior in the same year as the Synod.

St Aidan's early life is a mystery, but the Venerable Bede meticulously recorded his later ecclesiastical successes as Bishop of Lindisfarne. Aidan was supposedly born in Connacht in Ireland and travelled to the island of Iona to become a monk in Columba's monastery. In 633, King Oswald of Northumbria requested the help of the Ionian monks to Christianise the pagans of his kingdom after the Angles had discarded the influence of the Celtic Church. King Oswald was a principal exponent of Columba's teachings, having spent his youth in exile on Iona when raised as a warrior king.

Corman was the first monk to assist King Oswald, but his strict approach and indifferent reception failed to impress, and he duly returned to Iona, claiming the North Country pagans as *ungovernable and of an obstinate and barbarous temperament.* Later they agreed that Aidan's more liberal philosophy towards conversion would be more suited. He duly arrived in Northumbria around 635 CE, accompanied by twelve monks.

He first founded a church within the stronghold of Oswald's castle at Bamburgh. But the nature of Lindisfarne's tides provided a more suitable haven for the monks to continue their missionary work away from the royal court. Furthermore, Aidan preferred a simple life, caring little for worldly possessions and gave much of what he received from the king and the local landed noblemen to those in need. As Aidan spoke and understood little of the English language, King Oswald frequently accompanied him on his journeys as an interpreter. Aidan also created a school for young Anglo-Saxon boys to train for the priesthood, several of whom went on to make their ecclesiastical mark during that period, including St Eata, St Cedd and St Chad, who became Bishop of Mercia.

When King Oswald died fighting the pagan King Penda in 642, Bishop Aidan developed a good relationship with his brother King Oswiu. When the new king realised that Aidan was travelling to his various ministries on foot, he immediately presented him with a fine horse and trappings. Having encountered a beggar during his travels asking for alms, Aidan promptly gave the man his new horse and continued on his way, much to King Oswiu's consternation. Aidan died in 651 and interred beneath the church of St Peter on Lindisfarne.[17]

Later a stone church replaced the wooden church of St Mary, and a chancel was added in the 12th century. In the 19th century, it was subjected to a thorough restoration incorporating remnants of the original 7th-century structure, such as the quern stones at the base of the chancel arch. The removal of internal plaster revealed its striking multi-coloured stones and parts of a round-headed Saxon arch.

As you enter the south aisle, a large imposing sculpture called 'The Journey' greets you, comprising thirty-five pieces of elmwood carved mainly with a chain-saw. It depicts a life-size image of monks carrying St Cuthbert's entombed body from the island to safety after a Viking attack. Between 698 and 920 CE, the coffin rested at various places on its long journey, which was said to have lasted 222 years until it reached its final resting place at Durham Cathedral.

As we strolled around the interior of St Mary's, the setting sun cast orange beams of light through the stained-glass windows, illuminating the fine woodcarving of St Cuthbert's coffin. We noticed a small diagram of the present church hanging on the wall showing the whereabouts of the old Saxon foundations marked in red. The plan is the result of a dowsing survey by R M Bailey, H Cambridge and H D Briggs, which was published in *Dowsing and Church Architecture* in 1988.[18] According to their plan, the crossing of the female dragon current and the unknown male energy line under the chancel arch was marking the exact location of the Saxon high altar.

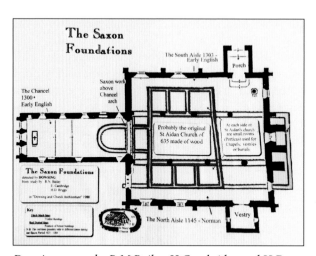

Dowsing survey by R M Bailey, H Cambridge and H D Briggs of St Mary's Church, Lindisfarne

Curious to know where this male energy line may lead us, we followed it through the priory grounds to the top of the Heugh, where archaeologists uncovered a stone chapel thought to be the very first church built on the island before the time of Aidan. According to Bede, St Columba sent missionaries to build churches at specific sites in northern Britain to spread Christianity across the heathen lands. Could this be the first seeding of Christianity from Iona?

The Priory and the Grail

We continued following the female current from St Mary's Church through its east wall into the graveyard to an ancient weathered stone socket, known locally as the 'petting stone'. It is a tradition for any new bride married in the church to be assisted over the stone by the island's fishermen. The practice has spanned generations and is said to bring good luck and fertility to newlyweds. The oldest tradition says the bride must stride over the stone without falling, or the marriage will fail. Perhaps these stories were unconsciously influenced by the female serpent energy line, as it amplifies the stone's power.

The socket once held a great cross erected by Ethelwold, Bishop of Lindisfarne (721–740). Interestingly, the cross was so revered that after it was damaged during the first Danish incursion, the monks skilfully pieced it together with cement and lead. Then, along with Cuthbert's relics, the monks took the cross on the long journey to

Durham, where it stood in the cathedral graveyard until its final destruction during the Reformation.

Curiously, carved on the cross base are cup-marks similar to those seen on numerous rocks and stones around Northumberland's hills dating to the Neolithic or Bronze Age, suggesting prehistoric origins. After further research, we discovered other cup-marked stones on the island, including one found during excavations of a Tudor building called 'The Palace' on the village's eastern boundary. In addition, cup marks appear on some of the masonry of the priory, perhaps recognised as holy by the Benedictine stonemasons or architects, who incorporated these stones into their newly-built monastery. Many examples of prehistoric rock art exist in Northumberland and throughout Scotland, their purpose a mystery, although our ancient ancestors revered them.

Inside the ruins, the female current continues through an impressive carved Norman dog-tooth arch, once the ceremonial entrance that led into the nave, of which little remains. The current widens as she travels down the central east–west aisle of the old priory church incorporating its lofty sandstone pillars. Within the evocative ruins, the line clips a deep well that supplied drinking water for the monks.

The Petting Stone in St Mary's Church graveyard, Lindisfarne

The Benedictines from Durham built their new priory in the 1120s just below the Heugh's basalt ridge over the Saxon St Peter's Church that once housed the shrines of St Aidan and St Cuthbert.

Kate Tristram writes that the architecture of Lindisfarne Priory is in the likeness of the old St Peter's church that became the new resting place of St Cuthbert's shrine. They used the same decoration for the pillars and the same design for the vaulted ceiling creating a grand and elaborate church, which would usually seem out of place for such a small island.[20] Although the roof and much of the old priory walls have gone, the weathered dark red sandstone pillars are still striking, showing the classic early Norman zig-zag patterning, perhaps copied from Durham Cathedral. Another outstanding feature is the famous ornately sculpted 'rainbow arch', a remnant from the high crossing vault that

Ruins of Lindisfarne Priory

hovered above the transepts and once held the weight of a tower until it collapsed in the 18th century.

In the north transept resting against the wall is another carved stone socket base dating to Saxon times showing entwined serpents, its original position unknown. The carving seems to mimic the serpentine nature of the female energy line that flows through here as it continues to the site of the missing tower and high altar.

As I passed through the priory doorway, I remembered a lucid dream I had a few nights ago. As a monk guided me around the ruins, he told me that, like Iona, this priory stands on a former megalithic site and that one or more of its revered stones are in the foundations. Furthermore, the powerful telluric energy of the megalithic site was transferred from the old site to the new. I asked my dowsing rods to show me one of these unique stones, and soon I was standing at the edge of the south transept where I found a sizeable unhewn megalith lying on its side within the flow of the current. Many have witnessed the ghost of St Cuthbert wandering around the ruins, particularly in the area of this stone.

Megalithic stone in the foundations of Lindisfarne Priory

While visiting the priory with the Ridings Dowsing Group, Nigel Twinn detected an etheric shape of two counter-rotating spinning infinity symbols close to the well in the centre of the nave. At several chambered tombs and long barrows around Cornwall and Wales, Nigel and his wife Ros had dowsed the same form, initially found by dowser Hamish Miller. However, up until then, they had never encountered such an earth energy feature outside of a megalithic enclosed space. Other dowsers dated the well to pre-Roman times, indicating that perhaps the large foundation stone originally came from a prehistoric monument that once stood on this spot near the well.

A tinge of melancholy is attached to these weatherworn ruins, the semi-circular walled sanctuary, the most sacred part of the church that once held the high altar, now empty and austere, any vestiges of its holy past removed long ago. The relics of

St Aidan and St Cuthbert and their elaborate shrines never graced the interior of the new Benedictine priory, having been removed before the arrival of the Normans. But, according to local tales, the ghost of Cuthbert took part in the dedication ceremony of the new Norman monastery when he was seen processing along with other ghostly priests and monks out of St Mary's Church to the priory to celebrate mass. Afterwards, the holy spectres returned to the church. This ghostly procession supports the tradition that St Mary's Church existed before the construction of the priory and was built over St Aidan's original church.

I also felt that a physical Grail was kept here, possibly a cup linked to the power of the female serpent energy. After reading *The Celtic Chronicles: The True Story of the Holy Grail* by Maurice Cotterell, the Grail connection here made sense. The author believes that the Ardagh Chalice, one of Ireland's most precious relics, is the Holy Grail and ended up in the hands of the monks of Lindisfarne for safekeeping. The monks later incorporated its secrets into the celebrated manuscript known as the *Lindisfarne Gospels* and possibly the *Book of Kells*.

The chalice's date is determined by the similarity of its inscribed lettering with those in the Lindisfarne Gospels, which date from *c.* 710–720. But many experts believe the chalice is from the 5th century Byzantine Empire or earlier and therefore may have influenced the style of the Lindisfarne Gospels. There are powerful crystals set into the cup, which I believe imbues any liquid inside it with healing qualities. After fleeing from the Vikings, the monks carried the holy cup to Ireland.[21]

Ardagh Chalice

The Grail cup symbolism and the discovery of a potent feminine serpent/dragon energy current on the island seemed significant. We later found that visualising the image of the healing cup aided the dowsing of the feminine flow across the wilds of Northumberland and Scotland.

Looking up at the sky through the roofless ruins, I remembered another strange event recorded by the monks here in 793 and written down in the 9th-century *Anglo-Saxon Chronicle*. It describes the first wave of Viking attacks on the early monastery, '*Here were dreadful forewarnings come over the land of Northumbria, and woefully terrified the people: these were amazing sheets of lightning and whirlwinds and fiery dragons were seen flying in the sky.*'[22] This extraordinary event heralded the downfall of the religious community and the dispersal of its famous relics. I wondered if the 'serpents' were comets or meteorites, for in history, comets were often prophecies of doom.

The tales of lightning, whirlwinds and fiery dragons are also akin to plasma-related phenomena. Plasma is highly luminous and can exist outside our space-time continuum, performing extraordinary manoeuvres, which many in the past interpreted as dragons or serpents. Lightning is an example of partially ionised plasmas, and whirlwinds could be plasma vortices that form during daylight hours. According to many witnesses of UFO encounters, the belief that they had seen spaceships, aliens or even the Virgin Mary seemed very real to them. Modern researchers claim that UFOs in the form of balls of light are plasma entities that can morph or rearrange their molecular structure into an acceptable apparition depending on the belief system of the observer. Perhaps the 8th-century serpents in the sky event on Lindisfarne was a warning of an impending Viking invasion from higher intelligences.

When the Normans took control of England and its religious fraternity, they demanded that the remaining Celtic Christian monks leave the island unless they converted to Benedictine rule. The pious existence of the Celtic Christian monks, renowned for living simply in isolated earthen floor buildings made of stone or wood, was an aversion to the more wealthy Norman religious orders. Neither would they approve of these monks preaching amongst the rural communities, helping and healing the poor and vulnerable. Unlike the Benedictines, who owned vast acreages of land and many churches and mills, the monks of Lindisfarne were never wealthy and held little in the way of land.

Leaving the priory behind, we dowsed the current meandering east through a complex of old stone cottages before crossing the picturesque bay called The Ouse. Here, we stopped to observe some of the many birds and wildfowl that frequent the island during certain times of the year, including ringed plovers, oystercatchers, lapwings and Brent geese.

The Castle and the Mound

On the opposite shores of the bay, we dowsed the feminine energy skirting the base of the whin sill upthrust known as Beblowe Crag before disappearing through the western walls of Lindisfarne Castle. As members of the National Trust, we were keen to look around the building to see where the serpent would take us. We first detected her in The Ship Room, named after a model of a ship suspended from the roof, and the dining room with its impressive stained-glass windows. This area was once part of the army barracks until the famous Victorian architect Sir Edwin Lutyens restored it into a home for the Hudson family in 1903. After following the current through the entrance hall, once the sitting room, we realised that it was attracted to all of the castle's main reception rooms, frequented by the thousands of visitors it receives annually.

From here, the serpent flow takes us to Little Beblowe mound just east of the castle with a flattened summit. Yet another male energy line intercepts the dragon's flow here, creating a radiating spiral of energy that incorporates the entire hilltop.

Intriguingly, there is no mention of this flat-topped rock in any historical or archaeological accounts of the island, except that it had been quarried in the past and used as part of the old Waggonway rail link to the north shore. More intriguing still is that, like Beblowe Crag, this minor unidentified feature emits a potent telluric energy.

Lindisfarne's rich and varied rocks have suffered from the consequences of frequent exploitation over the centuries, as evidenced by the old jetties that carried stone quarried on the island to other parts of Northumberland. Remarkably the island's geology is rich in all types of rock, including sedimentary limestones, sandstones and coal, and igneous rocks such as fine-grained quartz dolerite and metamorphic slate and shales. The proximity of this varied geology and a significant fault line of magnetic basalt radiates a subtle healing energy, amplified by the ebb and flow of Lindisfarne's unique tides. However, as mentioned earlier, this power exists on the superspectrum level and is only perceived by sensitive people. Interestingly, places on or next to the basalt seam are the only sites on the island that have encountered ghostly activity.

After Little Beblowe mound, the female serpent line curves towards the southeast, passing through the old lime kilns, the dark interior reminiscent of a cave. Finally, after crossing an area of grassland and a large patch of wildflowers called 'Grass of Parnassus', the serpent current meets the North Sea, marked by a group of rocks known as Castle Point. As we gazed out to sea upon the path of the female serpent, we could see the imposing stone ramparts of Bamburgh Castle in the distance.

While dowsing and connecting with the feminine serpent along the whin sill/basalt ridge, Caroline kept sensing the presence of the goddess Bride. We wondered whether the visions we experienced during our initial dreams were a form of communication from this ancient deity. Caroline also felt that our connection with Bride's Hole and Brigwell the previous day was significant. Perhaps our psychic friend had foreseen this connection when urging us to connect with Bride while staying on Lindisfarne.

From that moment, we called the feminine dragon/serpent energy Bride, which seemed appropriate as the ancient tribes of Northern Britain and Scotland once revered her. While standing on her flow at Castle Point, we felt compelled to offer her one of our precious green serpentine healing stones collected from the beaches of Iona in honour of this ancient goddess of

Mysterious mound by Lindisfarne Castle on the Bride current

the land. These particular stones originate deep inside Mother Earth and are imbued with the essence of her nourishing healing power. Little did we know that this would be an omen for what we were about to discover – an energetic connection between two sacred holy islands and the discovery of a potential pilgrim route.

The Goddess Bride and the Chapel of the Rose

The British and Irish Celts honoured the goddess in the land through their worship of Bride, later canonised by the Roman Catholic Church as Bridget to disguise her antiquity and actual status as 'the great mother', also known as An or Anu. As a result, early cultures called her 'Britannia' or Brit Anna, and she became the female personification of Albion or Britain.

She is the goddess of birth and fertility and the element of fire and represents the intelligence of nature. According to legend, the Irish pagan goddess Brigid had her main sanctuary at Kildare, where she guarded a perpetual flame along with nineteen virgin maidens during a 20-day cycle. Her flame was honoured at every hearth in every home and the smithy, whose fires create the utensils and tools of life and death.

Also known as Brigid, Brig, Brid, Brit, and Brigit, vestiges of this British goddess can still be found all over the UK, although mainly in the North of England, Scotland and Ireland. Another derivative of Bride is Brigantia, revered by the Brigantians, the most authoritative Iron Age tribe of northern England. Many cultures referred to her as the swan goddess and associated her with the constellation of Cygnus. At some point, the swan replaced the stork as a bringer of newborn babies, perhaps due to Bride's association with fertility. Therefore, maybe it is no coincidence that the place where the whooper swans rest on Lindisfarne before their migration north in the spring is named 'Bride's Hole'. Andrew Collins writes, *'In Britain, the cult of the swan is likely to have come under the protection of Bride, whose feast day, 1st February, marked the northern departure of the migrating swans.'*[23] Her other animal consorts were the cow and, in Scotland, the adder.

During our investigations of the Belinus alignment and the Celtic royal omphalos sites for our book *The Power of Centre*, we discovered that Bride's powerful feminine qualities still reside at many sacred places in the British landscape, particularly in the ancient lands of the Picts or Pictii.

The following day, during a last-minute stroll around the village before vacating the holiday cottage, we noticed the locals preparing for a grand open-air ecclesiastical event on the priory grounds. A large gathering of pilgrims was due to arrive from far and wide, representing six Christian denominations to celebrate the return of the 8th-century illuminated *Lindisfarne Gospels* to Durham. As we exited the island along the causeway, passing hundreds of pilgrims as they made their way by foot across the vast sandy causeway, we wondered whether the island's spirit had utilised us to help in some way to prepare it energetically for this grand ceremony.

On the advice of our psychic friend, we headed north along the A1 towards Edinburgh to visit Rosslyn Chapel. Here she envisioned Caroline taking a piece of amber, although we had no clue why and just trusted that a higher spiritual purpose was at play.

Just as we approached the River Tweed near Coldstream, which forms a natural border between Northumbria and Scotland, we noticed a sign pointing to the famous Battle of Flodden site. A strong feeling propelled us to go there, and we soon arrived at the village of Branxton. Standing at the gate of its historic church, we saw a large stone cross on a hill commemorating the bloodiest battle ever fought on British soil, also known as the Battle of Branxton Moor. The conflict saw the Scottish forces led by King James IV clash with those of Henry VIII led by Thomas Howard, Earl of Surrey. Although England's forces were victorious, over 14,000 men fell in one day.

We found an information board that showed a battlefield plan with clearly marked paths. We followed a track that meandered through a patchwork of fields to the granite monument viewed from the church. Here we sat and visualised pure healing light radiating across the traumatised landscape caused by this shocking and bloody event in 1513. As we stood in silence in this remote place, with only the skylark and a few humming bees to keep us company, it was hard to believe that it marked the centre of a tumultuous battle. Unlike the Scottish battle sites of Culloden and Bannockburn with their innovative information centres, gift shops and cafés, there is nothing here but a solitary cross to memorialise the loss of thousands of men. However, I couldn't help but feel that continuing to commemorate these bloody events, which in many cases are vividly retold and re-enacted, showing every gory detail, only perpetuates the negative emotional charge that scars the land. Our visit to this battle site seemed to be an omen of the dual nature of the powerful energy line we were about to uncover.

An hour later, we arrived at Rosslyn Chapel near the village of Roslin in Midlothian, located 7 miles (11 km) south of Edinburgh. As we approached the chapel, Caroline found a quiet spot to meditate, holding the piece of amber selected for the task. She then asked the chapel's spiritual guardian where to place the stone to help with any healing required. After a moment, an image of the northwest corner gave us the location. Here we visualised its healing power positively affecting the energies associated with the chapel. After the stone had completed its work, it was removed so as not to pollute the sacred place. Amber is the fossilised, hardened resin of trees millions of years old and has many metaphysical qualities. One is the absorption and transmutation of opposing forces into positive energies. But little did we realise that the amber at Rosslyn Chapel was preparing the way for our future quest across Northumberland and Scotland.

After a pleasant tour around the elaborately carved interior and a delicious lunch in the newly-built café, we readied ourselves for the long return trip to Dorset.

Discovering the Holy Axis

After arriving home and digesting all our experiences during the trip, we started researching the intriguing places we had visited. Sensing they had a link with Iona, I struck a line on Google Earth between Lindisfarne and Iona but interestingly found nothing significant along its path to mark it as a ley. However, when I moved the eastern end of the line south from Lindisfarne to the inner precincts of Bamburgh Castle, the site of Aidan's first church before he moved to Lindisfarne, a ley began to form. Finally, after moving the western end of the line a fraction to *Reilig Odhráin,* the burial ground of the kings, south of Iona Abbey, the ley revealed itself and the Holy Axis was born. The axis seemed impressive right from the start, passing through several important and renowned historical and spiritual places of power, including Rosslyn Chapel, the prehistoric sanctuary of Cairnpapple, Torphichen Preceptory, and two holy islands on Loch Lomond. Later, after examining the line in more detail, I discovered more places of spiritual importance that I had never heard of before.

The line points to the eastern horizon at 107 degrees, where the sun rises on or around 27 February and 15 October. In the west, the line points to where the sun sets at 287 degrees around the 26 August and 14 April. Interestingly during the 7th century, sunrise at 107 degrees marked the feast day of St Edwin of Northumbria, on 12 October. Edwin was King of Deira and Bernicia, later becoming King of all Northumbria and overlord of eastern Mercia, Isle of Man, Anglesey, Kent and Wessex, giving him the title 'Bretwalda' with Bamburgh Castle being his capital. Characteristics of this great king compare with those of the Hunter/God/Warrior Lugh and Orion, whose constellation rises in the east on his feast day.

The early Celtic Christian monks such as Columba, Aidan, Cuthbert and Eata, whose teachings have hugely influenced British history, are linked with Iona and Lindisfarne, Scotland's and England's most holy islands. Iona was the burial ground of numerous kings, more than anywhere else in Britain and revered as the 'Isle of the Dead' or the

Celtic realm of Avalon. Many Scottish folklorists believe the legendary King Arthur was taken here after being mortally wounded during his final battle.

While investigating the Spine of Albion in Scotland, the name Arthur appears in the ancient text *Y Gododdin*, written in poetic form as an epitaph to a tribe who ruled the Lothians in Scotland called the *Gododdin* as they prepared for battle against the Angles at Catterick in 600 BCE. One poem mentions their great cavalry warrior Gwawrddur, who was killed during the fight, *'though he was not Arthur … he was among the strong ones in battle.'* In another poem, Arthur's horse compares to *'Gwawrddur's mount.'* [25]

The Gododdin, like all Celtic tribes, had their own 'Isle of the dead' or Avalon, where they buried their kings. Authors such as Stuart McHardy [26] and Philip Coppens [27] believed this was either Invalone, Inchcolm or the Isle of May in the Firth of Forth. Coppens associates the word 'May' with 'the Maiden' referring to an island sanctuary tended by women similar to St Bridget's Nunnery at Kildare in Ireland. Yet, there is no evidence of such a settlement in Scotland during the Dark Ages when Arthur lived. Curiously, they discounted Lindisfarne even though it was within the Gododdin's territory. Legends and medieval Romances refer to Avalon as a fertile island of apple trees, unlike the rocky isles of May or Inchcolm. However, Lindisfarne has fertile land with a mild climate, where farming continues today.

Moreover, Avalon being a renowned pagan burial ground, would be a prime target for Christian settlement, which also corresponds to Iona and Lindisfarne. The former cave, Bride's Hole on Lindisfarne, might be a memory of goddess worship, suggesting the possible site of a sanctuary tended by maidens to heal the sick. Interestingly the island's earlier name Medcaut means 'Isle of Healing', and medicinal herbs still grow there.

Our next mission was to investigate Bamburgh Castle, a citadel of the Northern British tribes and Anglian kings that marks the start of the Holy Axis pilgrimage between these two legendary Avalons.

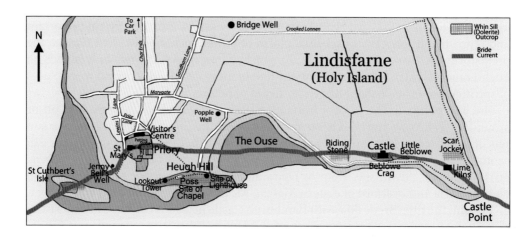

1. Magnusson, M. 1984. *Lindisfarne, the Cradle Island*. Oriel Press Ltd, Stocksfield, Northumberland.
2. McKeehan, I. P. 1933. *The Book of the Nativity of St. Cuthbert*. Cambridge University Press.
3. Krajewski, Elizabeth. M. G. 2017. *The Anonymous Life of Cuthbert: A Celtic Account of an Anglo-Saxon Saint*? Department of Celtic Languages & Literatures, Harvard University, USA.
4. 5. 15. Bede (Author), Simon Webb (Editor), 2016. *Life of St Cuthbert*. CreateSpace Independent Publishing Platform.
6. Bromwich, R. 1961. *The Welsh Triads*. The University of Wales Press, Cardiff.
7. Morris, J. 1980. '*Nennius*' *British History and the Welsh Annals*. Phillimore, London.
8. Malory, Sir T. Matthews, J. et al. 2003. *Le Morte d'Arthur*. Cassell, London.
9. Thorpe, L. 1966. *The History of the Kings of Britain*. Translated. Introduction to Geoffrey of Monmouth, p.17. Penguin Books, London.
10. Morris, J. 1978. *Gildas: The Ruin of Britain and Other Documents*. Phillimore, London.
11. Biltcliffe, G. and Hoare, C. 2012. *The Spine of Albion*. Sacred Lands Publishing, Weymouth.
12. Underwood, Peter. 1984. *This Haunted Isle: The Ghosts and Legends of Britain's Historic Buildings*. Harrap, London.
13. McKerracher, Archie. 2006. *Perthshire: In History and Legend*. John Donald Publishers Ltd, Edinburgh.
14. Dumville, D. 2003. Bede: *Ecclesiastical History of the English People*, translated by L. Shirly-Price and D. Farmer. Penguin Classics, London.
16. https://nigeltwinn.org/
17. Frodsham, P. 2009. *Cuthbert and the Northumbrian Saints*. Northern Heritage, Newcastle-upon-Tyne.
18. Bailey, Richard N. et al. 1988. *Dowsing and Church Archaeology*. Intercept Ltd, Andover. 20. Tristram, Kate. 2009. *The Story of Holy Island: An Illustrated History*. Canterbury Press, Norwich.
21. Cotterell, M. 2006. *The Celtic Chronicles: The True Story of the Holy Grail*. The Celtic Press, Dublin.
22. https://www.bl.uk/learning/timeline/item126532.html
23. Collins, A. 2006. *The Cygnus Mystery*. Watkins Publishing, London.
24. https://web.archive.org/web/20090607090718/
25. Moffat, A. 1999. *Arthur and the Lost Kingdoms*. Wiedenfeld & Nicholson, London.
26. McHardy, S. 2001. *The Quest for Arthur*. Luath Press Ltd, Edinburgh.
27. Coppens, P. 2007. *Land of the Gods*. Frontier Publishing, Amsterdam.

Chapter 2

Bamburgh and the Farne Islands

'At Bamburgh above all we are pilgrims
come to do our service at one of the great
cradles of our national life.
Round Bamburgh and its founder, Ida, all
Northumbrian history gathers.' [1]

View of Bamburgh Castle

The following spring, we arrived at the picture-postcard coastal village of Bamburgh in Northumberland to begin our journey researching the Holy Axis. The fairy-tale castle stands on a natural plateau of volcanic whin sill overlooking fine white sandy beaches that stretch far into the distance. The sprawling curtain walls of Bamburgh Castle include round and square towers that show different periods of masonry spanning over nine acres of land. Rising out of the centre of this Camelot-styled fortress is the original Norman Keep dating from 1164, with impenetrable 10–13 ft (3-4 m) thick walls. Such impressive architecture indicates the strategic importance of this isolated rock from ancient times when it was a significant royal citadel of the Anglian territory of Bernicia for three centuries. The castle became the theatre of early Christian saints and high kings, whose fame has inspired writers and poets up until modern times.

The Holy Axis alignment, plotted initially using Google Earth, enters the mainland through the castle's southeast entrance, passing close to St Peter's Chapel and through the Norman Keep, and leaves the fortress through the Belle Tower, also known as the Clock Tower, recently converted as holiday accommodation.

The 12th-century English chronicler, Symeon of Durham, wrote of Bamburgh Castle in *Historia Regum* (History of the Kings), which also draws from the writings of the Venerable Bede *c.* 731 CE:

> 'The city of Bebba is extremely well fortified, but by no means large, containing about the space of two or three fields, having one hollowed entrance ascending in a wonderful manner by steps. It has on the summit of the hill, a church of very beautiful architecture, in which is a fair and costly shrine. In this, wrapped in a pall, lies the uncorrupted right hand of St Oswald king, as Bede the historian of this nation relates. There is on the west and highest point of this citadel, a well, excavated with extraordinary labour, sweet to drink, and very pure to the sight.'[2]

The 'hollowed entrance' Symeon refers to is St Oswald's Gate, which still exists today, the opening cut through solid rock. It also has a set of very worn steps leading up to it. The entrance faces Lindisfarne Castle and Castle Point on the island's southeastern tip, where we dowsed the Bride serpent current the previous year. Symeon also mentions the first church built at Bamburgh, founded by St Aidan dedicated to St Peter, and an ancient well, now inside the medieval Keep, both on the Holy Axis.

Dowsing the Castle Node

We began our dowsing explorations of the castle by walking around its exterior. We soon detected Bride disappearing through a stone stack at the northwestern end of the walls from the direction of Lindisfarne. The tall pile of masonry stands close to the ancient arched doorway of St Oswald's Gate, which once served as the main entrance during the time of the Angles. Then, continuing along a path below the castle's west walls that looks down upon the cricket and bowling fields, we suddenly identified another serpent current, just as wide and strong as the female, flowing through the Belle Tower marked by the Holy Axis.

After further dowsing, we determined that this line had masculine and solar attributes,

Rock Stack and Windmill with St Oswald's Gate below

and when consulting a colour-spectrum dowsing chart, we dowsed it to be a golden yellow colour. The female serpent line we call Bride has the colour violet vibrating through her flow – both colours are similar to the male and female dragon energies Elen and Belinus that accompanies the north–south Belinus alignment.

Taking a footpath on the seaward side of the castle, we again met with the male current as it entered the castle grounds through a walled rampart, although no noticeable feature seemed to mark its passage. Meanwhile, a bit further south, we found Bride passing through the walls just north of the main visitor's entrance. Here we notice a blocked-up doorway with stone steps leading down to it. Next to the door was a carved stone stoup, possible remnants of an old chapel in one of the castle's lower levels.

Observing the trajectory of the male and female currents as they approached and departed the castle, we felt confident that they formed a node somewhere inside its precincts. However, despite our eagerness to explore the castle's interior and Keep, the lure of discovering Bride's journey from Lindisfarne to Bamburgh Castle was too strong. Strolling across Bamburgh's beautiful white sandy beach northwards towards Harkess Rocks, we detected Bride weaving along the outcrops of dolerite, shale and limestone. As we skirted the blue dolerite stones with the gentle ripples of the sea lapping at our heels, we suddenly came across an unusual figure of a white stag painted onto the flat vertical surface of a rock appropriately named Stag Rock. The research of this figure revealed a legend commemorating a stag that jumped into the sea to escape hunters after being chased from Spindlestone Heughs, a group of high crags a few miles west of here. However, another theory suggests that Italian prisoners of war painted it during WWII.

Despite its uncertain origins, many people who visit these rocks feel a powerful and mysterious atmosphere emanating from this place. The stag is a noble, intelligent creature that can outrun and outwit the hunter. In a group of Arthurian Romances known as the *Vulgate Cycle*, a white stag heralds the spiritual quest of the knights to pursue the Holy Grail. According to the story, Lancelot, approaching the Grail Castle, sees a vision of a white stag borne up by angels, indicating his closeness to the spirit world. Although the painted stag has no great age, the fact that Bride passes through this figure is interesting. Perhaps the serpent current is absorbing the spiritual symbolism of the stag projected by the artist. That we encounter an image of this enigmatic creature right at the start of our quest along this Holy Axis is also symbolic. From here, Bride journeys across the sea to Lindisfarne's Castle Point.

Returning to Bamburgh, we purchased our ticket and a handy plan of the inner wards of the castle and entered through the 'Great Gate'. We were somewhat overawed by the historical importance of this once great citadel, although exhilarated at the prospect

White Stag marking the Bride flow at Harkess Rocks

of discovering the first node of these powerful serpent lines. We felt the spirits of the past all around us as we proceeded to the East Ward and the ruins of St Peter's Chapel, their ever-watchful gaze judging our progress.

We first visit the Belle Tower to connect with the Holy Axis alignment and the current of the male serpent/dragon. Then, after reacquainting ourselves with the current's solar aspect, we followed its meandering trail with our dowsing rods over an area of excavated masonry to a modern, finely carved stone seat. This unusual sculpture outside the north wall of the Keep is a reproduction of an 8th-century throne used by the early Northumbrian kings. The carved arm of the original, discovered during archaeological excavations, is now on display in the castle's museum.

When meditating in this replica seat, I immediately started to see a series of images as if receiving a download of information. One included a pillar of rock, another a church with a tall tower, a male warrior figure and an open moorland dotted with cup and ring marked stones. None of these images made sense until we discovered they represented significant sites on the male current of the Holy Axis in Northumberland.

Looking down from the throne at a section of the unearthed archaeological relics, I wondered what other unique finds had been discovered. Dr Brian Hope-Taylor from Cambridge University spent many years excavating at Bamburgh between 1959 and 1962 and 1970 and 1974 but died before he could publish his work. Moreover, most of the results of his excavations are unknown, and curiously many of his discoveries have since disappeared.

One of Hope-Taylor's most significant finds was the 'Bamburgh Sword' in 1959, rediscovered in 2001 and declared the only one of its kind in the world. This regal sword dating from the 6–7th century contains six strands of twisted iron to form a herringbone pattern edged with steel, which would have taken over six weeks to complete – a blade certainly fit for a great king! We wondered if this Excalibur-like talisman belonged to one of the many symbolic wounded kings who perished in these lands. Could it be the sword of Urien, assassinated in Lindisfarne, or Oswald, who returned from Iona and performed the impossible by defeating Cadwallon, the last king of the Celtic Britons, and the illustrious Saxon warlord Penda to take back his father's lands? Perhaps it was a symbolic object to be venerated, like a Grail Sword, one of the most important of three Grail hallows associated with the Fisher King, the others being the spear and the cup.

Also found were finely worked solid pieces of gold, including one depicting a stylised animal known as the 'Bamburgh Beast'. Thankfully, the Bamburgh Research Project, set up in 1996 under archaeologist Graeme Young, is piecing together all the previous information concerning Hope-Taylor's archaeological discoveries. Further planned digs may uncover more evidence of Bamburgh's illustrious past.[3]

From the throne, the male current enters the Keep's west wall before heading out to sea through the Inner Ward towards the Farne Islands. As we stood looking over the battlements, we could make out this small group of islands in the distance, where once Aidan and Cuthbert lived in their tiny cells, now home to a beautiful array of sea birds, including puffins, terns, shags and kittiwakes.

Our next mission was to locate Bride's flow as she entered the stone stack near the old St Oswald's Gate, the original and only entrance to the castle in the 7th century. While strolling along a path between immaculately kept lawns, we noticed some sizeable blocks of stone in the archway of this historic Saxon gateway. The female current first connects with an old windmill before crossing the West Ward through a turret known as Waldehaveswell. She then disappears into the old stable building, now a gallery, adorned on its exterior wall with a stunning glass sculpture of a galloping horse called 'Silver' by the local glass artist Rena Holford. Silver is the lunar quality of the moon, a perfect representation of the feminine energy of the Bride serpent.

The edge of her flow overlaps with the male serpent at the replica stone throne before she also disappears through the nine-foot-thick walls of the Keep, suggesting that the two currents might form a 'node' inside. Hamish Miller was the first to discover that where dragon lines meet to form nodes at certain places of power, they narrowed down to a point in the ground, only to reappear a little further away.[4] This perfectly describes the Z-pinch node discovered in plasma tubes mentioned by Robert Temple in *A New Science of Heaven*, discussed in the introduction.

The medieval Keep sits on the highest point of the castle complex, over a well bored down to the deepest parts of the rock citadel. Perhaps a great hall stood where the Keep is now, belonging to the time of the Anglian kings of Northumbria or the magnificently carved basilica of St Peter said to have been founded by Aidan and King Oswald. Perhaps the ancient well, now on the ground floor of the Keep, may have previously stood inside the basilica or great hall.

According to *An Archaeological Investigation of Bamburgh Castle's Hidden Past* by Graeme Young, much of the Anglian fortress was destroyed after the Viking raids in 993 CE. However, the site remained a citadel during England's rule by the later Scandinavian kings, possibly due to its strategic position overlooking the North Sea close to the Scottish border.[5]

In 1095, after a long siege, the Earl of Northumbria finally surrendered Bamburgh to the Normans under King William Rufus, who built a new royal castle on the site. In 1164 the Keep was added along with a chapel rededicated to St Oswald. In 1610,

The Keep at Bamburgh Castle marking the node

King James I of England granted Bamburgh to Claudius Forster, whose father, Sir Nicholas, travelled from Scotland to England to claim the English throne on behalf of King James VI of Scotland upon the death of Queen Elizabeth I.

After eventually falling into ruin, it was purchased in 1704 by Nathaniel Crewe, Bishop of Durham. He allowed Thomas Sharp, the Archdeacon of Northumberland, to strip the castle of all its materials, leaving the remaining shell to deteriorate. Subsequently, a hospital, a school and later a hospice for shipwrecked sailors occupied this site. Finally, in 1894, it was bought by industrialist William

Armstrong, First Baron Armstrong, who reconstructed the castle as a stately home, which his descendants still own.

To explore the interior of the Keep, we entered the castle through its elaborate staterooms. With our dowsing rods discreetly hidden, we strolled through the impressive entrance room and the King's Hall with its ornate Victorian restoration, although the style is medieval. Its superb 19th-century vaulted hammer beam roof was constructed using teak donated by the King of Siam. King Henry III first ordered the construction of the King's Hall in 1221 as a reception room away from the Keep. He also installed glass windows and proper chimneys to protect against the fierce North Sea weather.

Dragon carving inside Bamburgh Castle (by kind permission of Bamburgh Castle Estate)

Making our way through various rooms that connect the Keep to the main house, we suddenly detected the feminine serpent energy passing through a small alcove just beyond the King's Hall, housing a cabinet displaying a full suit of armour. Above it, we noticed on the ceiling two magnificent carvings, one of a green man and the other a dragon. We soon noticed other dragon depictions around the castle, which seemed to allude to the famous story *The Ballad of the Laidly Wyrme of Spindlestone Heugh*.

The well came into view as we entered the Guard Chamber inside the Keep, with its vaulted ceilings and stone floors. The covered well-head has Victorian restoration, but according to various sources, the well-shaft dates to the Anglian occupation. Cutting the well-shaft was a tremendous achievement at the time penetrating 450 ft (21 m) of solid rock. An entry on the *Megalithic Portal* website includes a reference to the well provided by the castle's Collections and Conservation Manager:

Green Man carving inside Bamburgh Castle (by kind permission of Bamburgh Castle Estate)

'We don't know how the well was built but our archaeology team have thought it may have been made with fires on top of the dolerite, heating to a great temperature and then pouring cold water onto it, causing the rock to split. Sandstone is underneath the dolerite layer. The sides of the well are smooth, and about a quarter of the way down, there is an arched tunnel approximately 5 feet in height, which is reached by iron rungs set into the stonework. Running at a South Westerly angle, it travels to shrubbery outside the castle near the existing pump house and must have been made as an emergency exit. The exit is now blocked. During this time, there were at least two other wells within the Castle walls. Medieval records show that a corner tower near St Oswald's Gate was called The Tower of Elmund's Well. Walls were built in this area, possibly to defend the well. There was also Waltheof's well near the site of the present Clock Tower.' [6]

We dowsed the width of Bride's current at 10 ft (3 m), entering through a window in the Keep and shrinking as she disappeared through a door marked 'Private'. We also detected the male current very close to her, passing through a cabinet next to the same doorway that accesses the former private residence of the Armstrong family, where the currents form a node. Unfortunately, the apartment is now a permanent let and out of bounds to the public.

The node's inaccessibility was frustrating, and even when we checked for any distinguishing features on the floor above, we found nothing of significance. So perhaps the two serpents are drawn to something below the Keep.

According to the Ballad of the Laidly Wyrme, a cave exists under the castle. A chance conversation with one of the informative guides led us to believe that perhaps the Norman Keep was deliberately built here to harness the node's power enhanced by the chi of the underground water that supplies the well.

Whilst dowsing the Elen and Belinus dragon currents along the Belinus Line, we found that several of their nodes formed over underground springs or wells inside crypts, such as those at the cathedrals of Winchester and Carlisle. The currents are attracted to the potent telluric power emanating from these underground springs, which nourish and animate their divine force.

As we tuned into Bamburgh's hidden node, we felt the best way to connect with its power was by sitting on the replica throne just beyond the Keep's west wall. Returning to the throne, we noticed the beautifully carved images of entwined serpents and nicknamed it the 'dragon chair'.

Well inside the Keep at Bamburgh Castle (by kind permission of Bamburgh Castle Estate)

After exiting the alcove next to the King's Hall, we followed Bride's flow through the Inner Ward to the ruined remains of the restored medieval St Peter's Chapel. The Bamburgh Research Project found some evidence that certain buildings from the time of the Angles, including a chapel, lay in the Inner Ward:

'We have a set of annals, compiled as a follow-on to Bede's Ecclesiastical History, preserved in a later manuscript compiled at Durham. One describes Bamburgh and tells us that on the hill's summit stood a church that contained the relics of St Oswald and also mentions a well cut through a great depth of bedrock to its west.' [7]

Their excavations found early stone structures, including walls and at least one building, beneath the foundations of the 12th-century chapel. But unfortunately, in the early 19th century, it was re-modelled as a sort of folly to replicate romantic ruins, as was the fashion during the Victorian era. They also concluded: *'Inside this wall-line, to the south and beneath the current chapel ruins, we identified walls measuring approximately 52 ft (16 m) by 26 ft (8 m)'.* Could this be the earlier church mentioned by Bede, founded by St Aidan and containing the relics of King Oswald? They also believe that the buildings at the centre of the citadel would have been similar to the 7th-century royal villa complex of Northumbrian kings of *Ad Gefrin* at Yeavering, a few miles to the west of here. Edwin had a finely carved wooden hall highly decorated inside and out with gold leaf and solid gold fittings. Also, a similar royal palace is described in the epic Anglo-Saxon poem *Beowulf*, which may have been written in Northumbria and possibly recited in the great hall at Bamburgh.[8]

Until further excavations are carried out, the question of whether the original church founded by Aidan lies beneath the foundations of the Keep or the Victorian folly in the West Ward will remain unanswered.

After exiting through the southeast end of the castle and the blocked-up chapel doorway dowsed earlier, the female current crosses the North Sea towards the Farne Islands. I noticed Caroline looking longingly towards the tearoom and knew it was time to put our dowsing rods away, rest our weary legs and ponder on our fascinating day's findings.

We wondered whether the Northumbrian Anglo-Saxon kings were consciously aware that this highly magnetic outcrop of basalt was on a powerful ley-alignment and node of male and female dragon currents that linked their royal citadel to other important prehistoric and sacred sites all the way to Iona. Interestingly, a similar node point occurs on the Belinus alignment at St Catherine's Hill overlooking the ancient capital of the Wessex Anglo-Saxon kings.

We noticed that Lindisfarne lures the flow of Bride northwards away from the east–west alignment and wondered if Aidan had the skill of geomancy to entice the female serpent away from Bamburgh to enter and empower his new church.

We also sensed that the volcanic plateau on which Bamburgh Castle sits was an important ceremonial site long before the Angles arrived here. Similarly, St Catherine's Hill in Winchester was a sacred ceremonial place to the ancient peoples of Britain since at least the Bronze Age. After reading various history books purchased in the castle's bookshop and borrowed from local libraries, we discovered some remarkable stories attached to this ancient stately pile. Thanks to excavations by Brian Hope Taylor and the Bamburgh Research Project, recent digs in the grounds found evidence of occupation reaching back to at least the Iron Age. The *Votadini* or Gododdin, who ruled lands between the Forth and the Tees, may have utilised this basalt outcrop as a stronghold. Early records do indeed suggest some form of citadel existed here before the arrival of the Angles and almost certainly occupied by an early Brythonic tribe.

Ida was the first recorded Anglian King to utilise it as a royal fortification. He ruled the kingdom of Bernicia or Bryneich from around 547 until his death in 559. He was the son of Eoppa, nephew of King Ine of Wessex and established a line from which later Anglo-Saxon kings in this part of Northern England and Southern Scotland claimed descent. The *Anglo-Saxon Chronicle* (*c.* 891 CE) recorded that in the year 547,

'Ida assumed the kingdom, from whom arose the royal race of the Northumbrians, and reigned twelve years, and he built Bebbanburh, which was first enclosed by a stockade, and afterwards by a rampart.' [9] Excavations have proved that there was indeed a Saxon wooden stockade, using box ramparts to hold the upright posts instead of digging holes, which would have proved impossible due to the diamond-hard whin sill.

Lancelot and Lugh

The 9th-century chronicler Nennius in *Historia Brittonum* refers to Bamburgh as *Din Guaïroï* or *Din Guarie*, a Celtic–British placename meaning 'Fort of Guayrdi' renamed Bebbanburgh by King Aethelfrith after his queen Bebba. He was King of Bernicia from *c.* 593, and after claiming the neighbouring lands of Deira, controlled the kingdom later known as Northumbria. His queen Bebba, believed to be his first wife, must have been a significant figure to have this great citadel named after her and Beblowe Hill on Lindisfarne. Nennius also mentions her (ch. 63): '*Aethelfrith the Artful reigned twelve years in Bernicia and another twelve in Deira. He reigned twenty-four years in the two kingdoms and gave Din Guaire to his wife.*'[10]

Aethelfrith died after battling the exiled Edwin of Deira and Raedwald of East Anglia, who became the new ruler of Northumbria. However, his reign was brief, meeting his death at the hands of Penda and Cadwallon. Despite this, Edwin possessed the title Bretwalda, meaning 'Britain-ruler', and maintained peace in his lands. Bede records:

'It is told that at the time there was so much peace in Britannia, that whenever King Edwin's power extended, as is said proverbially right up to today, even if a woman with a recently born child wanted to walk across the whole island, from sea to sea, she could do so without anyone harming her.'[11]

Moreover, Edwin introduced Christianity to Northumbria with the help of St Paulinus, who may have built the first church on Lindisfarne long before Aidan's arrival. Edwin became venerated as a saint after his death, although his legacy in the region would be later overshadowed by that of St Oswald, son of Aethelfrith.

We wondered whether it was coincidental that in Saxon times, the Holy Axis at 107 degrees pointed to the horizon where the sun rose on 12 October, the feast day of St Edwin of Northumbria, a Bretwalda king of Britain.

After the death of Aethelfrith, his sons, Oswald and Oswiu, through his second wife, Acha of Deira, were exiled to Iona. They would later return to Bamburgh to reclaim the throne and lands of Northumbria.

It was during the reign of King Oswald (604–642) that Bamburgh became known as 'the very foundation stone of England' and a major stronghold of the Northumbrian royal family. Nevertheless, throughout all the male-dominated centuries of rule at the castle, its name retained its dedication to the mysterious Queen Bebba.

No written records exist regarding Bamburgh's original name, *Din Guaïroï* or *Din Guarie*, and to what or who Guarie/Guayrdi' might be is a mystery. However, the name may derive from a time when the stronghold belonged to the Gododdin, who fought the Angles. Din Guarie lay in the Celtic British region of Bryneich or Brynaich, from which the Anglian kingdom of Bernicia originates. Some of the earliest kings of Bryneich claim descent from Coel Hen, a 5th-century king of Northern Britain.

Sir Thomas Malory identifies Bamburgh in *Le Morte d'Arthur* as the fortress of Sir Lancelot called Joyous Garde, initially mentioned in the 'Matter of Britain'. In the 13th-century French *Vulgate Cycle*, Lancelot's father is King Ban of Benwick Castle.[12] According to the Arthurian Romances, before Lancelot, the castle was known as 'Dolorous Gard', meaning 'castle of sorrow' and inhabited by the notorious Sir Brian of the Isles. He entertains himself by imprisoning knights and maidens until Sir Lancelot successfully besieges the castle and releases them. 'The Isles' may refer to the nearby Farne Islands, seen from the castle's eastern walls. However, before being ejected from the castle, Sir Brian leaves a curse, which forces Lancelot to remain there for forty consecutive nights to defeat a monster in a cave beneath the chapel until a damsel dressed in copper appears and releases him from the spell. Interestingly,

Sir Lancelot at the Chapel of the Holy Grail from 'The Earthly Paradise' by Edward Burne-Jones, 1890s

another version of this tale mentions Lancelot gaining access to the castle through a cavern beneath the chapel. The cavern may refer to the cursed cave beneath the Keep, recorded in Bamburgh's legends.

While exploring the castle, Lancelot finds within its depths a hidden tomb, which only the rightful successor of the castle can open. After lifting the lid, he discovers a prophetic inscription that explains his true identity, including his illustrious lineage and that one day he will lie within the tomb. Lancelot changes the castle's name to Joyous Gard (Castle of Joy) and receives Arthur and Guinevere as his guests. From here, many knights, including Sir Tristram, set out in search of the Holy Grail, but as the legend states, Lancelot would later betray Arthur by taking Guinevere as his lover.

Now convicted of treason, Arthur's queen is taken to Carlisle, awaiting execution, but is soon rescued by Lancelot and taken to Joyous Gard. King Arthur demands his wife's return and forces Lancelot to flee to France, where he dies. His body is brought to Joyous Gard for burial in the chapel, after which its name reverts to Dolorous Gard – Castle of Sorrows. In another of the Romances called the *Queste del Saint Graal*, Lancelot is tricked into believing the Grail king's daughter is Guinevere, resulting in the birth of Galahad. Thus, out of Lancelot's sin is born the one true knight who will achieve the Grail and redeem the wastelands of Britain.[13]

Lancelot is a fascinating fictional character, and one theory regarding the origin of his name is that it stems from *Lan scion*, which translates as 'Son of the Land' or 'Servant of the Earth'. Some authorities believe that another version of his name, Lancelot du Lac, derives from the old Welsh *Llwch Lleminawc* or *Llawwynnauc*, from the Irish Lluch or Lleawc Lleminauc or Lugh Lonnbemnech associated with the Irish god Lugh Lamhfada or Lugh of the Long Arm. In Irish mythology, Lugh is portrayed as a warrior, a king, a master craftsman and a saviour with his famous spear, just like Lancelot and his sword. Interestingly, 'lance' is another name for a spear, and Bamburgh is often referred to as the 'castle of the warriors' and stands on a spear-shaped hill. The second syllable of his name, 'Lot,' could refer to the realm of Lot or Loth, also said to derive from Lugh. Lot was a ruler of the Gododdin during the time of Arthur, his territory encompassing Lothian in Scotland. The Holy Axis in Scotland appears to symbolically penetrate like a 'lance' through the lands of 'Lot' and pierces many sites associated with the archetypes of a spear and warrior.

Engraving of Lancelot on the Road to Shalott by Gustave Doré 1867

Attached to Bamburgh Castle is the legend of the Laidly Wyrme of Spindlestone Heugh, the name *wyrme* deriving from Old Norse, worm meaning a snake-like dragon. Often these legends refer to sacred areas associated with tales of serpents or dragons ravaging a region and then meeting their death at the hands of a brave knight.

According to the legend: There lived in Bamburgh Castle the Anglo-Saxon King Ida. His wife had died, leaving him with two children. His son, Childe Wynd, had gone to seek adventure abroad, but his 18-year-old daughter Margaret remained. She was a good and beautiful maid, well-loved by the people and courtiers. One day on a hunting trip in lands to the west, Ida met a beautiful woman, Behoc, whom he married, but the king was unaware that his new wife was a sorceress of dark magic. A great feast was planned at the castle, and Margaret welcomed the queen warmly. The new queen greeted her with a smiling face, but inside she was jealous and began plotting her demise. One day,

Lancelot and the Dragon by Arthur Rackham

58

the queen invited Margaret to come with her to a cave to look at some jewels, where she used her magic to cast a spell upon the princess, and she was never seen again from that day. The king grieved deeply for his beloved daughter, but more bad news would come. A large and terrifying worm or dragon had curled itself around a nearby hill called the Heugh at Spindlestone. There it lay, basking with its terrible snout in the air. It soon became known as the Laidly (loathsome) Worm as it terrorised the kingdom.

The beast roamed the countryside, burning and eating everything, even though the villagers brought it food. Then, one day, the news reached 'Childe Wynd', the brother of Margaret. He and his men built a ship with a keel made of the rowan tree, known as a protection against dark magic and sailed to Bamburgh. When the queen saw the ship approaching from her watch tower, she used magic to whip up a mighty storm, but the keel made from the rowan tree kept the ship safe. Meanwhile, the Laidly Worm stood on the cliffs and used his fiery breath to drive them back out to sea, forcing Margaret's brother to head for Budle Bay. Once ashore, Childe Wynd left his men and followed the dragon, finally overtaking it among the crags of Spindlestone.

Confronting the dragon, he lifted his lance to strike it dead but quickly paused when he saw tears flowing from its eyes. He was touched with pity, as he had never seen a dragon cry. He sheathed his sword and listened in amazement as, in a rumbling voice, the ugly creature told its story. To break the spell, Childe must kiss the dragon's face three times before sunset. So, bravely, he went forward and held his breath and kissed it twice, but the idea of kissing the creature for a third time proved almost too much. Then noticing the sun had begun to set, he closed his eyes and gathering up all his courage he kissed the worm for a third time. The scales fell from its skin and the dragon changed before his eyes into his lovely sister Margaret. He wrapped her in his cloak, and they returned to the castle together. When he reached the Keep, he found the queen and used her own magic against her. Immediately her skin became warty and she shrank in size until she became a giant toad. The king then banished it to the cave at the base of the well.

The king, his son and daughter lived long and happy lives. As for the queen, she still squats, waiting in the cave below Bamburgh Castle. For every seven years, on Christmas Eve, the cave opens in case any man is willing and brave enough to kiss the toad and free the wicked stepmother of the curse.[14]

This story has similarities with the Lancelot legend, who is forced to fight a gigantic monster in a cave under the castle chapel until a damsel dressed in copper appears and releases the curse. The well inside the Keep near the node point might refer to the one mentioned in this legend, situated above a cave deep below. An authoritative guide at Bamburgh informed us that a cave does indeed exist beneath the Keep with a secret passage leading to it, which emerges on the east crags above the war memorial, now blocked off. However, it may be just a good yarn, as there is no actual evidence of a cave below the castle. A tunnel leading off from the well shaft does exist, however, probably dug as an escape route. Perhaps a cave does exist beneath the castle yet to be discovered, as many castles in Britain had tunnels and hidden apartments beneath their Keep, and at Bamburgh sandstone exists at the deepest levels, a substance conducive to caverns.

The guide, undeterred by my questions concerning the dragon legend, spoke of the high crags of Spindlestone Heughs just a couple of miles southwest of the castle. He also told us that near the entrance to the crags used to be a stone-carved trough that the locals filled with milk to appease the dragon. Furthermore, below the crags is a freestanding rock pillar where Childe tethered his horse in the legend before attempting to slay the serpent, and a rounded hill further west retains the coiled marks of the sleeping beast.

Often truth can be veiled in allegorical stories where mythical places are transposed onto real physical locations in the local area and occasionally become linked with the same landscape mystery. After reading the Laidly Worm of Spindlestone Heugh ballad, we wondered if the site of Spindlestone Heughs was also connected with the dragon lines we were following. We made a note to visit this fabled place the following day, which according to the O.S. map, is 2.5 miles (4 km) to the southwest of the castle.

A large part of the castle's history belongs to Oswald, a great warrior king and saint who reintroduced Celtic Christianity to this part of Northern England. He invited Aidan to establish a church inside his fortress, perhaps at the site of the present chapel ruins. Bede describes it as a Roman basilica dedicated to St Peter, where the uncorrupted right hand of St Oswald was displayed after his death fighting King Penda at the Battle of Maserfield in 642. The story of Oswald is remarkable. His banishment as a child from his native Northumbria to Iona and his triumphant return many years later as the victorious warrior avenging his father and retaking his lands inspired Tolkien to create the character Aragorn in *Lord of the Rings*.

Bede refers to the courageous manner in which the king died surrounded by his enemies. He prayed for the lives of his soldiers and, with his last breath, said, *'God have mercy on their souls.'* Unfortunately, no mercy was shown to Oswald, for his body was dismembered on the battlefield, his head and arms impaled on stakes. Having retrieved one of his arms, hands and head, his brother Oswiu returned Oswald's remains to Aidan at Bamburgh. The head was preserved at Aidan's hermitage on Inner Farne, and his hands and uncorrupted arm were held in a silver shrine in the church of St Peter inside the citadel at Bamburgh. Oswald was later canonised as a saint, and miracles occurred at his shrine.

Oswald is an archetype of the spiritual warrior god Lugh and is often depicted with a raven. The bird symbolises the Celtic warrior, like Lugh Lámhfhada (Lugh of the Long Arm), Arthur, Urien and Owain of Rheged before him, all having the same attributes – brave, mighty and possessing magical spears or swords.

In Greek mythology, Orion, with his sword and shield, was symbolised as the warrior/god/hunter, reminiscent of the myths associated with Lugh and Oswald. The Ancient Egyptians equated the stars of Orion with Osiris, the sun god of rebirth and the afterlife and one of the most important deities of this ancient culture. The constellation of Orion was considered the abode of Osiris following his resurrection, and like Oswald, the body of Osiris was dismembered and buried in different places. Curiously, the shape of Lindisfarne mirrors an axe, and the hill on which Bamburgh stands mirrors a spear, both instruments of the warrior and sites accustomed to significant conflicts that settled the fate of England. Perhaps it is no coincidence that these characters had such influence over so many places on the Holy Axis, a line influenced by the risings and settings of the constellation of Orion.

The stars of Orion, anciently depicted in the heavens as a warrior with his extended right arm or sword, also resembles the Irish God Lugh of the Long Arm. In 2020, around the summer solstice, this constellation carried the sun across the ecliptic from east to west.[15] The sun's setting along the Holy Axis at 287 degrees over Iona is followed by the Virgo constellation, personified by the goddess Bride or Brigid. In legend, Bride tended her flock on Iona, living on the slopes of Dun-I. Therefore, the Holy Axis would appear to symbolically connect the warrior energy of Orion/Lugh with the power of the goddess in the form of Virgo/Bride.

Lugh also exemplifies the warrior traits of Oswald and Lancelot, whom Malory calls the 'best knight in the world'. Lugh is also contemporary with his Celtic feminine counterpart Brig, Brigid and Bride, a name we have given to the feminine dragon of the Holy Axis. Therefore, after much consideration, we named the male serpent current Lugh.

We soon discovered that the Holy Axis between Bamburgh and Iona features many great warrior gods, kings and knights, legendary and historical, including spiritual warrior monks such as Aidan, Columba and Cuthbert.

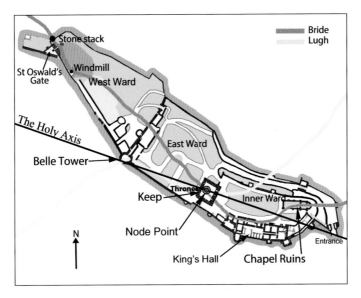

The Romances say many knights set out on the Grail quest from Joyous Garde or Bamburgh Castle. The spear, sword and cup of the Grail legends have their roots in the club and the cauldron of the god Dagda, the Irish equivalent of the Welsh Celtic Bran the Blessed. Dagda's god-like attributes were later assimilated with Lugh Lámhfhada, later immortalised as Lancelot.

The dramatic appearance of the castle, with its Arthurian mythos and throne of kings, is the perfect place to begin a spiritual quest. Bamburgh now adds a Grail Sword to our journey, symbolic of Lugh and Lancelot, as we head towards the Grail chapel at Rosslyn, where the pilgrim must undergo many tests and ordeals.

Before following the Bride and Lugh currents across Northumberland, our next destination was the Farne Islands, across the waters from Bamburgh, where both currents dowsed at the castle seemed to be heading.

Replica throne at Bamburgh Castle next to the Keep

Inner Farne

Inner Farne

We arrived at the large village of Seahouses just south of Bamburgh on a calm sunny day in May. Several boats in its quaint harbour offer trips to Inner Farne, once a place of sanctuary for St Aidan and St Cuthbert and now run by the National Trust. Hopefully, the island would determine the true beginnings of the Bride and Lugh currents.

The magnetic whin sill ridge on which Bamburgh Castle stands has its most spectacular aspects at the heart of the Farne Islands, the largest of this group being Inner Farne. Its remarkable natural features include steep vertical cliffs of weather-resistant igneous dolerite and a 60ft (18 m) rock stack. The island also provides a beautiful reminder of nature's immense power as enormous waves pound against its naked rocks creating great clouds of spray and resounding echoes of the sea. Although this island is bleak, it is home to an extraordinary array of seabirds and abundant flora and fauna. The neighbouring island of Outer Farne is home to a large colony of grey seals and their pups.

In the 7th century, the reclusive barren island of Inner Farne became the abode of St Aidan, who founded the first monastery on Lindisfarne and became its first bishop. Nearing the end of his life, he preferred to live in a cell as a hermit away from the pressures of secular life and eventually died here in 651. His tiny settlement comprised a cell, a small chapel and a well. It was still there when St Cuthbert arrived thirty-four years later, who also spent time on the island in isolation. Cuthbert reinforced the chapel and Aidan's cell by building a wall around them high enough to block out all but the sky above. According to Bede, the saint's cell was constructed of stone and turf and stood 'higher than a man'. The present Fish House or Hut is thought to be the site

of a *hospitium*. Cuthbert remained until March 685, when he returned to Lindisfarne to become its bishop, but soon resigned to return to his beloved Inner Farne, where he died a few months later.[16]

Despite his yearning for seclusion, St Cuthbert's reputed gift of healing brought many pilgrims and members of the Northumbrian royal family to the island who sought his wisdom and advice. Farne Islands supposedly derives from *Farena Ealande,* meaning `Island of the Pilgrims'.

During Cuthbert's time on the island, *'he wished to be self-sufficient, and grew his barley; when the birds ate the seed he instructed them to stop, which they duly did.'*[17] He also had a deep affinity with the island's wildlife, and as a saint, he became associated with otters, dolphins and other land and sea creatures. Even the eider ducks on the island are called 'Cuddy's ducks'.

Before St Cuthbert could live on Inner Farne, he had to 'banish certain 'demons' or 'devils' from the island to the nearby isle of Wideopens. Later inhabitants of Inner Farne, long after Cuthbert's death, occasionally caught sight of these strange demons, described as follows:

'.....clad in cowls, and riding upon goats, black in complexion, short in stature, their countenances most hideous, their heads long - the appearance of the whole group horrible. Like soldiers they brandished in their hands lances, which they darted after in the fashion of war. At first the sight of the cross was sufficient to repel their attacks, but the only protection in the end was the circumvallation of straws, signed with the cross, and fixed in the sands, around which the devils galloped for a while, and then retired, leaving the brethren to enjoy victory and repose.'[18]

Others saw them as spirits of early settlers or the original indigenous tribes cut off from the mainland. Perhaps these are the same ancestors who left behind the mysterious cup and ring marked stones found in many remote parts of the Northumberland countryside. Interestingly, the unusual and hideous-looking sanctuary knocker on the main entrance to Durham Cathedral is said to depict one of these intriguing little 'Farne Demons'.

After the time of St Cuthbert, other inhabitants of Inner Farne included a monk from Ripon called Ethelwald. The idyllic lives of these Celtic Christian monks were devastated in the 9th century by the invasions of the Danes. Many met their deaths during these tumultuous times, and those fortunate enough to escape fled to the mainland.

In 1093, Bishop William of St Carilef gifted the Farnes to the priory at Durham. In the 12th century, St Bartholomew of Whitby and Thomas de Melsonby dwelt on Inner Farne until their deaths. A hundred years later, a cell of Benedictine monks established itself on the island, which consisted of two monks, a master (Magister), an associate (Socius), and a few servants.

The Benedictines built a chapel dedicated to St Cuthbert in 1370 on the old settlement, its east window exhibiting a legendary scene of St Aidan praying 'in earnest' to stop Penda, the Pagan king of Mercia, from inflicting terrible damage upon Bamburgh Castle. The legend says the answer to his prayers came when the wind suddenly changed direction resulting in the fires lit by Penda's men turning against them, causing them to flee.[19]

Visible today are the medieval buildings of St Cuthbert's Chapel, St Mary's Chapel, Prior Castell's Tower, and another building further to the southeast built over the site of the hospitium. Bede describes Cuthbert creating two wells by digging pits and praying to God, which resulted in holes filling with water. According to *Historic England*, the site of one of the wells, depicted on Eyre's map of 1887, lies to the southeast of the hospitium, now the Fish House. Also, between St Cuthbert's Chapel and the hospitium is a circular depression, 16 ft (5 m) in diameter and 3 ft (1 m) deep with traces of stonework, believed to be the other well, but today there is no clear evidence to support the existence of a well on the island.[20]

Puffins on Inner Farne

The boat journey was a delight, stopping now and again at some of the other islands to show us many nesting birds on the towering columns of rocks. Arriving at the little jetty of Inner Farne, we avoided the crowds heading for the information centre and the chapel and instead walked to a secluded bench near the lighthouse to consult our map and decide upon a dowsing strategy. As we ate our sandwiches, a very friendly and opportunist eider duck pestered us for offerings, one of many that frequent this island. May is an excellent month to visit the island as many birds come to nest here, including arctic turns, cormorants, puffins, kittiwake, razorbills, guillemots and shags. If you are lucky, you may spot dolphins, whales, and porpoises swimming in the area.

As a cold easterly wind started to gust around us, we attempted to dowse the currents, which was particularly challenging due to the sheer number of birds. We also had to stick to specific paths to avoid interfering with the nesting sites, which we had to share with the numerous other sightseers and bird watchers, all of us vying for the best position to catch a glimpse of the sea birds, particularly the adorable puffins.

We detected the Lugh current arriving through a tall rock stack at the island's southern end, yet another nesting site. We continued to follow its flow across the rough boggy ground to the south walls of Prior Castell's Tower, now frequented by the private offices and accommodation for the National Trust staff.

We dowsed Bride at a beach on the island's eastern shores by the jetty where visitors disembark from the boats. We followed her to the Fish House, the possible site of the hospitium and down the central aisle of St Cuthbert's Chapel, first constructed in 1370 and later restored in the 1840s by Archdeacon Thorp. Earlier chapels have stood on this site, and remnants of 12th or 13th-century masonry are still visible in the lower part of the north wall. Many believe it stands over the area of Aidan and Cuthbert's cells. By the west wall are foundations of a small room, sometimes known as a 'Galilee Chapel' and typical of churches dedicated to St Cuthbert. The chapel has woodwork furnishings from Durham Cathedral, made for Bishop Cosin in about 1665 and brought to Inner Farne in the 1840s.

Just south of St Cuthbert's Chapel are the remains of another chapel dedicated to St Mary, now incorporated into the Visitors Centre. However, according to a 1930s survey,

St Cuthbert's Chapel, Inner Farne

it once extended another 22–26 ft (7–8 m) further west, the equivalent measurement of St Cuthbert's Chapel. In the late 19th century, a carved stone cross shaft was discovered lying half buried nearby, dating from the mid-8th to mid-9th century, now housed in the Monks' Dormitory at Durham Cathedral. In addition, a medieval cross base lies within the present lighthouse compound.

The female current then enters the tower's west wall to join Lugh, where they form a node. The tower was built for Robert Castell, Prior of Durham (1494-1519), to accommodate the monks who lived on the island, which supposedly stands over earlier foundations, another possible site of St Cuthbert's cell and holy well. Later, it became a fort, and in the 17th century, Charles II authorised its conversion to a lighthouse surmounted by a beacon.

There is great confusion about the actual location of St Cuthbert's cell and well, and the island's wardens have told some researchers that they believe it to be the Fish House. Others say the foundations of the cell lie beneath the tower's ground floor, along with St Cuthbert's holy well. Unfortunately, the tower is the private accommodation for National Trust wardens and is out of bounds to visitors. When we explained to the staff the nature of our research and whether we could have access, they refused and denied all knowledge of the existence of a well there.

So, like the Keep at Bamburgh, yet another node of Lugh and Bride lies hidden from view. We resorted to dowsing the node remotely and sensed the potent presence of the womb-like well beneath the tower, drawing the male and female serpents. The tower's stone structure seemed to amplify the energy at the node.

Prior Castell's Tower, Inner Farne

Interestingly, sometime later we watched a YouTube video of a St Cuthbert pilgrimage to Inner Farne, where staff guided the presenter to a hatch in the wooden floor of the tower, where they entered a cellar with a stone-lined ancient well dedicated to St Cuthbert. As the presenter sat by the well in semi-darkness, he remarked on the sacred atmosphere of this secret place. However, a few months later, the video was taken down.

In contradiction to the National Trust, the *Historic England* website says, '*The ground floor of the tower is tunnel vaulted and originally contained a well, sometimes called St Cuthbert's Well, which has now been covered over and is no longer visible.*'[21] The *Gatehouse Gazetteer* also records Leland's description of the Pele Tower of Robert Castell, which reads, '*Interior: keeled tunnel-vaulted ground floor with well in the corner.*'[22]

Naturally, we were disappointed that the first two nodes of the Holy Axis were out of bounds, both contained within thick-walled Keeps that concealed their presence. The node points of the male and female dragon lines are essential for us to connect with because of their potential healing and creative power, their harmonising effects ensuring fertility in the land and connection to higher realms. However, you can still remotely connect with the node from the nearby St Cuthbert's Chapel while standing on the flow of Bride, if you are lucky enough not to find it full of tourists.

As explained in the Introduction, Scientists have shown that the large plasma strings out in space create nodes called Z-pinches, where stars are born. Therefore, we believe the male and female dragon/serpent energy currents are microcosmic versions of plasma tubes, holding the consciousness and intelligence of the Universal forces, their nodes being earthly places of creation.

Lugh exits the tower north along a gully called St Cuthbert's Gut and continues west across the North Sea to Bamburgh Castle. Bride heads west from the node to another gully on the island's western tip called Churn Gut.

Despite being unable to connect directly with the node at the well, we sensed that the Farne Islands, with their large colonies of seals and nesting birds, particularly Inner Farne, symbolised the 'birthing' of the Bride and Lugh serpents.

These powerful geological islands birth other alignments of power, including a powerful vortex on nearby Staple Island, said to be the crown chakra of England. *The Truth Vibrations,* written by David Icke in 1991, describes a pilgrimage he undertook initiated by a psychic to heal and unblock a line of energy through England. The line included seven earth chakras points, three closely connected to the Spine of Albion or Belinus Line – Needles Rock on the Isle of Wight, Uffington Castle and Brailes Hill. The other chakra points were at Kenilworth Castle in Warwickshire, Jervaulx Abbey in Yorkshire, Durham Cathedral and Staple Island, one of the Farne islands. [23]

We drove back to Bamburgh to continue the Lugh journey from the castle's base and to follow Bride as she flowed west from Lindisfarne.

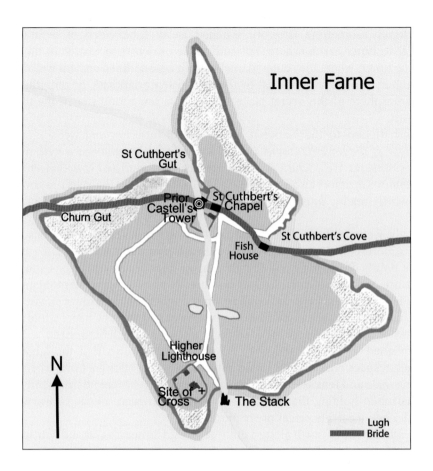

1. Freeman, E. A. 1876. *The History of the Norman Conquest of England.* Macmillan, London.
2. Symeon of Durham. 1965. *Historia Regum.* (reprint). Kraus Publishing, Iola, Wisconsin.
3. https://bamburghresearchproject.co.uk/
4. Miller, H. Broadhurst, P. 1989. *The Sun and the Serpent.* Pendragon Press, Launceston.
5. Young, G. 2003. *An Archaeological Investigation of Bamburgh Castle's Hidden Past.* Bamburgh Research Project.
6. https://www.megalithic.co.uk/article.php?sid=50547
7. https://bamburghresearchproject.co.uk/index.php/inner-ward-bamburgh-castle/
8. Tolkien, J.R.R. 2016. *Beowulf: A Translation and Commentary, Together with Sellic Spell.* Harper Collins, London.
9. Ingram, J. (translator). 1912. *The Anglo-Saxon Chronicle.* Everyman Press, London.
10. Morris, J. 1980. *'Nennius' British History and the Welsh Annals.* Phillimore, London.
11. Dumville, D. 2003. *Bede: Ecclesiastical History of the English People.* Translated by L. Shirly-Price and D. Farmer. Penguin Classics, London.
12. 13. Lacy, J, Norris. (Ed.). *Lancelot–Grail: The Old French Arthurian Vulgate and Post-*

Vulgate in Translation. Vol 1-4, Garland, New York.

14. Henderson, Joan. 1991. *The Laidly Worm of Bamborough.* Newcastle-upon-Tyne City Libraries and Arts.

15. https://mythicalireland.com/blogs/news/lugh-of-the-long-arm-carries-the-sun-on-the-summer-solstice

16. Webb, S. 2016. *Bede's Life of Saint Cuthbert: In a Modern English Version.* CreateSpace Independent Publishing Platform.

17. Frodsham, P. 2009. *Cuthbert and the Northumbrian Saints.* Northern Heritage, Newcastle-upon-Tyne.

18. Graham, F. 1987. *Bamburgh, Seahouses, Beadnell and the Farne Islands.* Butler Publishing, Morpeth.

19. https://seahouses.wixsite.com/farne/the-farnes

20. 21. https://historicengland.org.uk/listing/the-list/list-entry/1014771?section=official-list-entry

22. http://www.gatehouse-gazetteer.info/English%20sites/2750.html

23. Icke, D. 1991. *The Truth Vibrations.* Aquarian Press, Wellingborough.

Chapter 3

On the Path of Dragons, Towers and Sacred Rocks

Lugh's Journey from Bamburgh to the Borders

Bamburgh Castle with cricket and bowling green

As we tracked the male serpent inland from Bamburgh, we were excited at the prospect of discovering more of Northumberland's beautiful landscape. It is England's northernmost county and has a rich history stretching back to Mesolithic times. This once vast kingdom of Northumbria extended from Edinburgh to the Humber, hence its name, meaning 'north of the Humber'. Before the time of the Anglian kings, its ancient peoples left behind stone circles, cairns, sacred enclosures and enigmatic cup and ring marked stones. Brythonic Celts migrated here from continental Europe, such as the Votadini, the borders with their neighbour, the Brigantes, constantly shifting due to wars and local skirmishes.

70

The Roman occupiers began building Hadrian's Wall through the territory of these local tribes in 122 CE all the way to South Shields on Northumberland's east coast. The county's numerous castles and battle sites are a testament to the many upheavals experienced in the county over the last 1500 years, including Anglian invasions, marauding Vikings, attacks by the armies of William the Conqueror, Edward I and Henry VIII and the repeated border raids by Scottish Reivers.

Northumberland's imposing Cheviot Hills and idyllic river valleys, softly rolling hills and fertile plains contain a wonderful assortment of prehistoric monuments, sacred sanctuaries and pretty churches, many of them featured along the Holy Axis and its serpent paths.

From Bamburgh's cricket and bowling green below the castle, we dowsed Lugh passing through the grounds of Wyndings House on the outskirts of the village. It was the former home of the Darling family, whose daughter Grace, at age twenty-three, gained heroic status in Victorian times for her dramatic sea rescue near the Farne Islands of passengers in a stricken vessel in treacherous conditions.

The pretty village of Bamburgh features a triangular tree-covered green at its centre with a well at the apex. Surrounding the green are numerous pubs, houses, holiday cottages, shops and a parish church. Thankfully Bamburgh, with a population of three hundred, has retained its historical heritage and exudes an air of quiet sophistication and charm.

From Wyndings House, Lugh flows along the back of houses on the north side of the green to enter the parish church through the east window of the chancel. Dedicated to St Aidan, the site has Saxon origins and a Norman chapel was erected here for the villagers serving the castle and its extensive estate. Folklore attached to the church says Aidan's original wooden Celtic church stood on this site, and inside there is a preserved beam under which he supposedly sheltered before he died. In 1121, Augustinian monks from Nostell Priory in Yorkshire rebuilt the Saxon chapel.

The large chancel is unusual, for it is out of character with the rest of the church, having a higher roofline than the nave as though it was once a separate building of greater importance. Nevertheless, we were awe-struck by its magnificent reredos made of white Caen stone depicting sixteen characters from Bamburgh's early Christian heritage, including St Oswald, St Oswiu, St Edgar, St Aidan and St Cuthbert.

Also, within the chancel is the recumbent effigy of a knight, which legend says is Sir Lancelot du Lac, the son of King Ban of Benwick and Queen Elaine. I believe this well-known folktale originates from the myth that Bamburgh was his home, known as Joyous Garde. As romantic as it may sound, the tomb belongs to Sir John Forester, a crusader knight from the 12th century. He fought in the last crusade at the siege of Acre in 1191, accompanying King Richard the Lionheart. However, Sir John's brave exploits against the Saracens match the courage and prowess on the battlefield of the legendary Sir Lancelot and the Celtic warrior Lugh. According to accounts of the final conflict in the Holy Land, a party of Saracens attacked and surrounded King Richard. As he was about to be overpowered and made prisoner, Sir John Forester and his knights saw the danger from a distance and attacked with his 'lance', shouting, 'To the rescue! A Forester! A Forester!' Afterwards, he was awarded the Governorship of Bamburgh Castle, his descendants continuing to live there for another five hundred years. Forester died in 1220, so perhaps his exploits defending a king with such bravery inspired French writers of the *Vulgate Cycle* (1210-1235) to create the character

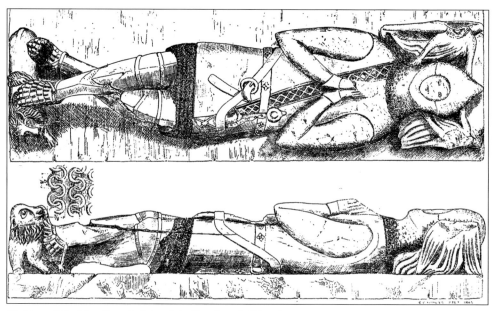

Etching of Sir John Forester's tomb in Bamburgh Church

Lancelot. If so, then Forester is the embodiment of this legendary knight of Arthur's Round Table and therefore, symbolically, the warrior Lugh.

Lugh's flow enters the chancel through the reredos and high altar, continuing to the nave altar at the centre of the church and to the font beneath the tower. Here, we find a window depicting St Cuthbert holding Oswald's head after being slain at the Battle of Maserfield in 642. The stained-glass windows in this church are some of the finest in the county. Above the font is the legendary holy beam said to have miraculously survived two fires and the buttress that Aidan leaned against when he died. Nearby is a modern shrine to St Aidan, erected in 2013 by the Archbishop of York John Sentamu with a plaque that reads, *'According to the Venerable Bede Saint Aidan, Bishop of Lindisfarne died near this place AD 651.'*

The guidebook states that the church was Aidan's burial place, the first true apostle of Anglian Northumbria, which became a place of pilgrimage for centuries. According to Bede, in his *Ecclesiastical History of the English People*, Aidan stayed in a tent outside the wooden church when he fell ill and died whilst leaning on the attached exterior buttress. His body was then taken to Lindisfarne for burial and sometime later translated to Bamburgh's newly built St Aidan's church for interment on the right side of the altar.

After the defeat of King Oswald, the notorious Mercian King Penda invaded the area and burned the village and Aidan's wooden church to the ground. The beam Aidan leaned against survived the fire and was later incorporated into the stone church. However, this building also fell to the flames, and the beam miraculously survived again. Its new position inside the church ensured that this important relic could continue attracting pilgrims for centuries to come. Soon more miracles followed after pilgrims touched the beam and drank water that contained slithers of its wood.[1]

However, this legend may be false, as the royal residence and church Bede describes was not here at Bamburgh, as many believe, but 16 miles (25 km) away at Ad Gefrin below Yeavering Bell, the old royal palace of King Edwin. Archaeological excavations there unearthed a wooden church, founded by either Paulinus or Aidan, with exterior buttresses and evidence of burning, as recorded by Bede. The beam in the church at Bamburgh may well be the one recovered from the site at Yeavering and transferred here in Norman times.

In the churchyard, we followed the current to an elaborate tomb that seemed out of place in a village graveyard and more reminiscent of a medieval shrine. However, it belongs to heroine Grace Darling, whose family home Wyndings House in the village, is also on the flow of Lugh. Grace was born in 1815 and lived on the Farne Islands, where her father was a lighthouse keeper. In 1838, she helped her father save many people from a wrecked ship using their tiny lifeboat. Sadly, four years after this dramatic rescue, she died of tuberculosis. Remarkably, they placed her grave on the male serpent, perhaps reflecting a courageous masculine act akin to the heroic actions of Lugh.

The dowsing continued beyond the graveyard, crossing a road to a house called The Friars, a reminder of an Augustinian monastery that once stood here. A couple of miles further west, we tracked Lugh along a footpath, which forms part of a pilgrimage route called St Oswald's Way, passing Shada plantation and a hill called Fairy Knowes. Witnesses may have seen mysterious plasma lights hovering over the mound and believed them to be fairies. Just past a junction near East Hill campsite, the current follows St Oswald's Way as it heads south through a narrow valley to a group of high crags of whin sill rock known as Spindlestone Heughs. The towering cliffs feature in the legend of the Laidly Wyrme, and I instantly recognised them as the rocks I had envisioned while sitting on the replica throne next to the Keep at Bamburgh Castle.

The Lair of the Dragon

As we made our way along the footpath, we noticed a marshy pond on the left of us marked on the map as Ladyworms Trough. Although now destroyed, there once stood a hollowed-out rectangular stone here called the Fairy Trough, which also features in the tale of the Laidly Worm of Spindlestone Heugh. According to the legend, locals would fill the trough with the milk of seven cows to appease the wrath of a local dragon. This legend is an often-told tale concerning dragons and the desire to appease them. It usually begins with the laying down of food to feed the dragon's endless appetite, until one day it demands a young female virgin, who the villagers willingly sacrifice. Milk and cows are also associated with Bride and the Celtic festival of Imbolc on 1 February, when the ewes start to lactate, perhaps symbolic of fertility and nourishment to aid the birth of spring.

We suddenly lost the current as we approached the rocks of Spindlestone Heughs along a muddy footpath surrounded by woodland. We could see that the path before us had turned into a quagmire due to heavy rain the previous night, and we were unsure whether to progress with our dowsing and wade through the thick mud or turn back and try another route. As luck would have it, at that precise moment of indecision, a well-equipped walker came strolling towards us from where we were planning to go. He warned us of the treacherous water-logged path ahead and advised us not to go further. We asked him if he was local and how well he knew this area, to which he replied, '*Yes, I take guided walks through this area.*' We further quizzed him about the legend of the dragon and enquired about the Spindlestone, also called the Bridle Stone, where the hero Childe tethered his horse before attempting to slay the dragon. He told us that it was, in his opinion, the tower of the old windmill two miles east of here. As he walked away, we both felt that the Spindlestone was somewhere in this woodland and not as he suggested, at the site of an old windmill and that somehow the sudden disappearance of the male current was a clue.

The Footpath at Spindlestone Heughs

Retracing our footsteps, we asked our dowsing rods to show us the path of Lugh again. Suddenly, the dowsing rods swung 45 degrees to the left, steering us away from the track towards dense woodland beneath the rocky cliffs. After scrambling through lush foliage and fallen branches, I reached a clearing and saw a tall pillar of whin sill rock jutting out of the cliff face. I climbed up to it and soon detected the male current passing through the rock stack. A few weeks later, whilst undertaking more in-depth research of the area's history, I discovered that the Spindlestone rock mentioned in the Laidly Worm legend was indeed the very pillar where I had found Lugh. Interestingly, the same rock stack is depicted in a painting by Walter Crane called *The Laidly Worm of Spindlestone Heugh* (1881).

A year later, with the help of better weather, we returned to Spindlestone Heughs to look for the cave said to be the dragon's lair. Unfortunately, we soon discovered it had been

The Spindlestone or Bridle Stone by Grahame Gardner

The Laidly Worm of Spindlestone Heugh, painting by Walter Crane 1881

destroyed by quarrying long ago. It seems a shame that the locals have forgotten such a powerful geomythical landscape. Thankfully, a local history society inspired by the magical surroundings of Spindlestone Heughs has created a web page about this unique area with links to old maps and even a photo of the Spindlestone or Bridle Stone hidden in the woods.[2]

Interestingly, just under half a mile to the southwest, we next dowsed Lugh passing straight through the windmill tower mentioned by the local walker. The rocket-shaped circular stone building called the Ducket stands on a mound, tapering to a height of 65 ft (20 m) with a conical roof, like a watchtower guarding the approach to Holy Island. Locals believed the mound was the lair of the Laidly Worm, its contours shaped by the sleeping dragon coiled around it. Old maps say a Roman Camp on this hill called Outchester defended an important northern route to Scotland, now the A1. The building's history began as an 18th-century windmill, then after the removal of its sails, it became a dovecote, which has since been converted into a luxury holiday let.

This phallic-like building is typical of the kind of structure the male dragon favours, such as the church tower Lugh had previously passed through at Bamburgh. In *Ancient Mysteries, Modern Visions*, Dr Philip Callahan hypothesised that the hollow-tube round towers with pointed caps were 'antennas' to collect and store electromagnetic energy waves, similar to orgone accumulators. The building also acts as a very powerful conduit for enhancing earth energies and focusing them specifically to bring fertility to the land.[3]

The Ducket is also reminiscent of a Grail tower described in the Romances as concealing a young maiden dominated by a male dragon, perhaps symbolic of terrestrial solar power controlling the divine feminine.

Interestingly, the male serpent visits all of the sites mentioned in the legend of the Laidly Worm. They include the castle, Ladyworms Trough, Spindlestone Rock, where Childe tethered his horse, the site of the dragon's cave and its other lair at the Outchester windmill.

From here, the Lugh current runs parallel with St Oswald's Way as it crosses rolling hills and dales towards the town of Belford. We soon spotted another church tower as we approached, seemingly drawing the male dragon to this once-thriving community. The 97-mile (156 km) long St Oswald's Way begins its journey to Lindisfarne from Heavenfield, close to Hadrian's Wall near Hexham. Here King Oswald erected a wooden cross under which he prayed before defeating the combined forces of the Welsh and the Mercians under Cadwallon and Penda in a decisive battle.

The Ducket windmill

Belford and the Holy Lance

Belford is a small market town nestling below the Kyloe Hills on the edge of the fertile Northumbrian plains. It has thrived because of its strategic geographical position, where the Great North Road meets an ancient east–west track that cuts through a natural pass in the hills towards the royal residence of the old Anglian kings at Yeavering. Over the centuries, its Georgian streets have witnessed a flourishing weekly market, the annual Whitsun Fair, its visitors brought by stagecoach as they travelled between London and Edinburgh. However, with the building of the A1 bypass, Belford's popularity faded, and the Blue Bell Hotel, once a famous coaching inn, is now just a pub in a quaint village. Margaret Tudor, daughter of English King Henry VII, stayed at Belford on her way north to marry her first husband, King James IV of Scotland, who later fell at the Battle of Flodden Field.

Lugh enters Belford through its golf course, once part of the grounds of Belford Hall, a classical-styled mansion dating from 1756. He then leads us to the parish church on another prominent mound in the centre of the village, where locals have worshipped since at least 1200 and perhaps earlier, as ancient earthworks surround the hills above. According to the church guidebook, Augustinian Canons, who rebuilt St Aidan's Saxon church at Bamburgh, built a Norman church at Belford.

The name Belford, formerly *Beleford,* perhaps indicates an early site of sun worshipers – Bel or Bele being the Iron Age Celtic sun god associated with ancient fire festivals at Beltane on 1 May.

Although the church, dedicated to St Mary, has Victorian restoration, remnants of medieval dog-tooth stones remain in the chancel arch. As we walked into the sanctuary, an impressive stained-glass window of King Oswald took our gaze. The warrior saint clutches a tall green cross in one hand and a long spear in the other, like the Wilmington Long Man hill figure in East Sussex or a Dodman surveyor referred to by Watkins. Although the green cross supposedly represents Christianity's restoration to

Northumbria after Oswald's victory at the Battle of Heavenfield, we also felt it was symbolic of the straight alignment of the Holy Axis, over which Oswald had such an influence during his reign. The spear is also associated with Lugh. I suddenly remembered my vision of a warrior while sitting on the Bamburgh throne outside the Keep and felt sure it was connected to this window.

Stained glass window in Belford Church of St Oswald and St Maurice or Mauritius

The window beside him depicts St Maurice or Mauritius, who holds the 'Spear of Destiny' or the holy lance of Vienna, believed to have pierced the side of Christ while on the cross. After the crucifixion, the spear became a much sought-after relic carried by the Roman emperor Charlemagne before his Frankish army in the 9th century. St Maurice rivalled St Michael and St George – a warrior saint revered by the Holy Roman Emperors during medieval times.

The current enters through the east window to flow along the central axis of the church and leaves through the tower. It also passes beneath the remains of the dog-toothed Norman archway, where we spotted carvings of a centaur and a lion. The centaur features in many churches on the Belinus Line, representing the astrological sign of Sagittarius, his outstretched bow pointing to the Pole Star or centre of the Universe. Sagittarius is the zodiac sign that appears when the sun reaches mid-winter, the carvings here perhaps representing the symbolic slaying of the earth dragon at the winter solstice.

From Belford Church, Lugh heads towards some earthwork remains next to West Hall, a 19th-century castellated house situated a little to the northwest of the village. The earthworks are remnants of an earlier moated fortification, mentioned in a 15th-century document as *Castrum de Belford*, possibly a former Norman motte and bailey.

The St Michael Line, Belinus Line and Apollo/St Michael Axis have numerous examples of castles built on their male dragon lines.

Leaving St Oswald's Way, the male dragon's path flows due west to enter woods at Blagdon Dean, having crossed a hidden linear earthwork

Carvings of a centaur and a lion in Belford Church

of some great age, possibly part of a defence system constructed by a local Iron Age tribe. Nearby, Lugh visits a place called Early Knowe, supposedly the location of several Bronze Age round barrows and stone circles, although other sources state that they were merely clearance heaps and sheep shelters.

Lugh then joins St Cuthbert's Way at Milky Well just to the southeast of North Hazelrigg Farm, a natural spring high in calcium that would have nourished the pilgrims as they journeyed to Lindisfarne. St Cuthbert's Way runs for 62 miles (99 km) between Melrose and Lindisfarne and includes the abbeys of Melrose, Jedburgh and Dryburgh. A mile west from here, the male current enters a wooded hill containing a small circular fort with concentric bank and ditch fortifications called Fox Covert. This Iron Age camp overlooks the most ancient road in Northumberland called The Devil's Causeway, said to be Roman but most probably a prehistoric way later utilised by them. A modern section of road overlays the ancient track for several miles, creating a straight northbound highway to Lowick, which lies close to the Holy Axis. In the distance, we could see the feminine dome-shaped hill of Doddington Moor, a bleak and remote landscape with curious weathered sandstone rocks that jut out around its circumference. The word 'dodd' is very ancient, and many believe it refers to the Scottish Q-Celtic word meaning 'plump or rounded hill', which is a good description for Doddington Moor.

The name may also originate from an ancient tribe that once settled the region. Before the Angles arrived, a tribe of Welsh-speaking Britons called the Gododdin ruled the Doddington area and much of ancient Northumbria and the Scottish Lothians. Some sources refer to 'Dodd' as a Brythonic P- Celtic word rather than Gaelic Q-Celtic, with the 'dd' pronounced as 'th'. So Gododdin becomes Godothin, similar to Lothian in Scotland, and Doddington becomes Dothington. Interestingly, *dodi* in the Brythonic P-Celtic means 'to lay' or 'place'.

Alfred Watkins, who rediscovered the existence of leys, noted the old name for staff is a 'dod', and an ancient surveyor was called a Dod-man who, in time-honoured tradition, sighted straight lines with the aid of two wooden staves. Names such as Dodestone, Dodmans Point, and Dodderhill may refer to sighting points used by ancient surveyors and Doddington Moor, a high hill seen for miles around, could be one such site.

Doddington Moor and The Ringses

Doddington Moor rises above the Milfield Plain near the town of Wooler, with the little village of Doddington nestling at the base of its western flank. The old settlement here dates back to the time of the Angles, and its little church dedicated to St Mary and St Michael has 13th-century foundations. An old spring nearby marked by a cross is known as Dod Well or Cuddy's or St Cuthbert's Well.

We parked in the village near the holy well and climbed the steep footpath towards the high moorland. Fine views of the sun-washed vale of the River Till and the glorious Cheviot Hills stretched before us, making the arduous windblown ascent worthwhile. However, dowsing the windy rugged moorland proved difficult, so we decided to head for its main feature, an earthwork enclosure called The Ringses. Here, we traced Lugh entering the earthwork from the east before narrowing to form a node at its centre with the Bride serpent. A well-worn cup and ring marked stone is on his flow, and an outcrop of rocks indicates his northwesterly path towards another cup-marked rock just beyond Doddington North Moor.

We wondered what drew the male and female dragons to a node inside the enclosure. Could something of a sacred nature be buried here or, perhaps a fault line runs through here, the currents using its telluric power from deep within the earth to gain nourishment?

We sensed that The Ringses was once the site of a grand ceremony where the ancient tribes would revere the Earth Goddess, honour the Celtic festivals and connect with the earth serpents' healing and fertilising power. Interestingly, the county of Northumberland has the highest concentration of these enigmatic cup and ring marked stones in Britain, and The Ringses earthwork seems to be their focal point.

Bride flows through The Ringses enclosure to the node from the northeast and then exits to cross open and wild moorland. As soon as we began following her path, we became disorientated and lost her trail on more than one occasion. The current felt weak and narrow, and we had a strong sense that all was not well with the female energy here, so we decided to find an appropriate spot to meditate to find the reason. After connecting with the moorland's spirit guardian, we both received a strong message that we had to leave immediately and return another day. This type of communication often comes when the accumulated energy at a sacred place such as a mound, stone circle or earthwork enclosure is about to discharge. Many visiting ancient sites have experienced this power accumulation with detrimental side effects such as nausea, headaches and dizziness. Those who ignored the sensations and remained during the moment of discharge developed flu-like symptoms or were physically sick. With this in mind, we decided to leave our dowsing of Bride at Doddington for another occasion.

Dowsing on Doddington Moor

Roughting Linn

We drove north towards Doddington North Moor and dowsed Lugh crossing the B6525 into Fenton Wood. He then follows a northwesterly ridge of hills towards more ancient earthworks at Roughting Linn, located between Doddington North Moor and Ford Moss about 2 miles (3 km) east of the village of Ford.

Having left our car at a layby, we entered an area of enchanted woodland called Linn Woods. Here we found one of Northern England's most impressive cup and ring marked stone slabs. Roughting Linn or Routin Lynn derives from the cascading waterfall in the woodland below the earthworks. In old English, 'Roughting' or Routin means 'bellowing' and 'linn' is a Brythonic word for a pool or waterfall. This large dome-shaped circular cup-marked rock is of light grey crystalline sandstone and carved with various symbols, some only seen in Ireland. Thought to date from the Neolithic to Early Bronze Age periods, these 4000-year-old patterns, of which there are over 160, range from a single cup, cup and ring, concentric circles and even flower-like shapes. Sadly, many have worn away due to their exposure to harsh weathering over thousands of years and bright sunlight is needed to appreciate the designs fully. Quarrying has also destroyed parts of this great slab, with one section missing altogether.

Canon William Greenwell first discovered the site in 1852 and wrote about his findings for the Archaeological Institute at Newcastle. Later, in 1865, George Tate undertook the first drawings of the site.

Cup and ring marked stones are numerous in Northumberland and Scotland. Many scholars and earth mystery writers have attempted to explain the purpose of such carvings. In his book, *Rock Art and The Prehistory of Atlantic Europe*, Richard Bradley argues that these stones are ritual monuments. The patterns are a series of symbolic messages shared between other monuments, including passage tombs and portable artefacts such as pottery and natural places in the landscape. He also compared the Roughting Linn markings with Irish megalithic art, such as the kerbstones at the Neolithic passage tombs of Newgrange and Knowth, particularly the 'horseshoe' motifs and cup and ring marks with parallel rays. He believes that the rock art character represents the unique landscape of their surroundings.[4]

We dowsed Lugh running across the dome-shaped outcrop and wondered whether the patterns or the rock

Roughting Linn cup-marked stone

had attracted him. The carved designs are mesmerizing, and it felt as if the cups, spirals and rings had electrically charged the stone.

Adjacent to the decorated slab is a large enclosure or hillfort, which has the remains of four rows of well-defined earthen banks and ditches. Moreover, a burial mound existed north of the site. As we dowsed Lugh along a well-worn path following the Broomridgedean Burn into the woods, we both sensed that we were entering an enchanted realm with the ever-watchful eyes of the woodland elementals around us. Suddenly we could hear the roaring sound of water, and as we turned a corner, a spectacular 18-foot-high (5.4 m) waterfall greeted us. Near this spot is said to be a holy well where King James IV washed his hands before the Battle of Flodden.

Roughting Linn waterfall

The sunlit waters of the waterfall, from which Roughting Linn derives its name, creates an idyllic scene as it cascades down the steep rock face surrounded by beautiful flora and fauna. We spotted the bobbing movements of a white-throated dipper as it fished about at the top of the waterfall for food snippets. The male current connects with a particular boulder that juts out from the rock face, its shape and features reminiscent of a serpent's eyes, nose and mouth. The width of Lugh's flow widens here, clearly invigorated by the chi discharged from the immense power of the cascading waterfall. As we immersed ourselves in the same energy, we visualised it clearing and cleansing our auras.

Reluctantly, we departed this fairyland to continue Lugh's westward journey across fields to the exposed Goatscrag Hill that stands high above Routin Lynn Farm. There are fabulous views of the Cheviots and the Kyloe Hills to the north from this high point, and on a clear day, you can see right across Northumberland's east coast.

Goatscrag is a typical Northumbrian sandstone outcrop, shaped by Ice Age glaciers and weathered by centuries of northern storms. To the north of the crag, prehistoric burial cairns and earthen enclosures punctuate the moorland. To escape the fierce wind, we moved to a rock shelter, and here we observed what looked like the faint outline of four crude animal carvings on the rear walls, which are reputed to be prehistoric. The rock art researcher Maarten Van Hoek first discovered these unique carvings in the 1980s, thought to be deer as horns or antlers are visible. Archaeologists have questioned their age, but some believe that stylistically they closely resemble Bronze Age carvings found in Scandinavia.

Stan Beckensall, in *Northumberland's Hidden History,* writes that rock shelters in Northumberland date back to Mesolithic times. Excavations here by Colin Burgess in the 1960s also uncovered evidence of an early Bronze Age cemetery, consisting of several cremated burials, two containing pottery vessels, now in the Great North

Museum, Newcastle. Carvings are also visible on top of the outcrop that appear horseshoe-shaped but could also be remnants of cup and ring marks.[5]

In Mesolithic times the rock shelter at Goatscrag was probably a cave that eroded over centuries until it collapsed and became the overhang we see today. Horns and antlers were symbols of the gods, and the shamans may have used this cave to connect with the spirit world, whose rituals possibly lured the Lugh energy here.

Goatscrag Rock shelter

Perhaps the ancients considered this remote cave a place of vision where geoplasma appears at certain times of the year. We have experienced many of these caves on our quests throughout Britain, such as Merlin's Cave in Tintagel in Cornwall and St Margaret's Cave in Dunfermline, during our research for our book *The Spine of Albion*.

To the west of Goatscrag, Lugh's flow meanders across the sandstone rocks of Broom Ridge within an ancient prehistoric landscape once dotted with tumuli. He soon arrives at the church of St Michael and All Angels Church in the small village of Ford, standing next to a sharp bend of the River Till near Ford Castle. Now heavily restored, the foundations of this church date back to at least the 13th century. Various fine examples of early Crusader gravestones are evidence of its early beginnings, located inside the church by the west wall. The smallest of them, the Piper's Stone, is incised with the Northumbrian bagpipes, having been moved there from its previous position in the churchyard. Another sculptured stone marks the male current, perhaps the remnants of a water stoup or cross.

Carvings on the pulpit depict figures of St Paul and a bishop, possibly St Aidan, Cuthbert, or even Paulinus, who baptised the pagan King Edwin of Northumbria and his earls in the Yeavering Valley. Lugh also enters the ruin of a square tower next to the church, known as the Parson's Tower, where the clergy of the manor lived. It has splendid views to the south of the Cheviots and the twin-peaked goddess hill of Yeavering Bell.

Nearby is Ford Castle, once the site of a manor house built in the 13th century by Odinel de Ford over a Saxon settlement. In 1513, James IV of Scotland made it his headquarters before the Battle of Flodden, and many believe he prayed at Ford Church before travelling to Branxton Hill to face the English. Unfortunately, he and 10,000 of his men died that day, the last time a Scottish monarch would fall in battle. The castle became the seat of the Marchioness of Waterford until its conversion as a residential educational centre.

The Duddo Stone Circle

Just over 2 miles (3.2 km) north of here, the Holy Axis lies close to the remains of a prominent landmark, one of Northumberland's most magical and atmospheric prehistoric sites. The Duddo Stones stand resolute on the western slopes of Mattilees Hill near the village of Duddo, within a dramatic setting overlooking Yeavering Bell. To the north are views of the River Tweed that defines the Scottish border just 4 miles (6.4 km) away.

This small stone circle is variously known as 'The Women', 'The Seven Turnip Pickers' and 'The Singing Stones' because of a strange whistling sound often heard from the stones when the wind blows from a particular direction. They bore the name 'Duddo Four Stones' for many years until around the 1800s when archaeologists found a fifth stone and had it re-erected.

These five powerful sandstone megaliths, standing exposed to the elements in the middle of a crop field, once comprised of seven uprights, the missing stones now long gone. Archaeologist Roger Miket describes the stone circle as *'Undoubtedly the most complete and dramatically situated in Northumberland.'* In contrast, Stan Beckensall describes it as *'One of the most attractive monuments in Britain.'* Excavations in the

The Duddo Stones

1890s uncovered cremated remains in a central pit dated between 1740–1660 BCE, although Cambridge University has since dated the stones as early Bronze Age (*c.* 3000–2200 BCE). The megaliths stand between 6–10 ft (2–3) m high, and the circle is about 32 ft (10 m) in diameter, with an elevated point at its centre. The harsh Northumbrian weather has created deep water-cut channels running down the face of each stone, but despite the amount of erosion, remnants of cup and ring marks are still visible on them.

As we followed the well-marked footpath through the fields, the stones soon appeared, rising dramatically on the hill's summit. Having the circle to ourselves for a while enabled us to sense the sanctity of the place. However, because of its small size, many have debated its purpose. Perhaps, as we have found at other similar sites in Britain, it serves to harness orgone energy from the atmosphere to fertilise the landscape once released. This natural energy, emitted by all living matter, can sometimes take the shape of balls of light.

Recently, locals have protested against plans for two 113 ft (34.5 m) turbines to be erected just over a mile from the site, which they fear will have a cumulative impact on the stone circle.

Just under a mile south of here, Duddo Tower marks the Holy Axis, now a ruin on the village's south side. Curiously, we dowsed an earth energy line connecting the two sites as if the circle wished to communicate with the alignment. The tower, built in the

16th century, replaced a similar structure erected in 1496, later destroyed by James IV's troops en route to meet the English army at Flodden. However, border raids constantly harried this area, by not only the Scots and English but also the notorious border-raiding families known as 'reivers'. Men from the Border regions of Scotland terrorised the area from the late 13th century to the beginning of the 17th century, stealing cattle and crops from their neighbours regardless of creed or cause.

Duddo Tower

The Battle of Flodden

Lugh continues to the restored St Paul's Church at Branxton, where it flows along its central aisle. The quaint little church lies within unspoilt and tranquil farmland, and inside are fine examples of 12th-century Norman pillars and a medieval chancel arch. However, there has been a place of worship here since at least the earliest days of St Paulinus, who baptised the pagan Angles at nearby Ad Gefrin, the 7th-century royal court of King Edwin of Northumbria.

The name Branxton or Brankeston originates from the old English word 'Branoc', meaning Branoc's settlement, but the area is better known for its proximity to the Flodden battlefield. The church served as a temporary mortuary for some of the thousands of English and Scots slain at Flodden Field. The body of King James IV of Scotland supposedly rested here, the last monarch to die in battle, and many of the fallen are still buried here. The nuns from Coldstream Priory travelled to the battlefield to offer care to the wounded and returned the bodies of Scottish nobles to their families. The king's remains went to Berwick and, after that, to London.

The monument on Pipers Hill that commemorates the battle is visible from the churchyard and is said to mark the probable centre of the English battle lines. It is hard to believe that this now peaceful and

12th-century Norman pillars at St Paul's Church, Branxton

idyllic rural scene was the site of one of the most important and bloodiest battles in Scottish history over 500 years ago.

The Flodden battle resulted from the failed diplomatic efforts of James IV of Scotland (1473–1513) to end any thoughts of war between England and France. This outgoing, sociable, charming and courageous king was the youngest son of James III, who took the throne after the assassination of his father at the battle of Sauchieburn. In 1502, the signing of a 'Treaty of Perpetual Peace' with the English King Henry VII brought with it the marriage between James and Henry's daughter, Margaret Tudor. However, his relationship with England soon soured when his brother-in-law Henry VIII came to the throne. Henry antagonised James further when he took up arms against France to support the Holy League, leading to the renewal of Scotland's 'Auld Alliance' with Louis XII of France in 1512, which promised mutual support in the event of an attack by England. James made many requests to Henry to cease with this plan of action, but his pleas went unanswered, forcing James to come to the aid of France.

Having crossed the River Tweed at Coldstream, the king of Scotland arrived at Flodden Hill on a wet day with 30,000 men, said to be the largest and best-equipped Scottish army ever to cross the border into England. Here he set up camp over the site of ancient earthworks with an entourage that included the archbishop of St Andrews, fifteen earls, twenty barons, many bishops and abbots, and hundreds of knights. Louis XII also supplied James with fifty French soldiers to train his army to use the long pike, heavy canons pulled by four hundred oxen from Edinburgh Castle, and ammunition carried by thirty packhorses.

On 9 September 1513, they faced Henry VIII's army led by Thomas Howard, Earl of Surrey, which included 26,000 English soldiers. The Earl carried the Sacred Banner of St Cuthbert, a symbol of protection. On the day of the battle, the English marched from Wooler, crossing the treacherous burn of St Paulinus or Palinsburn and surrounded Branxton village and church with their battle lines.

At first, the Scottish pikes seemed effective against the English as they pushed further towards their lines. However, after deciding to allow the rest of the Scottish troops to charge down Branxton Hill, James IV soon found them knee-deep in boggy terrain at its base, barraged by English cannon fire and a rain of arrows from Lord Stanley's skilled archers. As they became utterly overwhelmed, the Scottish king, much to his noble's horror, sprang from his horse, grabbed a pike and joined the fray.

James IV died with an estimated 10,000 men and most of the ruling class of Scotland. His badly mutilated body was wrapped in the royal standard and laid in Branxton Church before being taken to Berwick-upon-Tweed to be embalmed. Later, they escorted the king's coffin to London and interred him in an unmarked grave at St Michael's Church, Cornhill.

Many historians have criticised James' involvement in the battle, believing that he should have remained behind the lines to make the necessary changes to the tactics if needed. Instead, James was a 'participatory king' like Robert the Bruce, inspiring his men by fighting alongside them.

However, legends say that James IV had survived the battle and that the body taken to England was 'my lord Bonhard'. One account says that he was seen in Kelso and then went secretly on a pilgrimage overseas. Another legend claims that he received a warning against invading England by supernatural powers while praying in St Michael's Kirk at Linlithgow.[6]

Interestingly, the horrific events of that fateful day are commemorated by an annual cavalcade from the Scottish border town of Coldstream to the Flodden memorial of around 300 equestrians led by the Coldstreamers. This event highlights the town's Civic Week celebrations in August, culminating in the laying of wreaths at the monument with a short service accompanied by a piper in memory of the fallen.

Lugh seems to avoid the commemoration site on the hill above and instead diverts northwest towards a standing stone marked on the map as 'The King's Stone', just under a mile from the church. This 7 ft (2 m) standing stone of oolitic limestone, extracted from a nearby quarry at Carham, is situated in a field by a footpath just off the A698 near Crookham Westfield Farm. As we neared the stone, we could already feel an immense power radiating from it. As I tuned into the guardian spirit of this ancient stone, I felt compelled to touch it with the palm of my hand. Suddenly, a massive release of energy surged through my body as if I had reawakened a sleeping power within this silent megalith.

Most stories surrounding this stone tell us that James IV fell here during the battle of Flodden, romanticised by Sir Walter Scott, and where the Earl of Hertford supposedly met with his troops. However, it may have had a more sacred purpose as a tribal gathering or trysting stone. There are traces of ancient settlement in this area going back to Mesolithic times and evidence of other ceremonial monuments in the area, including prehistoric henges, burial mounds and roundhouses, and various rock cut carvings similar to those at Roughting Linn.[7]

The King's Stone

The Lugh serpent now heads west, passing just south of the old border town of Cornhill on Tweed to cross a significant bend in the River Tweed shaped like a massive Swan's Neck towards the Scottish town of Coldstream.

1. Dumville, D. 2003. *Bede: Ecclesiastical History of the English People*, translated by Shirly-Price, L. and Farmer, D. Penguin Classics, London.
2. http://heddonhistory.weebly.com/blog/the-laidley-worm-of-spindlestone-heugh
3. Callahan, P. 2001. *Ancient Mysteries, Modern Visions*. Acres, U.S.A.
4. Bradley, Richard. 1997. *Rock Art and The Prehistory of Atlantic Europe*. Routledge, London.
5. Beckensall, S. 2009. *Northumberland's Hidden History*. Amberley Publishing, Stroud, Glos.
6. https://familypedia.fandom.com/wiki/Battle_of_Flodden#Legends_of_a_lost_king
    Also, Goodwin, G. 2014. *Fatal Rivalry, Flodden 1513: Henry VIII, James IV and the battle for Renaissance Britain*. Weidenfeld & Nicolson, London.
7. https://www.themodernantiquarian.com/site/3164/kings_stone.html

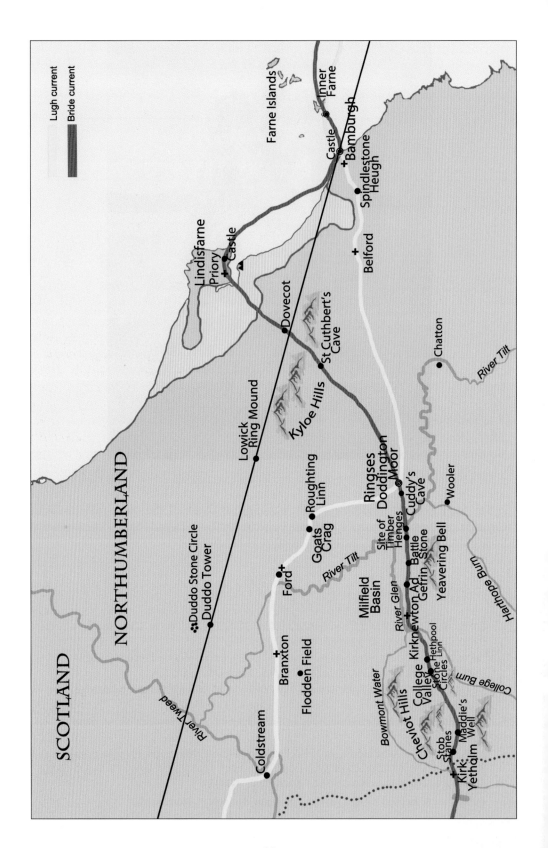

Chapter 4

In the Footsteps of Saints and Serpents

Bride's Journey to the Scottish Border

Returning to Lindisfarne, we resumed our investigations of the Bride serpent by following her flow west across Northumberland's picturesque landscape, leading us to hidden caves and secret valleys, ancient stones and hilltop sanctuaries. Driving along the A1 next to the coast, we dowsed the current crossing the road to a medieval stone structure known as Buckton Dovecot, now a scheduled monument. It stands almost hidden in a field close to the hamlet of Buckton, once the site of a medieval village that disappeared long ago. Another place on her path is an Iron Age earthen enclosure on Buckton Moor, partially surrounded by double earth and stone banks and an outer ditch. However, as she travelled south through Detchant Woods, we soon realised her destination was the remote and secluded St Cuthbert's Cave.

St Cuthbert's Cave

Situated on St Cuthbert's Way below Greensheen Hill, it was reputedly one of the many resting places for the monks of Holy Island as they carried the body of St Cuthbert to safety before finally settling at Durham Cathedral. Legend also says St Cuthbert spent time here as a hermit before retiring to the Farne Islands. As we would later discover, the Holy Axis is associated with many sites on this famous pilgrimage route. Established in 1996, it runs from Melrose Abbey in the Scottish Borders to Lindisfarne, climbing over the fringes of the Eildon Hills before following stretches of the River Tweed and the Roman Dere Street.

The Miracle of St Cuthbert

The body of Cuthbert was the holiest relic for the remaining Celtic Church, having proven to be miraculous. David Willem gives a good rendition of the incredible story in *St Cuthbert's Corpse, A Life after Death*. After Cuthbert died in 687, the monks entombed his body beneath Lindisfarne Priory for eleven years to fully allow his flesh to decay. Then came the day to exhume the bones on 20 March, the anniversary of this death. The bones would be washed, wrapped, and placed in a newly built tomb within the church for the reverence of monks and pilgrims. This ceremony was known as the act of 'elevation', a declaration of his sainthood. While Cuthbert was in the ground, the *Lindisfarne Gospels* were created and used for the first time at St Cuthbert's elevation ceremony.

However, when the monks opened the saint's coffin, they were astounded to find his body perfectly intact, having suffered no decomposition and the wrappings appearing almost new. The monks believed this was a clear indication of Cuthbert's great sanctity, and bishops from all over Britain came to witness and confirm this miraculous phenomenon.

In 875, after numerous Viking raids, the monks of Lindisfarne were forced to leave their beloved island, taking the body of St Cuthbert with them, led by Bishop Eardulf. The journey took them from one refuge to another, including St Cuthbert's Cave, and they even attempted to cross to Ireland, but foul weather forced them to abandon the trip. Instead, they continued south of Newcastle to the old Roman town of Chester-le-Street and its old parish church, where his body rested for 112 years. Here many miracles were recorded until further threats forced the removal of Cuthbert's remains for a short time to Ripon. When the danger subsided in 995, the intention was to return Cuthbert to Chester-le-Street, but the cart carrying his body stuck fast in a muddy track. After three days of fasting and prayer, the spirit of St Cuthbert revealed that he wished to be enshrined at a place called Dunholme, later revealed as a rocky crag situated in a loop of the River Wear. Here the monks built a church that eventually became Durham Cathedral.

Finally, in 1104, the Benedictine monks translated Cuthbert's remains to a new shrine behind the high altar. However, curious to see if the body was still incorrupt after 418 years, nine monks led by Prior Turgot examined the coffin's contents on the night of 24 August. A 12th-century account of its opening in Symeon of Durham's *Historia Ecclesiae Dunhelmensis* says that the nine monks nervously lifted the lid and removed the cloth to expose the body of Cuthbert. To their surprise, his body was lying on its right side, whole and un-decayed, as if he were asleep. They immediately fell to their knees and recited the penitential psalms. After removing King Oswald's skull and St Aidan's bones from inside the coffin, they gently lifted out the corpse. Onlookers noticed that it sagged with the suppleness of a living body, with flexibility in the joints, including the vertebrae, an occurrence not even seen in mummification. Some officials were sceptical of the miracle and ordered a further examination with independent witnesses. After viewing the body again, there was no doubt that it was indeed whole and showed no signs of decomposition. The body was then ceremoniously transferred to a beautifully ornate shrine, which hundreds of pilgrims visited throughout the Middle Ages.

The grave lay undisturbed in Durham Cathedral for another 400 years until the Dissolution of the Monasteries in 1537. Henry VIII's Commissioners destroyed most of Durham's Catholic shrines, including Cuthbert's, removing anything of value. However, when they opened the coffin, the body was still incorrupt. According to an eyewitness account published in the 'Rites of Durham' in the mid-16th century, three eminent men, Dr Ley, Dr Henley and Mr Blythman, instructed the opening of Cuthbert's coffin and brought with them a goldsmith. After removing all the cathedral's gold, silver and precious stones, the smith came to a chest firmly bound in iron chains. He broke the chains with a great hammer, damaging the coffin and one of Cuthbert's legs. Dr Henley called to him to throw the bones down, but he replied that he could not because they were still covered by skin and tissue.

After checking the goldsmith's claims, Dr Ley turned to Dr Henley and stated that 'he is lying whole'. However, Dr Henley refused to believe him and cried again, 'cast down the bones'. Dr Ley responded that he should come up and see for himself. The witness claimed that Dr Henley handled the body roughly but found it incorrupt.

The commissioners were uncertain about what to do, having never encountered such a marvel as this, which would be akin to a supernatural event. The body was moved to the vestry awaiting Henry VIII's instructions as to its fate. Meanwhile, the monks allegedly took the saint out of the coffin and reburied it secretly on the vast cathedral grounds. Another corpse then replaced St Cuthbert's body, also in a well-preserved state of mummification but not long dead. This story is certainly within the bounds of possibility as the monks must have known that the king would demand the destruction of perhaps one of England's most precious Catholic relics, equivalent to the Holy Grail.

The official story is that the commissioners returned with the instructions to bury the body in a new coffin in a freshly opened grave, believed to be behind the high altar. But, interestingly, three hundred years later, in the 19th century, the opening of St Cuthbert's coffin revealed an utterly decayed body, leaving only the bones – but were they those of St Cuthbert?

The legend persisted, and in 1896 William Brown published articles in *The Ushaw Magazine* in which he relayed the story of the three Benedictine monks hiding St Cuthbert's body in a place known only to them during the Reformation. He reasoned that because so many Catholic relics were secreted away during the Dissolution of the Monasteries, it would be only natural to hide the most precious relic of them all. The basis of much of his argument was that if the body remained incorrupt for 852 years, then there was no reason to believe that it would suddenly decay. Furthermore, it is said that even today, the superiors of the re-founded English Benedictine

Congregation and certain members of the Northern Catholic clergy know the secret of the saint's final resting place. Benedictine historian Abbot Cuthbert Butler (1858–1934) reported that when he first became acquainted with the mystery of Cuthbert's true gravesite, he travelled to Durham with specific instructions and identified the spot after shaking off a verger who regarded his movements with suspicion.

Durham Cathedral has magnificent architecture, symmetry and colourful stained-glass windows that enhance its ethereal atmosphere. But perhaps this intoxicating energy is not a result of the architecture and design but due to the healing powers of the incorrupt corpse of Cuthbert, which might still lie secretly hidden beneath the visitor's feet.[1]

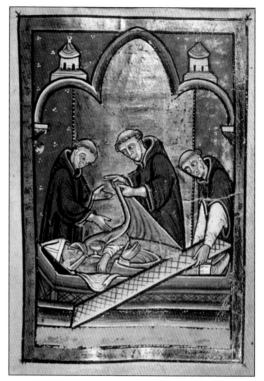

Illuminated manuscript from Bede's 'Life of St Cuthbert', showing the discovery of the saint's incorrupt body

Surrounded by Scots pines, the remote St Cuthbert's Cave is impressive, and a distinct air of otherworldliness enshrines this magical place where the incorrupt body of the old saint lay for a time. Finding it proved tricky at first, so we had to keep our wits about us and our dowsing rods at the ready to ensure we remained on the right path when entering the dense woodland.

The cave, also known as Cuddy's Cave, consists of an overhang of sandstone rock supported by an isolated stone pillar. In the mid-19th century, a stone wall enclosed the cave and found use as a 'lambing shed'. When the cave was in the ownership of the Leather family of Middleton Hall, the area became their burial place until 1981, when it was presented to the National Trust.

While tuning into the Bride serpent energy, we could feel the power emanating from the crystalline sandstone affecting our senses and provoking a higher state of consciousness. Just beyond the entrance, we follow the serpent current to a huge split boulder, the crack wide enough to walk through without touching the sides. As we walked reverently through the open fissure of this unusual rock, we felt a tingling sensation as if the electric field of the stone was interacting with our aura.

We experienced the same sensation at a limestone outcrop called the Fairy Steps near Silverdale in Cumbria. A narrow cleft with steps cut into it allows you passage through the centre of this ancient elemental formation. It once formed part of a 'coffin route' or 'corpse trail' for people from Arnside carrying their dead to St Michael's Church in Beetham for burial. Perhaps local tribes performed an ancient cleansing ritual here at St Cuthbert's Cave, passing the dead through the split rock. The ancient peoples of the area may have believed the rocks were special and would

Split boulder at St Cuthbert's Cave

purify the souls of the deceased before continuing their journey to the afterlife.

We were sad to read recently in the *Northumberland Gazette* that vandals had painted areas of the cave with white spray paint, and fire damage has caused the cave's sandstone wall to crack and fall.

The female current then led us southwest through the winding wooded glen of Poplar Burn before crossing over the hill called White Law to a Bronze Age burial mound, which the O.S. map curiously names 'Cox Graves'. It was the possible final resting place of a chieftain next to the old north–south trackway called the Devil's Causeway, which continues to Berwick-upon-Tweed.

Looking west along Bride's flow, we realised our next destination was Doddington Moor, where she forms a node with Lugh at the centre of an earthen enclosure called The Ringses. We were slightly apprehensive as we approached the boundary of the moor as during our last visit dowsing the female current, we felt the site guardian disapproved of our presence. However, we were in no doubt that a tremendous supernatural force is attached to Doddington Moor that does not take kindly to meddling dowsers, so we would ensure to tread lightly and honourably for our next visit.

The Node at Doddington Moor

The sheer abundance of prehistoric monuments dotted across Doddington Moor is a clear indication of its sacred significance. Archaeologists have recorded many more earth enclosures and settlements here, ploughed into non-existence long ago. The sandstone geology is conducive to high magnetic fields from piezoelectricity, a liminal place where the veils between the physical world and the spirit world are thin.

After connecting with the spirit guardian and informing it of our honourable intentions, we meandered across this windswept moorland. We started to sense its ethereal atmosphere after a short time, and suddenly the weather cleared just as we dowsed Bride heading for The Ringses earthwork last visited following Lugh. The large earthwork consists of three low ditch-and-bank concentric ringed ramparts set high above an escarpment that drops steeply on its western edge. The main entrance to

The Ringses, Doddington Moor

the enclosure is in the southeast, and traces of at least five smaller circles have been detected within the monument, varying in diameter from 11 ft (3.5 m) to 32 ft (10 m), some having dividing walls.

Re-dowsing the Bride current, we noticed it was narrowing in that familiar way before shrinking to a point with Lugh at the node. We then walked around the circumference of The Ringses to reacquaint ourselves with the path of the Lugh current as it enters the enclosure from the east and leaves through its northwest edge before diverting north to Doddington North Moor.

We were finally delighted to connect with a node on the Holy Axis in an open and accessible place. We dowsed its signature for the first time, and it gave us the shape of a rounded five-petalled flower. The node signature of the Elen and Belinus serpent currents of the Belinus Line is a six-pointed star; on the St Michael Line, Hamish Miller discovered a five-pointed star. The rounded shape of the Holy Axis node was curious yet unique. We found that nearly all node points connect with significant places of natural geological power, and often humanity has artificially enhanced them with stone circles, earthen mounds and shrines. The five-petalled rose represents 'spirit' as it contains five elements and is symbolic of the five human senses and the magic insignia of the pentagram.

The Ringses has little recorded history and is considered a minor Iron Age hillfort. However, there are no traces of a major fortification, and

Node signature of a five-petalled flower at The Ringses, Doddington Moor

94

the low earth banks would provide little or no defence against invading forces. There is no evidence that a reliable water source existed near the site to sustain a permanent settlement or to provide for those during a siege. We felt that the concentric rings of the earthwork were somehow ceremonially linked to the design of the cup and ring marked stones, which the moor seems to have in abundance. A local publication refers to traditions that this area was the abode of Welsh-speaking Britons called the Gododdin (Latinised as the Votadini) and further states that The Ringses enclosure seemed to be a focal point for this enigmatic rock art. Cup and ring marked stones are prevalent in other parts of Northumberland, having the highest concentration in the country, as outlined in Stan Beckensall's *Northumberland's Hidden History*.[2] These ancient symbols are in many parts of Scotland on prominent boulders, standing stones, rocks and flat stones often located on hilltops and meetings of trackways. They consist of carved-out cup shapes and concentric rings, sometimes with many rings encircling the cup with groves or channels. Their ancient purpose and age are still unknown, but as we continued following the currents along this fascinating axis of power through Scotland, we gradually began to understand its mystery.

Bride's path from the node continues southwest, her flow now stronger and easier to detect. As we walked across a complex pattern of pathways and earthworks, somehow avoiding the worst of the boggy terrain, Caroline suddenly stopped dead in her tracks, holding her finger to her lips and pointing to the ground. For there in front of us was a coiled adder that suddenly raised its head, hissed and quickly slithered away after realising our presence. This encounter was a rare treat indeed, as adders are generally shy creatures preferring shady rocks and grass verges. But, for us, the adder was highly significant for it is associated with the goddess Bride, especially in Gaelic traditions. In an article entitled *The Goddess in the Landscape*, Scottish historian Stuart McHardy tells us that several rhymes survive, linking Bride with the Druid traditions, one of which is a version of a poem associating her with the serpent. The snake is said to emerge from its hibernation on Imbolc, St Bride's Day, 1 February:

'Today is the day of Bride
the serpent shall come from the hole
I will not molest the serpent
Nor will the serpent molest me.'

Although many believe this saying is a relic of old serpent worship, McHardy believes the serpent/adder symbolises the Mother Goddess. Many cultures believe the serpent represents knowledge, and the shedding of its skin and hibernating underground signifies regeneration, rebirth, and fertility. Many world cultures depict serpent carvings, even within Christian traditions, but in particular on Pictish Stones. McHardy strongly suggests that the Picts believed the adder to be a powerful sacred symbol and associated it with their goddess, which they called Bride.[3]

Adder on Doddington Moor

In Eastern mystical tradition, the coiling of the serpent is symbolic of the kundalini or serpent fire, which is 'coiled' at the base of the human spine. This hidden energy force within the human body is likened to a sleeping serpent that, when awakened, produces spiritual enlightenment. The body has seven centres of power called *chakras*, and the kundalini resides in the Base Chakra. This energy flow is essential for good health, and the Greeks used the snake as a symbol of healing and wisdom. It is also symbolic of the primordial life force, encompassing the principles of yin and yang, representing duality and the search for balance, which is how we define the qualities of the Lugh and Bride serpent currents associated with the Holy Axis.

The shape and design of The Ringses enclosure also reminded us of a coiled snake, mirroring many aspects of the mysterious power in the land. From the air, the earthwork's rings mimic the concentric markings on the cup and ring marked stones, which can be seen all over the surrounding moor. Could the enclosure and stones lure the lights of plasma intelligence, often witnessed on the moor?

As we continue west to the highest area called Dod Law Moor, we locate Bride flowing through a circular earth enclosure known as Dod Law West. Nearby is a cottage called the Shepherd's House, situated at the end of a track that leads to a golf course. The female serpent intersects with another male energy within the circular remains of two earthen ditch and bank ramparts with entrances in the southeast and northwest. According to historical records, standing stones once stood within this earthwork, and a circular stone rampart surrounded the inner sanctum that remained until about 100 CE, along with several circular huts. 1980s excavations also unearthed prehistoric pottery, jewellery, flints and portable cup and ring marked stones. Such finds would suggest a ceremonial purpose indicating that these enclosures were considered sacred to the ancient cultures.

Cup and Ring Marked Stone at Dod Law on Bride current

Before Bride enters this western enclosure on Dod Law, the edge of her current clips one of the many stones carved with rock art, this one showing a double set of squared lines surrounding several cup marks.

Further to the east are scant remains of two more enclosures called Middle Dod Law and Dod Law East. Beckensall records some of the most impressive cup and ring marks here and cites past antiquarians' accounts of lost barrows and cist graves that once littered this area.[4] Just south of The Ringses and east of Dod Law is a small stone circle next to a footpath comprising one upright stone with others now fallen and hidden in the long grass.

From Dod Law, we follow a footpath south passing the Shepherd's House as it descends the moor's southwestern slopes. We soon realised Bride was leading us to a large sandstone outcrop overlooking the River Till called Cuddy's or Cuddie's Cave. If you take the narrow road beneath the hill between Westwood Bridge and Doddington Bridge, this striking natural feature appears like the head of a dragon emerging from the bowels of Mother Earth. Others describe it as a giant elephant's foot.

The cave's location provides spectacular panoramic views of Northumberland's fertile plains below. The cave roof is covered in cup markings now hardly visible, having been worn due to its exposure to Northumberland's harsh weather for centuries. In addition, its surface has been discoloured by years of water deposits percolating through the porous sandstone.

According to local folklore, *'the devil hanged his granny here on the bowed rock on the brae.'*[5] Although this story seems to paint a rather gloomy picture of this spectacular and enigmatic site, I believe that folklore often offers a glimmer of allegorical truth about a place, albeit slightly exaggerated. In this case, I believe the devil refers to a pagan god or even a giant, as we find in other folktales around the country, and the hanging of his granny is perhaps reminiscent of the slaying of the old crone goddess, the Cailleach. *Cailleach* comes from a Gaelic word meaning 'veiled one'. She is the winter goddess often associated with Bride in her winter role. In Irish and Highland lore, the Cailleach is the oldest being and creator of the landscape. Perhaps, goddess rituals took place here long ago, celebrating the death of winter and the birth of spring – moreover, naming a site after the devil was often a Christian way of deterring locals from worshipping at a pagan place of power.

Like St Cuthbert's Cave on St Cuthbert's Way further east of here, this cave was one of the alleged resting places of St Cuthbert's body. Another local legend says that Cuthbert kept his sheep here when he was a shepherd boy, although there is little evidence to support this tale. However, due to the proximity of Cuddy's or St Cuthbert's Well, located below the hill in the village of Doddington, this famous northern saint most likely had a connection with the Doddington area. Perhaps the power of this dome-shaped moorland that drew the ancient inhabitants to this area centuries before also lured Cuthbert as a sensitive young boy to commune here with Mother Earth in this small cave made from powerful sandstone and drink the water from the nearby well.

From the mouth of the little cave, you can see the sacred terrain of Milfield Plain, its fertile fields having grown crops since Neolithic times. A few miles to the southwest is Yeavering Bell, the holiest

Cuddy's Cave, Doddington Moor

peak in Northumberland. In spring, you can observe from Cuddy's Cave the setting sun falling behind this twin-peaked Mother Mountain, which is perhaps why this outcrop is associated with the death of winter.

After such an intense day of dowsing and with our energy levels waning after being exposed to powerful geology and highly magnetic sites, we noted our findings and left the moor searching for refreshments. To our surprise, there is a rather good café just outside the village of Milfield with a distant view of Doddington Moor. Over a late afternoon tea, we noticed information leaflets and books available on the archaeology of Milfield Plain and Doddington Moor.

History tells us that pilgrims would cross this part of the moor from Melrose Abbey to Lindisfarne to see the curious cup and ring carvings on the stones. So perhaps the Bride current responds to the pious consciousness of pilgrims walking from Lindisfarne.

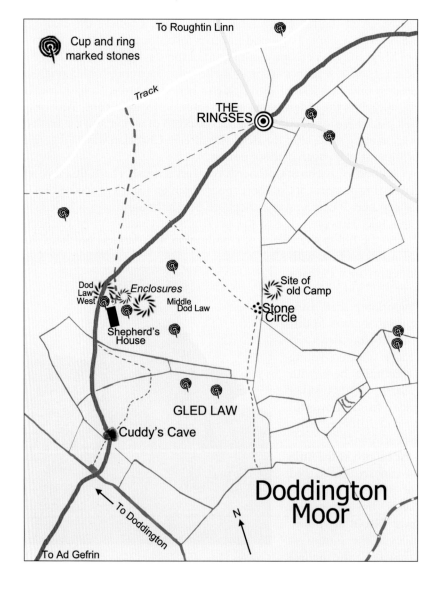

The Milfield Henges

Where the granite foothills of the Cheviots give way to the Tweed Valley, there lies a fertile plain steeped in history called the Milfield Basin. Three great rivers empty their fast-flowing waters into this valley, the Glen, the Till and Wooler Water. This region was a sacred place to the ancient priesthood, for they observed triple symbolism in nature to be representative of the goddess whose fertilising powers gave life to the land and all its creatures.

According to British historian Nennius, Arthur's first battle was at the mouth of the River 'Glein'. There are only two candidates for this elusive river in Britain – the River Glen in Lincolnshire and the River Glen here in Northumberland. The terrain in Lincolnshire during Saxon times was too boggy and therefore an unlikely site for Arthur's battle. There is evidence from the ancient text *Y Gododdin* that the British rode cavalry horses in action, which would be useless in the Lincolnshire marshes. Therefore, it would make sense that Arthur fought the Anglo-Saxons at a frontier where the Gododdin had their great fort at Yeavering Bell, beneath which King Edwin later built his grand royal palace of Ad Gefrin. The Angles arriving here from York may have been attempting to seize the sacred valley below Yeavering to primarily take control of the vital trade routes that intersected here.

The Gododdin were the only Celtic tribe not subjugated by the Romans but instead entered a trading partnership with them. The Romans made many alliances with the Celtic tribes, especially in the North of England, as their kingdoms included essential mineral and precious metal mines and quarries. The Gododdin held lands from the east coast south of the Forth, including Edinburgh and Falkirk, controlling a vital part of the central route across the Neck of Britain from the Firth of Clyde to the Firth of Forth. These pagan Celts were renowned traders in lucrative metals and commodities such as lead, silver and tin to many parts of Britain and mainland Europe. The Romans in Britain were keen to share or exploit their wealth and developed good relationships with the British for a time.

When the Romans withdrew from Britain, the Gododdin were the only tribe to retain their lands and remain wealthy and powerful, making them a target for other tribes, including the Scots and Angles. The prize was always about access to trade and controlling vital trade routes. The Gododdin eventually fell to the invading Angles at the Battle of Catraeth (modern day Catterick) in 600 CE despite fighting alongside their Welsh and Pictish allies. Those who survived fled into exile to Wales, settling amongst their Brythonic ancestors – their slain warriors commemorated in the *Y Gododdin*, attributed to Aneirin.[6] The fact that the Gododdin held on to their lands for so long against such mighty foes as the Scots and the Angles led to great stories about these courageous warriors, many of their names drifting into myth and legend.

From Doddington, we followed Bride across the Milfield Plain to West Akeld, connecting with the lost site of a late Neolithic henge monument called West Akeld Steads, next to the River Glen. The henge is visible on Google Earth as a crop mark with an internal enclosure measuring 114 ft (35 m) in diameter with a 24 ft (7.5 m) wide inner ditch with two entrances. She also visits another lost henge site now covered by the House Plantation near Akeld Lodge. These are two of many ploughed-out henges investigated by Anthony Harding in 1976 as part of a larger project in the Till Valley.

A reconstruction of one of these Neolithic henges can be found as part of the Maelmin Heritage Trail in Milfield, two miles north of Alkeld. The timber henge circle consists of tall wooden posts surrounded by two crescent-shaped ditches and encircled by an outer bank with two entrances. These timber henge structures were once dotted all over this fertile Basin, regarded as one of the best-known prehistoric landscapes in Britain. This extensive ceremonial complex stretched from Milfield village to the parishes of Ewart and Akeld in the south.

Reconstructed henge on Maelmin Heritage Trail in Milfield

Archaeologists excavating various locations in the Basin have revealed cemeteries with cremated human remains placed in pots and interred without cists, and aerial photography produced evidence of several more henges. They also discovered the remains of three settlements dating to the Neolithic period, the Late Bronze Age, and the Dark Ages. The latter dates between 410–570 CE, but whether native Britons or the Angles built them is uncertain.[7]

Most archaeologists who have studied this area believe the henges were part of a ritual landscape from Neolithic times extensively farmed. After visiting the reconstruction, we sensed it contained a specific energetic power. Its unusual design of wooden posts with banks and ditches was explicitly created to harness this energy and was still doing so in a modern reproduction.

We also felt that they attracted mysterious balls of light or plasma recorded in the area. Often lights rise out of prominent hills and mountains, and in this area, it would have been the towering eminence of Yeavering Bell south of here. Yeavering's summit has many prehistoric monuments and rock art to conjure these lights and spirits. But only the initiated or psychic people, such as shamans, could communicate with them through an etheric doorway opened by the high electromagnetic field of plasma. Perhaps the henges, with entrances pointing to the sacred mountain, were designed to draw plasma from the hill to bring fertility and balance to the Milfield Basin to provide regular harvests.

In the shadow of Yeavering Bell, Bride visits a standing stone known locally as the Battle Stone. As we dowsed around the tall megalith, we felt a strong emanating magnetic force, which we could sense using our hands. Perhaps its name derives from the legendary battle fought by King Arthur nearby or possibly the Battle of Geteryne (Yeavering) in 1415 between the English and the Scots.

However, this 6.5 ft (2 m) high megalith dates back to the Bronze Age, and archaeologists have found remains of burial pits and Mesolithic flint workings in the area. It possibly formed part of a much larger ceremonial complex of sites as

The Battle Stone near Yeavering

it aligns with another henge called the lost Yeavering Henge, once situated 153 yds (140 m) away. This circular embanked monument, another of the eight investigated by Anthony Harding, is also on Bride situated close to the river Glen on a prominent plateau of sand and gravel that straddles a road called the 'whaleback'. For over 5000 years, people have settled in the area, creating a ceremonial landscape to bury their dead and to meet their rulers.[8]

Ad Gefrin, Palace of Kings

The dowsing of Bride took us further along the whaleback ridge under Yeavering Bell to the site of King Edwin's palace called Ad Gefrin. According to the Venerable Bede, it was abandoned around 670 CE when Mercian invaders destroyed the royal court. The essence of Edwin, the Bretwalda king of the north, is connected to our quest as during Saxon times the Holy Axis at 107 degrees, pointed towards the horizon where the sun rose on 12 October, his feast day – today the sun rises at 107 degrees around the 15 October.

From the air, outlines of many significant buildings encompassing this royal township come into view. Between 1953 and 1962, archaeological excavations were carried out here under the guidance of Cambridge scholar Brian Hope-Taylor.[9] Findings revealed a massive complex of sophisticated wooden buildings constructed in the 6th and 7th centuries, some over 85 ft (26 m) in length, possibly halls or palaces and a pagan temple converted to Christian use. Several earlier monuments appeared to be incorporated into the palace complex, utilising an Iron Age enclosure for cattle or horses. They also found large quantities of horse bones and complete skeletons outside the main entrance in 1885.

The wooden halls had elaborately carved panels decorated inside and out with gold leaf and solid gold fittings with styling reminiscent of Theoden's great hall in *The Lord of the Rings*. The epic Anglo-Saxon poem *Beowulf*, written in Northumbria between 975 and 1025 and perhaps recited in the great hall at Bamburgh, could refer to the Great Hall at Ad Gefrin. The royal settlement also included an outdoor assembly theatre or grandstand, a rare feature, which was probably a parliament building, perhaps the oldest of its kind in Britain. There is also evidence that an early Christian church stood here, possibly built after the Roman missionary Paulinus visited the royal settlement in the early 7th century. The Roman bishop may have also created the first church on Lindisfarne before the arrival of Aidan. In 625, Paulinus, then Bishop of York, was said to have escorted Ethelburger, a Saxon Princess of the Kentish Kingdom, to marry Edwin King of Northumbria. In his *Ecclesiastical History of the English People*, the Venerable Bede records that while Edwin and his queen resided at Ad Gefrin, in 627, the queen's bishop Paulinus spent thirty-six days converting the pagans to Christianity baptising them in the nearby river Glen:

> 'Catechising and baptising; during which days, from morning to night, he did nothing else but instruct the crowds who flocked to him from every village and district in the teaching of Christ, and when instructed, he washed them in the water of absolution in the river Glen, nearby.' [11]

A digital reconstruction of the Anglo-Saxon settlement of Ad Gefrin (courtesy of Northumberland and Durham County Councils)

Ad Gefrin became a summer residence for some of the most notable kings and queens of the day, including Aethelfrith, the saintly Oswald and his younger brother Oswiu. It would be just one of many royal residences occupied by these kings as they moved around their kingdom. But, unfortunately, there is evidence that the Yeavering royal centre suffered much destruction after two battles during its 150-year history. By 670 CE, its total abandonment came after an attack by the joint forces of Mercian King Penda and Cadwallon of Wales.

During the reign of Oswald, St Aidan would have regularly visited this church at his summer residence, and it is possible that after the defeat of Oswald, Penda burned it to the ground. Therefore, the burnt beam in Bamburgh's parish church on the Lugh current probably came from the wooden church at Ad Gefrin, which Aidan later consecrated.

At the close of the 7th century, all physical traces of the Anglo-Saxon palace, once an imposing presence, faded away. The site was lost until its rediscovery through aerial photography in 1949. Today there are only fields with a layby and a stone monument with information boards to tell the story of this once magnificent wooden city ruled by the old Anglian kings of Britain.

Yeavering and the Three Kings

The distinctive conical twin-peaked hill of Yeavering Bell towers at 1158 ft (361 m) over Ad Gefrin and the flat plains of the Glen River. It was formed some 350 million years ago in the Devonian period in the violent volcanic eruptions that created the entire Cheviot range of hills. The hills were sculpted into their present rounded shape by a succession of glaciers during the Ice Age. The Bell, as it is affectionately called, has always fired the human imagination, and local people still use it to gauge the weather, time and the progress of the seasons. On its summit lies the largest hillfort in Northumberland with impressive 8 ft (2.4 m) high ramparts and the tumbled remains of what must have been an immense and remarkable wall over 10 ft (3 m) thick, encompassing twelve acres and both peaks of the hill. However, it was possibly originally constructed as a ceremonial enclosure similar to The Ringses on Doddington Moor. Inside was a small village with over 130 stone round houses, some paved. The British Gododdin (Votadini) tribe built the fort and named the hill Din Gefron, said to mean 'hill of the goats'. The eastern side contained a separate area enclosed by a wall with two main entrances, perhaps the site of the ruler's palace.

When newly constructed around 500 BCE, it would have had a dramatic appearance, for its walls made from local andesite pink granite stones in parts stood at around 30 ft (9 m) high. Yeavering Bell is a significant landmark seen over a wide area with views on a clear day of the North Sea. Rupert Matthews, in *Mysterious Northumberland,*

Twin-peaked Yeavering Bell (courtesy of Stuart Meek)

points out that during the time of the Celts, the county saw the construction of several dozen hillforts, including Bamburgh, Dunstanburgh and Tynemouth. However, the hillfort at Yeavering has remained untouched by later re-fortification and the building of medieval castles.[12]

As a place of kingship and governance, Yeavering was perhaps the greatest of all Northumberland's hillforts, serving as a powerful and prestigious statement for miles around. Its shape is also significant because twin-peaked hills are sacred to many cultures, with temples aligned to them, such as the famous Knossos temple on the Greek island of Crete.

The twin peaks or 'paps' also represent the mother goddess's breasts, examples being the sacred hills known as the Paps of Jura and the Devil's Gap in Scotland and the Paps of Anu in Ireland. The Gododdin had other power centres, including Traprain Law near Edinburgh and Eildon Hill near Melrose.

Author Philip Coppens discovered a geometric relationship between these sacred hills marking points on an equilateral triangle – the angle between the line running from the Eildon Hills to Traprain Law and then to Yeavering Bell being a perfect 90 degrees. Coppens called this the 'Gododdin Triangle' and stated that they mark essential points in the landscape at important meeting places of roads and rivers. So it would appear that nature unconsciously created landscape trigonometry when these three hills formed thousands of years ago.[13]

Whether the Celts knew of this perfect triangle of hills is uncertain. Still, such sacred geometry makes the land of the Gododdin special even when only noticed in modern times using mapping programs such as Google Earth.

Within the Milford Basin, we find a junction of valleys and major roads, creating a perfect meeting place for trade and ceremony, which further points to this area being a sacred landscape with Yeavering Bell as its focus. According to archaeologist Brian Hope-Taylor, by the 1st century CE, the settlement at Yeavering Bell had become 'a major political centre in the vast region between the rivers Tyne and Tweed.'

We climbed to the top of Yeavering Bell and witnessed an incredible view north and out over

Triangle showing the geometric relationship between Eildon Hills, Traprain Law and Yeavering Bell

the sea to the east, where Lindisfarne is easily visible. Views of the Cheviot range to the south are also spectacular. This quote from archaeologist Paul Frodsham sums it up:

'Recently, I led a day-long guided walk around Yeavering for thirty individuals, including schoolteachers, a retired GP, a Tyneside docker, farm workers and archaeology students. Some of these people live locally, while others have travelled considerable distances to take part in the walk. The weather was perfect, with a covering of crisp snow on the ground and bright sunshine all day. Having taken many guided walks to wonderful archaeological sites throughout the Cheviots over the years, I was quite taken aback by the reaction of these individuals to Yeavering. They were all spellbound by the place, and one couple even described the day as one of the best of their lives.'[15]

Just under a mile from Ad Gefrin, Bride visits the parish church at the small village of Kirknewton dedicated to St Gregory or Pope Gregory, the only dedication of its kind in Northumberland. The dragon current passes through the northeast corner of the chancel, considered the oldest part of the church, possibly dating back to Saxon times. Inside, Bride meanders through the famous relief carving of the Adoration of the Magi in the wall to the left of the altar, dated to before 960 CE but could be substantially older. The Magi are dressed in kilts or short tunics and seem to be wearing conical Phrygian caps, unlike the traditional depictions that show them wearing crowns. This type of headwear is synonymous with tribes of Eastern Europe, such as the Anatolian Phrygians. They are often depicted on Assyrian panels, which display similar caps on the heads of the enslaved people who supposedly were used to construct their empire. Later the caps would come to symbolise liberty and freedom from oppression.

The three kings are also associated with Orion and Lugh and are an allegory of the three stars of Orion. The biblical 'star in the east', which guides the Magi to the baby Jesus, is Sirius, the brightest star in the night's sky, which on 24 December aligns with the three stars of Orion's Belt. On 25 December, these stars point to the horizon, where the sun rises from its three-day standstill and begins its journey north towards summer and new life. The three kings in the form of Orion's Belt follow the star Sirius to the birth of the son of God, symbolic of the birth of the 'Sun' of God.

Bride flows along the nave's axis and out through the tower at the western end of the church. Outside, she visits the grave of social reformer Josephine Butler (1828–1906), widow of George Butler, Canon of Winchester Cathedral, who tirelessly campaigned for the injustice of women. The Scots have rebuilt the church several times courtesy of the numerous border raids that often occurred in this area. A Saxon church stood on the site, and the chancel bears signs of early masonry, possibly dating from after the destruction of Ad Gefrin. The name Kirknewton or 'church of the new town' may refer to a new place of worship built after Penda burnt the original to the ground at nearby Ad Gefrin.

Relief carving of the Adoration of the Magi, Kirknewton Church, Northumberland

The Hidden Valley of the Cheviots

To the southwest of Kirknewton, we find Bride flowing alongside College Burn, a tributary of the Glen River, as it streams south between two hills, one having a major Iron Age settlement on its summit called West Hill. Further up the valley we dowsed her at Hethpool Linn, a small waterfall that cascades deep within a narrow rocky gorge next to St Cuthbert's Way. It is an idyllic place surrounded by hazel trees and remarkable rocks where Mother Earth creates harmony and beauty. It is the perfect spot to stop and refocus your energy and absorb the healing chi and ozone generated by the friction of the cascading water. Further upriver, we cross the St Cuthbert Way at the tiny hamlet of Hethpool, with its pretty cottages, to remnants of two large stone circles.

College Valley stone circles

Breathtaking views awaited us in this secluded landscape, a well-known haven for local walkers and cyclists. The peaceful and unspoilt College Valley nestles in one of the foothills of the mighty Cheviots, dominated by the hillforts of the pyramid-shaped prominence of Great Hetha and the feminine-shaped Little Hetha. Hetha derives from the old Norse word *Heiðr*, *Heid*, *Hed* or *Heith*, meaning 'bright', 'strong' or 'bold. In Norse mythology, Hetha is also the name of a warrior-like queen mentioned in the *Gesta Danorum*.[15]

Opposite the National Trust car park are several megaliths forming two stone circles in a field. Only four stones remain from the original ten that made up the southern circle, broken up and scattered in grassland. It once measured 183 ft (56 m) in diameter, and the ring to the north had thirteen stones that would have measured 157 ft (48 m), of which only six remain. The thirteen stones may correspond to the 13 lunar phases in a year. Interestingly both circles have their centres aligned north–south. Very little remains to ascertain the true purpose of these circles, but dowsing Bride through both rings indicates the valley's importance as an ancient place of sanctity and power.

The female dragon current connects with all four stones of the south circle, almost precisely aligned towards Little Hetha hillfort. A flock of sheep zealously guarded one of the megaliths and seemed reluctant to surrender it to two suspicious-looking dowsers. Were they enjoying the presence and healing power of the Bride current? Reluctantly they moved, but only to a juicy patch of grass a few feet away. Under their ever-watchful presence, we dowsed Bride and soon realised that her flow had expanded by several feet on either side of the stone.

Sheep protecting one of the megaliths at College Valley

The current is then attracted to a group of stones in the car park, also possible remnants of the two circles, despite being moved from their previous site.

After spending time tuning into the female serpent flow and the spirit guardian of the site, we strongly sensed that Bride and the stones needed rebalancing. We were each drawn to different megaliths where we laid our unique green serpentine healing stones. We used them to imbue the stones with golden light, healing any past trauma affecting this sacred place and the Bride flow due to the destruction of these monuments or occult abuse. We visualised reconnecting the physical stones with the remaining etheric traces of their lost counterparts to restore the divine power of these circles that once played an essential role in aiding the fertility and well-being of this beautiful valley.

After removing the healing stones, we sensed from the spirit guardian that the ancients revered the valley because it was a focal point to commune with the mountain spirits or intelligent plasma. In other words, they built the stone circles to attract or draw spirit lights similar to the henges at Milfield but in this case, created by the surrounding hills of Great Hetha and Little Hetha, which, as stated earlier, means in old Norse 'light'. Perhaps the Norse settlers revered these lights as a symbol of their local earth goddess naming her Hetha.

The combination of the power of the Cheviot Hills and the gushing waters of College Burn may have provided the perfect conditions for the ancient cultures to commune with Bride's serpent energy and the consciousness of nature by drawing in the plasma to their stone circles from the mountains around them.

We then sensed that the mountain spirits were guiding us to collect the energy within the stone circles to take to the waterfall to help rebalance both sites. I was drawn to pick up a small white quartz stone found at the centre of one of the circles, which I carried back to Hethpool Linn. After placing the quartz stone into the fast-flowing waterfall, we blessed the waters and visualised sending healing light through the Bride serpent flow to the stones circles and the goddess hills of Hetha.

Visualisation has proven to be the most effective form of healing, a practice used by priests and magicians throughout the ages. There are plenty of instances where the power of the mind has created healing and positive change, including prayer, for the heartfelt intention accompanying the thought process during visualisation influences the outcome. Essential to this process is the awareness of the beneficial powers provided by the Universe, which can be channelled through intentioned thought to the troubled area by a shaft of pure healing light to flood and dissolve the harmful influences, restoring harmony to the body or land.

We were reluctant to leave this magical valley with its mysterious stones, goddess hills and fairy glen. However, we were excited by the thought of encountering other treasures as we continued west along the St Cuthbert Way towards Kirk Yetholm and the Scottish Border.

From the stone circles, the female dragon crosses the hillfort on the summit of Great Hetha, with its double-banked ramparts enclosing an area of about an acre. You can see from the summit fine views of several surrounding hillforts and settlements as part of a highly populated ritual and farming landscape in the Bronze and Iron Ages. Bride continues her journey to a round cairn cemetery just north of Trowupburn Farm. King John, son of Henry II and Eleanor of Aquitaine, once owned this land when it was Trolhopeburn, later transferred to the monks of Melrose Abbey. The hill to the right is Ell's Knowe, the word *el* or *ell* having its roots in many languages. In Irish and Scottish Gaelic, it refers to a unit of measure, but in old Welsh, the *ell-yllon* is a race of elves.

Interestingly, we have encountered many hills and mounds called 'fairy knowe' on Lugh and Bride during our travels through Scotland. Folklorists tell us that the Cheviots Hills are renowned for stories of the 'little people' and the witnessing of balls of light. The natural telluric power within these hills is conducive to producing mysterious lights because of underground water and its andesite stone, a hard volcanic crystalline rock that changes from a deep pink colour to pale grey when weathered.

Continuing west, Bride crosses the feminine-shaped Madam Law to Maddie's Well, the source of a stream called Tuppies Sike. Here an ancient well-trodden track leads to the border of England and Scotland. The Bride serpent visits many holy wells along the Holy Axis, and this one is special, being so close to an ancient border crossing.

Soon we approached a pair of megaliths on a path close to St Cuthbert Way, one standing and one recumbent, called the Stob Stanes. The Canmore website states, '*Both stones are of native porphyry and are locally called the "Gypsy Stobs" from the tradition that the kings of the Yetholm gypsies were crowned here*.'[16] Another story says they were border stones. However, from the weathering and size, they appear to be prehistoric, and the upright stone leans towards the sacred trinity of peaks in the distance near Melrose called the Eildon Hills, as if serving as a marker for the old pilgrims travelling between the abbeys of Melrose and Lindisfarne.

Re-joining the St Cuthbert's Way a little further west, we cross into Scotland and descend to the river crossing called Halter Burn, where the St Cuthbert Way joins the Pennine Way. We follow Bride to a standing stone that may be yet another of these medieval pilgrim markers or a prehistoric waymark. Here, the little hamlet of Halterburn has a magical quality, perhaps because it is the starting point of the Pennine Way. However, this remote spot may have been an important meeting or gathering

Stob Stones on St Cuthbert Way, near Halterburn

place for the Bronze and Iron Age peoples before heading south to the Pennines. At this point, we decided to resume Lugh's journey from the Scottish Borders towards the enigmatic Rosslyn Chapel.

1. Willem, David. 2013. *St Cuthbert's Corpse A Life after Death*. Sacristy Press, Durham.
2. 4. Beckinsale, S. 1983. *Northumberland's Prehistoric Rock Carvings*. Pendulum Publications, Rothbury.
3. https://electricscotland.com/history/articles/goddess.htm
5. https://archive.org/details/denhamtractscoll01denhuoft
6. https://www.gutenberg.org/files/9842/9842-h/9842-h.htm
7. https://www.maelmin.org.uk/
8. 9. https://gefrintrust.org/publications/
10. Tolkien, J.R.R. 2016. *Beowulf: A Translation and Commentary, Together with Sellic Spell*. Harper Collins, London.
11. Dumville, D. 2003. Bede: *Ecclesiastical History of the English People*, translated by L. Shirly-Price and D. Farmer. Penguin Classics, London.
12. Matthews, Rupert. 2009. *Mysterious Northumberland*. Breedon Books, Derby.
13. P, Coppens. 2007. *Land of the Gods*. Frontier Publishing, Amsterdam.
14. Frodsham, Paul. 2005. *Yeavering: People, Power & Place*. The History Press, Cheltenham.
15. Simek, Rudolf. & Hall, Angela. 1993. *Dictionary of Northern Mythology*. D.S. Brewer, Cambridge.
16. https://canmore.org.uk/site/59259/stob-stones

Chapter 5

Lugh and the Pilgrim Trail from the Borders to Roslin

Coldstream Priory

Lugh crosses the Tweed River into Scotland at a bend shaped like a swan's neck, and within the loop is a floodplain called Lees Haugh with a dyke built in the 1820s by POWs from the Napoleonic War. The fertile fields in this quiet and picturesque part of the river are an ideal habitat for oystercatchers, herons and leaping salmon. After flowing over Lees Haugh, the male current passes over a tributary of the Tweed called Leet Water that skirts the southern end of the town, where it mysteriously disappears through a high stone wall.

We entered Coldstream via an old stone bridge that spans the Tweed, passing through a centuries-old gateway that marks the border between England and Scotland. Our first mission was to find the stone wall beside Leet Water where we last dowsed Lugh. With the help of a map, we found our way to Market Street, passing the town's museum in Market Square. After turning right into Abbey Road, we soon found ourselves approaching the banks of Leet Water, and where the road bends to the left, we noticed the same stone wall detected earlier. Located next to a river path called Penitent's Walk, a metal gate in the wall encloses an old piece of masonry with an inscription that reads: *'This stone is one of the last remains of Coldstream Priory, also known as St Mary's Abbey, which stood on this site from 1165 to 1621. The Scottish nobility were interred here after*

the Battle of Flodden on 9 September 1513.' The priory's abbess, Isabella Hoppringle (1460-1538), rescued the bodies of many of the earls and barons who fought alongside the Scottish king on that fateful day.

The abbess was a personal friend of the Scottish dowager queen regent, Margaret Tudor, but also a clever spy who *'skilfully managed to balance between the two nations to benefit the*

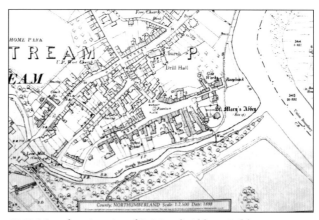

1898 Map showing site of St Mary's Abbey, Coldstream, Scottish Borders

abbey and was reputed as the best agent England had in Scotland.[1] In 1515, Henry VIII issued a proclamation to the English Wardens protecting the prioress and her convent. Her heroic actions are still marked today as part of the annual festival held in August to commemorate the Battle of Flodden. It includes riders led by the Coldstreamer, a young man elected to carry the town standard for the week's festivities, which processes to the battle site on horseback for the oration and service. A sod of turf is cut and taken back to Tweed Green in Coldstream, where a moving ceremony takes place to commemorate the actions of the abbess.

Lugh connects with the Coldstream Priory site, initially founded in 1165 as a nunnery by Gospatrick III, Earl of Dunbar, and his wife Deidre and remained intact until its dissolution in 1621. The Dunbars were descended from the Royal House of Wessex and Bamburgh. The priory church, the very first place of worship in Coldstream, was dedicated to St Mary by David de Bernham in 1243 and is referred to in early charters as '*the church of St. Mary of Calstrem.*'[2] A few pieces of masonry and the street names such as Nun's Walk, Penitent's Walk and Abbey Road are the only reminders of this old building.

Lugh then enters the museum in Market Square, where some of the priory's medieval masonry is displayed. We found to our surprise, some remarkable and unusual carvings of dragons. However, Lugh's primary focus is the Coldstream Guards' permanent exhibition, perhaps because it stands over the original site of General Monck's headquarters. The General marched to London from here with his army in 1660 to restore the Stuart King Charles II to the throne of England. In the corner of the museum yard, we spotted the Stone of Scone, also known as the Stone of Destiny or Coronation Stone, obviously a replica. We wondered how many fake stones exist, perhaps copied from the original stone stolen from Westminster Abbey in 1950.

Dragon Carving in Coldstream Museum

The 'Stone of Destiny' has a colourful history believed to have originated in Ireland, where it was known as the *Lia Fáil*. A mystical race called the Tuatha Dé Danann arrived on a hill in Northern Ireland out of thin air and brought with them four treasures – the Sword of Nuada, the Spear of Lugh, the Cauldron of the Dagda, and the Lia Fáil or Stone of Destiny. These treasures represent the four

Replica Stone of Destiny or Coronation Stone in Coldstream Museum

elements – the stone denotes earth, the cup signifies water, the sword symbolises fire and the Spear of Lugh is air. So far, we have encountered the cup and sword and now the Stone of Destiny here at the Border.

From Market Square, we continue west, following Lugh along the High Street to St Cuthbert's Kirk, now a community centre, its graveyard landscaped as a delightful garden surrounded by an old stone wall. The first church built on this site was in 1768, and in 1907 it became the West United Free Church. Perhaps the original builders sensed the presence of the earth serpent here and established their church on its flow.

Coldstream has seen many conflicts throughout history, from border raids by the Scots and English and the War of Scottish Independence in 1316. It even witnessed the theft of the Stone of Destiny by Edward I from Scone, carried over its old stone bridge on its way to London. It then saw its return in 1996 when the locals welcomed it back to Scotland, waving their national flag and shouting the word 'freedom'. In the 18th and 19th centuries, it became a famous centre for runaway marriages, similar to Gretna Green.

However, we could not help but wonder whether the stain of its turbulent past has affected the town's fortunes, with its streets empty of people and many of its shops either closed or boarded up. Perhaps continually commemorating such an atrocity creates low vibrational energy, infecting the local landscape and its inhabitants.

About 3 miles north of Coldstream, the Holy Axis is marked by the ruins of Simprim Old Parish Church within a circular graveyard. It fell out of use in 1761 when the parish was amalgamated with the nearby village of Swinton. The earliest known church on this site was one of the smallest religious houses in Scotland dating to the 12th century when it belonged to Kelso Abbey.

The Lost Sanctuary of Hirsel

Lugh travels along the tributary of Leet Water to the Hirsel Estate, just under a mile north of Coldstream, the present seat of the Earls of Home. We followed a path through the parkland from the car park, where a beautiful array of bluebells, daffodils and other spring flowers greeted us. As we surveyed the landscape, we felt Hirsel was once a unique sanctuary surrounded by ancient trees and meadows. The sycamore tree, located in the southeast corner of the walled garden, was said to have been planted to commemorate the Battle of Flodden in 1513 and nearby is a rare 300-year-old tulip tree.

We traced Lugh crossing a picturesque meadow just to the right of the main house, where Highland cattle silently grazed. According to the museum inside the information centre, the field was the site of a prehistoric enclosure called Dial Knowe. The scant remains of earthen ramparts are visible on high ground that would have given the dwellers a good vantage point overlooking a fording of the river below. Archaeologists excavated palisade trenches and postholes here, including timber structures and pottery dating from 3318–1000 BCE. The site continuance here has witnessed Roman, Saxon and medieval occupations.

In the 1970s and 80s, stones were unearthed within the enclosure belonging to a medieval chapel dedicated to St Cuthbert, similar in construction to many Celtic chapels found in Ireland. Archaeologists date the church to around 1165, though its graveyard saw the last burial in 1627. The chapel was initially gifted to Coldstream Priory by Gospatric III, the Earl of Dunbar, and his wife, Countess Deirdre. However, its foundations and the graveyard are much earlier, dating to the 9th century.

To our surprise, inside the little museum are several early crosses found at Dial Knowe that may date to Cuthbert's time. These are rare indeed, as few preconquest relics survive. Could this be one of the stopover places where the saint's coffin rested, or did he establish a religious settlement here?

Dial Knowe prehistoric enclosure and site of St Cuthbert's Chapel, Hirsel Estate

Lugh continues through woodland to Hirsel House, the private home of David Douglas-Home, the 15th Earl of Home. His family acquired the estate in 1611 from Sir John Kerr, who planted many trees during this time. The family's best-known member is Sir Alec Douglas-Home, 14th Earl of Home (1903 –1995), who served as Britain's Prime Minister from 1963 to 1964. After a narrow defeat in the general election of 1964, Douglas-Home resigned from his party's leadership. From 1970 to 1974, he served in the cabinet of Edward Heath as Secretary of State at the Foreign and Commonwealth Office. After the defeat of the Heath government in 1974, he returned to the House of Lords as a life peer and retired from front-line politics.[3]

One of the early crosses found at Dial Knowe, Hirsel

The original house stood nearer the old chapel site, known as 'Old Hirsel' or Hirsel Castle, probably built as a tower house. We believe that Lugh's flow incorporated the area of Old Hirsel between Hirsel House and the old chapel on Dial Knowe.

After struggling to dowse Lugh through the grounds, we realised that his flow was weaker than usual, so we found a quiet spot within the pretty woodland to conduct a healing ceremony. Here we visualised golden light revitalising and harmonising his flow. During our meditation, we were surprised to receive an image of The Ringses on Doddington Moor overshadowed by a dark guardian. Perhaps this was why we felt uneasy during our initial dowsing of Bride and Lugh on the moor. Although, when returning to Doddington Moor a second time and seeking permission to continue our dowsing of Bride, it seemed apparent that the male serpent also required healing and rebalancing. The spirits of Hirsel woodland were permitting us to do this within the safety and protection of this ancient sanctuary. As we projected pure love and light through the flow of the male serpent towards the node on Doddington Moor, we could see the dark and malevolent energy evaporating away to be replaced by a glowing fountain of pure white light.

Dial Knowe is on an old trail where pilgrims rested before and after fording the Tweed at Coldstream. The Celtic cross fragments found here highlight the importance of this sanctuary, possibly used by Celtic monks travelling between the sacred isles of Lindisfarne and Iona.

We enjoyed exploring the Hirsel estate, with its idyllic natural surroundings and parkland and were impressed by its informative museum and cafe. But, the highlight for us was discovering its sacred history hidden beneath the surface of this ancient landscape.

During our initial dowsing efforts in this area, we detected Lugh at a hillfort enclosure north of the Hirsel estate called Hirsel Law, also referred to as 'Hirslaw'. Some historians believe it is one of the largest enclosed sites in the region and a settlement of the Votadini tribe. Northwest of there, the current passes over a large, impressive artificial mound surrounded by a ditch and bank on Castle Law, called 'the Mount' or 'Mote Hill'. It stands on a high ridge above a fording of Leet Water and is recorded as the remains of a Norman motte and bailey castle, once on land owned by Sir Thomas Drienchester. The family built a castle to replace the Norman Keep a little further north of the site.

However, after the healing ceremony at Hirsel, we discovered that Lugh now follows an old pilgrim trail west towards Eccles and is no longer traceable at the Mount and Hirsel Law. Therefore, whoever built the Mount had deliberately drawn the power of the male dragon current away from its natural course. This endeavour may have been to empower the site or those associated with it. We wondered whether this change in Lugh's flow was the right action, so we asked various questions about the best outcome for the male dragon using our dowsing rods. To our relief, the answers indicated that it was more beneficial for the current to return to its original path following the old pilgrim route to Eccles.

Located just over five miles northeast of the Scottish border town of Kelso, Eccles was, like Hirsel, a Celtic Christian sanctuary. Its name originates from the old British word *eglwys*, meaning 'church', perhaps due to its notoriety as a major ecclesiastical centre. In 1156, Gospatric, Earl of Dunbar, founded St Mary's Priory here for a convent of Benedictine nuns, rededicated to St Andrew in 1248. Records show that an earlier church, dedicated to St Cuthbert, stood here, dating back to the 6th century. The chapel at Dial Knowe also has links to the saint – therefore, Lugh could be following a much older St Cuthbert pilgrimage trail than Bride.

The male current passes through the present Kirk, constructed in 1774 on the site of Cuthbert's Chapel. The church is designed on the Greek cross comprising four aisles of equal length incorporating remnants of old medieval masonry, possibly from the old convent, with more fragments visible in and around the village and Eccles House.

Marchmont and the Holy Axis

Just under 5 miles (8 km) north of Eccles, Marchmont House near Greenlaw marks the path of the Holy Axis. Set within the Blackadder Water Valley surrounded by the Howe and Swardon Burns, this grand mansion was erected in 1750 to a design by William Adam for Hugh Hume-Campbell, the third Earl of Marchmont. The site was formerly the estate of Redbrae Castle, now lying in ruins within the present grounds. Over the centuries, the lands of Redbrae belonged to significant Scottish families, including the Sinclairs and the Homes or Humes. Sir Patrick Hume of Polwarth, who lived at the castle in the 17th century, was implicated in The Rye House Plot of 1683, a failed attempt to assassinate King Charles II of England and his brother James, Duke of York. Sir Patrick was forced to hide in the vaults of nearby Polwarth Church, after which he fled to Holland. He made a glorious return with King William of Orange, who reinstated his lands and, in 1697, was created the first Earl of Marchmont. Later he was made Lord Chancellor, and then in 1698, was elevated to *the highest official position in the kingdom, that of the King's High Commissioner to the Parliament.*[4]

Plans to replace Redbraes Castle with a new and grander house began in 1726 with the planting of the Great Avenue, which consisted of 10,000 Dutch elms lining the 1.3-mile-long straight route, said to be the longest in Scotland. Remnants of it still exist today, although now mainly beech, planted after the great gales of 1881. It leads northeast from the front of the house and terminates at the Dovecot. Reminiscent of the Holy Axis, this straight track is a remarkable feature pointing northwest towards Eyemouth Fort on the east coast marking the rising sun at the summer solstice. In the opposite direction to the southwest, it travels directly to the hillfort on Eildon Hill north, one of the three sacred hills near Melrose where in legend King Arthur sleeps in a cave. Therefore, at the height of his power, the Earl orientated the avenue to imbue his grand mansion with the energy of the archetypal sun king. The Doocot or dovecot positioned on this line is also interesting as they are often found on leys and energy lines, perhaps symbolic of the holy spirit.

During WWII, the house became a school and later the Sue Ryder Foundation took it over in the 1980s for use as a nursing home. Since then, it has undergone restoration, winning the prestigious 2018 Historic Houses/Sotheby's Restoration Award. It now offers a series of events, monthly tours and accommodation.

Straight track at Marchmont House (courtesy of Mark J Richards)

Lauder Valley and the Vision of St Cuthbert

A couple of miles west of Eccles, we arrive at the imposing Hume Castle that stands in a dominant position on a volcanic outcrop with incredible views of the Merse, an area of Berwickshire between the River Tweed and the Lammermuir Hills. From its earliest times, it was a beacon station warning of invasion from England. Its design is like no other in Scotland, with its curtain walls reconstructed from its medieval predecessor in 1770 for the 3rd Earl of Marchmont. However, some walls, particularly around the central Keep, contain masonry dating from the 12th and 13th centuries.

The original Hume Castle was one of the most formidable fortifications in the eastern Borders, being the Hume family seat. An unlikely myth regarding the name change to Home allegedly occurred during the Battle of Flodden when Alexander, Lord Home, while leading his troops, screamed his battle cry, 'A Home! A Home!'

King James II of Scotland and his queen Mary of Gueldres stayed here on their way to Roxburgh Castle in 1460, one of the last Scottish castles still held by the English after the Wars of Independence. For centuries, Hume Castle defended the borders against the English until its virtual desecration by Cromwell in 1651.

The Third Earl of Marchmont, a descendant of the Earls of Home, rebuilt the present castle incorporating the old remains, adorning the walls with enormous crenellated walls that were more picturesque than practical. During the Napoleonic Wars, it was a lookout and beacon station, but *on the night of 31 January 1804, a sergeant in the Berwickshire Volunteers on watch here mistook the fire of some charcoal burners on the Cheviots for an invasion beacon, and ordered the lighting of the beacon at Hume Castle. The result was the "Great Alarm", during which beacons lit across southern Scotland, caused 3,000 volunteers to muster to repel a French army that never arrived.*[5]

Lugh travels east–west through the castle's battlements before heading to the Kirk of St Michaels set high up on a mound in the village of Gordon, just under 4 miles (6.4 km) to the northwest. Although the church dates to the 18th century, its foundations are medieval, as early as 1171, when a chapel here belonged to the monks of Coldingham Priory. Gordon derives its name from the Gaelic 'Gor Dun', meaning great fort. The de Gordons, who also owned lands at Huntly, held the manor here for two centuries in medieval times. A strange tale associated with them tells of Richard de Gordon's grandfather, a famous knight during the time of King Malcolm III of Scotland, who 'slew some monstrous animal in the Merse.' Inside the church, the male current flows through the tombs of the Fairholmes before continuing west to the nearby Greenknowe Tower, a roofless 16th-century tower house made of sandstone. It was built by James Seton of Touch in the early 15th century when his family acquired the land through marriage from the mighty Gordon clan.

Lugh diverts northwest to travel over the nearby site of an Iron Age hillfort on Knock Hill to the Dod's Corse Stone, located in a copse of trees at the base of Boon Hill. According to the Canmore website, the stone is all that remains of a sandstone cross shaft sunk into a square block, said to mark the site of a marketplace. Another entry by Canmore states: *'The cross was not religious but marked the spot where John Cranston of Corsbie died, slew by James Wicht, who was tried on 3 March 1612 and sentenced to be beheaded. The remaining stone fragment has the shaft of a cross on opposite sides, in relief on one side (southern face), incised on the other (northern face).'*[6] Interestingly, fragments of similar stones around the shaft may reveal a more important site of historical significance. Its name also fascinated me as 'dod' or 'dodd', like Doddington, is often associated with leys and alignments. Perhaps the stone marks the course of a local ley or, in this case, the male serpent of the Holy Axis.

Lugh crosses the high eminence of Boon Hill, once surrounded by ancient woodland consumed over millennia by the Picts, Romans, Britons, and Scots. Boon derives from the Breton word *bonn,* meaning boundary or limit, and during the reign of Queen Anne, a small fort was constructed on top of the hill to house another of Scotland's beacons.

Below the western slopes of the hill, Lugh flows over Boondreigh Water to the ruins of a peel tower called Old Thirlestane Castle, owned by the Lords of Thirlestane from the 12th century. It passed through marriage to the Maitland family in the 13th century, one of the oldest and most famous families in Scotland who originally came to England with William the Conqueror in 1066 and settled in Northumberland.

From here, we follow Lugh to the valley below, where Boondreigh Water meets Leader Water. We soon detected him passing east–west through the new Thirlestane Castle near the town of Lauder. This impressive building, constructed of rose-pink sandstone and adorned with numerous turrets, stands on Castle Hill, once the site of Crown Fort. The fortification dates from 1100, erected by the Lauder or Lawedre family to defend the approach to Edinburgh from the south. By 1585, it was in the ownership of Sir John Maitland, who built a new Keep on the site. He became Chancellor of Scotland under James VI, and his son John Maitland became Earl of Lauderdale in 1624, who later developed the old tower into a grand castle. It was further extended and restored in the 18th and 19th centuries and retained the magnificent 17th-century ceilings modelled by plasterers from the court of Charles II.

About 60 yards west of the castle's main entrance is a sycamore tree that marks the site of the ancient Church of Lauder. Many of the old Lauder family who built the Crown Fort were interred here, including William of Lauder (*c.*1380–1425), Bishop of Glasgow and Lord Chancellor of Scotland, and Alexander Lauder, Bishop of Dunkeld.

One gory story associated with the church states that in 1482, James III's favourites, including the architect Robert Cochrane, were dragged by envious nobles from the church led by Archibald Douglas, 5th Earl of Angus, and hanged from the old Lauder Bridge. In 1673 a new place of worship in the centre of the nearby town of Lauder replaced the old church.

Near the tree is a walled graveyard with a watchhouse built after a body-snatching raid in 1830. As we stood under the boughs of this giant sentinel, we could feel the strong presence of Lugh as it passed through the site of the old Lauder church before

Sycamore tree at Thirlestane Castle marking the site of the ancient Church of Lauder

entering the main entrance of the castle and the old Keep. This part of the castle retains the old slit windows dating back to its original construction.

As we drove north towards Edinburgh on the A68, the dowsing rods indicated that Lugh was flowing to the left of us. We soon found the current visiting the site of a Roman Fortlet at Mountmill, just north of the village of Oxton. He continues to the hamlet of Kirktonhill and the pretty little pink-painted church of Channelkirk. From the church, the views overlooking Lauderdale and the Lammermuir Hills are spectacular, and the clear skies enabled us to appreciate the stunning and wild countryside. Set high on a spur of land, the present chapel dating from 1817, stands over the remote site of one established by Dryburgh Abbey in the late 1100s. In the past, its former names were Childenchurch and Channonkirk, eventually becoming the Mother Kirk of Lauderdale.

However, a place of worship has been on this site since at least 700 CE, evidence of which emerged in 1897 when grave diggers unearthed an early Christian cist burial with a body surrounded by flat stones. Also significant is that it lies on or very close to the old Roman road of Dere Street, hence the

Channelkirk

presence of a Roman fortlet and camp nearby. This site in the Lammermuir Hills is the supposed place where the young St Cuthbert was abandoned by his mother and where he had a vision of St Aidan's death while tending sheep. A scene from the illustrated *Life of St Cuthbert* by Bede shows Cuthbert observing angels carrying the soul of Aidan to heaven with the Lammermuir Hills behind. The vision inspired Cuthbert to travel to Melrose and later Lindisfarne, eventually becoming one of the most renowned ecclesiastical figures of the early Northumbrian church in the Celtic tradition.[6]

Interestingly, a modern interpretation of Cuthbert's vision shows him encountering a 'fiery orb' or plasma intelligence, which the young saint observed as an angel. Plasma creates a window through which other-dimensional entities can enter. Encounters with these otherworldly entities, I believe, have occurred throughout history, influencing and inspiring a small number of people with the inherent psychic ability to become famous historical and saintly characters.

This non-carbon plasma intelligence lives on the fringes of our existence but interacts with us when given the opportunity. For example, in the Tree of Life cosmology, the spirits of the upper world are free to travel throughout the lower worlds, but humans find themselves confined to middle earth. This higher intelligence

can monitor certain gifted people and influence them to become greater than they are, for good or bad. Joan of Arc and Moses are among the many historical characters who had encounters with balls of light through which God allegedly spoke.

In the time of Cuthbert, there were no cultural archetypes of UFOs or alien beings. Instead, it was angels, devils, fairies and saints. The young Cuthbert, out at night in the highly magnetic and remote Lammermuir Hills, must have encountered plasma that manifested his cultural expectations. The vision of angels carrying a soul to heaven is similar to Jacob, who saw angels ascending and descending on a ladder to heaven.

A modern interpretation of Cuthbert's vision on the Lammermuir Hills taken from Bede's 'Life of St Cuthbert'

Lothian, the Realm of the Grail

Travelling further north, we soon arrive in a region known as the Lothians, its ancient rocks emanating a hidden power within its crystalline volcanic geology. These lands were once part of the ancient kingdom of the enigmatic Gododdin, a British tribe ruled by the mythical King Lot. The Gododdin ruled over a vast area south of the Firth of Forth, bordered by the Lammermuir Hills in the south and the Moorfoot Hills to the west. The origin of the name Lothian in the old British tongue is *Lugudūniānā*, translated into Modern Welsh as *Lleuddiniawn*, meaning 'country of the fort of Lugus', Lugus being an archetype of Lugh. His name appears in different forms, such as Lleu Llaw Gyffes, a warrior hero of Welsh mythology mentioned in *The Mabinogion*, and Lancelot and King Lot of the Arthurian stories championed by the American Arthurian scholar Roger Sherman Loomis. Furthermore, the Latin name for Lothian is *Leudonia* or 'realm of Leu or Lugh'.

Philip Coppens compares it with County Louth in Ireland, another name deriving from the sun god Lugh also called Lugh Lamhfhada (Lugh of the Long Arm), from his skill with a spear. Louth village was also a cult centre of Lugh in St Patrick's time. In Aneirin's *Y Gododdin,* the Welsh bard references the Gododdin as *'the people of Lleu's tribe, the people of Lleu's mountain fortress.'*[7]

Geoffrey of Monmouth in *Historia Regum* refers to Lot (or Loth) as king of Lothian, Orkney and Norway.[8] Lot weds the eldest daughter of Uther Pendragon and Igraine, called Morgause (also called Anna), sister of Arthur. Lot and Morgause produce many sons, namely Gawain, Agravain, Gaheris, Gareth, and in earlier literature, Mordred.

When Uther fell ill, Lot commanded the British armies to aid him in his struggle against the invading Saxons. Despite initially objecting to Arthur assuming the throne after the death of Uther, Lot eventually reconciled with the new king and joined forces against the Angles. Lot is also said to have been the grandfather of St Kentigern or Mungo, the apostle of the Lothians.

Another source mentions Lot as a descendant of Caradog, or Caractacus, the pre-Roman British king of the Catuvellauni tribe, who was taken captive in Rome in 43 CE by Emperor Claudius.[9] Lot's kingdom received recognition in old Welsh manuscripts as part of *Hen Ogledd* or the Old North, and his principal capital was at Traprain Law, near Haddington (Lothian). The stronghold of Din Eidyn on Castle Rock, now the site of Edinburgh Castle, was another of his main courts. After their defeat by the Angles, the Gododdin lands became part of Bernicia, which later united with Deira to form the Kingdom of Northumbria.

Very few written records exist of this great kingdom of the Lothians and the legendary King Lot, especially regarding their citadels and sacred places. However, since investigating the Belinus Line for our book *The Spine of Albion* and now the Holy Axis, we have discovered several of them. Included is Drumelzier Law in Merlindale near Peebles, the island of Inchcolm in the Forth, anciently known as Emona, which they regarded as their Avalon, Castlelaw in the Pentland Hills, the Eildon Hills near Melrose and Cairnpapple near Linlithgow to name but a few. Coppens feels that academics and researchers have overlooked the historical significance of the Lothians, and in his book *Land of the Gods*, he describes many sacred places of this magical kingdom connected to the Grail stories, in particular, the local mythology surrounding the legendary King Lot and the Celtic warrior Arthur.[10]

The Healing Shrine at Soutra

Continuing north from Channelkirk, the male serpent travels over the site of a Roman camp to Dun Law before descending to an exposed spot on the western slopes of Soutra Hill that marks the boundary of Midlothian and the Scottish Borders. Here we also encounter the Holy Axis alignment at an exposed lofty location of the Lammermuir Hills, rising to 1207 ft (368 m) above sea level, where the A68 between Edinburgh and Lauderdale makes a steep ascent. Although bleak and windswept, the area has many early Bronze Age burial remains, including a post circle. We were curious as to why the Lugh current chose this remote place, but we felt sure it would be historically significant whatever it was.

As we approached the hill, our dowsing indicated that Lugh was flowing to the left of us. Turning off the A68 Edinburgh road onto the B6368 heading south, we soon detected the serpent current flowing through a little church with impressive stone walls and roof called Soutra Aisle. Although the wind was howling around this exposed site, the views from here are spectacular, with the hills of the Pentlands, Ochils, Sidlaws and Lomonds visible all around us.

Soutra Aisle once formed part of one of medieval Scotland's largest and most influential medical establishments known in early times as the House of the Holy Trinity. The 'Master and Brethren' of the Augustinian Order ran the medical facility under the diocese of St Cuthbert as part of a much larger religious monastery. It served as a hospital, a friary and a church to assist travellers and pilgrims, the aged, sick, the infirm and the poor. King Malcolm IV instigated its construction in 1160 with *'the founder's intention to build a hospital for the reception of the poor rather than a religious place.*'[11] During a survey of the Roman Dere street by the Royal Commission on Ancient and Historical Monuments of Scotland using aerial photography, they discovered a clear outline of a building just north of the Aisle, typical of a medieval monastery complex complete with cloisters.

The monks grew medicinal plants and herbs from different countries worldwide, including henbane, hemlock, cloves from East Africa and even the opium poppy. Recent archaeology uncovered evidence that revealed the high level of medical care the friars could offer here. As well as looking after the sick, the friars took in travellers and pilgrims as they made their way to shrines in the Borders and many others seeking refuge from the numerous Border conflicts.

The remote location of Soutra Aisle was mainly due to the suspicion and fear surrounding disease and pestilence during medieval times. However, the fact that it lies next to a renowned pilgrimage route between Edinburgh and the rich abbeys of the Borders is also significant. In fact, at one time, Soutra Aisle stood on a crossroads where five important roads met, including the Roman Dere Street, which once stretched between Edinburgh and the old capital of Eboracum, now York. A network of major roads still exists today, including the A7 and A68, which incorporates parts of the ancient Roman road. During the Spanish Armada, Soutra Hill was used as a beacon site, forming part of a series of beacons that included Hume Castle, Dun Law, Edgarhope Castle and Edinburgh Castle.

In the 1460s, the Crown and the border abbeys withdrew Soutra's income and confiscated their lands after misconduct by the Master of the Hospital. Eventually, due to its dwindling fame, it closed completely in the 17th century. Sadly the buildings soon became a quarry for walls and dykes, leaving only the Aisle, which the Pringle family of Soutra utilised as their burial vault and a lintel above the entrance dates from 1688.

Another possible reason the monks would choose to build their hospital and monastery in such an inhospitable, bleak, remote and exposed landscape is the proximity of Trinity Well, its former site now in a field just to the north of Soutra Aisle. Before the Reformation, it received thousands of visitors for its healing properties, which included valuable minerals. However, irrigation of the surrounding fields at the turn of the century sadly destroyed the well. This holy spring was just one of many that surfaced around Soutra Hill, another being the Prior's Well, used mainly by the area's local inhabitants.

The underlying geology of Soutra Hill may be a factor regarding the well's curative powers. The spring would have contained a large amount of hematite ironstone, which consists of eighty-two per cent of pure iron or ferrous oxide. The Red Spring in the Chalice Well Gardens in Glastonbury contains ferrous oxide and is well known for its healing properties. Iron-rich geology emits a subtle magnetic field, which often creates an atmosphere of otherworldliness when subjected to seismic stress and is conducive to receiving visions during higher states of consciousness. This subtle energy becomes stronger at certain times of the year when the earth's magnetic field fluctuates due to solar flares or the magnetic pull of the full moon.

The combined presence of a healing well, powerful geology and mineral-rich soil close to a major crossroads would be critical factors for making this medical establishment successful. Furthermore, the presence of the Holy Axis and the solar energy of the male serpent would further enhance the area's collective healing power.

The area is also known as Fala, deriving from the Anglo-Saxon *fal, fah* or *faw*, meaning 'speckled', which in old Welsh is *brecc*. Some believe it is likely that the region's name came originally from an 8th-century 'speckled' reliquary known as *Breccbennach Coluim Chille*, a small multi-coloured and highly decorated metal casket from Iona that held a relic of St Columba. Many sacred places received this relic to empower them with the essence of this famous saint whose holy influence had left its mark throughout most of Scotland.[12] Perhaps, the 'speckled' artefact rested here within an earlier shrine, and the area adopted the name Fala when the Angles settled there. This shrine may have been a Culdee church or cell, which drew the Augustinian Monks to build their monastery and hospital here.

Just a short distance from Soutra Aisle and close to the alignment are the ruins of Fala Luggie Tower on an isolated, exposed peak of Fala Moor. Luggie is a Scottish word for a drinking vessel, bucket or lodge. Traditionally, the tower was a royal hunting lodge, but others say it is a 16th-century tower house held by the Douglases and Murrays. William St Clair of Rosslyn Chapel supposedly owned the land at some point. Nearby, two Roman urns were found in 1852 next to the Roman Dere Street from the remains of a Roman tower.

Sir Walter Scott's epic poem, *The Lay of the Last Minstrel*, mentions Fala Tower and its haunted surroundings in verse eight (canto IV).[13] Interestingly, another story mentions a time-slip incident common in UFO abductions. According to the Revd James Hunter in *Fala and Soutra* (1892):

'A gentleman on horseback was crossing the moor on one occasion when horse and rider suddenly disappeared. They were never seen in this country again, but they were found safe and sound three weeks later in New Zealand.'

The rider supposedly fell straight through the earth to the opposite side of the globe.[14] This curious story seems too far-fetched to be a folklore tale, so perhaps the horse and rider had entered a time window or portal caused by a magnetic anomaly associated with the water energy of the moor and its powerful geology.

Soutra Aisle

Crichton Collegiate Church

Just 7.5 miles (12.1 km) south of Edinburgh, we find the next destination of the male current at Crichton Kirk, set in the most picturesque valley of Tyne Water. The imposing Gothic and Romanesque cruciform-styled church is dedicated to the Blessed Virgin Mary, St Kentigern and All Saints and has a large central tower. Nearby is Crichton Castle, the seat of the Bothwell family in the 16th century. James, Lord Bothwell, was the third husband of Mary, Queen of Scots. Lord William Crichton, then Lord Chancellor of Scotland and the original Laird of Crichton Castle, established it as a Collegiate Church in 1449.

Crichton Collegiate Church

Many Scottish families founded Collegiate Churches for priests and choir boys to sing daily for the health and good fortunes of the souls of the families who built them. The old 'wizard of Winchester', Bishop Henry of Blois, brother of King Stephen, had one built on the Belinus alignment in Hampshire, where priests chanted continually for the success and wellbeing of their benefactors, particularly Henry. In *The Ancient Science of Geomancy*, Nigel Pennick mentions many of these places were '*geomantically sited chapels*' built by medieval geomancers, initiated into the secret knowledge of the dragon force.[15]

Lord Crichton belonged to one of three great Scottish families of the 15th century, the others being the Livingstones and Douglas', who were often in conflict with one another hence the appearance of the castle's fortified architecture. According to Colin F Hogg, who wrote the official church guide, Sir Walter Scott described the Crichtons in his *Provincial Antiquities* as '*ancient and honourable*'.[16]

However, Lord Crichton fell out of favour after being implicated in a conspiracy against King James III. On the accession of James IV in 1488, Crichton Castle passed to the Hepburns, now newly created as the Earls of Bothwell. Mary, Queen of Scots visited Crichton before her marriage in 1562 to James, the 4th Earl of Bothwell, for the wedding celebrations of Bothwell's sister, Janet.

The Reformation saw the removal of all the hangings, tapestries, paintings, stained glass and statues from the church and much of its medieval stone tracery, leaving it in ruin. Also removed were the burial tombs and effigies of the Crichtons and Bothwells from the north transept. In 1825 restoration began with the addition of an upper gallery and box pews. The only traces of the Collegiate Church are the nave's west wall, a small window at the east end of the choir, the vaulted stone roof and the carved stone heads on the exterior of the church.

To view the church, we had to ring ahead to make an appointment with one of the churchwardens, who proudly informed us that his father and grandfather were ministers here. Two other features that interested us were a cross-shaped window and a round hole in the roof similar to the Pantheon in Rome called an oculus – now containing a fan to help with condensation build-up. The purpose of the oculus was not only to illuminate the interior but 'let those in the temple contemplate the heavens.'

Oculus in Crichton Collegiate Church

The west wall shows evidence of a nave now vanished where allegedly the ordinary people of the parish and passers-by were allowed to worship. An excellent east window depicts Christ's arrest in the Garden of Gethsemane, under which the medieval high altar would have stood. The church has managed to retain the original stone vaulted ceiling, which allows for beautiful acoustics, and it so happened that a concert was being held in the church that evening. While dowsing Lugh's flow through this fascinating church, we had to avoid several people arranging chairs for the evening event. Nevertheless, it ran diagonally through the building from the southwest corner. We were surprised to read the following entry in the visitor information leaflet:

'Visitors with the skill of using the diving rod confirmed that there was once such kind of structure extending 48ft out from the existing building that probably had been less substantial than the main church.'

Interestingly, Rosslyn Chapel, located just five and a half miles (8.8 km) away, was built as a Collegiate Church five years earlier than Crichton Kirk and had similar dimensions. Also, both castles and chapels at Rosslyn and Crichton are equally distant and have comparable inter-visibility. Furthermore, as dowsers have previously found, the foundations once extended 40 ft (12 m) out from the existing building, which suggests that, like Rosslyn Chapel, it was never fully completed. Rosslyn's unfinished western wall has drawn comparisons with the Temple of Solomon, yet this church, with its similar architecture, has received little attention from historians. Also, like the chapel at Rosslyn, this church has a series of enigmatic stone-carved heads adorning its exterior.

Another comparison between the two chapels is a secret passage between the church and castle at Crichton called the Velvet Way. In 1867, a search for this tunnel proved elusive, and like Rosslyn, its existence remains shrouded in mystery.[17] There is speculation that Rosslyn Chapel stands over a Mithraic temple or a megalithic structure, and Crichton stands in an area rich in Roman and Pictish settlements. Also, many agree that Lord Crichton built his church on the site of a much earlier Celtic

Christian shrine which probably included the holy spring called the Scholars Well. In the church guide, an account in 1848 states, 'In the immediate vicinity of the church is a copious spring of pellucid water.' We came across a spring flowing a short distance from the church next to a footpath leading to the Crichton Castle and wondered whether this was the elusive Scholar's Well.

Exterior Carvings at Crichton Collegiate Church

Although Crichton Collegiate Church might seem dwarfed by Rosslyn Chapel's spectacular carvings, its interior would still have been notable before the Reformation and Victorian renovations, which saw the removal of its beautiful carvings and fineries. Despite its lack of ornamentation, it still retains an air of its former grandeur and religious importance.

Two miles west of Crichton, Gorebridge marks the Holy Axis alignment, a former mining village with strange tales of otherworldly creatures. A poem called *The Ballad of the Gore*, dating back to 1916, alludes to the 'auld races' and places of supernatural events.[18] Many UFO researchers believe that a secret meeting place of otherworldly beings exists here, known as 'the camp', located at an abandoned coal mine in Gorebridge called the Blinkbonny Mine. Here, two witnesses were allegedly chased from the area by a 'luminous, floating, green eye' while digging up Christmas trees nearby. Other strange events in the area include the loss of livestock, strange lights glowing above 'the camp', alien abductions and sightings of 'Greys' (grey aliens like those reported at the Roswell UFO incident in 1947) and 'Men in Black' in the local woods. An official investigation took place to look into these strange events. However, it was scuppered by the intervention of a local MP, leaving the mystery unexplained and the people of Gorebridge still none the wiser.[19]

Were these incidences encounters with balls of light in the form of plasma intelligence? Could the trickster element of plasma have deceived the observer into believing they were seeing little grey men and other strange beings? Indeed, the piezoelectric geology of the area is conducive to creating an etheric 'window' or 'thin veil area' where plasma can regularly manifest.

We follow Lugh north to an atmospheric ruin next to a sharp bend of the River South Esk, between Bonnyrigg and Newtonbridge. Here, we find the serpent current flowing along the east–west axis of what remains of Old Cockpen Church, first established in the 13th century and later renovated in the 16th century. It was the burial place of the Marquises of Dalhousie, and their family vault still exists in the north transept. A pink granite obelisk stands in the graveyard erected in memory of the Marquis of Dalhousie (1812-1860).

From here, Lugh makes his way northwest towards the River North Esk, passing through a most unusual building in the former coal mining village of Rosewell. St

Matthew's Roman Catholic Church has a curiously arranged roof erected by local volunteers in 1926, and its cloisters were added in 1935 by the famous Scottish architect Reginald Fairlie (1883-1952).

Ahead of us now lay the sacred valley of the North Esk River and the magical Roslin Glen, with its fascinating history and legends. But, before we delve into dowsing this wonderful area, including its complex and enigmatic chapel, we will return to follow Bride's journey from the Scottish Borders.

---

1. https://www.undiscoveredscotland.co.uk/usbiography/h/isabellahoppringle.html
2. https://archive.org/stream/chartularyofcist00cist/chartularyofcist00cist_djvu.txt
3. https://www.dandaestates.co.uk/history/hirsel-estate.php
4. *Marchmont and the Humes of Polwarth by One of Their Descendants 1894.* 2004. The Grimsay Press, Glasgow.
5. https://www.undiscoveredscotland.co.uk/greenlaw/humecastle/index.html
6. https://canmore.org.uk/site/55794/dods-corse-stone-boon.
7. 10. Coppens, P. 2007. *Land of the Gods.* Frontier Publishing, Amsterdam.
8. Thorpe, L. 1966. *The History of the Kings of Britain*, translated. Introduction to Geoffrey of Monmouth, p.17. Penguin Books, London.
9. Squire, L.C. 2000. *Celtic Myths and Legends.* Lomond Books, Broxburn
11. https://canmore.org.uk/site/54532/soutra-aisle
12. Caldwell, D. H. 2001. *The Monymusk Reliquary: The Breccbennach of St Columba?* Proceedings of the Society of Antiquaries of Scotland.
13. Scott, Sir W. 1900. *The Lay of The Last Minstrel, Canto I, With Life and Notes.* W. & R. Chambers Ltd, London.
14. Hunter, Revd J. 1892. *Fala and Soutra.* James G Hitt, Edinburgh.
15. Pennick, N. 1979. *The Ancient Science of Geomancy: Man in Harmony with the Earth.* Thames & Hudson, London.
16. Scott, Sir W. 1834. *Provincial Antiquities of Scotland, The Miscellaneous Prose Works.* Robert Cadell, Edinburgh.
17. Coppens, P. 2021. *The Stone Puzzle of Rosslyn Chapel.* Adventures Unlimited Press, Amsterdam.
18. https://gorebridge.org.uk/heritage/the-ballad-of-the-gore-1916/
19. McCue, P. 2019. *Britain's Paranormal Forests: Encounters in the Woods.* The History Press, Cheltenham.

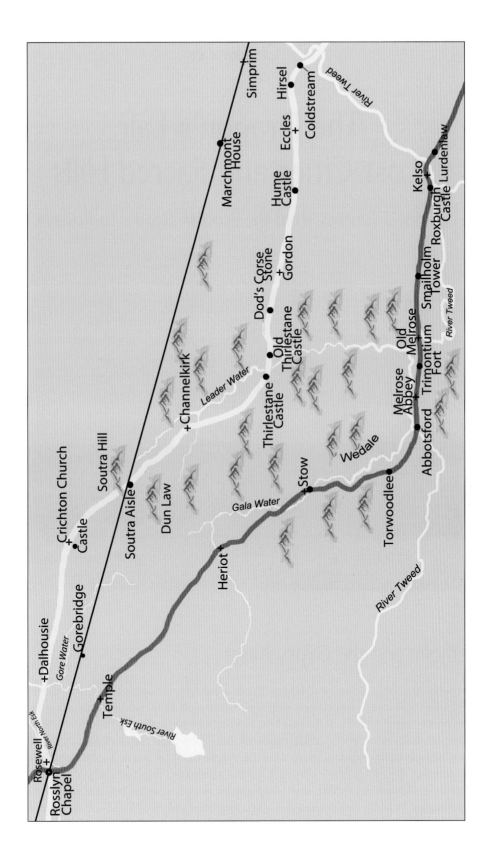

127

Chapter 6

The Dragon's Lair,
Lost Cities and Sacred Hills

Bride's Journey from the Scottish Border to Rosslyn

View of Kirk Yetholm

Yetholm and the Gypsy Kings

From the standing stone near Halter Burn, close to the Scottish Border, Bride travels west to a cairn on the northern slopes of Staerough Hill before descending into the Bowmont Valley to Kirk Yetholm. This Border village lies at the most northerly point of the famous Pennine Way, which runs for 267 miles (429 km) to Edale in Derbyshire. Kirk Yetholm also marks the southern terminus of the Scottish National Trail and features on the St Cuthbert's Way. Like the Cheviots, there are signs of prehistoric activity on almost every hill, including numerous enclosures, hut platforms and field boundaries. In 1837, two bronze shields dating from 1150 and 750 BCE were unearthed in the boggy ground at the edge of the village, now on display in the National Museum of Scotland, Edinburgh. The bog was once a lake into which offerings were thrown to the gods.

Yetholm or Zetholm derives from the Saxon word Zete, meaning 'gate' or 'gateway' and 'holm' being Norse for 'flat land by the river', the village's etymology perhaps alluding to it as a 'border gate' between England and Scotland. Yetholm consists of the twin villages of Kirk Yetholm and Town Yetholm that stand on either side of Bowmont Water, now linked by a bridge.

In the 7th century, Yetholm was part of the Kingdom of Northumbria when King Oswiu (612-670), brother of King Oswald, granted most of the Bowmont Valley to the monastery at Lindisfarne after defeating King Penda of Mercia. In 1304, King Edward I of England convened a large meeting here to receive the submission of many 'rebellious' Scottish noblemen. From this date until 1603, relations between England and Scotland were hostile, and Yetholm suffered several burnings when Henry VIII's launched a campaign against Scotland, most notably in the 1520s and 1540s.

Fortunately, today it offers a tranquil scene with picturesque thatched cottages and houses and a pub reminiscent of the Cotswolds rather than the Scottish Borders. We tracked Bride crossing the Pennine Way footpath to a house in the High Street adorned with a plaque of two entwined dragons before entering the parish kirk on Main Street. Although Victorian, the kirk has a history on this site going back to 1233 and has an unusual northeast–southwest orientation. It contains a fragment of a 14th-century tombstone carved with a Celtic cross and a sword.

Plaque of two entwined dragons in High Street, Kirk Yetholm

Kirk Yetholm is most famous for its community of Gypsies, known for having dark eyes, curly hair, high cheekbones, and olive skin. It is a mystery why they settled here, although some say the local laird, Captain David Bennet of Grubert, invited them to the area after one of them saved his life at the Battle of Namur in 1695. Another tale says that Sir William Bennet of Marlfield asked them to settle here in gratitude for recovering one of his valuable horses after being stolen by the Jacobites during the 1715 rebellion. According to *The Kirk Yetholm Gypsies* by A V Tokely, the first gypsies arrived in Scotland in 1500 from India.[1] They were tribal and had leaders who administered justice. However, in the 17th century, their presence in Scotland became less tolerated, and many men went to the gallows for the most trivial of crimes, and the women drowned. As a result, many adopted Scottish names to save themselves from this barbaric act.

Numerous gypsy families lived in Yetholm during the late 18th century, leasing houses in the village, although they still travelled away for months on end. In 1829, the Quakers forced them to leave their children behind if they wished to continue their education at the local school. From then on, as these children grew to adulthood, their gypsy culture and language began to fade, and now only tales and old photos recall their fascinating past.

The Gypsy King and Queen lived in a house called Gypsy Palace on High Street, now a holiday cottage, so we thought it would be interesting to rent the place for a few days to research the female current in the area. The last Queen was Esther, who reigned from 1861–1883, succeeded by her son Charles 'Faa' Blythe, who died in 1902. The standing stone at Halter Burn and the Stob Stones on the female current were sacred to the gypsies and used in their coronation ceremonies. Today they are utilized as markers for an annual ride over the Pennines from Kirk Yetholm.

Gypsy Palace on High Street, Kirk Yetholm

The nearby village of Town Yetholm sees Bride crossing the road by the Plough Inn and passing through the green before ascending a hill northwards to Lochtower and Yetholm Loch. The loch lies in a crescent-shaped valley, an important area for breeding and wintering wildfowl. A tower stood on an island within the loch connected by a causeway, destroyed by the Earl of Surrey in 1523. Causeway islands were considered sacred in ancient times as places of contest or burial, and we found Bride passing through the tower site. Examples of these holy isles are found all over Britain, including Lindisfarne, St Michael's Mount in Cornwall, Burgh Island on the south coast of Devon and the Isle of Portland in Dorset. When we arrived, the loch was full of swans gliding across the watery surface as it sparkled in the September sun.

Swans are often seen as symbolic of the goddess Bride, perhaps because they return from their winter habitats around the time of Imbolc, Bride, Brigid or St Bridget's Day. Prehistoric and Celtic shamans saw the swan as representing the soul and believed they assisted their journey to the Otherworld. They also used the wings of a swan to call on the spirit realm. The swan was sacred to the Bards, who wore cloaks with swan feathers. Caroline Wise writes in her article *The Swan, the Goddess, and Other Samhain Musings:*

'The winged souls, led by the winter goddess, enter the Grail cauldron of rebirth. As the souls transform in this dazzling darkness, it too is transformed into the womb-Grail of the spring goddess represented by the White Swan Bride. In human form, she opens her green cloak and shakes off the winter ice, and the newly reborn souls fly from her, enriched with the wisdom of many lifetimes.'[2]

The Linton Dragon

Beyond Yetholm Loch, Bride meanders over the northeast slopes of Linton Hill, where traces of an Iron Age hillfort or ceremonial enclosure are visible with three ramparts. Numerous cairns and tumuli in the area would suggest that this entire region is part of a forgotten sacred landscape. To the south of the hill, the female serpent current heads northwards towards Greenlees Farm through a hollow called 'Worms Hole'. This site is associated with the legend of the 'Linton Worm', a dragon or serpent-like monster that lived here. 'Worm', 'wyrme' or 'orme' is the ancient Norse word for serpent or dragon. A 12th-century writer described it as *'In length three Scots yards and bigger than an ordinary man's leg – in form and callour to our common muir edders.'* According to the local tale, this monster would emerge from its lair at dusk to ravage the countryside, eating crops, livestock and even people. The locals could do little to subdue the creature, proving invulnerable to the weapons ranged against it.

Eventually, the dragon's exploits came to the attention of John de Somerville, Laird of Lariston, and a man of great courage who happened to be travelling through the town of nearby Jedburgh at the time. When Somerville encountered the Linton Worm, he noticed that the creature opened its mouth to swallow anything in its path, but when faced with something too large to eat, the dragon would remain motionless, keeping its mouth open. Sensing an opportunity to slay the beast, he went to a local blacksmith and had him forge an iron-covered spear with a wheel at its tip impaled with a hunk of peat tipped in tar and brimstone. As the first rays of the sun rose over the horizon, the laird faced the dragon sitting on his mighty steed, knowing he and the horse would prove too big for the beast to swallow. As the great serpent drew near, de Somerville quickly plunged the spear with its flaming tar and brimstone tip into the monster's gaping mouth and throat, mortally wounding it.

The Orcadian folklorist Ernest Marwick, writing in *The Folklore of Orkney and Shetland,* highlights the similarity between the methods used to kill the Linton Worm and those recounted in the slaying of the Stoor Worm of the Orkneys, killed with burning peat.[3] It also reminded us of another local folk tale associated with the Belinus Line set in Unsworth, Lancashire. A dragon terrorised the townspeople and particularly liked women and children. The local lord Thomas Unsworth tried to shoot the dragon with his musket, but the hard scales deflected his shots. So for his next attempt, he loaded his gun with a dagger. As he approached the predatory beast, it rushed at him, and as it reared, he fired the knife into the dragon's throat, killing it instantly.

Dragon slaying or taming was a popular pastime for the early saints, the best-known being St George, St Michael and St Margaret. Another aspect of these dragon legends is the menacing of the local population until a brave knight slays it. Numerous stories of dragon slaying appear in many cultures around the world. Its true origins, however, lie within the principles of fertility. As an annual process, the Chinese saw the dragon produced from a seed born from earth, fertilised by the union of yin and yang within the elements of sky, wind and water. The dragon, nourished by the celestial influences, reanimates the landscape until its life force wanes at the end of the cycle. As the dragon grows, it devours the land until it dies at the hands of one initiated into the ways of the earth.[4]

Geopathic Stress healers often insert copper or iron rods at specific points in the ground to neutralise imbalance within the Earth's energy lines, called black streams.

A short distance from the Bride current is Linton Kirk, just below the hill, standing

on a grassy knoll reminiscent of one of the many fairy knowes in Scotland. A stone-carved tympanum over the north door, now very weathered, depicts a bearded knight with a falcon on his right shoulder thrusting a lance into the mouth of a beast, said to be John de Somerville slaying the Linton dragon. Inside the church, on one of the pillar capitals, is a Grail cup half obscured by foliage, a remarkable feature that seemed symbolic of our journey.

Tympanum at Linton Church showing a bearded knight with a falcon on his right shoulder thrusting a lance into the mouth of a beast

We next encounter Bride close to Blakelaw Farm, visiting the summit of Lurdenlaw, where a tower stood dating back before 1600. Here we have fine views of the distant town of Kelso to the northwest, nestling next to the spectacular banks of the River Tweed.

Kelso Abbey and the Tironensians

The Tweed River is a tremendous watery highway and one of Scotland's longest rivers at 96 miles (155 km). The great body of water has travelled from the Lowther Hills at Tweeds Well near Moffat, within the Dumfries and Galloway borderlands, to the North Sea at Berwick-upon-Tweed, once a major seaport.

In the Old Brythonic language, the word Tweed means border. However, Moffat in *Arthur and the Lost Kingdoms* states that all river names beginning with 'T', such as Thames, Tyne, Tees, Tweed, and Tay, have their roots in the Sanskrit word *tavas,* which means 'to surge'. He believes these rivers derive their names from migrating groups of Indo-Europeans that used these rivers to navigate inland from the east coast of Britain to find areas to settle. Moffat writes, *'In AD 80, the Roman historian Tacitus calls the Tay 'Tanus' or 'Taus', a much clearer echo of the Sanskrit.'*[5]

Interestingly the Tweed flows past such landmark places as the home of Sir Walter Scott at Abbotsford, together with several other country seats of the local aristocracy and the ancient abbeys of Dryburgh, Kelso and Melrose.

The female current crosses a great bend of the River Tweed to visit the atmospheric ruin of Kelso Abbey, an internationally renowned tourist town, attracting people worldwide for its salmon fishing. But in early medieval times, it was known for its markets, as evidenced in its street names. Kelso's name derives from the word *calx,* meaning chalk, from the white cliffs along the banks of the Tweed flanking the riverside

Kelso from the Tweed by Edward Dayes 1792

walk known today as the 'Cobby', overlooked by a terrace known as 'Chalk Heugh'. A catastrophic fire destroyed most of Kelso's historic buildings in the 17th century, leading to extensive renovations in the 18th and 19th centuries. Its recently developed town square attracts visitors to its many shops, cafes and restaurants.

The town's history dates back long before Kelso Abbey was established in 1128 when a small settlement surrounded an early Celtic Christian church dedicated to St Mary. Similarly, further west of here, the old Celtic church of St Cuthbert's at Old Melrose, also built on a loop of the Tweed, predates Melrose Abbey.

However, in 1128 the town's fortunes increased when it became part of the royal burgh of King David I of Scotland, who established his royal court at nearby Roxburgh just across the river from Kelso. Having disbanded St Mary's, he commissioned French Benedictine monks from Tiron or Thiron to build a new abbey further upriver from the old church.[6]

The impressive royal citadel of Roxburgh Castle stood on a high ridge next to the banks of the River Teviot, close to where it meets the Tweed, the rivers providing natural protection during the turbulent times of King David I's reign. Its outer walls encompassed a sizable settlement, including the churches of St James' and the Holy Sepulchre, consecrated in 1136. At the time, Roxburgh was one of the wealthiest cities in Scotland. However, by 1460, the castle and Kelso Abbey fortunes had waned, and after several attacks by the English, it was in ruins. Today only scant remains of this once bustling royal city remain, much of it now grazing land for sheep and cows overlooked by anglers as they haul in their catch of the day.

After the Reformation, many Scottish nobles owned Kelso Abbey, including Francis Stewart, Fifth Earl of Bothwell. He was the nephew of the notorious fourth Earl, the third husband of Mary, Queen of Scots. Robert Ker of Cessford later claimed ownership of the lands and gained the title of Earl of Roxburghe, building a new grand mansion on the north banks of the Tweed, known today as Floors Castle.

Sitting with the other guests over breakfast in one of Kelso's many B&Bs, we listened to proud accounts of their various catches of the day and wondered what they might have thought if they knew what we would be fishing for that day – dragons!

As we headed towards the old abbey ruins in the town, we strolled through the picturesque and atmospheric market square, lively with locals going about their daily business. With the help of lottery money, the recent refurbishment of Kelso's handsome cobbled market square has certainly lightened and enlivened this old Georgian town.

Kelso Abbey ruins

The abbey ruins, however, are perhaps Kelso's most endearing feature. After establishing an abbey at Selkirk in 1113, David I invited the Tironensian monks to build a new religious house at Kelso, the Royal Abbey Notre Dame of Roxburgh. Its fine Gothic and Romanesque architecture made it one of the most magnificent ecclesiastical buildings of its time, and today would be considered the finest in Britain.[7]

Kelso Abbey stands next to the meeting of the Tweed and Teviot rivers. The old Druids venerated such places by junctions of rivers, building temples and places of worship close to them. The powerful force generated by the collision of two bodies of running water attracts subtle chi energy, which brings health and good fortune.

The Tironensian order also founded abbeys at Dryburgh in 1162, Arbroath in 1178 and Kilwinning around 1190 and by 1175, had completed the main structure of Kelso Abbey. Soon, it became one of the wealthiest and most influential abbeys in Scotland, mainly because of its proximity to King David's thriving royal burgh at nearby Roxburgh. In addition, the old village of Kelso that once surrounded the little Celtic church of St Mary's was now part of the abbey's lands.

The monks acquired a considerable acreage of land through the king's patronage, including St Michael's Church by the east bank of the Tweed and Thomas à Becket Chapel near the present Wooden House, east of the town. By the time David's grandson, William I, took the throne, Kelso was rivalling Roxburgh as a thriving trading centre.

Kelso Abbey witnessed many historical events, including its last, the hurried crowning of a young James III, after his father, James II, died from his wounds at Roxburgh during a siege against the English in 1460. Soon after, the Scots destroyed most of the castle to prevent it from falling into enemy hands. This period also saw the gradual decline of Kelso Abbey.

Kelso would continue to suffer from the conflicts between the Scots and the English. During the 'Rough Wooing' of 1545, the abbey was virtually destroyed by a terrible fire during an attack by the Earl of Hertford's army, with only its west end surviving. The Rough Wooing was a name used for Henry VIII's war with Scotland partly to destroy its 'Auld Alliance' with France and force Scotland to agree to a marriage between the young Mary, Queen of Scots and his son, the future Edward VI.

Early etchings show that this majestic abbey had highly sophisticated and intricate carvings, far more impressive than many English abbeys. A documented account in 1517 by a priest from the diocese of Glasgow called John Duncan describes Kelso Abbey before its virtual destruction as having:

'…two high chapels on each side, like wings, which give the church a likeness of a double cross….It has two towers, one at the first entrance to the church, the other in the inner part like the tower of the Basilica of St Peter….in the whole church, twelve or thirteen altars on which several masses are said daily.' [8]

Etching of Kelso Abbey after David Roberts 1852

The abbey also included a large cloister area, a chapter house, the monk's dormitory, two refectories, an infirmary, many household and guest quarters and a beautiful garden. Moffat states that the double cross design of the abbey is rare, and Kelso was the first to use it in Scotland.

While relaxing in one of the square's new trendy cafes, we witnessed the erection of two three-metre-high horse head sculptures in front of the Town Hall, hand-crafted by renowned Scottish sculptor Andy Scott. They are smaller models of 'The Kelpies', the famous equine statues erected at the new Helix Park in Falkirk, and were on loan as part of a travelling exhibition at the time.

Before crossing the River Tweed, we detected the female dragon current passing through the 19th-century Wooden House, built to resemble a medieval castle on or near the old site of Thomas à Becket's Church. This river area was once a significant fording place called Hempseedford, captured in the name of nearby Hempsford House in Abbotsford Grove that once belonged to the family of the famous Scottish novelist and playwright Sir Walter Scott. Continuing west, we follow Bride to another house called Abbey Bank in Maxwell Lane in an area known as the Knowes, meaning knoll or hillock. Dr James Douglas built the house in 1815 and inherited nearby Ednam House, now a hotel.

Before entering the ruins of the old abbey, we dowsed the current flowing through the site of the old Grammar School, built over the high altar at the eastern end of the chancel. In medieval times, a grammar school existed at Roxburgh but transferred to Kelso Abbey in the 15th century. Sir Walter Scott received his education here while staying at Waverley Lodge on the corner of Maxwell Lane, the home of his uncle Captain Robert Scott, which Walter later inherited, close to the Bride current. Behind the old school site, you can see footings of the old abbey and remains of the abbey graveyard where some of the Scott family lie buried.

Bride passes through a beech tree as she enters the abbey ruins, just missing the Memorial Cloister of the Dukes of Roxburghe of Floors Castle (also known as 'Roxburghe Aisle'), added in the 20th century. She exits through the main entrance, taking a southwest course towards the Victorian St Andrew's Church and the Ednam House Hotel's attractive garden before crossing another loop of the Tweed exactly where it meets with the River Teviot. Ednam House was first built as a fine mansion by James Dickson in 1761, having made his fortune in London as a spice trader. Next to it, an old stone bridge once spanned the river before collapsing in the great flood of 1797.

As we stood on Rennie's Bridge, we observed anglers wading in the river up to their chests as they fished for salmon. In the near distance, we have a fine view of the magnificent Floors Castle, the seat of the present Dukes of Roxburghe, set within a stunningly beautiful landscape. We could almost see the pathway of Bride as she headed for an area of land squeezed between the Tweed and the Teviot rivers, the site of the original medieval royal burgh of Roxburgh.

The Mason Monks

The Tironensians are an intriguing order of mason monks, and Francine Bernier, the author of *The Great Architects of Tiron,* writes:

> 'These monks were master craftsmen of all trades: architects, bridge-builders, painters, carpenters, woodcarvers, goldsmiths, blacksmiths, stonemasons... However, they left no marks that could identify them as such because they worked in absolute humility and solely for the glorification of God. For this reason, their masterpieces were often attributed to other, more "visible craftsmen."'[9]

The Tironensians derive their name from their founder, Bernard de Tiron, who established his *Abbatia Sanctae Trinitatis de Tirone* (Abbey of the Holy Trinity of Tiron) in 1109. It stood in the forest of Tiron, near Chartres, on land donated by crusader knight Rotrou III, Count of Perche (*c.* 1080–1144), whose wife, Matilda, was the illegitimate daughter of King Henry I of England. Previously, Bernard lived as a hermit at the monastery of La Roë in the forest of Craon in Brittany. Having rebelled against the supremacy of the Catholic Church in favour of the teachings of the old

Celtic Church of Brittany, Bernard founded this new order following the rule of St Benedict that observed the 'Celtic Rite', used widely in Britain, Ireland and Brittany. Bernier cites historian A J Wylie (1886), who explains:

> 'The 12th century, particularly in Scotland and Brittany, was a time when two Christian faiths of different origins were contending for possession of the land, the Roman Church and the old Celtic Rite. The age was a sort of borderland between Culdeeism and Romanism. The two met and mingled often in the same monastery, and the religious belief of the nation was a mumble of superstitious doctrines and a few scriptural truths.'[10]

Like the Culdee monks, the Tironensians adopted the Celtic tonsure, shaving only the front part of the head following a line drawn from ear to ear. They became known as *tirones*, meaning students, and taught the 'basic elements of a craft or science'. The medieval term for a person learning a trade or an apprentice was *tiro*.

By establishing many great abbeys, they gained much respect from the nobility and royalty. By the end of the 12th century, they controlled one hundred and seventeen religious houses in France and the British Isles. Their building skills and appreciation of the local culture and customs of the old Culdee church were remarkable, bridging the legal, ritual, artistic and political gap between the Church of Rome and the Celtic Rites. Furthermore, Breton Celts were allies of the Irish, Scots, and Welsh. Bernier writes,

> 'While the old Church of Brittany was losing ground and power to the advantage of Roman supremacy, the Tironensian abbeys of Scotland, independent and distant enough from the Holy See, quickly rose in prestige, power and fortune while becoming a most welcome refuge for the local "Celtic heretics."' [11]

There is evidence that the Culdee order was still alive and well in Scotland in medieval times, and many believe they remained there until the 14th century. Many Druidical colleges converted to Culdee Monasteries, including those at Govan and Kilwinning near Glasgow. Isabel Elder writes that this priestly order successfully merged their teachings with Druid lore, corresponding to the original structure of the Celtic Church in Glastonbury, having become its most important centre. Often referred to as the Pythagorean Essenes, Gnosticism inspired the Culdees, a form of Christianity linked with the Petrine Church of Rome known as Coptic. Many learned writers have also sought to derive Freemasonry from the Druidical and Culdee orders.[12]

English Freemason John Yarker writing in 1909, states that many of their customs survived until the Reformation within the walls of several powerful abbeys, including Kilwinning Abbey in North Ayrshire, founded between 1162 and 1188, often referred to as 'The Birthplace of Freemasonry'. It was supposedly here that the Knights Templar first visited after fleeing France in 1307.[13]

After establishing the abbey at Arbroath in 1178, special privileges were awarded to the Tironensian monks, particularly the possession of the *Brecbennach*, meaning 'the speckled peaked one', the consecrated banner of St Columba. Brought from Iona, this 8th-century holy relic was *'the most visible and potent symbol of the post-Columban Church.'* It was kept *'in an ark-shaped box of Pictish style, supposedly containing a relic of Columba .... About the size of a plum, this portable shrine was worn around the neck, usually by a guardian monk.'* The Scots held the relic during the battle of Bannockburn in 1314.[14]

The Tironensians introduced the Gothic style of architecture in many of their abbeys and cathedrals, with its distinctive pointed arch and ribbed vault, one of the first being Notre Dame Cathedral at Chartres. In *The Hiram Key Revisited*, Knight and Butler state that this order of masonic monks had close links with the Knights Templar, who passed on their knowledge and skills to new generations of ecclesiastical stonemasons that became the next generation of master craftsmen. The authors also noted that *'the building of Kelso [abbey] took place in the same year as the Council of Troyes and the return of the Templars from Jerusalem.'* They also suggest that the famous Dead Sea scrolls written by an Essene order in Qumran were re-discovered by the Templars, who brought them to Scotland and eventually hid them in the abbey at Kelso.[15]

Old Engraving of Kelso Abbey's North Doorway by R W Billings

Roxburgh Castle, the Fortress of Arthur

Roxburgh Castle is set high upon a ridge 98 ft (30 m) above the River Teviot and extends over 349 yds (320 m). The once royal citadel was 'the most powerful and prosperous stronghold between the Forth and the Tyne', its history lost to the ravages of time. Along with Edinburgh, Sterling and Berwick, it was one of medieval Scotland's four great political and religious centres.

Moffat states that this precious and impressive site has been largely forgotten or ignored by generations of historians because its owners, the present Dukes of Roxburghe, have never permitted archaeologists to dig there. As a result, its history is consigned to old documented accounts by the monks of Kelso Abbey.[16] Even so, the remains of its 6 ft (1.8 m) thick walls are imposing, which at one time stood in places 30 ft (9 m) high and included an enormous Keep and four massive towers.

King David originally founded the castle around 1125. He was the younger son of King Malcolm III and Queen Margaret and brother to Matilda, wife of Henry I of

England. David utilised the natural defences of this tall sloping ridge surrounded on its north and south sides by the Rivers Teviot and Tweed. An earlier fortification called Marchidun or Marchmont stood on the site, meaning 'fort of the Marches' or 'Mount of the Marches', as recorded by the Scottish 14th-century chronicler John of Fordun. However, Moffat believes Marchidun derives from the Old Welsh for horse or cavalry fort and was a citadel of the Gododdin, referred to by the Romans as the Votadini. The name Roxburgh originates from the time of the Anglian Kings of Northumberland

and, according to Moffat, derives from *'a warlord known as "Hroc" or "The Rook", which eventually became "Hroc's burgh" or Roxburgh, the Rook's fortress.'*[17]

Within the main medieval castle walls was a church dedicated to John the Evangelist, probably for the sole use of the king, his sheriff and the castle guard. It was the scene of several royal weddings and significant political and

Old Engraving of Roxburgh Castle ruins by William Miller

religious events, which enabled Scotland to be fully independent of England. The castle also hosted many important historical events, such as Edward Baliol, son of Sir John Baliol, King of Scotland from 1292 to 1296, proclaiming his right to the Scottish throne after the death of Robert the Bruce in 1329. In 1232, during the reign of King Alexander II, Franciscan monks founded a friary just beyond the outer walls dedicated to St Peter.

King David's original aim was to build a thriving market burgh around the castle. The town of Roxburgh had a lattice of streets with two churches, a grammar school and five mint masters. Its prosperity meant expanding the walls to accommodate many European merchants from as far away as the Baltic. Ancient manuscripts suggest the town provided for a wide range of artisans, including goldsmiths and silversmiths.

However, Roxburgh declined after the English captured Berwick-upon-Tweed in 1482 and blocked vital trade to its port. In fact, because of its strategic position close to the Scottish and English border, Roxburgh and its famous markets were constantly under attack. Henry II of England captured it in 1174, and Edward I, 'Hammer of the Scots', besieged the castle during his reign of terror in 1296. He captured Mary, the sister of Robert the Bruce, and imprisoned her at Roxburgh Castle, supposedly holding her in a lattice iron cage.

Records show that the burgesses petitioned King Edward II to build a wall around the town 'to save us from the brigand Wallace'. However, it was re-captured in 1313 by Sir James Douglas, known as the 'Black Douglas', by scaling the walls dressed in black and taking the guards by surprise. The Scots recaptured it again from the English in 1460 but lost their king, James II, in the process. His Queen, staying at Hume Castle on the Lugh dragon flow, raced to the siege with her son, the young Prince James, to encourage the disheartened army. Douglas crowned eight-year-old King James III (1460-1488) several days later at Kelso Abbey. Gradually, the Royal Burgh's importance as a royal centre dwindled, and Scotland's once great medieval castle became a ruin for sheltering cattle and horses.

Studying local traditions, topography and place names, Moffat claims that these lands were just as important 1,500 years ago when in the hands of the Scottish Celtic tribes of the Selgovae and the Gododdin. It was also part of the Kingdom of Rheged after the Roman Conquest. When the local inhabitants abandoned the Roman fort of Trimontium below the Eildon Hills a few miles west, they migrated downriver to Roxburgh.

Moffat writes that this place has associations with the legendary King Arthur and suggests that Arthur's seventh battle, fought at Celidon Woods, was in an area now called Ettrick Forest to the west of Selkirk, once Selgovae territory. According to legend, Arthur fought alongside King Lot of the Gododdin against the Picts and the Angles. However, according to other Scottish sources, there was an Arthur or Artuir, son of King Aedan of the Dal Riata, who lived and fought battles in the territory of the Gododdin. Perhaps stories of the British Arthur and the Scottish warrior Artuir merged into the same character after the introduction of the medieval Romances. Moffat further states that on the grounds below Marchidun, Arthur kept and trained his cavalry horses. This area was renowned for its horse fairs centuries later, including the medieval St James' Fair, eventually taken over in the 16th century by the gypsies as a place for horse dealing.

In his article *Arthur and the Lost City*, Tony Grace believes that one of Arthur's first battles was fighting and defeating the Picts. He quotes Lambert de Saint-Omer, who wrote in 1120, in *Liber Floridus*, *'there is a palace of Arthur the soldier, in Britain, in the land of the Picts, built with various and wondrous art, in which the deeds and all his acts and wars are seen to be sculpted.'* Grace surmises that:

'A detailed analysis of all the available documentary evidence indicates an overwhelming bias to actions in the north. When this is added to other evidence, there is little question that it locates Arthur's base in the south of Scotland, probably in the Tweed basin. Roxburgh's voices are silent now, its stories lost in the grass where the sheep graze and where twice a year horses thunder between the hurdles. And yet it was a place of determinant importance to the whole history of Britain. It was the place where Arthur came back to, where he held his own power, where he kept safe his precious cavalry horses, where he drew his lines of communication together, where he sat in his castle hall feasting with his loyal warriors. It was, to use a mythic term, his Camelot.'[18]

This equestrian tradition has continued with a prestigious International Horse Trials hosted annually by the Duke of Roxburghe on Fairgreen. Likewise, Kelso's 'Whipman Ceremony', where over two hundred horsemen and their followers after gathering in Kelso's market square ride to Yetholm visiting various villages on the way. This ceremony of the Whipmen's Society is an all-male affair reminiscent of old festivals where warriors would display their prowess as great cavalrymen.

After the ceremony, the cavalcade travels across the old site of Roxburgh's medieval city and gathers around the 'wych elm', a common elm species in Scotland. Moffat

The remaining walls of Roxburgh Castle

states: '*The original wych elm at Roxburgh was massive, measuring thirty feet in girth, and furniture and tools were made from its wood while it lived.*' The old Gododdin tribe, who ruled this kingdom during the time of King Arthur, would also have known the importance of the Roxburgh elm.[19]

St James' Fair, first established in 1113, was named after the medieval St James' Church, sited at the base of Roxburgh Castle and miraculously continued until World War II. According to Moffat, the fair originally celebrated a Christianised version of the Celtic festival of Lughnasa or Lammas, associated with the harvest god Lugh. Traditionally, such celebrations started at sundown on 31 July and ended at sunset on 1 August when bonfires were lit, perhaps because of Lugh's association with the power of the sun and light. Herdsman would drive their cattle through the fire as a cleansing ritual. Moffat recalls how this tradition continued for centuries on the Eildon Hills at Lughnasa. The celebrations included selling farm stock, although, by the 1930s, you would more likely see hoopla stands and puppet shows.[20]

Before visiting the ruins of Roxburgh Castle, the feminine current passes over the site of St Michael's Church next to the banks of the Teviot known as Maxwellaugh. Records show that it was still in use in 1649 but had disappeared by the early 19th century, the land used as a horse racing track from the 1960s. Bride then crosses over a loop in the river to the site of the lost religious house of St Peter's Friary, located next to the Teviot's north banks. After climbing the summit of the ancient glacial ridge, Bride visits another sacred spot where the Church of the Holy Sepulchre once stood within the castle precinct.

Dowsing the remains of this vast citadel was a challenge due to the overgrown terrain. Nevertheless, Bride's current maintains an east–west flow towards a high mound called 'Bell Mount' at the western end of the motte and bailey. The interior is relatively undisturbed, allowing an almost ethereal quality to permeate its atmosphere.

Having struggled through the dense undergrowth, our friend Rob, who accompanied us that day, reminded us to 'walk lightly' out of respect for Roxburgh's spirits. Once our senses were attuned to our surroundings, we felt the enigmatic site was revered long ago by the ancient inhabitants who worshipped the Earth Goddess here. Moffat believes grand ceremonies took place on the hill, with the lighting of a giant bonfire at Beltane. The meeting of the two great rivers, the Tweed and the Teviot, would also enhance the magical power of this high ridge.

After tuning into Bride, her energy felt stagnant and weak, which seemed to reflect the general decline and neglect at this once sacred sanctuary and capital of the old kings of Scotland. Centuries of desecration and misuse by the Scots and the English have also left their mark. According to the principles of Chinese feng shui, if an area suffers from neglect or deliberate abuse, the energy will stagnate and become detrimental to the environment. We often find that the earth's vital energy communicates its distress to sensitive individuals, particularly those who work with the healing of the landscape.

Standing at the centre of the castle ruins, we felt compelled to send healing thoughts along the path of Bride to release any remaining negative energy and restore balance and harmony to this ancient site. We also placed on her flow a healing stone from Iona, and a white quartz stone from Merlin's Cave in Tintagel, charged by the energy of the sea. The feminine serpent appeared to benefit from our healing thoughts and actions as her current now dowsed wider than before. Essential to this process is the respect shown to the Universe's beneficial powers, which we can direct to troubled areas with intentioned thought. Visualising a shaft of pure healing light to flood and dissolve harmful influences is one method that works for many. Although we are experienced in visualisation to help heal these sites, many people prefer invocation, song, drumming or other specific ceremonies to direct the healing.

An atmosphere of serenity began to permeate the castle, and as we walked back to our car, a heron suddenly took flight out of the Teviot and circled the castle. In Celtic lore, the heron or crane represents shamanic journeying and symbolises the hidden knowledge of the otherworld. In the fields below us, we also observed a hare leaping across the old site of the Friary, another sign perhaps that we had triggered an energy release. The hare brings fertility and abundance, often regarded as a symbol of birth and rebirth.

Old Melrose and Scott's View

Just over 5 miles (8 km) away on exposed moorland is the remote Smailholm Tower, a squared Pele tower through which Bride flows east–west. The dramatic building stands on a ridge of dolerite volcanic rock called Lady Hill. This seam of highly magnetic stone is the same material found beneath Lindisfarne Castle and Bamburgh Castle. The stone used in the tower's construction is a mixture of sandstone and dolerite, attracting cosmic energies and amplifying the power of the feminine earth serpent. The climb to the uppermost floor was well worth the effort, as the outstanding western views that greeted us across to the enigmatic three peaks of the Eildon Hills were breathtaking, and on a clear day, you can even glimpse Bamburgh Castle.

The tower is a masculine phallic symbol and not the usual site to attract the feminine serpent, being more the domain of the male current, which prefers high places and structures such as mountains, hills and church spires.

A tower has stood at Smailholm since 1430, built by George Pringle, who prospered as squire to the mighty Earl of Douglas, also known as Black Douglas. In 1635, Sir Walter Scott's ancestors purchased it, and as a child, Scott became greatly inspired by the area's history while visiting his paternal grandfather. The Scottish poet would feature Smailholm in one of his poems, which romanticised life in the Scottish Borders. The family finally abandoned the tower in 1710 when they moved to a more comfortable house at Sandyknowe Farm. One of Scott's imaginary ballads was called *The Eve of St John,* written during his time at Smailholm Tower. His uncle, Sir Hugh Scott of Harden, jokingly accepted the verses to 'pay' for its repairs.[21]

Smailholm Tower

A little way north of here is New Smailholm Farm, which marks the old and now lost settlement of Wrangholm, where a local tradition states that St Cuthbert spent his childhood before entering the abbey at nearby Old Melrose.

Bride flows west from the tower to a great loop in the River Tweed, once the site of Old Melrose Abbey. Here Aidan of Iona established a Culdee monastery in *c.* 635, long before King David I built his new abbey in the nearby medieval town of Melrose.

Before visiting this idyllic spot, now part of the Old Melrose Estate, we consulted our map. We were intrigued by Scott's View, located just below Bemersyde Hill, overlooking the Old Melrose site. It is a renowned landmark viewpoint in Scotland and, supposedly, Sir Walter Scott's favourite place, perhaps because it has spectacular views towards the Eildon Hills and the ruins of Melrose Abbey.

According to one story, Scott would stop at this point so often on his way home that his horses would halt without command. After he died in 1832, his funeral cortège passed this way to his burial at Dryburgh Abbey, the horses stopping for one last look. A plaque now commemorates this spot, and a viewpoint indicator and several benches

The Eildon Hills (courtesy of Colin Baird)

are there for pilgrims travelling in Scott's footsteps to absorb this sacred landscape in comfort.

After parking our car in a layby next to the viewing point, we savoured the stunning view Scott loved so much. We soon found ourselves chatting with a local couple about the history and mystery of the area. Now a retired ghillie, the elderly gentleman told us about the old landowning families in the area, having worked the fishing beats on their various estates most of his life. While we were staring at the view and listening to his eloquent stories describing local life, we spotted what appeared to be a line of 'light' running from the ledge through the peninsula of Old Melrose within the loop of the Tweed and continuing along the base of the Eildon Hills to Melrose Abbey. Perhaps this luminous line was an optical illusion due to the prevailing atmospheric conditions, or was Bride showing us the direction of her earth current? We tried to contain our thrill at seeing this faint mark in the landscape, but when we shared our discovery with the ghillie and his wife, they could not see what was so apparent to us.

Many years ago, I had a similar experience at Swinside Stone Circle in Cumbria when after spending the day of the summer solstice at the stones, a straight burned line appeared etched into the green grass at sunset. Nigel Pennick says that in the West Country, fairy paths or *trods* leave a straight mark in the grass, and you should avoid building on them less ill luck befalls you. Moreover, some people used to walk trods to cure rheumatism, although animals avoided them.

Later research of the 'line of light' using Google Earth revealed a great mystery. From Scott's View, the line aims for the site of Roman Trimontium and passes straight

Looking from Scott's View along the Scott Line

through Melrose Abbey. It then continues to Abbotsford, Scott's home, and, interestingly, further west to the location of Merlin's grave at Drumelzier, which Scott mentions in his poem *Thomas the Rhymer*. To the east of Scott's View, the line passes through the old capital of Roxburgh to Kelso, where Scott went to school. Therefore, this equinoctial line we witnessed manifesting before our eyes is a trail through Walter Scott's life, so I named it the 'Scott Line', which also corresponds to the journey of Bride as she travels through this area. I also noticed that the ley passes through gaps in hedges and aligns with some roads, so it might be one of those old straight tracks first proposed by Alfred Watkins in 1921.

On Bemersyde Hill to the east of Scott's View, Bride connects with a tall pointed standing stone. It stands about 10 ft (3 m) high but lay for many years on its side before being re-erected relatively recently. Although the stone is supposedly not old, it still lures the female current like an ancient megalith. A short distance further to the east, we followed Bride to a fallen and dying oak tree that must have been magnificent in its day.

The old Celtic monastic site of Old Melrose lies within a U-shaped bend of the Tweed, protected on three sides. *Mailros,* its original Gaelic name, means 'the bare promontory in the bend of the river'. When referring to Melrose Abbey, built by the Normans on a new site further upriver, historians believe it derives from '*mel*' meaning a mason's hammer and '*rose*' representing the Virgin Mary. However, Alistair Moffat refers to the word *maol*, which means 'bald', perhaps describing the monk's bald

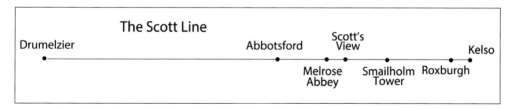

heads or tonsure's rather than the region's topography. Therefore, Mailros translates as 'promontory of the bald monks.'

Incredibly, the holy peninsular forms another vital link in the chain of St Cuthbert sites between Iona, Lindisfarne and Bamburgh. King Oswald of Northumbria had instructed St Aidan to take twelve Culdee monks from Iona and establish a holy sanctuary at Mailros in the same year he created a monastic community on Lindisfarne. Of Irish descent, Aidan began his life as a monk on Iona at a young age. Having been invited by King Oswald, he slowly introduced Christianity to Lothian and Northumbria, founding many churches, monasteries and schools, including Mailros.

Its first abbot was Eata, a disciple of Aidan, and in 651, young Cuthbert arrived supposedly led here after his vision of Aidan being accompanied to the afterlife by angels. He studied under Boisil, eventually becoming prior in 664. St Boisil gave his name to the nearby settlement of St Boswells and was known for his healing and psychic powers. He supposedly predicted the miraculous recovery of young Cuthbert after being struck by a plague and prophesied his influential role in the Christian conversion of the people of Northumbria.

Aidan's monks would have lived a simple and solitary existence here, their community consisting of individual cells like beehive huts made of wood or mud and wattle similar to those recorded in Ireland and Glastonbury and later replaced with stone. They chose this land within a sharp bend of the Tweed, surrounded by a high-sided gorge, for protection and the beneficial energy nature creates. In the absence of a cave, the beehive-like structures made of natural material would be a fitting place to commune with the divine powers of the earth directly.

Kenneth MacAlpin burned the monastery to the ground in 859 after creating a combined Pictish and Scottish state. However, it was rebuilt in 875, later becoming one of many temporary resting places for the monks carrying St Cuthbert's coffin. By 1073, the monastic community had left, but a stone chapel arose over the earlier wooden church dedicated to St Cuthbert. It soon became a place of pilgrimage, continuing over many centuries until the English demolished it in 1321.

On the peninsula's west side, where the Tweed forms a narrow neck of land, there is an earthen vallum or ditch boundary probably from 1130 when King David I utilised the monastery to build a castle. However, given the sanctity of this place, it possibly marks the perimeter of a sacred sanctuary. The king later granted the land to the Cistercian monks of Rievaulx Abbey, but they preferred a new site further west where they established Melrose Abbey overlooking the Eildon Hills. Finally, in 1560, the land was awarded to Robert Ormeston, who used the stone from St Cuthbert's Chapel for his new manor house. Several buildings now stand on the monastery's site, and the present Old Melrose House remains private, so there is no access except for marked footpaths from the tearoom.

Today, only a feature known as chapel knoll, located in the grounds of Old Melrose House, and traces of the earthen vallum remain. According to the Old Melrose & Environs Archaeology Project (2019), 'a gardener dug up a stone in about 1894 in the proximity of what was believed to be the Medieval Chapel of St. Cuthbert (in the late 19th century this became the site of greenhouses and currently it is the location of the piggery).' The stone was carved with a double spiral and is now on display in the Commendator's House at Melrose Abbey. The Canmore website also reports that some of the chapel's

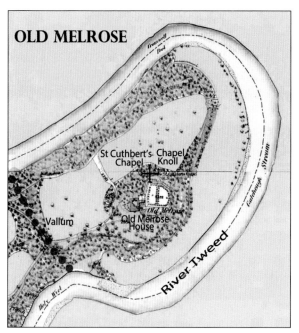

OLD MELROSE

St Cuthbert's Chapel
Chapel Knoll

Vallum

Old Melrose House

River Tweed

Plan of Old Melrose showing the vallum and site of St Cuthbert's Chapel (adapted by the author from an extract from Ordnance Survey map, c. 1859)

foundation stones are '*in a flower bed skirting the southeast side of Chapel Knoll, with three graves lying under the lawn.*'[22]

Leaving the car park next to Old Melrose's tearooms and bookshop, we followed a heritage trail, avoiding the private grounds of Old Melrose House to the river below. We strolled around the tranquil grassy isthmus that once provided a sacred sanctuary for St Aidan's Celtic Christian community. Grazing sheep and the anglers fly fishing in the Tweed occasionally broke the peaceful atmosphere. An oak woodland now surrounds the peninsula, filled with descendants of the old deciduous varieties that once filled the valley, forming a loving protection for the monastery.

We dowsed Bride flowing through a magnificent copper beech tree on the eastern banks of the Tweed as she travels from Scott's View. She meanders through the grazing sheep before disappearing into the private grounds of Old Melrose House and possibly to the site of St Cuthbert's Chapel. Bride's continued connection with places associated with St Cuthbert is remarkable and magical, like the saint himself.

An unusual legend recounted in *Description of the Abbeys of Melrose and Old Melrose, with their traditions,* says that abbey's founder was a princess from one of the archipelago islands in the Mediterranean who fled to Scotland after losing her virginity – an act punishable by death on her native islands. Therefore, she set sail with her priests to Britain, landing at Dunbar in East Lothian, where she travelled to the Tweed crossing at Monks Ford. Here they built a settlement and an abbey on land opposite in the river loop later called Maleros – 'a rose sullied or tarnished by a male', alluding to her misfortune.[23] Perhaps this story provides an allegory or code to alert us to the presence of the divine feminine force in the form of the Bride serpent energy.

Further upstream from Old Melrose, the female current visits the private grounds of Ravenswood House. A grand house stood on this site in 1824 built for Major John Scott, a cousin of Sir Walter Scott who made his fortune in the East Indies. He sold the house to Adam Fairholme in 1830, after which it fell into several hands until William Younger eventually bought it in 1900 along with the Old Melrose estate. He was a member of one of Scotland's most successful brewery families, who once supplied a quarter of Scotland's beer.

Trimontium Fort and Scotland's Holy Hills

We soon realised that the female serpent's flow was taking us to the iconic landmark hills of the Eildons that overlook the town of Melrose. The Romans called the Eildons *Trimontium*, meaning 'three mountains', although there is a fourth smaller peak. Like Edinburgh's majestic craggy hills of Castle Rock and Arthur's Seat, which mark the east end of Edinburgh, the Eildons are volcanic plugs, eroded remains of separate outpourings of lava from a volcanic eruption some 350 million years ago.

These once-sacred hills dominate the landscape for miles around, and it is here, at the base of the Eildons, that the Romans chose to build their largest camp in Scotland. Their arrival in 80 CE saw the establishment of an encampment to house the auxiliary cavalry force. Having constructed the Roman road of Dere Street, which stretched from the south, the camp also acted as a supply base for operations while building the Antonine Wall. During the height of the Roman occupation, Trimontium's population numbered between 2000 and 5000.

Nothing remains of this historical site today but for the various information boards placed strategically along a footpath. However, long before the Latin invaders took up residence here, Bronze Age peoples settled the base of the Eildon Hills. Moreover, on its

northernmost peak, archaeologists uncovered the remains of one the largest hillforts in Britain, dating back to 1000 BCE. Eildon means, in the old P-Celtic tongue, 'old fort' and at one time may have been the domain of the Brythonic Selgovae tribe, 'the hunters', who were a sub-tribe of the great Brigantes nation of Northern England. Some historians believe it later became a stronghold of the Votadini, whose tribal centre was Edinburgh and Traprain Law further east.

There are several holy springs around the base of the hills, once places to honour the local goddess and later dedicated to Christian saints, such as St Dunstan and St Mary and another called Monkswell.

Stone Monument marking the site of the Trimontium encampment

Perhaps these names originated when pilgrims followed an old route across the summit of these peaks as they descended to the valley below to visit the ancient abbey at Melrose. Around all three hills are the outlines of huts, defensive earthworks and ramps, and according to some sources, certain features are considered sacred temples or groves.

Moffat believes the Eildon Hills were places of sacred ceremony similar to the Hills of Tara and Uisneach in Ireland, not inhabited in the traditional sense. Here, royal enclosures witnessed the inauguration of high kings, the dispensing of laws, feasting and games during solar festivals such as Samhain Eve when the tribes gave thanks for the year's harvest and prepared for the winter with the slaughtering of cattle and sheep. Likewise, at Imbolc, Bride's Day, the farmers and herders climbed up to the summit of Eildon Hill North to pay their rents to the king and the priests who resided there throughout the year. The lighting of bonfires at Beltane here was a sign to commence the fertility rituals. Moffat disputes its use as a hillfort and writes:

'Zigzagging in several directions, the earthworks are mainly ditches and banks. Although they use the contours and features of the land, running out at the bottom of very steep slopes or just as they reach the stream, they cannot have been defensive. There is simply no military logic to their layout with ditches running at all angles, connected but not consistent in presenting an obstacle of any challenging aspect to an oncoming enemy.' [24]

Local folklore attached to these hills includes one that tells of Eildon having once been one hill until the famous 13th-century wizard and court philosopher Michael *Scott 'cleft it in three with a spade and bridled the river Tweed with a curb of stone.'* The Devil then wiped the spade of mud to make Eildon Little Hill. Curiously, another local tale says the Eildons are hollow and home to Elfland:

'At the beginning of each summer, when the milk-white hawthorn is in bloom, anointing the air with its sweet odour, and miles and miles of golden whin adorn the glens and hill-slopes, the fairies come forth in grand procession, headed by the Fairy Queen. They are mounted on little white horses, and when on a night of clear soft moonlight the people hear the clatter of many hoofs, the jingling of bridles, and the sound of laughter and sweet music coming sweetly down the wind, they whisper one to another: "Tis the Fairy Folks' Raid", or "Here come the Riders of the Shee". The Fairy Queen, who rides in front, is gowned in grass-green silk and wears over her shoulders a mantle of green velvet adorned with silver spangles. She is of great beauty. Her eyes are like wood violets, her teeth like pearls, her brow and neck are swan-white, and her cheeks bloom like ripe apples. Her long clustering hair of rich auburn gold which falls over her shoulders and down her back, is bound round about with a snood that glints with star-like gems, and there is one great flashing jewel above her brow. On each lock of her horse's mane hang sweet-toned silver bells that tinkle merrily as she rides on.' [25]

Perhaps the most famous legend attached to these hills originates from a 13th-century bard from Berwickshire called Thomas the Rhymer, who met the Fairy Queen by a hawthorn tree known as the Eildon Tree while walking towards Eildon Hill at Halloween. Having seduced him, Thomas follows her to Elfland, where he stays for three days before being allowed to return, having received the gift of prophecy. However, when he returned to his village, the shocked locals informed him that he had been gone for seven years. These time-slip events are reminiscent of many fairy and UFO abduction cases recorded worldwide.

At certain times, the electromagnetic energy of this trinity of hills is conducive to altered states of consciousness, and the presence of balls of light or plasma intelligence may explain the abduction story of Thomas the Rhymer. Plasma lights can read the consciousness of anybody coming into contact with this unearthly energy and will morph into any form depending on the observer's expectations. Thomas the Rhymer, who may have read old Norse tales of fairies, elves and goblins, would have believed he was experiencing a fairy realm.

King Arthur is said to lie sleeping in a secret cave beneath the Eildon Hills with his ghostly knights, who await his call to arms to save Britain in its hour of need. Perhaps the early tribes witnessed many lights coming from the hills and believed them to be their warrior hero Arthur.

Sir Walter Scott, Scotland's most famous historical novelist and playwright, embellished this tale and created the myth of a horse trader called Canonbie Dick who, having been taken inside the hill at night, discovered King Arthur and a band of knights asleep. The horse dealer was travelling across Bowden Moor one day and met a stranger who, unbeknownst to him, was King Arthur himself. Arthur asked whether

he would sell his horse to him, and after striking a deal, Dick was paid. This encounter continued every night for several days until Dick invited this stranger to his home. During their journey, they encountered a magic door in the hillock of 'Lucken Hare', which opened to reveal a vast cavern under the Eildon Tree, where lay a sword and a horn. Having been told to pick one of them, Dick chose the horn. Unfortunately, it was the wrong choice, and he was instantly tossed into the air and thrown out of the cave. The reason for his rather unceremonious rejection was that picking the horn was not the action of a warrior. A passing shepherd found the dazed Dick, who promptly told him this extraordinary tale before passing away.[26]

Under the Eildon tree Thomas met the lady, painting by Katherine Cameron (1864–1965)

We came across a similar legend at Alderley Edge in Cheshire on the Belinus alignment concerning sleeping knights, the striking of a deal for a horse and a magic door. But in this tale, it was Merlin who approached the individual. These stories may relate to changes in the earth's local magnetic field, creating window areas and time anomalies, especially in the location of fault lines of crystalline geology such as basalt or sandstone. As mentioned earlier, at such places, our three-dimensional reality, with all its hopes, fears and superstitions, can be accessed by intelligent energies entering our realm and adopting a form that we might find acceptable to interact with. For instance, if we know that dragons or black dogs haunt this area, they will morph into that archetype. If a person is highly religious and disbelieves in the existence of fairies, they will appear as a religious figure, such as the Virgin Mary. If people are aware of UFO encounters, they may see alien beings.

American Ufologist and journalist John Keel (1930-2009) extensively researched thousands of UFO cases. As a result, he rejected the extraterrestrial hypothesis, believing that it is easier to accept that lights in the sky are aliens in ships than animated-intelligent bundles of energy traversing the scale of the electromagnetic spectrum, of which we only perceive a fragment.

Luring a physical person into another reality or fairy world is an age-old tale. Sometimes the person experiences time and space displacement, like in many UFO abduction cases. Perhaps the site of the old Eildon tree is a doorway that can open to another multiverse or parallel world under specific conditions. Today, the Rhymer's Stone, erected in 1929 by the Melrose Literary Society, marks this enchanted spot.

The Romans may have chosen this site because they understood the magical qualities of the Eildons. However, such a large settlement, close to the busy highway of the River Tweed, must have come at a time when there was a prolonged period of peace between the Romans and the local tribes, having established lucrative trade deals. Moffat thought it likely that, being skilled at politics, the Romans agreed that the local kings kept control of their land and continued with their solar festivals.

Although the Romans left the area in 180 CE, there is evidence of occupation until the end of the 4th century. Around this time, the local tribes amalgamated with the Pictish peoples of the north to fight a new enemy – the Angles and the Saxons. Perhaps a great warrior called Arthur or Artuir came to the aid of the Picts and the Gododdin to save Trimontium and Britain during its time of need. The legend of King Arthur sleeping within the Eildon Hills with his warriors might echo old memories of when this legendary hero fought alongside the local tribes in the 4th century.

According to Coppens, Arthur married the sister of King Lot or Loth of Lodonasia, Latin for Lothian. He argues that the twelfth battle at Badon Hill, where Arthur killed 960 men in one single charge securing his military reputation and peace over the land, may have been at Bowden Hill on the territorial border of the Gododdin.[28]

We traced the female dragon current flowing through the site of the Roman baths within the Trimontium encampment, continuing to a Shap granite column at Newstead designed as a Roman Milestone that marks the western edge of the fort, placed there in the year 2000 to commemorate the millennium. An 'ancient Lodge of Masons' existed in Newstead long ago, possibly founded by the stonemasons who built Melrose Abbey and a nearby bridge over a crucial fording place of the Tweed. On a trackway between here and Melrose was also a famous venerated cross planted within an oakwood called the Prior Wood Cross. From here, Bride heads west towards the medieval precincts of one of Scotland's most famous abbeys.

Melrose Abbey

Nestling in a tranquil valley of the Tweed River is the picturesque ruins of Melrose Abbey dedicated to St Mary, its towering arches reaching up towards the sun-drenched sky. As we strolled around the well-kept grounds of this old Cistercian Abbey, we could see clearly to the south the high peaks of Eildon North Hill and Eildon Mid Hill. We soon detected Bride meandering along the abbey's central axis, now open to the elements, connecting with the site of the high altar, her width taking up most of the aisle.

Melrose Abbey, an engraving by John Stoddart 1801 from 'Scenery & Manners In Scotland'

In 1136, David I invited a group of Cistercian monks from Rievaulx Abbey in North Yorkshire to establish an abbey at the site of St Aidan's old monastic settlement at Mailros or Old Melrose. However, they preferred another location called Little Fordell, later renamed Melrose. Perhaps, they understood that it was an ideal place to draw upon the energies of the Eildon Hills to enhance the divinity of this grand Norman stone edifice.

Soon a large town grew up around it, and with the Cistercians implementing new farming techniques, the abbey and town thrived as one of Scotland's most prosperous wool producers. It also became the burial place of Scottish kings and nobles, such as Alexander II and the final resting place of King Robert Bruce's heart. Many of its abbots were men from distinguished families, including the last abbot James Stewart, 'natural son' of King James V, who died in 1559. *The Chronicle of Melrose* mentions its second abbot Waltheof (*c.*1095–1159), son of Simon Senlis, the Saxon First Earl of Northampton and Matilda, grandniece of William the Conqueror. In *The Sword and the Grail*, Andrew Sinclair mentions that Waltheof's father was related to the St Clair family of Rosslyn Chapel.[29] His relics were associated with many miracles, and his body, like St Cuthbert, remained incorrupt after burial. The *Chronicle of Melrose Abbey* states:

> 'The tomb of our pious father, Sir Waltheof, the second abbot of Melrose, was opened by Enguerrand, of good memory, the bishop of Glasgow, and by four abbots called in for this purpose; and his body was found entire, and his vestments intact....'[30]

In other words, like St Cuthbert, his body was embalmed.

Built in the gothic style, in the form of the St John Cross, historical evidence suggests that Melrose Abbey was a straightforward structure with few adornments, in line with the principles of the Cistercians. However, during the 13th and 14th centuries, intricate carvings of great detail were introduced, including ornate stone vaulting over the presbytery and elegant tracery around the windows. Even today, you can still see many beautiful pieces of masonry within the ruins, including various fascinating sculptures of saints, dragons, gargoyles, demons, hobgoblins, lute-playing angels, a cook with a wooden spoon, a bagpipe-playing pig and intricate foliage.

However, because of its situation next to one of the main routes to Edinburgh, Melrose Abbey became vulnerable to attack. Like Kelso Abbey, it suffered during the numerous conflicts between the English and the Scots. Moreover, Edward II's English army destroyed much of the abbey and town in 1322, killing many monks.

Robert the Bruce was responsible for much of its rebuilding, and perhaps it is no coincidence that his heart was buried here after he died in 1329. The remainder of his body was interred at Dunfermline Abbey, close to a node of the Elen and Belinus currents of the Belinus Line. Legend says King Robert requested that his great friend Sir James Douglas, also known as Black Douglas, transport his heart to the Holy Sepulchre in Jerusalem after his death. He did so by carrying it in a silver casket around his neck. Unfortunately, while passing through Spain, he and his entourage were called upon to fight alongside Alfonso XI of Castile against the Moors of Granada near Teba. After attempting to rescue one of his stricken comrades during the battle, Douglas found himself surrounded by a rallying cluster of Moors. Before being slain, he tossed the silver casket into the thick of the fight and shouted: *'Now pass thou onward before us, as thou wast wont, and I will follow thee or die.'* Later, the Moors gave back his body and Bruce's heart. In 1996, an archaeological excavation at the abbey unearthed a conical lead container with an engraved copper plaque that read, *'The enclosed leaden casket containing a heart was found beneath the Chapter House floor, March 1921, by His Majesty's Office of Works.'*[31]

In 1385, during an invasion by the Scots in Northern England, Richard II of England defeated David II of Scotland and, consequently, burned down Melrose Abbey. Over a hundred years of reconstruction took place, with various architectural styles employed at different stages, suggesting that the work was carried out first by the English under Richard II and later continued by the Scots. However, the building remained unfinished when James IV visited over a century later, in 1502 and 1504.

The abbey was badly damaged again by Henry VIII's armies in 1544 and 1545, and by the time of the Reformation, it was rapidly deteriorating. The last resident monk died at Melrose in about 1590 when local landowners began stripping the abbey of its stone, valuable lead, glass, and wood. The final assault came with the arrival of Oliver Cromwell's troops during the English Civil War.

In 1618 part of the central portion of the nave of the abbey was converted into a newly renovated parish church for Melrose. However, by 1810, it was no longer in use, and its congregation preferred a new place of worship on Weir Hill just to the west, now the Parish Church of Bowden and Melrose.

At the beginning of the 19th century, during his appointment as Sheriff Depute of Roxburghshire, Sir Walter Scott, with the financial assistance of the Duke of Buccleuch, supervised extensive repair work to preserve the ruins. In 1918, after further restoration and repair, it was awarded to the state and is now in the care of Historic Environment Scotland.

Also buried here is a real-life 12th-century wizard called Michael Scott, along with his books on magic. He predicted his own death from a stone falling on his head.

He practised black magic and claimed he could fly. The stone coffin of the famous conjurer was found in the aisle of the south chancel in 1812, and even today, his ghost is said to haunt his grave within the ruins. Although Sir Walter Scott embellished much of Michael Scott's magical feats, he was a famous and well-travelled scholar in real life. He became known as a wizard due to his strange attire, favouring a long robe tied at the waist and wearing a pointed hat like Dumbledore in Harry Potter. He frequented the Sicilian court of one of the most powerful men in Europe at the time, the Holy Roman Emperor Frederick II, where he produced several original works on astrology, alchemy and the occult sciences. His tomb no longer exists, but old postcards depict a turban-headed statue in the chancel labelled 'Tomb of Michael Scott'. Other ghostly apparitions have been witnessed here, including a group of monks that walk amongst the ruins at night.

Old postcard showing the tomb of Michael Scott, Melrose Abbey

Many Knights Templar graves appear in and around the abbey – one described as a Templar and Grail tombstone by Andrew Sinclair is on display in the Abbey Museum. The gravestone is a smaller version of one inside Rosslyn Chapel, designed with an eight-pointed cross *fleury* with a cup or Grail. The Templars were closely associated with the Cistercians, so perhaps it is unsurprising that many are buried here. Sinclair writes that just seven years before the founding of Melrose Abbey by the Cistercians, Hugh de Payens, co-founder and first Grand Master of the Knights Templars, established property close to Rosslyn Chapel at Balantrodoch or Temple, as it is known today.[32]

At the east end of the abbey, Bride connects with two elegant tombs carved with skulls and crossbones, the mark of master masons. Continuing west from the ruins, she passes through the ticket office at the main entrance before crossing the road to a white-washed cottage that was the original information centre. She then diverts to the northwest to visit the 'bulb lawn' of the idyllic Harmony Gardens of Harmony Cottage built in 1887, now holiday accommodation, a peaceful setting to meditate on the feminine energy.

Almost directly west of here, Bride visits Melrose Parish Church on Weirhill, built in 1810 to replace the old place of worship at Melrose Abbey. As if by divine coincidence, its beautiful east window depicts St Cuthbert and St Margaret, mother of King David, characters associated with the female serpents of Bride and Elen of the north–south Belinus Line.

Before leaving this picturesque town, Bride visits a 15th-century three-storey tower house close to the Tweed River built by the Heiton family in 1425. Originally from Normandy, the family resided here until 1986. Now surrounded by residential dwellings, Darnick Tower is set within its own grounds, hidden by a high stone wall. James V stayed here during the Battle of Melrose in 1526, but was burnt down during

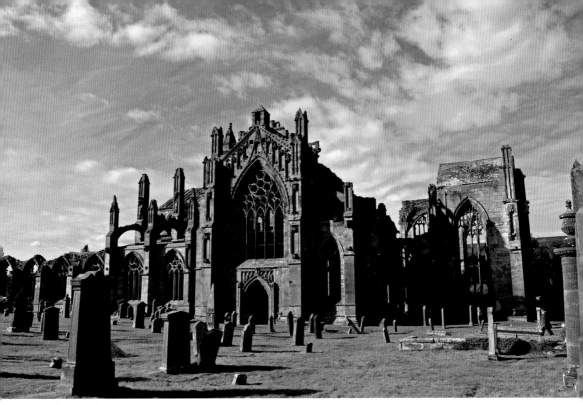

Melrose Abbey Ruins

the Rough Wooing by the Earl of Hertford. In the 20th century, it became a guest house and then a museum and is now a private residence. A ghost is said to still haunt the grounds.

Interestingly, Sir Walter Scott's attempt to purchase the property was unsuccessful. Perhaps he sensed the same feminine serpent energy previously experienced at his school in Kelso, his favourite view above Old Melrose and Smailholm Tower. However, he found the perfect place for his new home just under 2 miles (3.2 km) to the west at Abbotsford, which also happens to be the abode of his favourite female earth serpent, Bride. Interestingly, Darnick Tower is near the newly discovered Scott Line, just over one hundred yards north.

Abbotsford House and Sir Walter Scott

Abbotsford House was originally the site of a farmstead, and in 1811 became the new home of Sir Walter Scott (1771–1832). At the time, he was an internationally renowned poet and novelist, and his works included *Ivanhoe*, *Rob Roy*, *The Lady of the Lake*, *Waverley* and *The Heart of Midlothian*. Although primarily remembered as a great literary man, Scott was by profession an advocate, judge and legal administrator and at one time Sheriff-Depute of Selkirkshire.

Born in Edinburgh, he was the ninth child of Anne Rutherford and Walter Scott, a solicitor and member of the Scottish society known as the 'Writers of the Signet'. Having contracted polio as a young child, the young Walter was sent to live with his paternal grandparents at their farm at Sandyknowe near Kelso, neighbouring the atmospheric ruin of Smailholm Tower. He then attended the local grammar school on the site of Kelso Abbey, where he met James and John Ballantyne, who later became his business partners and publishers.

Abbotsford House

From a young boy, Scott became fascinated by the oral traditions of the Scottish Borders and collected and recorded many local stories and folk tales. Being associated with so many energetic sites on the Holy Axis, we were fascinated to learn that in 1797 Scott married his wife Charlotte Charpentier in Carlisle Cathedral, which so happens to be on a node of the male and female dragon lines of the Belinus alignment. He often visited his aunt at the Garden House and later Rosebank in Kelso, now called Waverley Lodge, both on the Bride current.

He renamed the farmstead Abbotsford after a fording place nearby where abbots of Melrose Abbey once crossed the river. He extended the building in 1818 as a small villa, later carrying out further work to create the fine Scottish Baronial mansion you see today, likened by some to a 'fairy palace'. He incorporated many architectural features copied from such Scottish landmarks as Rosslyn Chapel and Melrose Abbey.

On the house's exterior are parapets and gargoyles, and the main entrance is from Linlithgow Palace. Even the screen wall in the garden mimics the Melrose Abbey cloister. Also built into the house and garden walls are numerous carved or inscribed stones 'rescued' from sites in south east Scotland, such as a 16th-century door, a 15th-century niche from Edinburgh's Tollbooth and parts of Edinburgh's original Mercat cross. But, of more interest to us was a series of stone carved panels of five Roman deities, Mercury, Jupiter, Venus, Apollo and Mars, part of a series representing the days of the week, taken from Old Penrith, near Carlisle in Cumbria. Many years ago, we dowsed the male serpent current of the Belinus Line here, passing through the scant remains of the Roman fort of Voreda, which served as a station for a task force from the 20th Legion during the entire period of their occupation of the north of England. Finds from this site include altars honouring the Roman gods Silvanus and Mars and the Brythonic gods of Belatucador and Mogons. We felt that Scott was extremely fortunate to acquire these treasures.

Abbotsford became a place of pilgrimage even during Scott's lifetime and remained open to the public long after his death, when 'it rapidly assumed the character of a literary shrine.' However, in 1825, Scott's fortunes took a massive downturn due to a nationwide banking crisis, which resulted in the collapse of the Ballantyne printing business, in which Scott was the only partner with a financial interest. The debts incurred were crippling and caused his very public ruin. However, rather than declare himself bankrupt, or accept any financial support from his many supporters and admirers, including the king himself, he placed his house and income in a trust belonging to his creditors. Adding to his burdens, his dear wife Charlotte died a year later.

Determined to write his way out of debt, Scott produced six novels from 1826 until 1832, as well as two short stories, numerous plays, eleven works or volumes of non-fiction, a journal and several unfinished works. Unaffected by his financial problems, he became a literary superstar, and his writings have continued to *'fire the imagination of a generation'*. He was *'..a man who had done much to re-establish the idea of a distinctive Scottish identity at a time when "North Britain" was in danger of becoming indistinguishable from any other region of Great Britain.'*[33] Although Scott died owing

Figure of a Roman God with a spear, Abbotsford House

money, his novels continued to sell, and the debts encumbering his estate were discharged shortly after his death. By the 1850s, the house required modification to accommodate the increasing number of visitors, including its dedicated tourist entrance.

Before visiting the house, we enjoyed a light lunch in Abbotsford's visitor centre, which opened in 2012, with beautiful views over the grounds. Afterwards, we strolled to the well-kept gardens and soon spotted the various classical carved stone carvings and panels collected by Scott, including those from Old Penrith.

We detected Bride flowing through a copper beech tree before entering the house, where she passes through the library and part of the drawing room. The library has some of the finest books in Scotland and is considered one of the most significant and complete writer's libraries. Scott was renowned for obtaining old Scottish manuscripts to preserve Scotland's ancient history. As we wandered through the reception rooms, we noticed the many replica carvings found in Rosslyn Chapel and others of a more pagan nature, including a crowned 'green man'.

We also observed Scott's somewhat eccentric tastes in the furnishings and the various relics and curiosities displayed throughout, imbuing the rooms with a unique magical atmosphere and charm, which many believe still evokes this famous Scottish icon's spirit. In addition, Scott collected memorabilia associated with the tragic Scottish monarch Mary, Queen of Scots and various occult items. Scott was a member of a secret society in Edinburgh founded in 1764 called the Speculative Society, whose select members were called 'Specs'.

We follow Bride through the Armoury, featuring guns belonging to Bonnie Dundee and Rob Roy, including his broadsword and dirk. We also noticed the carving of a 'sheela-na-gig' on her flow opposite a comical dragon that looks down over the door, all replicas of those found at Melrose Abbey. She also passes through the private area of the house, including a courtyard garden, as she heads for the family chapel.

We wondered whether divine inspiration or psychic intuition led Scott to buy the old farmhouse at Abbotsford on a ley connecting places he has lived and loved. At Abbotsford, Scott produced some of his best work amidst such dire circumstances and stayed here until his death in 1832.

Perhaps Scott, having such a close connection with the Bride dragon energy throughout his life, could tune into the Scottish collective unconsciousness. The theory of quantum entanglement may explain the connectedness of all things, for subatomic particles can communicate with all other particles at any distance and time. Perhaps Scott had a sense of universal connectedness that helped to elevate his literary genius to superstar status, having often been compared to Shakespeare. His legacy has helped define Scotland's illustrious history and that of its landscape and people, which has endured to the present day.

Torwoodlie Tower and Broch

Bride travels northwest away from the Tweed Valley to the remains of Torwoodlee Tower next to the scenic banks of Gala Water and the site of an Iron Age Broch. The Pringles of Smailholm also settled on the female current here at Torwoodlee in the 15th century. William, the first Laird of Torwoodlee, was killed at the Battle of Flodden in 1513.

The tower was rebuilt in 1601 after rival clans destroyed the original house during a skirmish in 1568. It is now a romantic ruin next to Torwoodlee Mains, abandoned when the Pringles built a fine Georgian mansion closer to the Gala River in 1783. On a bank adjacent to the tower is an ancient yew tree, which may indicate a previous site of sacred importance before it became a clan house.

Torwoodlee Broch and Fort (courtesy of Tom Parnell)

The serpent current continues to an Iron-Age earthen enclosure on high ground just north of the tower. Here, it passes through the scant remains of a large circular drystone dun or broch on its southwestern edge. The broch is now less than 3 ft (0.9 m) in height, and its overall diameter measures 76 ft (23.2 m), but its impressive walls once measured over 16 ft (5 m) thick, farmers and road builders having taken its stone long ago. A ditch was also evident around its base. Archaeologists believe its original entrance was on the east and, during investigations by James Curle in 1891, Roman pottery and glass were found together with a 1st century CE coin.

Torwoodlee Tower (courtesy of Ian Lees)

There is much debate about the age and purpose of the brochs, and many historians believe them to be grain stores or fortified shelters against attack. However, following the dragon currents of the Belinus alignment for our book *The Spine of Albion* back in 2012, we encountered similar more intact structures around Scotland attributed to the Picts, often marking nodes. So we were curious as to

why these defensive brochs were mysteriously abandoned in the 1st or 2nd centuries CE when the Romans invaded Scotland. The design of the Scottish broch is similar in style to the round towers found on the Balearic Islands, Sardinia and Malta, but much wider at the base. They are also reminiscent of the Irish Round Towers, which many researchers believe act as antennae for focusing cosmic energies to bring fertility to the land.

The round towers in Ireland are unique in using superlative engineering. Many historians consider them older than the churches they stand next to, some lying in ruins next to them. We wondered whether the Torwoodlee Broch somehow amplifies the fertile power within the serpent earth energy lines.

During his ground-breaking research of the Irish Round Towers, American scientist Dr Philip Callahan studied the subtle influences emitted by certain types of geology. In his remarkable book *Ancient Mysteries, Modern Visions*, Callahan wrote that the Neolithic or Bronze Age builders and the later Celts utilised specific stones during the construction of the round towers because of their magnetic qualities. He discovered that all substances are diamagnetic, meaning 'repelled by a magnetic field', or paramagnetic, meaning 'attracted to a magnetic field'. Organic materials such as plants, water and rocks formed from the same matter, such as chalk and pure limestone, are diamagnetic. However, sandstone, granite and metals, such as ironstone and slate, are paramagnetic due to their quartz silica content. Soil with a high concentration of iron-rich clay is highly fertile due to its balanced consistency of both diamagnetic and paramagnetic ingredients, a quality akin to chi, having the correct balance of yin and yang. He found that the stone in most of the round towers were highly paramagnetic types of limestone and granite.[34]

Stow and the Ancient Shrine of Our Lady

The Bride current is drawn to the flowing waters of Gala Water, a tributary of the River Tweed, as she travels north to the quaint village of Stow, situated next to the historic route of the A7 to Edinburgh. This ancient road stretches from the border towns of Longtown and Canonbie to the capital city of Edinburgh, passing through some stunning scenery and fascinating towns and villages.

Here, the current passes north–south through the chancel of the 17th-century ruin of St Mary's Church with 15th-century foundations. However, a place of worship existed on this site from the 7th century and in 1242, David de Burnham, Bishop of St Andrew's, consecrated a new church to replace it. Over a wall to the southeast of the ruin are the scant remains of the Bishops of St

St Mary's Church ruin, Stowe

Andrew's summer palace. A few feet south of here, set upon a high mound, is the new parish kirk constructed in 1876.

The area was initially called Stow-in-Wedale, and according to some sources, 'Stow' in old English means a holy or consecrated place of assembly, and 'Wedale' translates as 'dale of the holy house'. Wedale also derives from the word 'Wiche' meaning shrine – therefore, Stow in Wedale translates as 'holy place in the valley of the shrine.'

Stow's holy well and chapel were highly revered, located just south of the town dedicated to Our Lady, its foundation dating back to the 6th century. In contrast, others believe it existed during the Roman occupation of the area. Interestingly, a translation of *Historia Brittonum* written in around 828 CE by the Welsh monk Nennius mentions that Arthur left a relic at the well at Wedale:

> 'For Arthur proceeded to Jerusalem, and there made a cross to the size of the Saviour's cross, and there it was consecrated, and for three successive days he fasted, watched, and prayed, before the Lord's cross, that the Lord would give him the victory, by this sign, over the heathen; which also took place, and he took with him the image of St. Mary, the fragments of which are still preserved in great veneration at Wedale, in English Wodale, in Latin Vallis–doloris. Wodale is a village in the province of Lodonesia, but now of the jurisdiction of the bishop of St. Andrew's of Scotland, six miles on the west of that heretofore noble and eminent monastery of Meilros.' [35]

This documented account of King Arthur visiting a sacred place in Scotland is fascinating. Folklore says that Arthur had a vision of the Virgin Mary at the well of Wedale before a great battle promising him victory. After winning the fight, Arthur returned and built a chapel next to the well. Other tales say a chapel already existed here, and Arthur placed a statue of Our Lady from Cappadocia at 'the Holy House of Wedale' in thanks for his success. Unfortunately, a Danish raid of the area in the 9th century destroyed the chapel, although the well remained relatively intact.

Stow is believed to be the scene of Arthur's battle at *Castello Guinnion*, Guinnion being another possible derivation of the name Wedale. In the *Four Ancient Books of Wales*, William Skene writes:

> 'The eighth battle was "in Castello Guinnion." The word castellum implies a Roman fort, and Guinnion is in Welsh an adjective formed from gwen, white. The Harleian MS. adds that Arthur carried into battle upon his shoulders an image of the Virgin Mary, and that the Pagani were put to flight and a great slaughter made of them by virtue of the Lord Jesus Christ and of Saint Mary his mother. Henry of Huntingdon, who likewise gives this account, says the image was upon his shield; it has been well remarked that the Welsh ysgwyd is a shoulder and ysgwydd a shield, and that a Welsh original had been differently translated. Another MS. adds that he likewise took into battle a cross he had brought from Jerusalem, and that the fragments are still preserved at Wedale. Wedale is a district watered by the rivers Gala and Heriot, corresponding to the modern parish of Stow, anciently called the Stow in Wedale. The name Wedale means "The dale of woe," and that name having been given by the Saxons implies that they had experienced a great disaster here. The church of Stow being dedicated to St. Mary, while General Roy places a Roman castellum not far from it, indicates very plainly that this was the scene of the battle.' [36]

According to Moffat, the old Brythonic word Guinnion changed to Gwedale from its Q-Celtic translation, *Guidh-dail*, meaning the 'valley of prayer'. However, 'dail' is a word for 'battlefield'; therefore, Gwedale may translate as 'the prayer battle' or 'the holy battle', referring to Arthur using the image of the Holy Mother Mary on his shield to bring Christian enlightenment against the barbaric Saxon forces.

This holy place was said to have been one of the few in Scotland to provide rights of sanctuary for fugitives and felons in the Middle Ages and where the Virgin Mary appeared to pilgrims. A later chapel known as Our Lady's Chapel once stood a short distance to the southeast of the well at the foot of Torsonce Hill and survived until 1963 when despite local protests, it was bulldozed for its stone to use in the foundations of a field road.[37]

A stone roof once protected the well, which was demolished in 1864 by the local farmer to make it easier for his cattle to drink. A large white stone was also a feature of the well, which 'bore the imprint of St Mary's foot' as she alighted from the well to speak to King Arthur. Sadly this holy relic was broken up in 1810 to use as hardcore on the Turnpike Road. In his *Arthurian Localities*, John Stuart Glennie refers to a poem in *The Book of Taliesin*, which mentions a battle between Urien of Rheged and the Angles: *I saw a brow covered with rage on Urien when he furiously attacked his foes at the white stone of Galystem.*[38] Glennie argues that the Galystem has to be Gala-stream, and the white stone is the object of veneration that stood by the holy well.

To our delight, we discovered that the well still exists and access to it is via a footpath from the 'Bridge to Heaven' opposite the ruin of St Mary's. An old stone bridge over Gala Water, constructed in 1655, linked Stow to the main route between Edinburgh and Galashiels, which, unlike the modern A7, used to follow the west bank of the river.

From here, a footpath took us south, hugging the banks of the river before continuing through fields until we noticed a stone-walled enclosure to our left. On closer inspection, we realised it to be the ancient Our Lady's Well mentioned in so many early chronicles. However, traffic zooming along the busy A7 above seemed incongruous with this tranquil and sacred setting, although we were thrilled to encounter one of Scotland's most historic Christian sites.

Nennius wrote that the shrine suffered damage during a great conflict, possibly Urien's battle, but was still held 'in great honour and veneration' and, according to Moffat, continued as a place of pilgrimage for many centuries. Although the Catholic shrine was closed to the public after the Reformation, locals still used its healing waters, for in the 1650s, a group of women were tried for witchcraft after drinking water from the well to cure minor ailments. Finally, after many years of neglect, the local community fully restored this ancient pilgrimage site in the year 2000, which included a new stone roof.

The Wedale landscape, formed by the convergence of sandstone and near vertical crystalline rock strata, creates an enchanted environment, emitting high electromagnetic energy emissions. Many pilgrims were said to have witnessed the Virgin Mary here, including King Arthur. But as we have mentioned previously, the cultural expectations or archetypes at that time were religious figures, legendary kings and elementals such as fairies or goblins.

Despite its suppression and neglect, the holy well of Our Lady, which still has incredible power, has managed to survive the ravages of time and still attracts the Bride current. Perhaps those who continually venerated Our Lady at the well were

Restored Holy Well at Stowe by Rob Wildwood

somehow influenced by the presence of the divine feminine power in the form of the Bride female earth serpent. We believe this well is a perfect place of honouring for the modern pilgrims searching for reconnection, balance within the land and a bit of magic.

Before leaving, we stood for a moment and imagined walking in the footsteps of Arthur, one of this island's most chivalrous leaders, who, according to 'The Matter of Britain', will rise again to save Britain in its hour of need.

Just a few miles north of Stow is a tiny isolated church at the hamlet of Heriot, which you can reach by turning off the A7 onto the B709. We dowsed Bride passing through the Victorian church, which replaced a medieval place of worship on lands once belonging to the monks of Newbattle Abbey.

Temple of the Knights

Bride crosses the Moorfoot Hills to enter the South Esk Valley and another beautiful historical setting with the enigmatic name of Temple, formerly Balantrodoch. The village is famous for housing Scotland's principal seat and preceptory of the Knights Templar. David I, who met their Grand Master Hugh de Payens in Scotland, granted these lands on the east bank of River South Esk to the Templars in 1128. However, some sources suggest that the land was donated by the St Clair's of Roslin, located just 4 miles (6.4 m) away. Interestingly, de Payens fought in the First Crusade with Sir Henry St Clair, so it seems reasonable to assume they may have discussed a possible site to establish a future Templar headquarters in Scotland.[39]

Following the Papal Bull of 1312, King Edward II of England abolished the Templars in England, seizing their assets and handing them over to the Knights Hospitallers. However, many Templars who escaped capture on the continent came to Scotland, partly due to its ruler at the time, Robert the Bruce declaring his country a haven for them. The Pope had previously excommunicated Bruce for his role in the murder of John Comyn of Badenoch at Greyfriars Kirk in Dumfries.

A legend suggests that during the persecution of the Order, its members in France secretly removed the treasure of the Knights Templar from Paris to Balantrodoch. A local tale referring to the graveyard in Temple says, *'Twixt the oak and the elm tree, you will find buried the millions free.'*[40] However, some researchers dispute this and suggest that as most of the Templars residing at the preceptory were English and not Scottish, anything of value would be handed over to King Edward I. However, many writers describe the Templars as faithful to their order, so it is pretty likely that politically they switched allegiance to preserve their relics and inheritance – which, for them, was everything.

With the fall of the Order, the Knights of St John in Jerusalem took their lands and buildings. Also called the Hospitallers, their chief Scottish seat was at Torphichen, a place we later discovered to be a node point on the Holy Axis.

In 2004, while attending a Sauniere Society conference with Henry Lincoln and other famous authors on the Templars and Rosslyn Chapel, I was allowed to visit Temple House next door to the church built over the site of the early preceptory. One of the speakers at the conference knew the owner and asked me if I would be willing to dowse 'something unusual' in the house.

After brief introductions, the owner led us to a small empty subterranean vault supported by two pillars. We wondered if the cellar belonged to the preceptory and if it was the alleged hiding place of the treasure alluded to in the local tale. At the time, we suggested that the pillars represented the two pillars of Freemasonry. Although we left none the wiser, I did sense the strong presence of a female dragon current flowing through the crypt, which sixteen years later proved correct, as it is here that we dowsed the Bride current.

Bride also visits the old parish church nearby, which like the house, is built over part of the 12th-century preceptory that initially took the form of a monastery – the building dates from the 1300s, probably built by the Knights of St John or the Hospitallers.

In 2002, *The Scotsman* newspaper reported that 'a mysterious carved stone' had been uncovered in the graveyard by workers reinforcing one of its walls. It appeared to be the top of a sarcophagus with Norse inscriptions. Local historian and author John Ritchie stated that carvings on it were crude and primitive and unlike anything he had seen before. He further commented that the symbols on the stone *'look like Viking sun compasses, while the dials at the top look a little bit like a Celtic cross but with notches carved on them.'* Other experts believe it is from the 13th or 14th century and represents the burial of a Templar knight or Hospitaller.[41]

In the 1990s, I came to Temple with my late friend John Beasley and dowsed an energy line from the Temple Church to St Mary's Chapel at Mount Lothian. We eventually discovered that the line was part of a small but incredibly accurate four-point ley precisely 12 miles (19 km) long. It starts at St Mary's Chapel, then travels north through Temple Church to Crichton Collegiate Church on the Lugh current, and

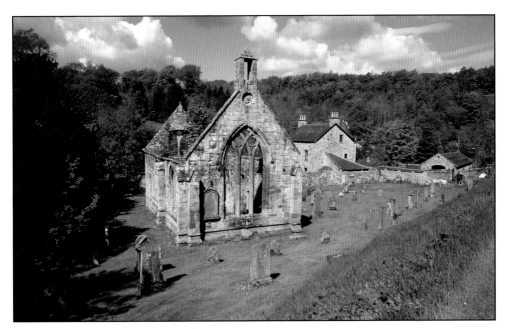

Ruin of Old Parish Church at Temple

finally to the ruined church at Keith Marischal in the parish of Humbie, East Lothian, built by Harvey de Keith. This chapel has serpentine spiral carvings on the windows and an unidentified tombstone of a crusading knight, probably a memorial to Sir William Keith, who accompanied Sir James Douglas and William St Clair as they carried the heart of Robert the Bruce to the Holy Land. The ley also passes over a hill called Dodridge Law just to the southeast of here.

Interestingly, the name 'dod' is often associated with many leys across the UK. So for what purpose does this short alignment marking these four fascinating sites serve? Could these places be connected to the old Knights Templar or possibly the early Freemasons of Scotland?

After dowsing Bride at the church ruins, we follow her flow through the village and across playing fields on the east side of the main road. Here, the current passes through a single carved stone arch said to be the remains of an entrance leading to Temple House, built in the 17th century by Laird Stephen Boyd. From here, the current heads northeast to Rosslynlee Hospital and Roslin Glen.

1.   Tokely, A. V. 2004. *The Kirk Yetholm Gypsies*. Hawick Archaeological Society, Hawick.
2.   http://mirrorofisis.freeyellow.com/id153.html
3.   Marwick, E. 1975. *The Folklore of Orkney and Shetland*. Rowman and Littlefield, Washington, DC.
4.   Michell, J.1983. *The New View Over Atlantis*. Thames & Hudson, London.

5. 16. 17. 19. 20. 37. Moffat, A. 1999. *Arthur and the Lost Kingdoms*. Wiedenfeld & Nicholson, London.

6. 7. Moffat, A. 2006. *Kelsae: A History of Kelso from Earliest Times*. Birlinn Ltd, Edinburgh.

8. https://canmore.org.uk/site/58418/kelso-bridge-street-abbey

9. 11. http://www.themasonictrowel.com/ebooks/fm_freemasonry/Bernier_The_Great_Architects_of_Tiron.pdf

10. Wylie, J. A. 1886. *History of the Scottish Nation* Vol. I. Hamilton, Adams & Co, Boston, USA.

12. Elder, I. H. 1962. *Celt, Druid and Culdee*. Covenant Publishing, London.

13. https://archive.org/details/b24886002

14. https://www.englishmonarchs.co.uk/monymusk_reliquary.htm

15. Knight, C. & Butler, A. 2010. *The Hiram Key Revisited*. Watkins Publishing, London.

18. https://www.calgaryburnsclub.com *Arthur and the Lost City*

21. https://www.bartleby.com/333/451.html

22. https://canmore.org.uk/site/55631/old-melrose-st-cuthberts-chapel

23. Bower, J. 1827. *Description of the Abbeys of Melrose and Old Melrose, with their Traditions*. Self Published, Edinburgh.

24. Moffat, A. 2002. *The Borders: A History of the Borders from Earliest Times*. Deerpark Press, Selkirk.

25. https://www.sacred-texts.com/neu/celt/tsm/tsm15.htm

26. https://allpoetry.com/Thomas-the-Rhymer

27. https://www.gutenberg.org/files/9842/9842-h/9842-h.htm

28. Coppens, P. 2007. *Land of the Gods*. Frontier Publishing, Amsterdam.

29. 31. 32. Sinclair, A. 2002. *The Sword and the Grail: The Story of the Grail, the Templars and the True Discovery of America*. Birlinn Ltd, Edinburgh.

30. Broun, D. Harrison, J. 2007. *The Chronicle of Melrose Abbey: a Stratigraphic Edition*. Volume I: Introduction and Facsimile Edition (Scottish History Society 6th Series)

31. Bower, J. 1813. *Description of the Abbeys of Melrose and Old Melrose, with their traditions*. Self-published by the author.

33. https://en.wikipedia.org/wiki/Walter_Scott

34. Callahan, P. 2001. *Ancient Mysteries, Modern Visions*. Acres, U.S.A

35. Morris, J, 1980. *'Nennius' British History and the Welsh Annals*. Phillimore, London.

36. Skene, W. F. 1868. *The Four Ancient Books of Wales*. Pantianos Classics.

38. Glennie, J. S. 1869. *Arthurian Localities*. Llanerch Press, Somerset.

39. http://www.knightstemplar.org/KnightTemplar.

40. Coppens, P. 2021. *The Stone Puzzle of Rosslyn Chapel*. Adventures Unlimited Press, Amsterdam.

41. https://www.scotsman.com/news/mystery-stone-found-near-church-linked-knights-templar-2443278

Chapter 7

Rosslyn
The Chapel of the Grail

Rosslyn Chapel, officially known as the Collegiate Chapel of St Matthew, stands on College Hill, precisely marking the Holy Axis, overlooking the deep gorge of Roslin Glen. Sir William St Clair (1410–1484), First Earl of Caithness, 11th Baron of Roslin and Third Earl of Orkney, built the incredibly ornate gothic building between 1446–1486, although he died before the laying of the final stone. William was a 'Master of the Work' and supervised every stage of its construction, including each carving and decoration.

Researchers believe the geomantic location of the chapel on the hill's summit high above a U-bend in the North River Esk adheres to the principles of feng shui. By harnessing the hidden energy beneficial to the well-being of nature called chi, Sir William created his family seat as a 'place of power', thus ensuring balance, harmony and well-being in life and for his future dynasty, like the ancient emperors of China.

Rosslyn Chapel

Lewis Spence (1874–1955), respected writer, folklorist and researcher of occult mysteries, wrote, '...*nothing can shake my conviction that Rosslyn was built according to the pattern of the Chapel of the Grail as pictured in Norman romance.*' He also noted that William St Clair had in his poet's mind a vision of the 'Chapel Perilous' when designing his new chapel.[1] The term 'chapel perilous' first appeared in Sir Thomas Malory's *Le Morte d'Arthur* (1485) as the setting for an adventure where the sorceress Hellawes unsuccessfully attempts to seduce Sir Lancelot. It also refers to a psychological state in which an individual is uncertain whether some experience was affected by a supernatural force or imagination. After some research, I discovered that the chapel certainly tests your belief in the supernatural, and here Lugh, the Lancelot archetype, meets with Bride.

The chapel stands south of the village of Roslin, its name according to *Scottish Place Names* translates as 'morass at the pool'[2], although this landscape feature no longer exists. In the 18th century, Forbes believed the original name was *Roskelyn* from the Gaelic meaning 'hill in a glen'.[3] Others claim *ros* means promontory or ridge and *lin*, a waterfall, remnants of which still cascades from the hill below the chapel. However, the meaning of ros is ambiguous when converting Gaelic to English. Many sources believe it refers to 'rose' rather than promontory, and *lin* or *linn* translates as 'generation' or 'lineage', which has led some alternative researchers to deduce that the name refers to a holy bloodline or indicates a north–south ley that runs through the chapel from Arthur's Seat, known as the Rose Line.[4]

Over the years, this tiny yet grand and ornate building has inspired and intrigued those who seek a deeper meaning to life, nature, spirituality and the otherworldly, for amid the intricate carvings and symbolic architecture are clues that may unlock these mysteries. However, this secret knowledge is not given freely, as it is veiled in allegory to challenge the layperson and the initiated to decipher the hidden code. Trevor Ravenscroft, who wrote *The Spear of Destiny,* says, '*Rosslyn Chapel is a temple to the spirituality and mysticism that transcends all of the great religions and yet pervades each one of them.*'[5]

For decades, Rosslyn Chapel has inspired artists, poets, musicians and writers to visit and record its mysteries, including Burns, Wordsworth, Byron and Sir Walter Scott. More recently, iconic books such as *The Holy Blood and the Holy Grail* in 1982,[6] *The Hiram Key* in 1996 [7] and *The Da Vinci Code* in 2003 [8] have propelled it onto the global stage.

The chapel's foundation as a collegiate church in 1446 enabled its members to form an organised society or college not presided over by a bishop and with no diocesan responsibilities. During that time, Scotland's leading families established more than thirty-seven collegiate churches, including the Crichtons, just a short distance south from here on the Lugh current and the Forresters at Corstorphine in Edinburgh on the Elen current of the Belinus Line. In *The Stone Puzzle of Rosslyn Chapel*, Coppens states, '*They were probably secular foundations intended to spread intellectual and spiritual knowledge, and the extravagance of their construction depended on the wealth of their founder, which in the case of the Sinclairs was more substantial.*'[9] Therefore, the building of a collegiate church was a feasible and subtle way to encode a message in stone for future generations without the scrutiny and control of the Catholic Church.

My first visit to the chapel in 1996 was in the company of my late friend John, a fellow quester of esoteric mysteries. At that time, no visitor's centre, bookshop, cafe or large car park existed. The main entrance was through a cottage, once the old Rosslyn Inn, where I remember a cheerful elderly lady taking our entrance fee and giving me an information leaflet. Upon entering the gloomy interior, I noticed the quality of the intricate stone carvings above the pillars depicting a Green Man and various fauna. There was so much to see that I wandered around in a daze, not focusing on any particular carving. So much of it was extraordinary and impressive, like its solid stone barrelled roof with stars carved in relief and the exquisite Lady Chapel with its elaborate Apprentice Pillar and Master Mason Pillar.

For over an hour, I gazed at the finest stone carvings I had ever seen. Then John came over and explained that Freemasons from around the world revered this chapel, and many believed it was a symbolic representation of King Solomon's Temple. As I wandered around, shuffling through the crowds of visitors, I noticed three pillars at the entrance to the Lady Chapel, which reminded me of an ancient Greek temple. The entire building, with all its fabulous carvings of exotic foliage and flowers, its green men and dragons, felt more like a pagan shrine than a Christian chapel. The spiral carved Apprentice pillar is the finest feature of the chapel that many believe represents 'The Tree of Life' symbolic of the 'axis mundi' and a focal point of the whole building. Its original name was the Prince's Pillar, named after the chapel's founder, William St Clair, Prince of Orkney. I had the impression that the pillar and many of the carvings were trying to tell me that the Earth is just one of many levels of existence, and after attaining enlightenment, we can move between them.

That first tour with John sparked a life-long fascination with Rosslyn, inspiring me to read almost every book published about its mystery and history. I also attended, whenever possible, organised lectures and tours concerning the chapel and listened to presentations by excellent researchers and authors, including Andrew and Niven Sinclair, Robert Knight and Christopher Lomas, Henry Lincoln, Alan Butler, Robert Brydon, Jim Munro and the late John Ritchie.

During the building of Rosslyn Chapel, Europe was experiencing an age of enlightenment that embraced a new renaissance of artistry, ideas and political and economic rebirth, breaking the thread of conventional thinking. Many believe that its stonemasons encoded these new ideas and practices into Rosslyn's carvings, many following the principles of Hermeticism.

The numerous legends and theories surrounding the chapel make for fascinating reading, but for every book that reveals a mystery, there is one to debunk. For example, many academics claim that Rosslyn is not concealing a secret or hidden knowledge but is merely a folly or a 15th-century place of Christian worship for a devout Catholic family. Others believe it is the Holy Grail in stone, where the Knights Templar stored their treasure, including the mummified head of Christ.

The quality and quantity of the carvings inside the chapel are hard to ignore and surpass all known 15th-century British masonry – only the Alhambra in Spain and some of the Renaissance carvings in Italy come close. John Ritchie and Alan Butler in *Rosslyn Chapel Decoded* believe that the Tironensian monks who built the magnificent Kelso Abbey on the Bride current and later Kilwinning Abbey, southwest of Glasgow, had a hand in creating some of the carvings at Rosslyn.[10] The word Freemason derives from the right of skilled working masons to travel without needing permission from an overlord.

The Tironensian monks, as mentioned earlier at Kelso, were a 12th-century order of stonemasons from France who favoured the teachings of the old Celtic Church. They were at the forefront of Gothic architecture, particularly in France and were directly involved with building and designing the great cathedral at Chartres, fifty miles southwest of Paris. Sadly, all of the

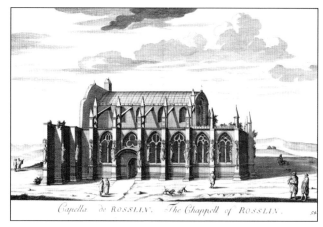

Etching of Rosslyn Chapel by John Slezer, 1693

Tironensian abbeys in Scotland were stripped of their finery and stone carvings after the Reformation, making it almost impossible for us to compare. However, from what we learned at Kelso, they were highly skilled stonemasons demonstrating their art as an act of piety over general monastic worship.

The St Clair Dynasty

When William St Clair laid the foundation stone at Rosslyn Chapel in 1410, he had more wealth than the royal family, owning vast areas of Scotland. He was highly decorated and influential as Lord High Admiral of Scotland, Lord Chancellor of Scotland and the first Lord St Clair. He was also a protector of the young James Stuart, the future James I of Scotland. According to antiquary Father Richard Augustine Hay (1661–1736), St Clair was appointed the hereditary office of patron and protector of Scottish Masons by King James II.[11]

The St Clairs trace their lineage to Rognvald the Mighty, the Earl of More, who lived near Trondheim in Norway. His second son Rollo invaded northern France and created the dukedom of Normandie in 928 CE. He married Grizele, daughter of King Charles the Simple of France of the Carolingian dynasty. Walderne or Waldernus (1006–1047), grandson of Richard II Duc de Normandie, became the first Count de St Clare. According to the authors of *The Holy Blood and the Holy Grail*, the Saint-Clair's were part of the so-called 'Rex Deus' families behind the Merovingian dynasty, a ruling family of the Franks of Gaul from the 5th century until 751.[12]

In 1068, Walderne's son William 'the Seemly', accompanied by another knight, Ladislaus Leslyn, escorted the exiled Princess Margaret Atheling to Scotland to meet her future husband, King Malcolm Canmore. A carving on the south wall of Rosslyn Chapel, often referred to as 'two brothers on one horse', is said to be William with the young princess riding pillion holding a relic known as the 'Holy Rood' as part of her dowry. The Holy Rood was, according to historians, a piece of Christ's crucifixion cross contained within a golden cruciform casket. After marrying King Malcolm in 1070, some sources believe that Margaret gifted the settlement of Roslin to the St Clair's and placed the Holy Rood there, declaring that a chapel should stand on the spot. Some say the Holy Rood is still within the chapel today in the vaults awaiting some destined discovery.

William the Seemly (c 1028–1078) became a steward in Malcolm and Margaret's royal court and married Dorothy, daughter of Gospatric Earl of Dunbar and Earl of Northumbria. Their son Henry fought alongside King Malcolm in 1093 and died during the siege of Alnwick in Northumberland. He also participated in the First Crusade to the Holy Land with Godfroi de Bouillon in 1096, who became the first ruler of the Kingdom of Jerusalem.

In 1700, Father Hay compiled the St Clair's early history, or the Sinclair family as they became known, called *A Geneologie of the Sainteclaires of Rosslyn*, from a set of papers since destroyed in a fire. As such, much of Hay's history is unproven, including the St Clair's descent from Norwegian nobility. Many authors have tried to substantiate his information with differing success. So it remains unverified but enigmatic, for Hay's writings still inspire those who seek the St Clair dynasty's fascinating history and impressive lineage.

The St Clairs continued to be very influential within the royal courts of Scotland during medieval times. Sir Henry, 7th Baron of Roslin and his sons William and John, fought alongside the great Scottish warrior hero Robert the Bruce at Bannockburn. When the king died in 1329, William and John accompanied Sir James Douglas and four other knights, one being Sir William Keith mentioned earlier, to take his heart on a holy quest to Jerusalem. Unfortunately, they were all killed during an attack by the Moors at Teba in southern Spain, and Bruce's heart returned to Melrose Abbey on the Bride current. The mounted grave slab near the north door of the chapel inscribed 'Willhm de Sinncler' is said to have belonged to the William killed at Teba. His tomb initially lay within the graveyard of the old chapel of St Matthews below the car park. Its carvings depict a foliated cross and sword, symbols often associated with the Knights Templar.

However, many writers claim that although the St Clairs had links with the Knights Templar, they were never members of the order. Moreover, given the power of the St Clairs in political and religious affairs, it seems unlikely that they would be part of such an organisation that preached chastity and poverty and protected pilgrims along the routes to the Holy Land. More likely, as 'movers and shakers' of society, they secretly sponsored the order.

Sir Henry (c.1345–1400), 9th Baron of Roslin, First Prince of Orkney, Lord of Shetland, Admiral of the Seas and more titles besides, was second only to the king and, due to his rank and influence, was allowed to mint coins and make laws within his territories. There are claims that he sailed to the Americas with Venetian explorer Antonio Zeno, one hundred years before Columbus, and that the carvings of maize and aloe cactus in the chapel are testimony to that voyage.

Sir Oliver St Clair, the 12th Baron, led the Scottish army against the English at Solway Firth in 1542 but was captured and taken to London, where he swore allegiance to Henry VIII. However, after breaking this oath, he disappeared. His brother Henry, Bishop of Ross, became one of the twelve Privy Councillors to Mary, Queen of Scots, and in 1541, he was named abbot of the monastery at Kilwinning. Oliver's son John became Bishop of Brechin and presided over the disastrous marriage of Mary, Queen of Scots and Henry Stuart, Lord Darnley.

The St Clair's of Rosslyn remained close advisors to the Scottish kings, particularly Marie de Guise, the French mother of Mary, Queen of Scots. In 1546, she wrote in a letter to Sir William, the 13th Baron, that included a somewhat mysterious message: *'Likewise that we shall be a loyal and true mistress to him, his council and secret shown to us we shall keep secret.'*[13]

They continued to support her daughter Mary to help retain her throne. But, interestingly, rather than Sir William pledging his allegiance to the Queen Regent, the Queen Regent pronounced her obedience and loyalty to him. But, what was the 'secret' Marie de Guise swore to keep?

Reading through the lineage of the St Clairs and their connections, I soon realised that they were one of the most powerful families in Europe and probably helped to influence governments and kings.

How the chapel escaped destruction from all the many Scottish wars and local conflicts is a miracle unless it had some special 'Masonic' protection. Even Cromwell ordered his troops to spare the chapel, something out of character for him, but he was a Master Mason.

With no male heirs, Sir William, the 19th and last Baron of Rosslyn (1700 – 1788), resigned as hereditary Grand Master of the Grand Lodge of Scotland Freemasons. His only surviving child Sarah inherited the lands and chapel and married Sir Peter Wedderburn of Chester Hall. Their son Alexander Wedderburn St Clair carried out several repairs to the chapel and became the First Earl of Rosslyn. After he died in 1805, his nephew Sir James St Clair-Erskine succeeded him. Queen Victoria visited the chapel in 1842 and, after witnessing its ruined and overgrown state, requested that the present owner James Alexander St Clair Erskine, the 3rd Earl, restore the chapel. He introduced stained glass windows, added an altar to the sacristy and repaired many of the carvings.

Dowsing the Chapel

After spending some time dowsing in and around the chapel and castle, we began to sense that Roslin Glen's geography and geology were crucial to understanding its mystery, a rarely-mentioned subject by many Rosslyn researchers and authors.

We arrived at the chapel early midweek, hoping it would be relatively quiet, but by 10.00 am, several tour buses had already arrived from Edinburgh. So we quickly entered through the visitor centre, bypassing its lovely café and fascinating exhibition to explore the chapel courtyard. The sight of the chapel is always breathtaking, whatever the season, but on this sunny day, we were mesmerised by how the sunlight brought out the stone's evocative myriad of colours.

Dowsing can often be tricky within highly monitored places like this, and some sadly view the practice as disrespectful. Also, others see the pointed metal rods as dangerous, especially around children in crowded areas. But, we produced our little copper rods from the rucksack, easy to hide in our pockets if needed. We decided to dowse around the chapel's exterior first to see if the Holy Axis' male and female serpent lines connect with the building.

Once we tuned into the site, we reacquainted ourselves with the serpent energies by visualising the female Bride as the Earth Goddess with her Grail cup and Lugh, the male, as the warrior god with his spear. Once our dowsing had confirmed they were present, we took turns locating their path by walking around the chapel's perimeter and then compared our results. Although we detected many earth energy lines passing through the building, we were excited to find the Bride current entering through the south door and leaving by the north entrance, her flow strong and width expansive. Moreover, we noticed overlooking her flow the carving of William the Seemly, supposedly carrying the young St Margaret to Scotland. The early stonemasons may

have left us a clue to Bride's presence here, as an exquisite dragon carving on the chapel's exterior at the base of a window next to the south door also marks her flow.

When focussing on Lugh, our rods swung towards the west door of the baptistry, his width slightly narrower than his female counterpart. We picked him up again at the east end of the chapel, passing through the crypt. Here the current incorporates the boss carving of a Green Man by the east window and a winged head of Mercury. Above it is an alcove that perhaps housed a statue, where we noticed a hidden carving of a pentagram set into the underside of its upper ledge.

Carving of a dragon at Rosslyn Chapel

Carving of a green man at Rosslyn Chapel

Carving of the head of Mercury at Rosslyn Chapel

At this point, we decided to locate the node inside the chapel and were surprised to find only a handful of visitors remaining, the perfect moment to start dowsing the interior. First, we detected Lugh encompassing the whole of the baptistry, including its font, before travelling along the central axis of the chapel. Then we noticed his width started to shrink to a point just east of the north and south

doorways, where he formed a node with Bride at what appeared to be an unmarked spot on the floor. But, as we looked directly above, we noticed a pyramid-shaped pendant with Sinclair cross shields at the apex of an arch, which pointed down at the crossing place of the two currents. I immediately asked a guide what the pendant

Pendant Keystone, Rosslyn Chapel (courtesy of Kjetil Bjørnsrud)

represented, and she informed us, '*It's the chapel's keystone, the building's pivotal core.*' We both looked at one another wide-eyed and then she added, '*It is supposed to be the last stone inserted into the building.*'

Whilst researching Rosslyn's keystone, we came across some interesting theories. Some say that it represents a holistic integration of 'X', 'sacred' and 'matter', and 'Y' or 'Yod', symbolising the manifestation process and the appearance of the mystical in the physical. Others say it points to secret vaults below the floor, the hiding place of the Holy Grail.

Authors Knight and Lomas discovered that the foundation plan of Rosslyn Chapel is similar in design to that of Herod's Temple complex in Jerusalem, built on the foundations of the destroyed King Solomon's Temple. In addition, they noticed that the eight eastern pillars created a triple tau cross.[14] The *tau* is the last letter in the Hebrew alphabet, which like the Greek letter *omega*, signifies the ending of something, perhaps the quest for the Grail. They also found a six-pointed star or hexagram representing Solomon's Seal within the temple's design through the positioning of certain pillars.

Coppens noted that the proportions almost match when superimposing a plan of Solomon's Temple over Rosslyn Chapel.[15] Interestingly, we noticed that the inner sanctum or 'Holy of Holies' of Solomon's Temple corresponds with the exact spot in Rosslyn Chapel where we discovered the node of Lugh and Bride. The inner sanctum in Solomon's Temple also housed the enigmatic Ark of the Covenant.

Knight and Lomas believe the vaults under the chapel marked by the keystone contain ancient scrolls of forbidden history, and ultrasound ground scans have established cavities under the chapel's floor. They also suggest that the landscape around Rosslyn Chapel overlooking a deep glen mirrors the topography of Jerusalem, with the Kidron Valley to the east and the Valley of Hinnom to the south. King Solomon's Temple had pillars on either side of its eastern entrance, and Rosslyn Chapel's Apprentice Pillar and Master Pillar are at the east end of the Lady Chapel by the entrance to the crypt.[16]

On a lintel next to the Apprentice pillar is the only carved inscription in the chapel, and its Latin translation reads: '*Wine is strong, a King is stronger, Women are even stronger, but truth conquers all.*' Many believe it to be a key to decoding the mystery of the chapel. It derives from a passage in the Bible (*Esdras 9:37*), written as a trail of wisdom for the three youths who formed the bodyguard of Persian King Darius the Great. One of the three was Zerubbabel, Prince of Judah, who requested to leave captivity and return to rebuild the temple of the 'most high' in Jerusalem, which the king would permit and fund if he solved the riddle: '*Which is the strongest, the strength of wine, the strength of the King or the strength of Women.*' The verse is a reminder of a pivotal event leading to the rebuilding of the Temple of Jerusalem that historians have dated to 520 BCE.

When observing a ground plan of the present chapel, the later addition of the baptistry in 1881 created a new geographical centre, which happens to be the location of the node of the Holy Axis marked by the keystone above. Knight and Lomas believe the baptistry is an 'invasive carbuncle' constructed of a different coloured stone. But did the architect intentionally change the chapel's dimensions to improve its acoustics, adding the keystone to signify its new omphalos?

Francis Robert St Claire-Erskine, the fourth Earl of Rosslyn, added the baptistry and renovated the chapel with new stained-glass windows during the 1860s. In 1871, he became the 69th Grand Master Mason of Scotland, head of the Supreme Royal Arch Chapter of Scotland and member of the Royal Order of Scotland, the Religious and Military Order of the Temple and the Supreme Grand Council of the Thirty-Three and last degree of the Ancient and Accepted Scottish Rite. Queen Victoria also appointed him as her Captain of the Gentlemen-at-Arms. After St Claire-Erskine completed the restoration, he attended the chapel's rededication on Tuesday, 22 April 1862 and hosted

a grand Masonic gathering in 1870 with the attendance of over 600 Freemasons.[17] Again, we sensed that this man was another 'mover and shaker'.

He requested a spot in the southwest corner of the churchyard at Rosslyn for his magnificent 10ft (3m) high tomb. A curious epitaph from a poem written in 1889 on the monument reads, '*Safe, safe at last from doubt, from storm, from strife. Moored in the depths of Christ's unfathomed grave.*' Researchers believe it is an allegory alluding to Christ's resurrection and having no final resting place. Being a high-ranking 33-degree Mason, the Fourth Earl did not appear to be someone who would carelessly build a baptistry to look like a 'monstrous carbuncle'. He would almost certainly have known about the importance of sacred proportion and harmony of structure and direction, including his grave's location.

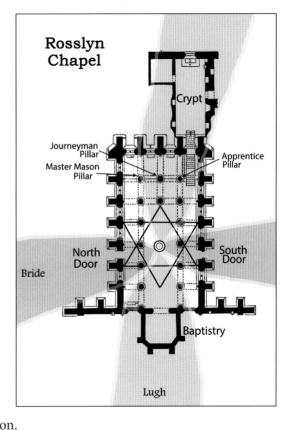

During our second dowsing trip to the chapel a year later, we noticed a line of visitors queuing up to stand on the node below the keystone. After approaching the guide in charge of the group, she explained that '*many people feel something extraordinary whilst standing on that spot, and I often tell visitors to stand there during my talk to test their reaction.*' Intriguingly, the guide mentioned that a few people had sensed two 'ley lines' crossing there; some even call it the 'Grail point'. Other dowsers, including our friend Stuart Dow, who runs a popular Facebook group, *Ley Lines and Earth Energies*, independently dowsed the chapel and found the same node of the Bride and Lugh serpent lines under the keystone.

The vault below the node supposedly contains several St Clair burials, including the chapel's founder. Coppens cites a 1774 account by John Sleezer: '…*at the foot of the third and fourth pillars, between them and the north wall, there is a large flagstone that covers the opening of a vault which is the burial place of the family of Roslin.*' He also states, '*The vault is so dry that their bodies have been found entire after 80 years and as fresh as when first buried of old in their armour, without any coffin.*'[18]

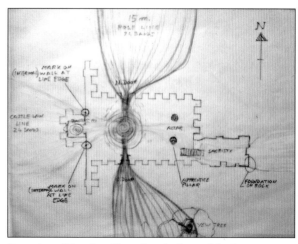

Drawing of Rosslyn Chapel node dowsed by Stuart Dow

Sir Walter Scott described the vault in *The Lay of the Last Minstrel*:

'Seemed all on fire that chapel proud,
Where Roslin's chiefs uncoffined lie:
Each Baron, for a sable shroud,
Sheathed in his iron panoply…
There are twenty of Roslin's barons bold
Lie buried within that proud chapelle.'[19]

Coppens concludes that these long-dead St Clairs were '*everlasting Knights of the Grail, on sentry duty over the mysteries entrusted in their keeping.*'

The chapel was probably not the first on this site, and Knight and Lomas claim that a Roman temple of Mithras lies beneath the chapel. Others say that, like Chartres Cathedral, it stands over a subterranean megalithic chamber, which the St Clairs used as their burial vault. However, it is more likely that an underground vault already existed here, belonging to the original castle built by an earlier St Clair.

Entwined dragon carving on external wall of baptistry, Rosslyn Chapel

Many dragons or serpent carvings adorn the interior and exterior of the chapel, including intricately carved entwined dragon figures. One overlooks the chapel's northwest corner on the baptistry's exterior wall, and another is located above William Sinclair's grave, both carvings on Lugh's flow. When we pointed them out to the tour guide, she explained, '*The dragons are supposed to represent the fighting dragons of legend either in the story of Ludd or Merlin*'. I then told her that if they are 'fighting dragons', why are they harmoniously entwined? The guide gazed at the beautifully carved creatures and became intrigued by my observation. She showed us a similar carving overlooking the Apprentice Pillar. The elaborately carved Apprentice Pillar has eight entwined serpents at its base, also visited by the Lugh current as he flows towards the crypt. Perhaps William St Clair, who personally organised the chapel's carvings, must have known about the serpent earth energy lines that intertwine here over the St Clair burial vault.

The width of the female serpent inside the chapel incorporates another dragon carving and the gravestone of William St Clair, who died fighting the Moors in Spain in 1330. Also on her flow are two stained-glass windows depicting dragon slayers, one of St Michael overlooking the south door and the other of St George over the north entrance, a dragon entwined around his feet with one eye open. St George and St Michael were considered the heavenly twins, the protectors of humankind. Michael is the ruler of the heavens, whilst George is his earthly counterpart – perhaps the guardian of the earth's energy matrix. There are many images of the dragon slayers St George and St Michael around the world, which depict them pinning the dragon to the ground without piercing it. Perhaps they are an allegory of man's control over the serpent lines within the land. Moreover, St George holding a spear may represent a ley that has drawn the dragon lines to twist around it like a caduceus, like the Lugh and Bride lines of the Holy Axis.

Dragon carvings at the base of the Apprentice Pillar, Rosslyn Chapel (by kind permission of Rosslyn Chapel Trust)

Entwined dragon carving, Rosslyn Chapel (by kind permission of Rosslyn Chapel Trust)

In *The New View Over Atlantis*, John Michell reminds us that the true origins of 'dragon slaying' lie within the principles of fertility. The role of the slayer-saints was replaced in medieval times by local noble families and their descendants. [20]

Depicted in windows on either side of St George are St Longinus and St Mauritius, two notable Christian archetypes of Lugh and his magic spear. Longinus was a Roman soldier said to have pierced the side of Christ with a lance while on the cross. The lance's spearhead became a powerful occult relic called 'The Spear of Destiny' that at one time fell into the hands of Adolf Hitler. Just as the Holy Grail transitioned from being a Celtic otherworld cauldron to the cup of Christ, the Spear of Lugh transformed into The Spear of Destiny or 'Lance of Longinus'. Mauritius was an Egyptian military leader who headed the legendary Theban Legion of Rome in the 3rd century and became a patron saint of the German Holy Roman Emperors. He also possessed The Spear of Destiny, which he carried into battle.[21]

Lugh flows through the crypt exiting through its altar and the beautiful coloured stained-glass window of Christ, said to transmit healing powers. The window dates from 1954 and is dedicated to the 5th Earl of Rosslyn (1869-1939). The window portrays Christ within a double-diamond-shaped cartouche with arms raised in the act of blessing. Beneath is a Latin inscription: '*In your light we shall see the divine light*'. According to Barry Dunford in *Vision of Albion: The Key to the Holy Grail*, the diamond configuration is an alchemical mandala transmitting what may be called the 'Diamond Light Body' blessing of Christ, known to Taoism, Buddhism and the Rosicrucians.[22]

This lower vault was built by Lady Margaret Douglas, the first wife of the chapel's builder, although some researchers say the crypt is much older than the chapel. The fireplace on the north wall has led some to speculate that it was a residence for the priests. However, the most curious feature here is the incised patterns on the south wall, believed to be working drawings for many of the carvings in the chapel, including a pentagram.

The Pillars of Rosslyn and the Venus Connection

From the node, Lugh continues along the axis of the church, his flow widening to encompass the three pillars. Before the 18th century, the Apprentice Pillar was the Prince's Pillar and the Master-mason's Pillar the Earl's Pillar. The central pillar, known as the Journeyman Pillar, was called the Shekinah Pillar. These original names, I believe, are a clue to the mystery of the chapel.

At one time, the Apprentice Pillar was the only ornately carved pillar in the chapel, the Master Mason's Pillar having been hidden under plaster to conceal its Masonic significance. Its full glory was revealed in the 1860s by Master Mason David Bryce.

Knight and Lomas believe the three pillars represent the Freemasonic ritual of the 'three degrees' that the initiates have to undertake to become a Master Mason. These degrees are the 'Entered Apprentice', 'Fellow Craft' and 'Master Mason'. In addition, the three may represent the trinity, Father, Son, and Holy Spirit.[23]

If we compare the three – the Apprentice Pillar is circular, the Master Mason's Pillar square and the Journeyman Pillar is octagonal. Here

Interior of Rosslyn Chapel, painting by Louis Daguerre (1787–1851)

178

we have a circle, square, and octagon, three significant shapes in sacred geometry. The circle represents heaven, the square earth, and the octagon is the perfect balance between them, signifying 'eternal life'. In Freemasonry, the Journeyman is a qualified apprentice who has evolved and been set free. Curiously, the Dome of the Rock temple on the original Temple of Solomon site is also a perfect octagon.

Tim Wallace-Murphy compared the Apprentice Pillar to the world tree or *Yggdrasil* of Norse Mythology associated with the ash tree and representative of the Christian Tree of Life – related to incarnation within the traditions of the Kabbalah.[24] In Scandinavian mythology, the gnawing dragons at the tree's base symbolise controlling the spread of knowledge. This tree's crown comprises the twelve zodiac constellations, the spiralling branches represent the planets, and the roots dig deep into the elements of the earth and the underworld. At the bottom of the pillar the Níðhöggr serpents or dragons can be seen gnawing at the roots to rob the tree of its fruitfulness and stunt its growth. This concept, I believe, relates to entropy.

Entropy is the gradual decline from order to disorder, a force that rules the third-dimensional plane on which we live. No matter how hard we try to create a utopia or perfection, the power of entropy will disrupt our endeavours. Gregory L Little, who co-authored *Origins of the Gods* with Andrew Collins, states that according to Native American mythology, there is a constant interplay between the spiritual energies of the upper and the lower worlds on Earth. One element seeks to create order and the other disorder. These opposing powers can manifest in different guises and shapes and account for many natural and supernatural forces.[25] The creatures of the sky, such as eagles, hawks and swans, represent spiritual and creative powers from the upper world, and creatures that live underground, like snakes, represent the lower world and entropy. The middle world or earth dimension is the domain of spirits that help and hinder humankind, epitomised by the 'trickster' or 'joker' that manifests order and disorder.

The powers of the three worlds merge here on the physical Earth plane in a symbolic dance of opposites, and the role of humans is to balance these forces. The Rosslyn snakes nibbling at the roots of the Tree of Life pillar represent disorder that mirrors our life's 'ups and downs'. We have learned that giving back to the earth through loving thoughts and actions is essential instead of constantly taking from it. Doing so can heal the land, cleanse the negativity we have caused as a race, and help balance the land and our lives. But we can never completely cure the world's problems, as the lesson is to understand the concept of entropy and balance here on this plane of existence and how it affects our lives.

Interestingly, there are fourteen freestanding pillars in Rosslyn Chapel, and Zoroaster, the founder of Zoroastrianism, the world's oldest monotheistic religion, carved the seven liberal arts on fourteen pillars, seven of bronze and seven of brick, to preserve them from flood and fire.

The original name of the middle pillar or the Journeyman Pillar was the Shekinah Pillar, 'Shekinah' being the Hebrew word for the glory of the divine presence or the dwelling place of the feminine essence of God, which perfectly explains the concept of the light ball phenomenon or plasma intelligence. Gnostic writings also refer to the Shekinah as God's hidden aspects, later becoming the Holy Ghost. Therefore, the original names of the Rosslyn pillars relate to the Father, Son, and the feminine fertilising essence of God that creates life called the Holy Ghost. They also relate to the

Sun, Moon and Venus, a trinity of celestial bodies worshipped in the ancient world from Babylon to Rome. From statements in the Bible and Freemasonic documents, Knight and Lomas in *The Book of Hiram: Freemasonry, Venus and the Secret Key to the Life of Jesus* deduce that the Shekinah is the periodic arrival of a bright light or mass of energy that would appear at ominous occasions and ceremonies. The authors suggest that the bright light was the planet Venus, known in Freemasonry as 'the morning star', also referred to as Lucifer, which in Latin means the 'light-bringer', that rises before the sun and follows it in the evening as the 'evening star'.[26]

Knight and Lomas further state that the worship of Venus is a practice seen in the Masonic ritual of the Third Degree. The Worshipful Master Mason directs the candidate to glance toward the east to observe a five-pointed star (pentagram) rising before the sun at dawn. Moreover, when the candidate rises from his symbolic death, the Worshipful Master embraces him at five points. This ceremony derives from the movements of the planet Venus around the sky as observed from the Earth. The orbit of Venus traces the design of the pentacle or five-pointed star, or more precisely, a five-petalled rose, as it touches the path of the sun every eight years when it returns to the same place in our sky on about the same date. After five repetitions, the planet returns to where it begins another 40-year cycle.

Thirteen Venusian orbits (8 x 224.8 days) almost equate to eight Earth years. So is it a coincidence that great Biblical kings such as Saul, David and Solomon worshipped Venus, and all ruled a complete Venusian cycle of forty years?[27]

Venusian numbers and symbolism are in abundance in Rosslyn. The chapel construction took forty years – thirteen angels are carved into the top of the three pillars – the Shekinah or Journeyman Pillar has eight sides with pentagonal carvings around the top, said to be Gordian knotwork. There are also eight dragons at the base of the Apprentice Pillar and numerous depictions of the five-petalled rose in the chapel.

Richard Merrick in *The Venus Blueprint* believes Rosslyn Chapel is a fertility temple to Venus,[28] a theory that Alan Butler and John Ritchie proved in their seminal book *Rosslyn Revealed: A Library in Stone*. The authors discovered a small pentagonal lightbox at the apex of the east window through which a blood-red light flooded the chapel at sunrise on St Matthew's Day. The chapel's dedication to St Matthew is significant. His feast day is the 21 September, the autumn equinox, when the hours of day and night are equal. However, as Venus is the third brightest object in the sky after the sun and moon, its light is strong enough to cast a shadow.[29]

The Apprentice Pillar, Rosslyn Chapel (courtesy of Cornell University Library)

For four years of its eight-year cycle, Venus rises before the sun with a bright luminescence that at first appears red due to the Earth's atmospheric conditions. This light illuminates dark passage tombs such as Newgrange on the winter solstice in Ireland and Bryn Celli Dhu in Anglesey, documented by Robert Lomas. Moreover, certain chapels and churches also have apertures that will capture the predawn light of Venus, including Masonic temples. According to Masonic rituals, the light of Venus represents fertility and rebirth. However, we believe the worship of Venus later substituted man's early encounters with intelligent plasma, possibly witnessed at the Temple of Solomon, of which Rosslyn is a modern representation.

In the Old Testament, the Shekinah (plasma intelligence) is said to appear to the tribes of Israel randomly and has the power to communicate with priests like an oracle. In many passages of the Old Testament, the Ark of the Covenant was considered very dangerous and capable of laying waste armies and cities, such as Jericho. When Moses climbed Mount Horeb, God appeared as a fiery ball of energy, described as a burning bush. God instructed Moses to build an Ark to certain specifications and cubit measurements so he could accompany the Tribes of Israel on their journey. In other words, the Ark was designed to contain and transport a ball of plasma called the 'Glory of the Lord'.

The Bible says the Lord appeared as a cloud during the day and a ball of fire at night. Interestingly UFO research is full of cases that describe either cloud anomalies in daylight hours or bright lights at night. Many UFO cases could be explained as plasma sightings, not nuts-and-bolts spaceships, but a conscious energy of a highly electromagnetic nature born out of mountainous regions, seismic areas, and the upper atmosphere. The highly electromagnetic nature of plasma creates an opening in time and space that will allow upper or lower entities to enter our dimension. There is also the possibility that aliens from another dimension or a parallel universe are visiting us.

Lomas and Knight, believe the function of the Temple of Solomon was to contain the Ark that housed the Shekinah (or plasma), which entered through a dormer window.[30] Certain ceremonies known only to early Freemasons supposedly summoned the Shekinah to the temple through the roof window to settle on the mercy seat of the Ark. The exact dimensions and design of the Ark enabled its electrostatic properties to prevent the plasma it held from losing its power so that it could remain in this lower vibrational world for longer and be more effective as an all-seeing, all-knowing oracle.

A document quoted by Lomas and Knight from 'The Royal Order of Scotland' claims that Masonic rituals go back to those established by Moses, and the Shekinah is the Glory of the Lord:

> 'The descent of the Divine Shekinah, first at the consecration of the Holy Tabernacle, and afterwards at the dedication of the Temple of the Lord by King Solomon, placing itself on the Ark or Mercy-seat of the Holy of Holies, covered by the wings of the Cherubim, where it continued to deliver its oracular responses for several generations.' [31]

The Freemasonic Royal Order of Scotland claims it can trace its royal roots back to Moses. Interestingly, the order maintains that the earliest lodge formed in Britain was not Kilwinning but Icolmkill, an early name for Iona.[32]

If Rosslyn Chapel is a replica of Solomon's Temple, its sacred structure may draw plasma from the glen or local geological faults to provide an oracle for the St Clairs, like the Ark of the Covenant. Perhaps a Masonic ritual was performed when the light of Venus shone into the chapel on St Matthew's Day. Exposure to high electromagnetic fields from plasma can affect the brain's 'temporal lobe' area and stimulate our latent psychic ability. Perhaps the summoning of this fourth state of matter somehow rewires our brains, enabling us to perceive a broader perspective of the electromagnetic spectrum. Maybe Rosslyn Chapel's dimensions and design create an etheric doorway to other existences, such as parallel worlds. Perhaps Sinclair's real secret was the ability to travel between worlds.

Interestingly, the name St Clair derives from *Sanctos Claros*, meaning 'holy light', a magical luminescence that, according to many writers, has haunted the Sinclair dynasty and the buildings they inhabit for generations. Perhaps people with specific DNA attract plasma intelligence, which explains why certain UFO witnesses have experienced multiple sightings of these balls of light throughout their lives. Maybe those born with a higher level of consciousness also attract plasma.

Many writers have described the Grail as a blinding light moving about in mid-air, perfectly representing the many accounts I have read relating to plasma. If Rosslyn's design and layout are to attract plasma intelligence, then it has all the hallmarks of a Grail Chapel.

Where Lugh exits the baptistry, we noticed three stone piscinae and a section of later masonry used to block up the aisles at the western end of the chapel. These are remnants of a larger church that continued westwards, its foundations now marked by a perimeter wall. According to guidebooks, this extension included the beginnings of a tower and nave planned by the chapel's founder but abandoned after his death.

It was discovered in the 19th century when excavations uncovered traces of a building that extended 91 ft (27.7 m) beyond the chapel's original west door, an area incorporating the baptistry and St Matthew's churchyard. These findings were further substantiated using ground-scan radar analysis in 1980. Curiously, these ground scans also showed that the buried foundation stones were not substantial enough to hold the weight of a more significant structure and only provided a mere outline of its intended footings.

When Knight and Lomas asked Dr Jack Millar, head of geological studies from Cambridge University, to examine the chapel in 1997, he believed the west wall to be a mere folly, not an unfinished section of an intended larger building. Millar stated:

'Whilst those buttresses have visual integrity, they have no structural integrity; the stonework is not tied into the main central section at all … Any attempt to build further would have resulted in a collapse… and the people who built this chapel were no fools. They simply never intended to go any further.… The stones of the unfinished ends have not weathered like that, they have been chiselled to make them look worn, like a ruin.'[33]

Was this design feature deliberate or yet another piece in the puzzle of Sir William's enigmatic Grail Chapel? We were also curious how Sir William learned to build this Temple to Venus. One particular, almost legendary character, who possibly had links with Rosslyn and the St Clairs, may hold the clue to this mystery.

The Rosicrucians and the Grail

Christian Rosenkreuz or Rosenkreutz (*c*.1378–1484) is the legendary founder of the Order of the Rosy Cross, also known as the Rosicrucians. His secret teachings were published in three anonymous manifestos between 1614 and 1617, eventually spreading into Europe. In the early 17th century, they caused much excitement by declaring the existence of a secret brotherhood of alchemists and sages preparing to transform the arts and sciences and Europe's religious, political, and intellectual landscapes.[34]

Several parallels exist between this character, which many believe is fictional, and William St Clair, founder of Rosslyn Chapel. Both died in 1484, travelled widely across Europe, and were members of the 'Fraternity of the Rose Cross'. Rosenkruez's body is said to lie in a vault in the Rosicrucian temple of 'Sanctus Spiritus' perfectly preserved like the Sinclairs and St Cuthbert. The temple is said to contain ancient knowledge or 'serpent wisdom' within its carvings and design, similar to Rosslyn Chapel. Did the Rosicrucians base their fictional master on William St Clair? Was William the secret founder of the ancient order of the Rosicrucians?

Author Trevor Ravenscroft studied the chapel at Rosslyn for many years. He noticed several symbols belonging to the Rosicrucian Order, particularly a rose at the centre of a cross on railings in front of the Lady Chapel. He stated, *'The sculptures of Rosslyn are magnificent manifestations of spiritual insight or vision, given substance in stone.'*[35]

Lewis Spence also believed that William St Clair built Rosslyn as a Grail Chapel and that seekers of the Grail mysteries considered it held a secret encoded within its carvings.[36] Adolf Hitler believed Rosslyn held the Grail secret inside the Apprentice pillar. Hitler was fascinated with occult artefacts, including the Spear of Destiny and the Holy Grail. In *The Discovery of the Grail*, Andrew Sinclair writes that Rudolf Hess, Hitler's second in command and member of the infamous Thule Society, identified himself with Percival. He believed Rosslyn was the Grail Chapel of the Arthurian Romances.[38] A member of the Thule Society, Dr Karl Hans Fuchs, visited Rosslyn Chapel in 1930 with a mysterious colleague who signed the visitor's book as D Hamilton. Fuchs claimed that Hess believed he was related to the Duke of Hamilton. During his visit, Fuchs and his companion showed a great interest in the Apprentice Pillar, which they thought concealed the Grail.[39]

Rosicrucian temple of 'Sanctus Spiritus' from the Temple of the Rose Cross, an engraving in 'Theophilus Schweighardt Constantiens' 1618

In *Parzival*, a medieval romance by the knight-poet Wolfram von Eschenbach (*c* 1160–1220), the Knights Templar and their successors were guardians of the Grail. In 1933, Walter Johannes Stein, an Austrian

183

Jew who fled to England, believed the *'Templars had taken the Grail from a spiral pillar near Cintra in Portugal to its sister chapel in Rosslyn.'* Hess communicated with Stein, and many believe their mutual interest in the Grail brought him to Rosslyn in 1941.[40]

Many researchers state that there is no objective evidence of any connection between the Knights Templars and Rosslyn Chapel, even though, in 2005, a Knights Templar seal was discovered in the village of Roslin less than a mile from the chapel. The seal depicts the classic image of the Templars with two riders astride a horse holding shields and lances encircled by the Latin inscription SIGLLVM MILITVM XPISTI meaning 'Seal of the Soldiers of Christ'. This inscription can be accurately dated because of its unique provenance, having once belonged to Renaud de Vichiers, 19th Grandmaster of the Knights Templar from 1250 to 1256. The seal dates to the time of William, 6th Baron of Roslin (1230-1297), who was an advisor to Alexandra III and Sheriff of the shire of Edinburgh. He acquired the Knights Templar lands of Gourton from Walter Fitz Stephen de Melville around the same time he received the lands of Roslin.

Roslin village was supposedly settled in 203 CE by the Picts, ruled by a king called Asterius. The Picts chose this place due to its geographical situation near a vital junction of ancient tracks linking important routes north, south, east and west, including the Great North Road.

From the 11th century, Roslin was an important mining town. Its population later expanded with the large influx of labour building the chapel and castle, becoming the third largest town in the Lothians. By 1456, it was granted the status of a burgh by King James II, and its road layout took the shape of an upside-down cross. Looking down at the village of Roslin on the Google Earth program, the main roads resemble a wavy cross reminiscent of the cross of the constellation of Cygnus, the swan, with Rosslyn Chapel located on the head of the swan, itself a sacred symbol of the Rosicrucians. Coincidently, during the period of the chapel's construction, the Holy Axis pointed to the sunrise on 13 October, when the Templars were disbanded.

Rosslyn Castle and the Mysteries of the Glen

The next stage of our quest was to dowse the Bride and Lugh currents from the chapel to Roslin Glen. From the south door, we detected Bride diverting to the graveyard below and the old chapel of St Matthew's, which has only two of its buttresses remaining. Little is known about this church, although Andrew Sinclair states that the Black Canons of the Augustinian Order settled in Roslin in the 12th century and built a religious settlement here.

Behind the ruins, Bride disappeared through a stone wall into a wooded glade, where we could hear the faint sound of trickling water. After circling the wall, we cut through trees to clamber down a steep slope to a pair of concrete pods containing pipework, once the site of St Matthew's Well. The spring supplied the village of Roslin until the end of the 19th century but possibly dates back to the glen's earliest settlers.

A local guide, who accompanied us on one of our visits to the chapel, mentioned two stories that recall the well's demise. One report says it was due to a cholera epidemic in the 17th century, and another that the locals blocked it up to prevent the local gypsies from taking its waters. The last king descended from the Yetholm gypsies died at Rosslyn in the 1920s.

Bride continues to the partly ruined Rosslyn or Roslin Castle in a romantic position overhanging a beautiful area of the glen. A narrow bridge over a deep gully is the only access to the castle, which today is a holiday rental. We dowsed the current through the courtyard to a ruined tower in the southwest corner,

Rosslyn Castle Ruins

believed to be the remains of the original Keep. An early engraving displayed in the visitor's centre depicts the castle standing high on a rock pinnacle with an avenue of trees leading to it. Sir William later improved and enlarged the Keep while building his chapel.

According to Father Hay, after the Battle of Roslin in 1302, Sir Henry St Clair was encouraged by one of his English captives to move his castle from College Hill to its present location because of its advantageous defensive position with the gorge and the North Esk surrounding it on two sides.[40] The Battle of Roslin Moor was one of Scotland's most significant victories but rarely mentioned. During the battle, 8,000 Scots led by John Comyn waited in the glen and around the chapel and castle to face a 30,000-strong English army. Outnumbered almost four to one, it ended in victory for the Scots and gave new hope for independence from England. But unfortunately, Rosslyn Castle was no match for the English forces of General Monck, who destroyed much of it with cannon fire in 1650.

Many mysteries surround this site, including a legend that says it is home to a sleeping white lady who will one day awake and show the whereabouts of a fabulous treasure buried deep within its vaults. When this happens, the castle will again rise from its ruins. This story is reminiscent of a tale concerning Christian Rosenkruez, who encounters a strange castle similar to Rosslyn on one of his travels. On arrival, he witnessed a royal marriage and was awarded 'The Order of the Golden Fleece', a title held by Sir William St Clair at the time. His curiosity led him to a secret chamber with Venus asleep on a bed and a library where he obtained the 'King's secret books of wisdom'.[41] The mention of the goddess Venus asleep on the bed could be an allegory of the secret light of the planet Venus illuminating the way or the energy of Bride.

According to some sources, the castle had a scriptorium, a secret library containing many precious manuscripts and books the St Clair family collected. The manuscripts were saved in 1447, after a disastrous fire almost destroyed the library, by a quick-thinking chaplain who threw them down from a window into waiting hands below, much to the family's relief. Perhaps the ruined tower or Keep through which the feminine current passes was the original hiding place of these ancient manuscripts.

James Jackson mentions an Italian General called Count Poli visiting Rosslyn in 1834, bringing with him an ancient book. It was said to describe the chapel and castle before its abandonment in the 16th century, including the lost library's secret whereabouts. Poli claimed to be a descendant of the last Provost of Rosslyn Chapel, who fled Italy after the Reformation. A clue to its location is in a poem that mentions a hidden entrance:

'From the inner edge of the outer door,
At thirty feet of old Scotch measure,
The passage there, that's made secure,
Leads to the holy Roslin treasure.'

They found the hidden door in the graveyard, and after breaking through, they followed a corridor that led to the old library. It still contained many ancient books and historical manuscripts, including a copy of *Rota Temporum* and a history of Scotland from 'the beginning of the world until 1535', now said to be in the Vatican Library.[42]

Roslin Glen is an ancient woodland, first settled in the Bronze Age, and, like other sacred places on the Holy Axis, has cup and ring marked stones. A cave here is said to be one of many hiding places of the Scottish hero William Wallace, reached by rock-cut steps leading down from the grounds of a private house. Further along, the river, there are more rock carvings, including one showing concentric rings now inaccessible. These carvings often occur at natural places of telluric power enhanced by the vital force of fast-running water.

The many ghost appearances in and around the chapel, castle, and glen indicate powerful geology, which is evident here. The rivers of the North and South Esk, which encompass the area of Roslin Glen and Temple, are in a geological zone of Upper Carboniferous, iron-rich sandstone. This zone is under extreme pressure from two major faults, one south of the Pentland Hills and one north of the Moorfoot Hills. The sheer quantity of crystal and iron in the sandstone may produce a magnetic field under certain conditions, particularly during Earth movements or stresses from these major faults and anticlines, causing the release of plasma or balls of light.

Over the past few hundred years, these mysterious earth lights have been called Will of the Wisps, fairy lights, Jack o' Lanterns and White Ladies. But, in addition to the Earth's movements producing plasma, water is another essential factor. Here in the deep and narrow glen, the powerful force of the fast-flowing North Esk River against the magnetic sandstone rocks creates high magnetic fields. These forces can produce, under certain conditions, a distortion or curve in the space-time continuum, which can instantly transport anything or anyone that comes into contact with it forward or back in time.

One time-slip story told in *Rosslyn and the Grail* by Mark Oxbrow and Ian Robertson tells of a visit to Roslin Glen by a group of teenagers who decided to rest on a mound next to the river opposite Wallace's Cave. As the light faded, they made their way to the exit, where a search party of policemen and worried parents met them. Convinced that they had only been gone for a few hours, the teenagers were surprised to discover they had been missing for twenty-four hours.[43] This incredible time-slip event is a familiar tale encountered at many sites associated with the Holy Axis, particularly in areas of geological magnetism, such as the Eildon Hills near Melrose.

Rosslyn Castle, ink and watercolour by John White Abbott (1763–1851)

Oxbrow and Robertson also relate the experiences of the late John Ritchie and his friend while playing in the dark corridors of Rosslyn Castle when they were about twelve years of age. While exploring the lower levels, the pair suddenly became aware of a strange light coming from the far end of a corridor. The light grew brighter as they stared at it and began to move towards them. Horrified, the boys turned and ran as it chased them through the corridor, and as it got closer, it morphed into a wolfhound that ran underneath them and straight through the wall by a blocked-up doorway.

This experience may relate to the story of the Black Dog of Rosslyn. During the Battle of Roslin in 1303 between the English and the Scots, one of the English soldiers had a sizeable black hound to defend him. During the conflict, the English soldier lost his life, and the dog viciously set upon the Scot who killed his master. So ferocious was the attack that the soldier had to kill the hound to save his own life. Having won the day, the Scottish army celebrated their victory with drink and song in the castle guardroom. Suddenly, an enormous black dog appeared out of nowhere, snarling at the frightened group, causing them to flee in terror. The angry, vengeful ghost dog became known as the 'Mauthe Dog of Rosslyn' and still haunts the area.[45]

Phantom black dogs are often seen in areas of extreme trauma, particularly at battle sites or where murders and dark occult activity have occurred. Many people link black dog sightings with energy points such as crossings of leys or earth energy lines. I believe the bright light witnessed by Ritchie and his friend was a ball of plasma that morphed into the dog because of the boy's preconceived knowledge of the famous black dog hauntings of Rosslyn Castle.

Dowsing through the Glen

From the castle, we follow the Bride flow beneath its south walls to a magnificent yew tree. In ancient mythology, yews are associated with death and rebirth, their branches and foliage cut for ceremonial occasions.

As we descended deeper into the glen, we came to a sharp U-bend of the North Esk River where a waterfall or linn once cascaded down into the valley, which some say gave Roslin its name. Now reduced to a tumble of boulders, we dowsed the Bride current passing through this sharp bend encompassing a group of large loose rocks known as the 'Devil's Cauldron'. One of the stones juts out of the bank, known as the Witch's Head. We also found large stone slabs deliberately carved or chiselled with squared holes and ridges, possibly part of a mill that stood here long ago.

Yew tree below Rosslyn Castle

Returning to the chapel, Lugh passes through the sacristy window at the east end and travels towards a group of Scots pine trees on the upper ridge of the glen. We detected him again flowing across a footpath to an outcrop of rock high above the river known locally as 'Lover's Leap'. Its other name is the 'frog stone' because carved into its side is a small round elemental face that some interpret as that of a frog. However, we believe the carver was capturing the spirit of this highly electromagnetic stone. According to a local guide, people sitting on the stone have had otherworldly experiences. Local traditions say it is the abode of the fairy queen and where kings and priests would sit to commune with elemental spirits.

While exploring the many fascinating features of the glen, we noticed several magical rocks formed over centuries by the cascading river to emulate elemental faces, including one of the head of a warrior. The enchanted nature of this place, with its highly paramagnetic geology, is amplified by the surging North Esk River as it forces its way through the gorge.

Rock face with elemental head of a warrior, Roslin Glen

The male current continues east from the elemental rock seat to cross the North Esk at a place marked by two large jutting rocks as if showing us the way to its next destination, Wallace's Cave. The cave is set halfway up a cliff above the river's east bank, almost hidden by trees, and can only be accessed by a path on the private grounds of Gorton House. The cave is said to be the hiding place of William Wallace after losing the Battle of Falkirk in 1298. However, a series of prehistoric rock carvings in a recess a short distance away, including circles, triangles, spirals and other geometric shapes, suggest that this cave has a much older sacred significance. Many people who have visited the cave report its resonating qualities and experience a dream-like energy conducive to meditation when spending time inside it.

Stone with elemental face in Roslin Glen

From the baptistry, Lugh flows west to Roslin's parish church located at the village's southern edge, dating from 1881. Meanwhile, Bride meanders along Roslin's main street to the Roslin Innovation Centre at Edinburgh University's Easter Bush Campus.

Roslin Glen with rock shaped like the elemental head of a goddess

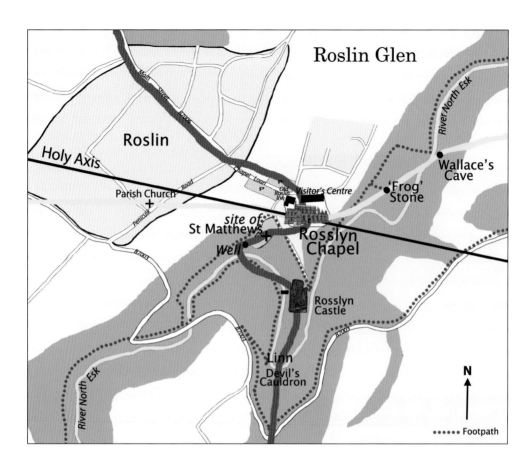

1. 36. Spence, L. 1993. *Mysteries of Britain*. Leopard Books, Bristol.
2. Wood, N.1993. *Scottish Place Names* (Chambers Mini Guides). Chambers, Edinburgh.
3. Forbes, Dr R. 1778. *An Account of the Chapel of Rosslyn*. Reprint ed. Cooper, R L D. Grand Lodge of Scotland, 2000.
4. 9. 13. 15. 17. 18. Coppens, P. 2002. *The Stone Puzzle of Rosslyn Chapel*. Adventures Unlimited Press, Amsterdam.
5. 21. Ravenscroft, T. 1983. *The Spear of Destiny*. Red Wheel/Weiser, Newburyport, US.
6. 12. Baigent, M, Leigh, R & Lincoln, H. 1982. *The Holy Blood and the Holy Grail*. Corgi Books, London.
7. 14. 23. 25. Lomas, R. Knight, C.1997. *The Hiram Key*. Arrow, London.
8. Brown, D. 2003. *The Da Vinci Code*. Doubleday, New York.
10. Butler, A. Ritchie, J. 2013. *Rosslyn Chapel Decoded: New Interpretations of a Gothic Enigma*. Watkins Publishing, London.
11.40. Hay, R. A. 1661–1736. *The Genealogie of the Saintclaires of Rosslyn*. Edited by Brother Robert L. D. Cooper with Latin translations by Brother John Wade. Available through https://www.grandlodgescotland.com/product/the-genealogy-of-the-saintclaires-of-rosslyn/

19. http://www.walterscott.lib.ed.ac.uk/works/poetry/minstrel.html

20. Michell, J.1983. *The New View Over Atlantis.* Thames & Hudson, London.

22. Dunford, B. 2008. *Vision of Albion: The Key to the Holy Grail.* Sacred Connections, Perthshire.

24. Wallace-Murphy, T. Hopkins, M. 1999. *Rosslyn: Guardian of the Secrets of the Holy Grail.* Element, London.

25. Collins, A. & Little, G. L. 2022. *Origins of the Gods: Qesem Cave, Skinwalkers, and Contact with Transdimensional Intelligences.* Bear & Company, Rochester, US.

26. 27. 30. 31. 32. 33. Knight, C. Lomas, R. 2003. *The Book of Hiram: Freemasonry, Venus and the Secret Key to the Life of Jesus.* Stirling, New York.

28. Merrick, R. 2012. *The Venus Blueprint: Uncovering the Ancient Science of Sacred Spaces.* Evolver Editions, Berkeley, US.

29. Butler, A. Ritchie, J. 2006. *Rosslyn Revealed: A Library in Stone.* O Books, Winchester.

34. https://order.rosy-cross.org/node/22

35. 40. Ravenscroft, T. 1990. *The Mark of the Beast: The Continuing Story of the Spear of Destiny.* Penguin, London.

37. Sinclair, A. 1998. *The Discovery of the Grail.* Century, London.

38. Ralls-Macleod, K. Robertson, I. 2005. *The Quest for the Celtic Key.* Luath Press, Edinburgh.

39. 41. Brydon, R. 1994. *Rosslyn: A History of the Guilds, the Masons and the Rosy Cross.* Roslin Chapel Trust.

42. Jackson, J. 1837. *Historical Tales of Roslin Castle, from the Invasion of Edward I. of England to the Death of Mary, Queen of Scotland.* James Jackson, Penicuik.

43. 44. Oxbrow, M. Robertson, I. 2006. *Rosslyn and the Grail.* Mainstream, Edinburgh.

Chapter 8

The Sacred Lothians and the Omphalos

Lugh from Rosslyn Chapel to Falkirk

Heading west from the village of Roslin, we followed Lugh towards the Pentland Hills just south of Edinburgh. The natural beauty of these hills has inspired some of Scotland's most celebrated artists, poets and authors. While visiting Carnethy Hill, the Pentland's second highest peak, Sir Walter Scott wrote, *'The hills glowed like purple amethyst; the sky glowed topaz and vermillion colours. I never saw a finer screen than Pentland.'* Robert Louis Stevenson called them *'the howes of the silent, vanished races'*, the lost races being the old tribes of the Salgovae, Votadini (Gododdin) and the Picts. Some sources believe 'Pentland' derives from the Brythonic *pen*, meaning head and *llan*, for church or enclosure. However, others suggest it derives from *Pettaland*, the Norse word for Pictland. [1]

The Pentland Hills

The Pentland range of hills stretches for 20 miles (32 km) from the outskirts of Edinburgh towards Biggar and Upper Clydesdale in the south, and of its twelve peaks, the highest rises to 1900 ft (579 m). The hills arose from ancient rocks beneath the ocean floor 430 million years ago. Within the sediments of mudstones, siltstones and sandstones are highly magnetic seams of igneous rocks, including basalt and andesite, full of crystalline structures such as feldspar.

A 19th-century Gothic Revival church at the village of Glencorse near Milton Bridge draws the male current, built to replace Glencorse Old Kirk, now a wedding chapel at nearby Glencorse House. But rather than the church, the male current prefers a cup-marked stone set within metal railings in the graveyard. This curious feature lies against the wall to the right of the church's tower. The carvings on the rock show excessive weathering, as you would expect, but long ago, at least ten cup and ring marks were visible on its surface.

Interestingly, the stone was transferred here from the Old Kirk along with the font. However, the font initially came from an even older place of worship dedicated to St Catherine in the Hopes, just over a mile to the west. This ancient chapel now lies at the bottom of Glencorse Reservoir at the heart of the old medieval religious and administrative centre of the Pentlands. 'Glencorse' may derive from Glencross, a local name associated with an ancient cross that once stood within the burial grounds of St Catherine in the Hopes.

Sir Henry de Brade bestowed the chapel and lands around Glencorse upon the monks of Holyrood Abbey in 1230. By 1314, it was in the hands of Sir Henry St Clair, having won a wager with Robert the Bruce. The bet required two hounds to bring down a renowned white deer before it reached a particular burn or stream. At a critical moment in the chase, Henry invoked the spirit of St Catherine, which ensured the dogs succeeded in their mission. His victory awarded him the barony of the Pentlands, and as a token of gratitude, he built a chapel at the very spot of invocation. Although there may be no truth to the tale, it could represent a geomythical memory alluding to female sovereignty in the land signified by the white deer. In the Grail mysteries, the white stag is a sign for the pilgrim when seeking enlightenment. So likewise, a quest or chase after the stag in world mythology symbolises a tremendous spiritual discovery.

Cup-marked stone at Glencorse Kirk

From here, Lugh makes a sharp turn north towards Glencorse House and the old Kirk, where the famous author of *Treasure Island,* Robert Louis Stevenson, once worshipped. The kirk stands on an impressive mound with at least two cup and ring marked stones still in situ, suggesting the site's sacred importance as a place highly revered by the prehistoric peoples of the area and the later Celts and Picts. Lugh enters the chapel from the west and travels down its axis and through the east window.

The lands of Glencorse belonged to notable Scottish families, such as the Abernethys, who built a castle here in 1464. From 1610, it came into the possession of the Bothwells, descendants of the Lords of Holyroodhouse and later the Inglis family.

Moving the old carved stone and font from the old church imbues the new place of worship with the sanctity of the previous site and draws the male dragon current. Famous author and dowser Tom Graves dowsed a line of energy from a stone circle to a particular stone in a nearby wall where it stopped. Upon further investigation, he discovered that the stone in the wall initially came from the stone circle, removed long ago by the farmer to create a larger entrance for his cattle or plough. It would appear that the stone circle and the stone were still energetically communicating like old friends, which I believe is the case at Glencorse.[2]

Between the new and the old Glencorse churches is Loganbank House, also visited by Lugh, once the site of the tower house of the Sinclairs dating back to the 12th century. Loganbank House was originally a thatched cottage built in 1810 by Revd John Inglis. The building also lies upon an equilateral triangle of sites that links a church in the village of Currie, on the southwestern outskirts of Edinburgh, associated with the Knights Templar and a mysterious cross-shaped wood looking like a splayed Templar cross from above. Some authors, therefore, speculate that the Knights Templar originally owned the site of Loganbank House.

The Castlelaw Node

Castlelaw Hill Fort

Lugh visits an impressive hillfort overlooking Glencorse Reservoir on the side of Castlelaw Hill, marking the Holy Axis alignment. The surrounding area is a prehistoric landscape with many cairns, hillforts, earthen enclosures, and ancient field systems. The views across this part of the Pentland Hills, with its soft contours and sparkling blue reservoir, are breathtakingly beautiful, attracting walkers, cyclists and wild swimmers from many parts of Southern Scotland. We know this area well, having visited it over ten years ago while dowsing the female serpent Elen of the Belinus alignment at the site of St Catherine in the Hopes Church at Glencorse Reservoir.

Three concentric rings of ramparts and ditches surround a mound within the hillfort, once a stronghold of the Votadini and Picts. Archaeologists set the date of its initial occupation as the 1st millennium BCE. With the impending threat from the Romans, the fort received two additional earthen ramparts and ditches. However, traces of practice trenches are also visible, built above the fortification in WWI and still used as a military firing range today. Before undertaking any dowsing investigations of the hillfort, we had to check that no red flags were flying that day.

Excavations of the hillfort in 1931 by Gordon Childe and in 1948 by his successor Stuart Piggott, Professor of Archaeology at Edinburgh University, revealed Roman finds dating to the early 1st century CE. Some discoveries included an enamelled bronze brooch, Roman pottery, and a Romano-Celtic mounting, suggesting that the local tribes may have traded with the Romans and possibly buried offerings to their deities here.[3]

Within the fort is a curving passage leading to a large underground chamber or souterrain called an Earth House, which has been modernised for the visitor and includes a concrete roof and a window. Most archaeologists believe its prime function was as a storage facility for agricultural produce and dated its construction to the 1st century CE. However, these underground passages and chambers found all over Scotland are still an archaeological mystery, including their actual date and function. In fact, according to some sources, there is no solid evidence that Castlelaw Fort ever served a defensive purpose. Instead, many believe the engineering of the passageway and chamber is too advanced to be just a mere storage area for grain. Incredibly, the passages are carved out of solid rock and lined with 5 ft (1.6 m) wide drystone walling.

We believe the Picts constructed souterrains for a ritual spiritual purpose, possibly to communicate with Mother Earth, the spirit world and the cosmic realms to receive ancient knowledge and wisdom. Also, the souterrains compare with earlier Neolithic passage tombs and chambered long barrows such as Wayland Smithy at Uffington and West Kennet at Avebury.

After leaving the parking area, we walked a short distance to an information board explaining the history of the fort and Earth House. Looking across this stunning lowland area, we realised that these fertile plains would have been heavily farmed by its inhabitants established over millennia. We walked around the ramparts where Lugh approached from the east. We also located Bride's current entering from the northeast through a breast-shaped hill called Castle Knowe, where archaeologists found traces of a palisaded prehistoric structure. We soon realised they were meeting inside the souterrain.

After crawling our way along the low, narrow passageway to the souterrain's circular chamber, illuminated by the modern skylight built into the roof, our dowsing soon confirmed the presence of a node. The Earth House is reminiscent of a beehive chamber similar to those found on Irish and Scottish islands built by the Culdees. It also reminded us of tholos tombs in Greece. Perhaps the souterrain was utilised for grain storage during and after Roman times. But because Lugh and Bride cross here, we firmly believe that the chamber was once an important ceremonial centre of power for the earlier tribes to communicate with the spirits of their ancestors and the serpents, Bride and Lugh. It is a place to meditate and dream in

Souterrain or Earth House on node at Castlelaw Hill Fort

absolute silence and darkness, where the conscious mind becomes free from everyday thoughts and impressions, allowing one to obtain higher states of consciousness.

Having travelled to many Native American sites, I could not help but recognise the similarities between the circular Earth House and the Kivas found in the Mesa Verde National Park in Colorado. Kivas were places of ceremony that Pueblo elders called *te'i*, 'the place of the cottonwood tree', thought to be a bridge between the underworld, Earth, and the skyworld.

Coppens observed that the Pentland Hills from Longniddry Beach looks like a sleeping giant.[4] Perhaps the ancient shamans saw this as symbolic. They used caves and underground chambers to create the perfect environment for communicating with the spirit world and astral travel along spirit paths such as the Holy Axis. Perhaps, the location of the underground Earth House here at Castlelaw is a focal point that provides a portal to another level of existence.

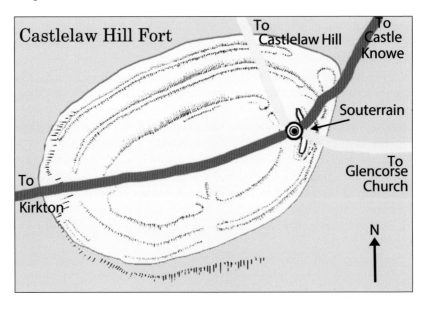

Currie and the Dalmahoy Stones

Lugh meets the Holy Axis at Castlelaw Hill before continuing west over Harbour Hill and crossing the Kinleith Burn, just south of the village of Currie. This north–south tributary of the Water of Leith is known locally as Poet's Burn or Glen. At the head of this idyllic wooded dell, we encounter a house called Mount Parnassus, named after the oracle mountain on which lies the ancient Greek temple of Apollo at Delphi. In the 18th century, the house belonged to a weaver called James Thompson, who infamously composed songs and poems in his spare time. Perhaps Thompson was inspired by the dragon energy of Lugh, as it flows through the nearby glen, the serpent acting as an oracle, reminding Thompson of Delphi's spirit mountain.

Lugh also visits Currie's graveyard and church, standing on an elevated position above the Water of Leith. Known as 'The Lang Whang', this river stretches 22 miles (35 km) from the heather-covered moorlands of the Pentland Hills to Edinburgh.

The village's original name was Kinleith, deriving from Killeith or 'chapel of Leith'. The present church dates from the 18th century, but Christians have worshipped here since at least medieval times, and the area was a favourite hunting ground for the Lords and Knights of Edinburgh Castle. A church dedicated to St Kentigern receives a mention in 1296, a saint who, in *c.* 550, established a religious community in Glasgow to convert the British tribes of Strathclyde before becoming its first bishop. Adjacent to the kirk, we encounter St Mungo's Well on the bank of the Water of Leith with an 18th-century stone surround. This ancient spring is still revered today, as people have decorated a bush nearby, but on this occasion with Christmas baubles rather than the traditional clootie.

The dedication may derive from legends of the saint establishing a chapel or cell here as part of his missionary journeys through the Lothians. The monk Jocelyn of Furness Abbey, who wrote *The Life of St Kentigern* around 1180, mentions him as the son of '*the daughter of a certain king most pagan in his creed who ruled the northern parts of Britannia.*' As a boy, he received his education from a community of monks

St Mungo's Well, Water of Leith, near Currie Kirk

run by St Serf, who nicknamed him Mungo, meaning 'the beloved one'.[5] A Saxon silver ring, considered part of a crucifix or an altar candlestick, now in the National Museum of Antiquities of Scotland, was unearthed while digging the foundations of the present church.

At the church's west end are the medieval foundations of an earlier religious site, and 13th-century calvary cross-slabs are incorporated into the north wall of the interior. Many more can be found in the churchyard, having been broken and set as a border to the path. In *The Secret Scroll*, Andrew Sinclair suggests that some belonged

13th-century calvary cross slabs, Currie Kirk

to Knights Templar members buried in the churchyard. Many have fascinating carvings, including a Grail cup, a compass and a knight's sword with a rounded pommel and square hilt. Sinclair states that the Templars built an industrial base at Currie using the power of the Water of Leith '*to grind flour and crush iron and silver ore from their Hilderston quarry near Linlithgow*'.[6]

We dowsed the male serpent current flowing southeast–northwest through the church connecting with what we believe was the original position of the high altar of the older church. It continues through the nearby war memorial and, after crossing the river, heads towards the grounds of Dalmahoy Hotel and Country Club near the village of Ratho.

However, Lugh's primary focus is a standing stone hidden in dense woodland on the southeast corner of its grounds. Although not shown on any O.S. maps, this hidden diamond-shaped megalith stands 6 ft (1.75) m high, with a large section missing at the base. The woodland was once part of a large estate owned by George Dalrymple, Lord Dalmahoy (1680–1745), who built a fine baronial mansion over the site of an earlier castle. James Douglas, 14th Earl of Morton, acquired it around 1750 and renovated the interior. However, there were further modifications when Dalmahoy House became a luxury hotel, golf and country club in 1990.[7] It is said to be haunted by Lady Mary Douglas, daughter of the 8th Earl of Morton, whose portrait still hangs in the hotel. Known as the White Lady, her ghost is said to wander the hotel's corridors, so beware if you want to stay there.

In *The Celtic Place-Names of Scotland*, W J Watson suggests the name Dalmahoy derives from *Dail mo Thuae,* meaning 'my Tua's meadow' – dāl being the Pictish word for meadow or haugh. Tua was supposedly a Celtic saint from Ulster who came to Scotland sometime in the 8th century.[8] However, John Garth Wilkinson wrote in *West Lothian Placenames* that Dalmahoy derives from *Dal Mochoe, mochoe* being the old British name for Mungo, otherwise known as Kentigern, Bishop of Glasgow.[9] Either way, Wilkinson believes that a meadow associated with a saint may indicate the site of an early Celtic church.

To our surprise, Lugh ignores the old site of Dalrymple Castle and instead meanders through the gardens towards a pretty Victorian church next to the northern entrance of the country club. St Mary's of Dalmahoy was established in 1850 by Lord Aberdour, son of the 17th Earl of Morton, for the local Episcopalians. After flowing diagonally through the church, we follow the current to what appears to be yet another megalith standing in the northeast corner of the churchyard, carved with a crude cross. It supposedly stood in a field about a mile west of St Mary's on a ridge, part of the old eastern avenue of Hatton Hall, which incidentally also marks the north–south Belinus alignment.

From the cross-slab, Lugh's flow is deflected north towards Edinburgh. We soon located it at another St Mary's Church at Ratho, just a few miles from the city centre, yet another site associated with the Spine of Albion. The male serpent current we call Belinus travels north–south through the centre of the church.

The refurbished Victorian church incorporates the remains of one established in 1436 under the auspices of the Collegiate Kirk of Corstorphine in the western suburbs of Edinburgh. Older remnants of an arch from a Norman church also survive and are incorporated into the west wall. However, the circular boundary wall that encloses the churchyard may suggest that this site was a pre-Christian sanctuary. An ancient spring, now lost, known as the Ladywell, existed next to the church. Also, a Celtic cross found during the Victorian refurbishment stands within the entrance porch next to a grave slab bearing the sword and cross-pattêe emblem of a Knights Templar, said to have owned Ratho in the 12th century.

Interestingly, we dowsed Lugh flowing north–south through the western end of the church parallel with the Belinus current.

Cross-slab at St Mary's Church, Dalmahoy

We noticed that Lugh's flow includes what appears to be megalithic stones built into the exterior foundations of the west wall, possibly from a stone circle that either once stood here or very close by. We have seen large pagan stones in the foundations of many churches, a method used to harness the power of the old sanctuaries and Christianise pagan deities. Although there is little evidence of its pre-Christian history, our ancient ancestors must have revered this site with its two major dragon lines as a place of ancient sanctity.

Huly Hill and the Lothian Triangle

Lugh continues north to Huly Hill, part of one of the most important prehistoric sanctuaries of Southern Scotland. Sadly, it lies close to a major traffic junction of the M8 and M9 motorways and enclosed within a roundabout overlooked by business premises, a well-known burger restaurant and a busy petrol station. Furthermore, the site aligns with the main runway at Edinburgh Airport, half a mile away. Despite its name, Huly or Holy Hill is a mound or a large burial cairn, 98 ft (30 m) in diameter and about 10 ft (3 m) high, defined by a modern stone retaining wall. Excavations of the cairn in 1830 uncovered a bronze spearhead and small fragments of animal bones. However, there was no trace of burial cists, urns or any human remains. In 1878, Joseph Anderson argued that the spearhead was a dagger with rivets, as *'no authenticated instance of bronze spearheads had been found with interment in Scotland.'*[10]

A stone circle once surrounded the mound, and according to one antiquarian, it consisted of twelve standing stones that survived until the 18th century.[11] Today, only three remain made of greenstone, one marking its east side and the others in the southwest and northwest. Two of the standing stones are approximately 6 ft (1.8 m) tall, and the third measures 4 ft (1.2 m), although based on the type of damage it has sustained, it may have been higher. An eastern outlier, 9 feet (2.7m) tall, called the Gauger Stone, is located on the premises of Bodycote Materials Testing Ltd and separated from the Huly Hill tumulus by the M9 motorway and Newbridge roundabout.

We first visited this site in 2007, led by the Belinus alignment and its male serpent. We dowsed the Belinus current entering the tumulus from the south and connecting with the northwest standing stone before exiting towards the small town of Kirkliston. We detected Lugh entering the complex from the southeast and through the eastern stone, crossing with Belinus on the mound before continuing his westward journey. Interestingly, there was no sign of a node, but we did detect some interaction as if they were operating at different frequencies.

A complete Celtic chariot was uncovered south of the tumulus during the industrial estate's building in 2001. This rare find was considered part of a burial dating to around 250 BCE. Although little survives of the organic remains, it is of a type previously unknown in Scotland, being more akin to those found in mainland Europe. The many spearheads and the chariot found around Huly Hill are associated with the male warrior, symbolised by the presence of the male serpent of the Holy Axis that carries traits of the brave and mighty warrior Lugh and his magical spear.

On the north side of Edinburgh Airport runway is the Cat Stane, with an inscription Sir James Young Simpson translated in 1861 as '*On this Mound lies Vetta son of Victi*'. Also in the vicinity, Robert Hutchison, in 1864, uncovered nine rows of fifty-one burial cists of varying types, further substantiating that up to the Roman period, this site was in constant use as a burial ground by different races over millennia. Historians suggest the area was a borderland of Iron Age tribes called the Vecturians, Meatea and Damnonii.

Further excavations in the 1970s, led by Trevor Cowie, uncovered several more prehistoric graves. In addition, numerous tumuli existed around the Cat Stane towards the Huly Hill tumulus, which suggests that before extensive farming and the building of the airport runway, this was a massive and significant complex of prehistoric monuments.[12]

Standing Stone at Huly Hill tumulus on the Lugh current

When viewed from the top of Huly Hill, the streamlined shape of the Gauger Stone outlier forms part of an equinoctial line linking both sites with Arthur's Seat, located in the centre of Edinburgh to the east of here. Dowser Grahame Gardner, former Chairman of the British Society of Dowsers, accompanied us on one of our visits to the site. He pointed out an east–west alignment found by Harry Bell that links the Huly Hill tumulus and the Gauger Stone with Edinburgh Castle and Cairnpapple Hill near Bathgate to the west.

During the Spine of Albion research, we discovered that the equinoctial line connecting Huly Hill with Arthur's Seat formed part of the 'Lothian Line' initially found by Philip Coppens. He noticed that the prehistoric sites of Cairnpapple Hill and Arthur's Seat also align with Traprain Law, an Iron Age hilltop citadel and capital of the Gododdin near Haddington in East Lothian. Standing on Traprain Law at the equinox, you can see the sunset over Cairnpapple, and from Cairnpapple, you would see the sun rise over Traprain Law. As well as Huly Hill, we also realised the old parish church at Corstorphine, now a western suburb of Edinburgh, also sits on this east–west alignment. St John's Church at Corstorphine, which incidentally is visited by the female dragon current of the Belinus Line, stands within a circular graveyard, the possible site of another prehistoric henge. We felt sure that the ancients deliberately built the Huly Hill tumulus and the possible henge site at Corstorphine on this equinox alignment to harness the power of the three sacred hills while celebrating the equinox sunrise on 21 March and sunset on 21 September. Incidentally, Lothian means 'Land of the Sun God'.[13]

Interestingly the three equinoctial hills referred to by Coppens are almost equidistant from one another, with Cairnpapple 18 miles or 28.97 km from Arthur's Seat and Arthur's Seat 18.8 miles or 30.25 km from Traprain Law. What is remarkable here is how nature creates three equidistant hills aligned with the equinox solar festival when day and night are of equal length. Perhaps the ancients, who buried their dead on these hills, also revered them as sanctuaries. Here they could commune with natural telluric energy and the combined power of three sacred hills at the solar equinox.

Furthermore, the Lothian Line between Arthur's Seat and Cairnpapple, the Holy Axis between Rosslyn Chapel and Cairnpapple Hill and the Rose Line between Rosslyn Chapel and Arthur's Seat create a triangle. In addition, it almost mirrors a triangle formed by Traprain Law, Rosslyn Castle and Arthur's Seat. The Rose Line is a true north–south meridian line that connects Rosslyn Chapel to Arthur's Seat and the Orkneys and south to Mount Lothian (*See Fig. 3*).

The importance of Huly Hill is punctuated by its position, standing at the junction of modern roads, old straight tracks and leys such as the Belinus Line and the Lothian Line. It also has Bronze Age and Iron Age burials, which denotes a significant sacred place connected to the spirit world, like the many shamanic spirit paths dating back to Neolithic times.

After Huly Hill, Lugh unexpectedly takes us into the beautiful gardens of Newliston House, which is only open to the public in May. The house was among the last to be designed by the famous 18th-century architect Robert Adam. In the 15th century, the estate became the property of the Dundas family of nearby Dundas Castle then it passed through marriage to politician and lawyer John Dalrymple, 1st of Stair. The gardens were the inspiration of his son John, Second Earl of Stair (1679–1747), after experiencing the grandeur and beauty of Versailles when serving as ambassador to the

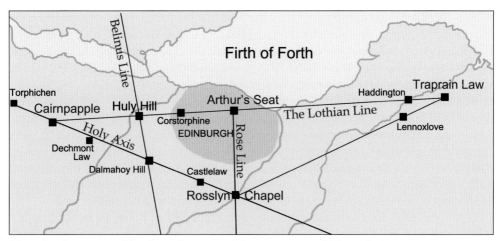

Triangle of sites created by the Lothian Line, The Rose Line and The Holy Axis

French court. Within the gardens of Newliston House, we find a Hercules Wood with a statue of the Roman god standing proud at the centre of a landscaped 'Union Jack'. However, Lugh prefers the unusual stone-built dovecote or doocot, now a private dwelling in the corner of the Hercules Wood, which appears to be a much earlier building. It is renowned as the largest doocot in Scotland, with two compartments and 2,663 nesting holes and predates the present house.

Newliston Doocot, (courtesy of M J Richardson)

We have encountered several dovecots on leys, alignments and dragon lines, and Alfred Watkins, the father of the Ley phenomenon, also mentions their significance. Their primary function was to house doves or pigeons for their meat and eggs or to send messages, and even their droppings provided fertiliser. However, long ago, they played an essential role in temple sacrifice. The dove symbolises the Holy Spirit and divine authority and is known throughout the ancient Near East as an emblem of the mother goddess. Crucially, the dove signified the rebirth of Earth after the great flood when it returned to Noah's ark carrying an olive branch in its beak.

The old Celtic church at Ecclesmachan, a few miles west of Huly Hill, recounts the legend of its foundation by St Machan, a 6th-century missionary and contemporary of St Kentigern or Mungo. Machan was a disciple of Welsh prince St Cadoc of Llancarvan who is said to have encountered King Arthur. However, it was not a friendly meeting as the saint awarded Arthur with a herd of cattle as compensation for protecting a man who had killed three of Arthur's soldiers.

We followed the Lugh current inside the church, where stained-glass windows depict Machan and Cadoc. A hollowed stone on display here, used for grinding corn, is a relic from Celtic times when a wooden church with a thatched reed roof stood on this spot. Later a stone church, erected here around 1200 CE, was re-dedicated to St Machan by the Bishop of St Andrews. Before the Reformation, the church belonged to the Knights Hospitallers of the Preceptory of St John at Torphichen, another significant place of power on the Holy Axis a few miles west of here.

Behind the church once stood the Bullion Well, a name possibly derived from *buller* meaning to boil, perhaps describing how the spring 'bubbled' out of the ground. Some wells emit sulphurated hydrogen toxic gas that smells like rotten eggs, which were revered because of their medicinal qualities, similar to the sulphurous wells in London. Monks would sell the London spring water as a kind of spiritual nectar, impregnated with the *spiritus mundi*. Perhaps the healing qualities of Ecclesmachan's well attracted St Machan to build his church here, using its healing powers to cure the locals.

Lugh continues westwards towards the high eminence of Binny Crag, the steepest hill in West Lothian, formed from an extinct volcano and one of several along the Holy Axis to attract the serpent lines. Nearby is Chapel Hill and the site of Binny Church, located next to a flattened circular mound, possibly the remains of a large tumulus or burial mound, where we also dowsed Lugh. The church had a dedication to St Giles, but little of its earlier history remains. In the distance, we could see the Bathgate Hills and a tall mast standing atop one of Scotland's most important Neolithic monuments and ceremonial complexes.

Cairnpapple Hill and the Middle Sanctuary

Leaving the busy network of routes between Edinburgh, Glasgow and Stirling behind us, the beautiful vista of the Bathgate Hills, with its green rolling hills and soaring igneous rock pinnacles, is a sight to behold. Here you can escape into another world of mystery, legend, folklore, and stories of the great warrior Arthur. According to local tradition, he fought his greatest battle on Bowden (Badon) Hill in the Scottish Borders, securing forty years of peace for the Celtic tribes in the region.

The Bathgate Hills are also known for strange light phenomena. According to one newspaper feature, a family driving through the winding lanes of the Bathgate Hills in 1988 saw a glowing figure running in the opposite direction, moving at high speed.

The prehistoric Cairnpapple Hill, one of the area's most dominant features, is well known as a 'hot spot' for UFO or plasma sightings. However, the great importance of this monument historically, geographically and culturally is not immediately apparent as you approach the site along a footpath leading from the layby below. A tall communications mast now dwarfs the moderate-sized mound, and a military nissan hut houses the information centre.

The Holy Axis alignment passes through the northeast corner of the hill, missing the prehistoric henge on its summit by 250 ft (70 m). The Neolithic henge is the domain of both Lugh and Bride, where they node within the great cairn.

Cairnpapple rises over 984 ft (330 m) above sea level, commanding Lothian's most spectacular views to the east and west. On a clear day, you can see Bass Rock in the River Forth to the east and as far as Goat Fell on the Isle of Arran, off the West coast. Although it barely stands out from its surroundings, the cairn is the highest point in West Lothian.

Aerial Photo of Cairnpapple Hill, Cairn and Henge (courtesy of Dr John Wells)

The earthworks at the summit represent one of the most important sites of sacred burial and worship in Scotland, if not in Britain. We soon realised that Cairnpapple is an omphalos site on the Holy Axis, and excavations by Professor Piggot from Edinburgh University in 1947 revealed that it had been a focal point for ritual and communal activity from at least 3500 BCE through to 500 CE. It is also the most significant Celtic Druid centre in Scotland.

The earliest structure on Cairnpapple Hill was a Neolithic henge monument 196 ft (60 m) in diameter, similar to those found on Orkney and in the south of England at Avebury and Stonehenge. Twenty-four large wooden posts encircled it, identical to the reconstructed henge monuments encountered at Milfield near Yeavering Bell in Northumberland. The henge also had north and south entrances similar to a henge called Arthur's Round Table in Penrith on the Belinus Line.

The actual function of these structures is still a mystery. Some believe the henge and the posts served as a shadow clock for the sun and moon, creating a line to a specific section of the raised bank that marks a particular solar or lunar festival. However, they may be for ceremonial ritual purposes, the henge being a protective ring and the posts acting like aerials to attract some form of cosmic energy triggered by specific sounds or intentions. Later the wooden pillars were replaced by standing stones.

At the end of the Neolithic period, a new era began called the Bronze Age, and here we find the first burial on the site, known as the 'North Grave (Cairn I)'. It consisted of a rock-cut grave aligned east–west, covered by stones, and a tall standing stone stood at its western end, probably taken from the original stone circle that replaced the wooden posts.

The contents of the North Grave are unparalleled in Scotland, as the bodily remains found there were wrapped in organic material and strewn with flowers, the face covered with a burnt wooden mask with a charred club or mace placed alongside the body. The finds evoke strong emotions among many local people, who believe the person buried was female and connected to a fertility ritual.

Sometime later, archaeologists found two cist burials near the grave, roofed with large capstones and covered by an impressive stone cairn (Cairn II) measuring 49 ft (15 m) in diameter and edged with twenty-one kerb stones. A modern concrete dome now encloses the area where Cairn II would have been.

Finally, a much larger cairn was added (Cairn III), measuring 98 ft (30 m) in diameter, containing two cremation burials. The most modern burial sites at Cairnpapple are the rock-cut graves within the eastern half of the henge. They are aligned roughly east–west, said to be Christian burials dating to the 1st millennium CE. The early Christians reused this sacred ground to bury their dead as a deliberate act of site continuance at a renowned spiritual omphalos of the many cultures that settled here over millennia, perhaps believing it provided them with a spiritual link to their ancient ancestors.

Professor Piggot, who excavated the site, believed that Cairnpapple is the 'Middle Sanctuary' recorded in these parts by the Romans. An anonymous cleric who lived in the northern Italian town of Ravenna around 700 CE produced a map of Roman Britain compiled from earlier charts. He catalogued a list of sites from 'ocean to ocean' along the narrowest isthmus of Britain between the Firth of Clyde and the Firth of Forth. Many historians believe the cleric's list refers to several forts along the Antonine Wall built by Antoninus Pius, successor to Hadrian, who needed the prestige of a military triumph to boost his imperial reputation in Rome.

In 138 CE, just twenty years after the construction of Hadrian's Wall, Pius ordered his legions to construct the Antonine Wall as a new frontier, but unlike the great stone

wall built by Hadrian, it took the form of a ditch and bank earthwork with a wooden fence. Of the ten sites listed by the Italian cleric, number six was *Medio Nemeton*, meaning 'open or middle sanctuary', suggesting neither a fort nor any other form of Roman defence.

Nemeton is a Gaulish word meaning grove or sanctuary associated with holy places, temples and shrines. Cairnpapple has the reputation of being a sacred sanctuary from at least 3000 BCE up to the Christian period and lies at the centre of Britain's narrowest neck of land between the Forth and the Clyde. Therefore, it would undoubtedly be a strong candidate for the middle sanctuary of Medio Nemeton.[14]

Cairnpapple is on an east–west equinoctial alignment with Arthur's Seat and Traprain Law called the 'Lothian Line' mentioned earlier. Coppens ponders whether Cairnpapple also served as a beacon lit twice a year at the equinox, similar to the fires lit on Arthur's Seat and Traprain Law. During the spring and winter equinox, when day and night are of equal length, the midway passage of the sun crosses the celestial equator. One phenomenon observed at Cairnpapple is that the sunrise and sunset at the equinoxes, 21 March and 21 September, are precisely due east and west. Is it just a coincidence that these three sacred hills mark the latitude of the true solar equinox?

'Pap' or 'Papple' refers to a breast or nipple-shaped hill and is used in Celtic place names to describe suitably shaped hilltops, such as the Paps' twin breast-shaped hills of Jura and the Paps of Anu in Ireland. So it seems appropriate that this central shrine should have a name associated with the nourishing aspect of the 'Great Mother'. While researching sites for our book *The Power of Centre*, we found many geographical centre points linked with the Earth Goddess, such as Anu at the Hill of Uisneach in Ireland and Ffraid and Bride in Wales and Scotland.

Local author and researcher Jackey Queally describes the henge at Cairnpapple and its later circle of stones as oval-shaped, reminiscent of the female ovulation circle dictated by the moon. Due to the proximity of the Hilderstane Silver Mines, perhaps Cairnpapple Hill was originally a place of goddess or moon worship.[15] According to Barbara Kacicek, '*The reflected light of the moon glows with the same luminance as the metal silver, and in the ancient world, there were no coincidences. The alchemical symbol for silver is a crescent moon, and the moon and silver were associated with the brain.*'

Cairnpapple Henge

Interestingly, the Hilderstane mines have yielded the best quality silver in Scotland used to make the Scottish Crown Jewels, now on display in Edinburgh Castle.[16]

There are several single standing stones in the surrounding area of Cairnpapple, which the late Jack Smith, a local author and a member of the Knights Hospitaller from Torphichen, believed marked radial lines from Cairnpapple as if the place was extending its invisible energetic powers to different locations in the local landcape.[17]

Since our initial discoveries of the Holy Axis and the Bride and Lugh dragon lines in 2013, we have been dowsing and researching the Holy Axis in relative obscurity. So when the invitation came to participate in the Great Scottish Dowse at Linlithgow, organised by Grahame Gardner and Bill Holding in 2014, we were delighted to share our experiences, especially as they planned to visit Cairnpapple and Torphichen Preceptory, two of the sites on the Holy Axis. We had yet to investigate these sites in detail, so we felt the event was an opportune moment to group-dowse the serpent energies for the first time.

With the help of Grahame, we plotted several energy lines converging here. Grahame began with dowsing a ley featured in the 1977 book *Forgotten Footsteps* by Harry Bell.[18] He then accompanied us while dowsing the Lugh and Bride serpent currents. Caroline and I followed Bride while Grahame dowsed the male and discovered they crossed at a node inside the concrete dome where other energy lines converge, including the Harry Bell Line.

Inside the dome, a short ladder leads you down to the preserved remains of the North Grave and one of the later cist burials. On a day when a gale is whipping across the top of the exposed hill, the atmosphere inside the cairn is remarkably tranquil, and, in some way, this ugly modern dome has provided ideal conditions to meditate right next to the node. Here, Lugh also connects with a giant protruding megalith, possibly an entrance stone of the old North Cairn or from the original stone circle that once stood inside the henge.

Bride travels over a knoll called The Knock before entering the prehistoric complex through its ditch and banks close to the south entrance. Meanwhile, Lugh meanders to the node from the east and exits the cairn in a southwesterly direction while Bride flows northwest.

Cairnpapple is particularly significant because it lies halfway along the Holy Axis and is a possible omphalos of goddess worship for our ancient ancestors. It is one of those 'thin veil' places which can help us connect to the higher vibrational realms and universal consciousness, the

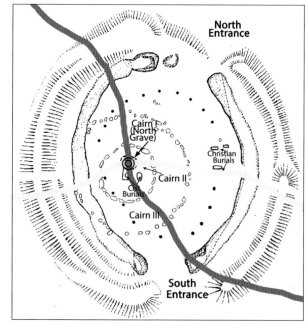

Plan of currents at Cairnpapple Hill

origin of our souls. In this higher vibrational state, we can receive subtle information to help us on our allotted spiritual journey.

As we continued west, we sensed that Cairnpapple represented 'the heart' of our Grail quest.

Temple of the Raven

The path of Lugh and Bride only separate for a short distance as they descend Cairnpapple Hill towards the Holy Axis alignment and a medieval preceptory in the village of Torphichen.

David I, son of King Malcolm III and St Margaret, founded Torphichen Preceptory in the 1100s as the Scottish headquarters of the Knights of the Order of St John of Jerusalem, also known as the Knights Hospitaller. The Hospitallers came to Scotland to recruit and collect funds for the Crusades. They built the preceptory as their central base, which comprised administration, monastic and domestic buildings and a small hospital. Within the preceptory lived several brothers, headed by a Preceptor, who oversaw the estates and collected the rents in cash or goods. Much of the daily work of the brethren would have involved growing food and herbs for medicine. In addition, the Order expanded to meet the needs of the pilgrims journeying to the Holy Land. In the 1130s, the Hospitallers also took on the military duty of protecting the pilgrims and Christian settlers from Muslim attacks. To help them with this undertaking, kings and magnates endowed them with riches, land and churches.

Torphichen Preceptory

'Torphichen' derives from the Gaelic *Tóir Féichín*, meaning the 'boundary/ sanctuary or hill of the Raven'. Some believe that Feichin refers to St Fechin, a 7th-century Irish saint, although there is little evidence of his existence in Scotland. Welsh traditions tell us that the raven was the totem of Bran the Blessed, Britain's primordial deity and guardian. In Greek mythology, ravens have a link with Apollo, the god of prophecy and a symbol of bad luck. They also represent the connection between the material world and the spiritual realms, a mediator animal between life and death. To certain cultures, they were messengers of the gods, associated with Lugh, Urien and Arthur, the emblem of the spiritual warrior.

The preceptory stands over a vast wooden platform, believed to be an artificial island with a causeway dating back to the 1st century CE before Christianity came to Scotland. Some suggest it was a place of pagan worship with a circle of standing stones around a wooden building that served as a sanctuary and ceremonial roundhouse, perhaps an oracle site, hence its name, 'sanctuary of the raven'. Some of the old stones were found in a nearby field to the east but later destroyed by a local farmer, who feared archaeologists would disturb his lands.

According to various online sources, a wooden church was established here in 400 CE by St Ninian and visited by King Arthur in 516 CE. In *The Dream of Rhonabwy*, the knight Owain battles King Arthur in a dream world assisted by ravens, and Arthur transforms into a raven upon his death. The story of Arthur's visit may stem from the legend that he fought his greatest battle at Bowden or Badon Hill, only 1.2 miles north of the preceptory.

Between the 12th and 15th centuries, Torphichen was rebuilt and enlarged as a cruciform church, its nave becoming the parish kirk after the Reformation. It was also a courthouse, and its last preceptor, Sir James Sandilands, was given the title of Lord Torphichen. To this day, the Scottish Knights Templar retain the position of Preceptor of Torphichen.

In 1756, the nave and other Hospitaller buildings suffered demolition. Then a new parish kirk was built over their foundations, incorporating some of the best-preserved late 12th and 13th-century stones of the original preceptory and its fine architectural detail.

With the help from dowsers attending the Great Scottish Dowse, we detected Bride entering the old preceptory church from the north through the tower before shrinking to form a node with Lugh in the south transept. Lugh enters from the southeast through the site of the old chancel. On the way, he visits St John's Well, located at the base of the southern slopes of Torphichen Hill, although no trace remains today. According to the Canmore website, it once supplied the preceptory, and the waters were renowned for their healing qualities. The male current then meets Bride inside

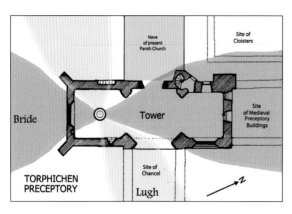

the south transept and exits through its west wall. Bride leaves through the south wall incorporating a massive monument of the Gowan family. According to Jack Smith, in his booklet, *Torphichen*, the area of the node in the south transept is almost certainly the site of St Ninian's wooden church.[15] We also dowsed the five-petalled rose node signature here, similar to Doddington Moor.

Observing our dowsing, the guide showing us around that day was also intrigued by the node's position. As if to affirm our findings, he announced that a circular stone structure lies beneath the floor exactly where we dowsed the node. Was this structure the pagan roundhouse or sanctuary like the Earth House on the node at Castlelaw? Many of the early Culdee cells were also circular and set into the earth, a design later adopted by the Knights Templar within many of their European churches, the Temple Church in Fleet Street being a fine example. It seemed very significant to us that the node of Lugh and Bride should mark the very site of Torphichen's earliest holy shrine.

Smith also mentions the existence of a sanctuary stone close to a path in the churchyard, possibly predating even St Ninian's arrival. According to local folklore, the megalith marked the centre of the pre-Christian sanctuary that would have extended out to other outlying stone markers, one Scots mile or 1.123 English miles to the north, south, east and west. The east and west sanctuary stones still stand in their original positions. The sanctuary may be part of a much larger ceremonial complex that includes the Neolithic henge and burial mound at Cairnpapple Hill. Perhaps these sanctuary stones originally belonged to the Cairnpapple cairn sites and were transferred to a new contemporary religious shrine to reinstate its sacred power at Torphichen. Smith believes the sanctuary protected every felon or debtor who entered and remained within its precincts, a place unique in Scotland's history which deserves more recognition. One of the stones shows signs of cup and ring marks, and it seemed remarkable to us that the east and west sanctuary stones still stand in their original positions, given that many farmers in the area were renowned for using such sites as their quarry.

Sanctuary stone at Torphichen Preceptory

There is evidence of beehive cell structures built within shelters of crags around Torphichen, probably by the Dysert Culdee Monks. Jack Smith suggests that the early Christian burials at Cairnpapple were those of Dysert monks who disappeared during the early incursion of the pagan Angles. Interestingly, an area of woodland bordering the Avon River to the northwest of the village is called 'The Desert' with a hidden cave, possibly occupied by the Dysert monks.

As both currents make their way northwest, they cross the River Avon towards the outskirts of the historic town of Falkirk, the nearest large settlement at the heart of central Scotland with its tales of the Scottish King Arthur or Artuir and another long-forgotten sanctuary.

---

1. Scott, A. B. 1918. *The Pictish Nation, its People and its Church*. T. N. Foulis, Edinburgh.
2. Graves, T. 1978. *Needles of Stone Revisited*. Gothic Image, Glastonbury.
3. https://portal.historicenvironment.scot/designation/SM90064
4. 13. 14. P. Coppens. 2007. *Land of the Gods*. Frontier Publishing, Amsterdam.
5. Jocelyn of Furness http://www.ancienttexts.org/library/celtic/ctexts/kentigern_frag.html
6. Sinclair, A. 2001. *The Secret Scroll*. Sinclair-Stevenson, London.
7. https://www.scottish-places.info/features/featurefirst8661.html
8. Watson, W. J. 2001. *The Celtic Place-Names of Scotland*. Birlinn Ltd, Edinburgh.
9. Wilkinson, J. G. 1992. *West Lothian Place-names*. Torphin House
10. www.cybercotia.com
11. Fyfe, W. W. 1852. *Guides to the Scottish Watering Places or Summer Life on Land and Water*, no 1: South Queensferry, Hopetoun and Firth of Forth, west of Edinburgh. Edinburgh. Page(s): 198.
12. www.canmore.rcahms.gov.uk
13. Bell, H. 1977. *Forgotten Footsteps*. Ley Line Publications, Glasgow. https://glasgowsecretgeometry.uk/
14. https://bathgatehills.co.uk/torphichen-preceptory-sanctuary-stones/

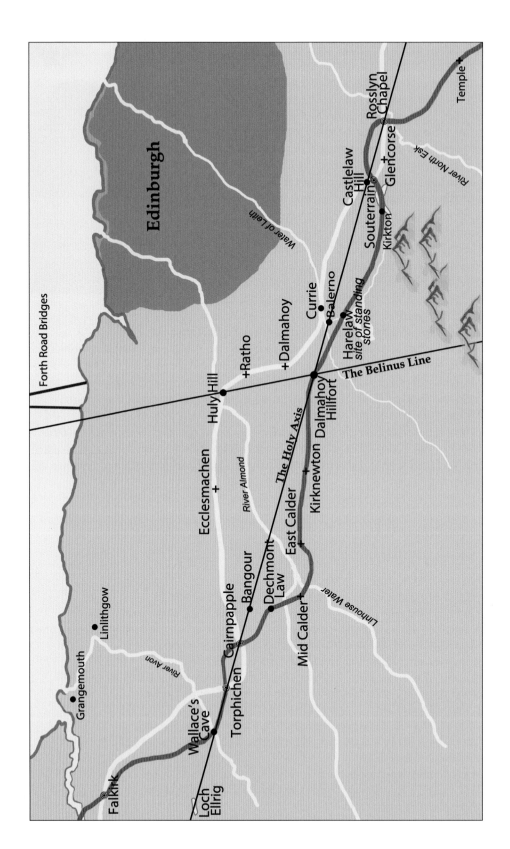

Chapter 9

Saints, UFOs and Megaliths

Bride from Rosslyn to Falkirk

From the nodes at Rosslyn Chapel and Castlelaw Hill Fort in the Pentland Hills, the Bride current continues to Kirkton on the western shore of Glencorse Reservoir, passing through the old site of St Catherine in the Hope as she crosses with the serpent energy of Elen of the Belinus Line. Nothing remains of the drowned chapel today except perhaps a few stones on the bed of the reservoir.

Bride's flow then meanders northwest over Bell's Hill towards Harlaw Farm, located on the northern tip of Threipmuir Reservoir at the foot of the Pentland Hills. At this location stood a group of five standing stones and a large cairn, destroyed in the early 1800s. Paul Bennett, writing for *The Northern Antiquarian* website, states the only known reference of the site comes from the *New Statistical Account* of 1845: '*About a quarter of a mile to the south of the large cairn was five very tall and large stones set perpendicularly in the earth.*'[1] Some sources say the megaliths formed either part of a stone circle, a megalithic stone row, or boundary markers.

Dragon Lines at Dalmahoy Hill

About a mile northwest of Threipmuir Reservoir, the Holy Axis connects with Malleny House and its delightful gardens in the small village of Balerno, next to the meeting of two rivers called Bavelaw Burn and Water of Leith. Unsurprisingly, various powerful families held property on this site and in 1478, it came into the possession of Alexander Knychtsoune or Knightson. The present house was built in 1617 when acquired by Sir James Murray of Kilbaberton, architect to King Charles I. However, it soon passed into the hands of Edinburgh lawyer William Scott and in 1882 it was purchased by Archibald Primrose, the 5th Earl of Rosebery. Primrose was a favourite of Queen Victoria and served as Prime Minister from March 1894 to June 1895. Eventually, Commander and Mrs Gore-Browne-Henderson acquired the house and gardens and gave them to the National Trust for Scotland in 1968.

Although the house is private, its idyllic gardens are open to the public. Its entrance is through an impressive ironwork gate with a spread eagle, the family crest of Commander Gore-Browne-Henderson. In the garden are four beautifully manicured yew trees called the Four Apostles, the last survivors of what was initially known as the Twelve Apostles. It also has a doocot (dovecote) with 915 nesting holes and an unusual saddle-backed roof.

Balerno became a settlement in the 1200s, known then as Balhernoch or Balernach. By the 1700s, it had grown to prominence due to the establishment of numerous mills powered by the Water of Leith, the last of them, a Bank Paper Mill located near the centre of the old village, closed in the early 1990s. Before leaving, we visited one of its churches dedicated to the 6th century St Kentigern or Mungo, established in 1863. Many years earlier, we dowsed the male serpent flow of the Belinus Line here, suggesting that a place of worship may have existed on this site during Celtic Christian times.

The female current meets the alignment further west at a long twin-peaked ridge called Dalmahoy Hill. The hill has the remains of two Iron Age hillforts; one survives on the edge of a vast quarry and another on Kaimes Hill, where Mesolithic people settled.

Looking at the map, we soon realised the importance of this hill, as it marks the meeting of the east–west Holy Axis and the north–south Belinus Line, researched in our book *The Spine of Albion*. But, unfortunately, an active quarry has destroyed about a third of it, and giant electricity pylons now dominate the skyline.

The ancient geology of this area is the main draw for the quarriers, the hard igneous rocks rich in iron and magnesium, called 'Dalmahoy Sill', are estimated by geologists to be 330 million years old. Such powerful minerals are a source of sustenance for leys and dragon lines, the natural telluric energy serving to invigorate and nourish other local sites on their flow.

Dalmahoy Hill from Kaimes Hill by Ronnie Neilson

Because two great leys and Bride meet here, the hills of Dalmahoy must have been considered 'special' by the earlier cultures. Perhaps the forts were ceremonial enclosures of deity worship. However, the violation of such a sacred hill associated with the Holy Axis, Belinus Line and the Bride serpent current on such a massive scale by the big business of industrial quarrying will inevitably have a detrimental effect on the local energy matrix. When earth energy lines and water streams are out of balance, the negative energy they create can be harmful to our health.

The Trail of Cuthbert's Churches

Before entering the densely populated River Almond Valley, Bride crosses the Water of Leith near Glenbrook House to an ancient church ruin at the village of Kirknewton. Here, she flows east–west through the mausoleums of the Maconochies of Meadowbank House, now known as Kirknewton House, and the 18th-century Scottish Judge Lord Robert Cullen. This once tiny church a few miles west of Balerno is dedicated to St Cuthbert but abandoned when East Calder and Kirknewton parishes combined in 1750, by which time it was in a badly decayed state. Bounded in the north by the River Almond, the parish of Kirknewton included an old cattle-droving route. As a result, the little Kirk was often the scene of many attacks by the 'reivers', families from the Border regions of Scotland who terrorised the area by stealing cattle and crops from local farmers.

Today little remains of its early Norman foundation, but it once housed a wonderful carving of a sheela-na-gig set within an arch or doorway, now on display in the National Museum of Scotland, Edinburgh. It depicts two figures, one of a man and the other a woman displaying her genitals. However, to have a male and female represented in an image of a sheela-na-gig is rare. He is helping to open her vulva with one hand, and his other appears to be caressing her head. Perhaps it represents the complementary forces of yin and yang: yin represents the feminine elements (watery, dark, negative), and yang the masculine aspects (airy, light, positive).

However, sheela-na-gig carvings, found in many churches around Britain and Ireland, are pagan fertility carvings representing the fecundity of the Earth Goddess and a perfect symbol of the fertile telluric power of the Bride serpent. The carving possibly denotes the site as a significant place of pagan worship later usurped by followers of St Cuthbert.

Until the 1950s or 60s, a hogback tomb existed in the graveyard but has since disappeared. These gravestones typically date from the 10th–12th centuries and appear all over northern England and Scotland, many associated with burials of Norse warriors. Several fine examples in Lancashire and Cumbria depict spiral and serpent carvings.

Further west, we tracked Bride to East Calder and another church ruin dedicated to St Cuthbert located at the very western edge of the village close to a tributary of the River Almond called Linhouse Water. Its foundation dates back to 1148, when Randolph de Clere owned the lands and the village was known as Calder Clere. East Calder developed as a stop-off for merchants transporting their cattle from Edinburgh, Crieff and nearby Falkirk and Linlithgow. Pretty trails within the nearby Almondell and Calderwood Country Park, once owned by the Lords of Torphichen, take you through enchanted woodland along the banks of the River Almond and its tributaries.

Before the 1900s, seven wells existed in the village, and a wooden bridge spanned a ford across East Kirk Burn. Unfortunately, the burn disappeared under the road and urban development destroyed the wells. In the 19th century, John Sommers wrote that there were many springs in this area, including the villages of East and Mid Calder and *'many of them consisted of pure, soft, and excellent water.*[2]

Crossing the Linhouse and Murieston Waters, the female serpent flows to the parish church at Mid Calder, which is only open for Sunday services. However, we were able to access valuable information about this historic site from writings by several local antiquarians and historians.

Hardy McCall writes that the name Calder refers to the Celtic *Coil* and *Dour*, meaning a wooded or wild region by water, which this area has in abundance even today.[3] Local Victorian archaeologist John Sommers in his *Account of the parish of Mid-Calder,* suggests that the name derives from another Celtic word *Cadair,* signifying a place of meeting or assembly.[4]

The church lost its original dedication to St Cuthbert when it was renamed Kirk of Calder in 1560. In 1150 it was recorded as the Kirk of Caledour or Kaledoure, built in the Romanesque style, and stood within the royal hunting grounds of King Malcolm IV and the Earls of Fife. It passed to the Douglas family in 1350 and then to the Sandilands, Lords of Torphichen.

The present church was built in 1541 and renovated in 1863. The old families may have realised its auspicious setting, surrounded by the beautiful scenery where the three rivers of Linhouse, Murieston Waters, and the Almond meet.

In the vestry wall are the remains of a Celtic cross dating from 1160, and carved into the stone window supports are the shields and armorials of the various noble families of the parish.

Kirk of Calder (courtesy of Stephen C Dickson)

Just north of the church is the remarkable presence of a natural mound or tumulus on Cunnigar Hill, probably dating from the Bronze Age and standing close to the meeting of the River Almond and its tributaries. McCall recalls several Bronze Age earthen barrows or tumuli existing in this area, some along the bank of the River Almond before they fell to the plough.

Further evidence of the sacred importance of the wooded valley of the Almond is the discovery of several stone coffins unearthed in the 19th century along the river bank, some carved from a solid piece of stone with tightly fitted lids. Excavated alongside them were a Bronze Age battle-axe and spearhead.

The Cunnigar tumulus witnessed the execution of many witches, hence its later name, 'Witches Knowe'. James Hendrie writes in his 2009 article: *'Hew Kennedie,*

Calder Kirk's firebrand minister appointed to the post in the 1640s, was a passionate persecutor of witches. He vigorously and ruthlessly tracked down those who practised the Black Arts, and any caught were hauled before Kennedie and the Kirk Session for trials in the church itself. Those who were found guilty were condemned to burning at the stake and met a horrific end on the Cunnigar Hill, which today still remains on the edge of the village.[5]

Standing just south of the Kirk of Calder is the 16th-century Calder House, once Calder Castle, built by the Sandilands, which Sommers states was linked to the church by an underground passage. James Sandilands was a Preceptor of the Knights Hospitaller of the Order of St John of Jerusalem from 1550 until the Order's suppression in 1554. John Knox openly celebrated the reformed communion for the first time there in 1556, during a period of tremendous religious intolerance in Scotland. Hendrie writes that during these times, the plans for Mid Calder church had changed from a grand collegiate-style Catholic Church with naves and cloisters to the more traditional church we see today.

The female current loops around to the northwest to connect with the old site of St Mungo's Well on the banks of the River Almond. The well still flowed in 1974 and had a dry-stone structure 4 ft (1.2 m) in diameter. Bride then continues through the district of Ladywell in Livingston, its name deriving from a well that once existed in the area dedicated to the Virgin Mary. The spring may have been used and revered by the Knights of St John, who once owned the land here.

When dowsing the churches of East Calder and Mid Calder, we noticed Bride's flow was weak and difficult to detect and felt she would benefit from some healing to release and cleanse any detrimental energy that might be stifling her flow. So we stood at a specific spot inside the church ruin at East Calder, determined by dowsing, and carried out a healing ceremony using our green serpentine and jade healing stones to help rebalance and rejuvenate her energy and the surrounding landscape.

Later research revealed a clue that may explain the disrupted energy here. We discovered intense mining activities once dominated this area in the 19th century. This region yields rich deposits of shale that for millions of years had lain undisturbed deep within the earth. But the effect of blasting it from its beds and heating it to produce oil damages the environment. It was the brainchild of Glasgow Chemist Dr James Young (1811–1883), who devised a method of distilling paraffin from coal and oil shales. By 1963, the Oakbank Works of the Mid Calder Oil Company had transformed the beautiful rural countryside bordering Linhouse Water into a grim industrial landscape, reducing the once natural and vibrant copse of Calder Woods.

The Bride serpent current has suffered the harmful effects of mining and quarrying at Dalmahoy Hill and the Calder Valley. Such a destructive force often causes sickness in the land, which geomancers term as geopathic stress, from the Greek *geo* meaning 'of the earth' and *pathos* meaning 'suffering' or 'disease'. It relates to irregularities in the Earth's magnetic field, such as deep mining and quarry blasting. The fracking process also pollutes the underground water, creating further disharmony in the local energy matrix.

Underground water streams are essential, for they hold energy similar in vibration and frequency to overland earth energies. Therefore, these water and earth energy streams must flow harmoniously to maintain balance and well-being.

Many water streams come to the surface as springs and holy wells. The ancients knew the importance of pure water if the land and its people were to thrive. However, if the springs become blocked, contaminated or neglected like those at Kirknewton and Mid Calder, the magnetic field becomes distorted and out of harmony with the earth's natural frequencies, the waters no longer having the life-giving powers to balance the land and maintain health for its people.

When dowsing Elen, the feminine serpent of the Belinus line, through the battle site at Culloden, she connected with a holy spring at its centre renamed 'The Well of the Dead' because of the slaughter there of a chief Highland clansman. Moreover, we discovered the well connected to a significant water course that ran parallel to the female serpent flow. Where paths of water and earth energy have experienced the trauma of battle, a distortion in their electromagnetic fields occurs, and their flow is no longer in balance with the earth. Therefore, sending healing thoughts through earth energy lines and water courses using powerful healing stones and crystals can positively transform and harmonise their energy.

There is a wealth of information about the memory of water, and Japanese author and pseudo-scientist Masaru Emoto (1943–2014) proved that human consciousness affects water's molecular structure. Emoto wrote in *The Hidden Messages in Water*, published in 2004, that water was a 'blueprint for our reality' and that emotional 'energies' and 'vibrations' could change the physical structure of water. He believes we can heal the water with positive thoughts, prayer, music, and visualisation.[6]

Like the art of acupuncture, which focuses on specific points of the body to stimulate balance and begin the curative process, we can also find the right spot in the landscape to promote healing with remedies, such as crystals, chanting, song or blessings. Similarly, dowsing can help you find the appropriate place to perform the healing, provided it is carried out at the right time and day or during specific sun and moon cycles.

Dechmont Law and the Alien Encounter

Bride next takes us through the modern urban sprawl of Livingston to another volcanic plug called Dechmont Law, located on its northern outskirts. This impressive high eminence lies between the busy M8 motorway to the north and the residential areas of Deans and Nether Dechmont to the south. We parked next to Deans Community High School, where we followed one of the many pathways to the top of the hill.

We dowsed Bride flowing east–west through the summit, where traces of Bronze and Iron Age earthworks and a causeway are visible on its steep slopes. Some sources believe it was the site of a hillfort, now marked by a triangulation pillar. However, quarrying has destroyed most of the hill's archaeology over the centuries, leaving it relatively featureless. Nevertheless, the views here are spectacular, particularly to the east towards the Pentland Hills and Arthur's Seat.

Trails through the parkland surrounding Dechmont Law are numerous, but one labelled 'Dechmont UFO Trail' certainly caught our eye. A plaque attached to a large rock placed there by the Livingston Development Corporation in 1991 marks the famous 'Livingston Incident'. It reads: '*This is the site referred to in Arthur C Clarke's*

"Mysterious World" which describes an encounter between a forestry worker out walking and what appeared to him as an unidentified flying object.'

The forestry worker in question was Robert Taylor, who, on 9 November 1979, having parked his truck nearby, walked up a path through a newly-planted forestry area on the northern outskirts of Dechmont Law. He was suddenly accosted by what he described as a metallic 'flying dome' some 20 ft (6 m) in diameter hovering above the forest floor, dark grey in colour and with an outer flange with arms on which were mounted propellers. Two smaller spheres detached themselves from the central dome and chased after him.

Having caught him, they knocked him over and attached themselves to his legs, tearing his trousers. The spheres then tried to drag him along the ground towards the rotating dome. He also reported a powerful, choking smell 'like burning brakes', which may explain why he lost consciousness for twenty minutes.

When he came round, the object had gone. He returned to his truck but had to walk to his home in Livingston because it failed to start. According to the *Undiscovered Scotland* website, when he arrived home, his wife was shocked to see him covered in mud and his clothes torn, so she called a doctor, who treated him for abrasions to his chin and thighs. She also called the police, who took Taylor back to the site of the incident. They found indentations on the ground from what looked like ladders where Taylor had encountered the large dome and the smaller spheres. The police recorded the incident as a criminal assault, making it the only UFO sighting in the UK subject to a criminal investigation.[7]

At the time of the incident, few doubted the claims of war hero Robert Taylor, who has since passed away. Even today, UFO enthusiasts consider it among the most convincing UFO sightings on record. Others have attributed it to an attack of epilepsy accompanied by hallucinations brought on by Robert Taylor, having suffered from

Dechmont Law (courtesy of Taras Young)

meningitis in the past. A YouTube video entitled '*Robert Taylor UFO Encounter*' shows him returning to the scene with a film crew and describing what he saw.[8]

Interestingly, Dechmont is located within the mysterious 'Falkirk Triangle', where people have reported many strange lights and UFOs sightings over the years. The triangle originally covered the skies between Falkirk, Stirling and the small town of Bonnybridge, dubbed the UFO capital of the world and crowned 'The Roswell of Scotland', having over 300 sightings reported every year.[9] Today, the triangle has expanded eastwards to include Fife and the outskirts of Edinburgh due to the increased number of sightings.

While investigating earth light phenomena at power centres on the Belinus Line, we discovered that the object seen during this UFO encounter may have been intelligent plasma. This multi-dimensional ionised energy surfaces along fault lines where piezoelectricity is produced, particularly around volcanic plugs such as Dechmont Law and rocks such as granite and sandstone with inherent magnetic qualities. We later discovered two fault lines run through East Calder and Dechmont Law.

People often relate light balls with earthquakes, but when seismic activity occurs within fault lines, the energy disperses evenly and efficiently. Therefore, plasma balls form when the stresses build up before an earthquake.

As mentioned earlier, plasma emits strong magnetic fields that affect the human brain and can give us varying degrees of psychological disturbances, including hallucinatory or visionary experiences. In *Space Time Transients and Unusual Events*, the authors Dr Michael Persinger and Gyslaine Lafreniere scientifically demonstrate a correlation between areas of unusual paranormal events, such as strange creatures, UFOs and time-slips, and geological anomalies that produce plasma, such as fault lines.[10]

On this occasion, the plasma intelligence briefly crystallised into physical form to interact with the witness. There is generally a trickster element to plasma manifestations, recorded by many authors researching fairy and UFO abduction cases, such as Jacques Vallee [11] and John A Keel.[12] A UFO encounter can vary depending on a person's psychic ability and hopes and fears. For example, Robert Taylor may have previously read about aliens and abductions and viewed them with trepidation, which allowed his fears to manifest. From the stories I have studied, plasma lights seem keen to interact with us and reveal themselves in whatever form makes sense to the individual based on their views and expectations, whether it be an angel, fairy or alien craft.

The research of Andrew Collins and Gregory L Little has indicated that governments and military forces know about this natural phenomenon and are quietly investigating it. For example, a four-year study by the Ministry of Defence in 2000, kept secret for six years, entitled *Unidentified Aerial Phenomena in the UK*, drew on approximately 10,000 sightings and reports. The 400-page report revealed no evidence suggesting that the phenomena witnessed were hostile or under any control other than that of natural physical forces. On the contrary, they concluded that most of the sightings were down to atmospheric occurrences generated by the electromagnetic fields of plasma. Furthermore, close encounters with plasma-related energy have caused responses in the human brain's temporal lobes, inducing perceptual alterations or hallucinations in those affected.

Just under a mile north of Dechmont Law, the Holy Axis alignment passes through the abandoned Bangour Village Hospital and a disused quarry at Bangour Knowes.

As you can imagine, the psychiatric hospital has a distinctly eerie atmosphere with its numerous derelict buildings spread out within an overgrown 960-acre site surrounded by woodland.

It was built in 1902 in the 17th Century Scottish Renaissance style under the directive of the Edinburgh District Lunacy Board to provide a new kind of mental care based on the 'Continental Colony' system. This ground-breaking development offered patients a positive and pleasant environment where they would stay in well-spaced 'villas' in a picturesque rural setting and work within the grounds in workshops and on the neighbouring farm. Its closure was due to the opening of St John's Hospital in nearby Livingston in 1989 and an increasing emphasis on 'care in the community'.

A derelict neo-Romanesque style church built between 1924 and 1930 lies on an elevated site at the centre of the complex, said to be the largest church in the Lothians during this period. Dedicated to Our Lady, the church was designed by renowned Edinburgh architect Hippolyte J Blanc, using brown whinstone from a local quarry and stone from The Duke of Hamilton's recently demolished palace.

We wondered what prompted the founders of this hospital to select this location. Were they consciously aware of the power and healing potential of the Holy Axis? Despite the noble intentions of its creators, the emotional and mental trauma experienced by its patients will remain in the fabric of the ruined buildings long after they have gone. We felt the detrimental effects of this suffering on such a powerful alignment as the Holy Axis would inevitably negatively influence the surrounding area and the psyche of the people who live there. Therefore we decided to help by projecting healing and loving thoughts through the energy matrix of the site and along the Holy Axis.

Bride continues west from Dechmont Law and makes a sudden 45-degree turn north to connect with a standing stone near Gala Braes on the summit of an exposed ridge just north of Bathgate. Another stone once existed close to it, but all that remains today is a filled-in socket hole and two fragments on the adjacent slopes. The broken pieces of the second stone were present in 1903, when the father of Mr Carlaw, the farmer of Gala Braes, found human bones when digging beneath it.

From here, she diverts her flow to the northeast, taking us to The Knock, which at 1,023 ft (311 m), is the highest natural plateau of the Bathgate Hills. Views from its summit, especially towards the north and east, are superb. For years this craggy ridge has attracted picnickers and ramblers from miles around and is formed from the same hard quartz-dolerite or basalt rock as Lindisfarne and Bamburgh.

Below, we were surprised to see a stone circle in a field next to Knock Farm. Having made our way there, we went to seek permission from the farmer to visit the site. Luckily, at that moment, he appeared and kindly stopped to chat about the stone circle. At first glance, we thought the stones were old, but the farmer assured us they were constructed for his fiftieth birthday in 1998, 'fifty stanes for fifty years'. The dolerite megaliths form two concentric circles, with one horizontal stone supported on three vertical ones at the centre, reminiscent of a dolmen. Surrounding it are the remains of a lime kiln and an old silver mine that, according to one source, once belonged to the Knights Hospitallers from the Preceptory in Torphichen.

A short distance to the northeast is an outlier, which the farmer had found lying on its side in the quarry, possibly a boundary or sanctuary stone. Having resurrected

Knock Farm stone circle near Cairnpapple Hill

it, he arranged for it to stand as near as possible to what he thought was its original position.

I had a strong impression that Bride was present, and as we walked around the edge of the stone circle, we dowsed her entering from the direction of the Knock and leaving to travel towards the nearby Cairnpapple Hill. The farmer seemed thrilled to witness our findings and to hear of its connection with the Holy Axis. It took us a while to drag ourselves away from this beautiful site and the spectacular views on this glorious sunny day. We could see the Forth Bridge and Arthur's Seat to the north and the island of Inchcolm, which features on the Elen serpent current, connecting with a Culdee cell. After saying our farewells to the farmer, we followed Bride north to the ancient sanctuary of Cairnpapple, where she forms a node with Lugh.

After dowsing her at the node at Torphichen Preceptory in the valley below, we follow her to the banks of the Avon River and Wallace's Cave, a typical dragon lair near Crawhill Farm. The cave also marks the alignment as it stretches over the River Avon to a woodland known as The Desert, possibly referring to the Dysert Monks who dwelled here in beehive cells during the Dark Ages. The cave is said to have been a hiding place of Sir William Wallace after the Battle of Falkirk in 1298. However, unlike Wallace's Cave in Roslin Glen, this cave is a natural geological formation composed of a large pillar of rock about 12 ft (3.6 m) high that supports a roof-like structure formed at the end of the last glacial period.

The shelter may have been a sanctuary for the Culdee hermit monks while on pilgrimage from Iona to Old Melrose or Lindisfarne. There is no direct evidence that Wallace hid in this cave, but many such sites are attached to various heroes throughout the ages, their names often changing to suit the times.

Standing in the arch of the cave, we sensed the vital energy from the sandstone rock and the chi force of the Avon River. Perhaps, like the other caves previously visited on the Holy Axis, it was a place to commune with the feminine earth serpent energy and plasma intelligence. A lone Scottish flag waving in the wind indicated its national importance due to its association with Robert the Bruce.

As Bride continued northwest, we soon realised that her focus was to join Lugh in the historic town of Falkirk.

1. https://www.thenorthernantiquarian.org/2018/12/09/harlaw-stones/
2.4. Sommers, J. 1838. *Account of The Parish Of Mid-Calder: With Miscellaneous Remarks.* Republished 2009, Kessinger Publishing, USA.
3. McCall, B. H. 1894. *History and Antiquities of the Parish of Mid-Calder.* Turnball & Spears, Edinburgh.
5. Hendrie, J. *Witches, Composers and Preachers - the Story of Kirk of Calder.* Article in Scottish Home & Country 2009.
6. Emoto, M. 2004. *The Hidden Messages in Water.* Beyond Words Pub. New York.
7. https://www.undiscoveredscotland.co.uk/livingston/livingstonincident/index.html
8. https://www.youtube.com/watch?v=WDGe62dR1tE&t=12s
9. Halliday, R. 1998. *Beyond The Falkirk Triangle.* Black & White Publishing, Edinburgh.
10. Persinger, M. Lafreniere, G.1977. *Space-Time Transients and Unusual Events.* Nelson Hall Publishers, USA.
11. Vallee, J. 1993. *Passport to Magonia: On UFOs, Folklore, and Parallel Worlds.* McGraw-Hill Contemporary, USA.
12. Keel, J. A. 2013. *The Eighth Tower: On Ultraterrestrials and the Superspectrum.* Anomalist Books, San Antonio, USA.

Chapter 10

Falkirk and the Temple

Lugh and Bride from Callendar to the Carron

Falkirk stands strategically next to the meeting of two ancient rivers, the Forth and the Carron and lies at the geographical centre between Edinburgh and Glasgow. At first glance, this built-up urban area appears to have little to offer our magical quest. However, after deeper investigation, we were surprised to discover that the region was once full of significant historic and mystical sites and legends of King Arthur. The Antonine Wall also ran through Falkirk, and stretches are still visible today through the southern part of the town.

Falkirk is also situated on a convergence of significant east, west and north routes, including several drove roads. Modern highways replaced these ancient tracks and the Forth, the Clyde Canal and the Union Canal also used this vital trade corridor across Central Scotland called the Neck of Britain.

View of Falkirk, engraving by John Heaviside Clark 1824

From the 12th century until shortly after the Reformation, Falkirk was administered separately in the baronies of Callendar and Abbotskerse. In 1646, Falkirk was made a Burgh of Regality during the reign of Charles I, and the erection of a Mercat cross represented his authority for the town to hold markets.

It was once renowned for its cattle fairs until industry dominated the area, including the Forth and Clyde Canal construction in 1790, designed by the famous engineer John Smeaton. It created a 35-mile (56 km) long through-route for seagoing vessels between the Firth of Forth and the Firth of Clyde at the narrowest part of the Scottish Lowlands. In 1760, an Englishman called Dr Roebuck founded Scotland's first significant iron foundry next to the Carron River. James Watt used the Carron Iron Works in 1765 to cast some of the beams for his early steam engine designs.

Today, the town is probably better known for the Falkirk Wheel, opened in 2002, an engineering masterpiece and the world's first and only rotating boat lift, reconnecting the Forth and Clyde Canal with the Union Canal for the first time since the 1930s.

According to written records dated c.1080, the original Gaelic name for Falkirk was *Egglesbreth* or possibly *Egglesbrech*, meaning 'speckled' church, breth or brech deriving from *brecc*. Some sources believe this word means 'many-coloured stones' whereas Falkirk historian John Reid suggests the name translates in old Welsh, spoken in this area before Gaelic, as the 'church of Brych' or 'Brychan'. The Anglo-Saxon word for specked is *fala, fah* or *faw*, hence one of the church's earliest names *Faw Kirk*.[1]

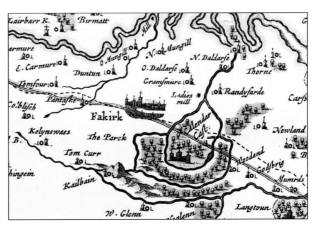

Map of Falkirk from 1645 Joan Blaeu Antique Map of the County of Stirling, Scotland

The 'speckled' or 'spotted' or varicoloured church refers to Falkirk's first church built in the 7th century on a high ridge founded by St Modan or Mo-Aidan', meaning 'my Aidan'. However, as local historian Ian Scott reminds us, the followers of an earlier saint, Ninian, travelled through this area from Rome as far back as the 5th century to convert the northern Picts and wipe out earlier forms of Christianity established by the Culdees.[2] Perhaps Aidan founded his church over the site of one established by St Ninian while journeying from Iona to Bamburgh to re-establish Celtic Christianity.

Falkirk soon developed as a substantial settlement around the old church, stretching from the River Carron in the north to the moorlands in the south, inhabited by the ancient Caledonian tribes. Moreover, it lay on the direct route between Edinburgh, Linlithgow and Stirling, with no more than a day's journey between these ancient places. Therefore, the town lay on a highly beneficial road for trade and Christian pilgrimage.

Archaeological evidence proves there have been 9000 years of occupation in this area, with early finds particularly prevalent in and around Callendar Park just south of the town centre. In fact, over the last twenty years, archaeology has uncovered many new sites, such as the Neolithic roundhouse at Weedingshall to the east of Falkirk, the Roman fort just north of the town, and a 9th-century timber Thane Hall on the northern edge of Callendar Park.

Falkirk's famous archaeological landmark is the well-preserved section of the Antonine Wall in Callendar Park, dating from the 2nd century. English trader, journalist and author of *Robinson Crusoe*, Daniel Defoe (*c.* 1660–1731), wrote:

> The town of Falkirk is near Calendar House, but nothing in it remarkable; but the other old decay'd house of the Earl of Calendar…..Here I must take notice, though, as I have often said, antiquity is not my business, that we saw the remains, and that very plain, of the ancient work, which they call Severus's Wall, or Hadrian's Wall, or Graham's Dyke, for it is known by all these: the short of which story is this; that the Romans finding it not only difficult, but useless to them, to conquer the northern Highlands, and impossible to keep them, if conquered; contented themselves to draw a line, so we now call it, cross this narrow part of the country, and fortify it with redoubts, and stations of soldiers to confine the Picts and Irish, and those wild nations which were without, and defend the south country from their incursions. This Wall reached from Dunbriton Firth, so they called the Firth of Clyde, to the Forth, and was several times restored and repaired till the Roman empire's declining, as is well known in the story. Tho' neither this, or the yet stronger Wall at New-castle, called the Picts wall, could preserve the country from the invasion of the Picts, and the barbarous nations that came with them.' [3]

Unfortunately, only small sections of the wall remain due to modern development and the building of the M9 motorway. The Howgate Shopping Centre also destroyed sections of the north ditch of a Roman fort and an Iron Age hillfort is now under the parking area for the Falkirk Wheel.

Alas, this seems to be the case in most cities and towns throughout Britain, where commercial interests have superseded history. Even in our home town of Dorchester in Dorset, a Waitrose supermarket stands over what would have been the largest Neolithic timber henge in Britain.

The Howgate Shopping Centre site was known as Bantaskine Port, one of the main entrances to the medieval town. Lord George Murray led part of the Jacobite Army through here in January 1746 after their victory at the second Battle of Falkirk. Bonnie Prince Charlie spent the night in Falkirk, and stained-glass windows in the shopping centre commemorate this Jacobite victory known as 'The Soldiers of Fortune'.

There is little mention of Falkirk's early history, despite pre-Roman finds, historians preferring to concentrate on the successful conquest of the area by Roman general Agricola. During the Roman period, a sub-tribe of the Gododdin called the Manau or Maeatae ruled the area encompassed by lands of the Picts, Votadini and the Damnonii. Northwest of Falkirk, the Romans built a line of Roman forts along the southern shores of the River Carron, one of the main tributaries of the Firth of Forth. The purpose of the defences was to keep the 'marauding' Caledonian tribes at bay and to protect Agricola's Legions from retaliatory raids.

In 142 CE, the establishment of the Antonine Wall reinforced these forts, which consisted of a turf ditch built on a stone foundation. It stretched across the central belt of Scotland, between Borrowstounness near Carriden in Edinburgh to Old Kilpatrick in the outskirts of Glasgow near Dumbarton. This incredible feat of engineering became the Roman Empire's northernmost frontier spanning approximately 39 miles (63 km). It supposedly took twelve years to complete but was abandoned eight years later, with the garrisons relocating back to Hadrian's Wall. However, in 208 CE Emperor Septimius Severus repaired the wall and re-established his legions there; the new boundary was now called the Severan Wall. But, again, occupation by the Romans only lasted a few years before it was left to decay.

Dowsing at Callendar Park

In the 11th century, Callendar was part of a barony called Abbotskerse, under the ownership of Holyrood Abbey in Edinburgh. Callendar is a name far older than that of Falkirk. King Malcolm Canmore (1058–1093) replaced St Modan's 7th-century church, possibly under orders from his Saxon Queen, Margaret, when he received the lands of Callendar.

Callendar House

As we drove west along the A803 towards Falkirk, we suddenly realised that we had crossed a section of the Antonine Wall where the railway line intersects with the road. Further along, we could see to our left a grand driveway that led to a French Renaissance château-style mansion surrounded by formal lawns. We turned into the car park, excited at the prospect of where Lugh and Bride might lead us in this historic setting.

The Callendar Estate, which covers over 170 acres, was the principal seat of power in the Falkirk area for almost a thousand years, the Thanes of Callendar being the first to hold lands here in the 10th century. Their original wooden hall occupied a prominent position at 'Palace Hill', just behind the Antonine Wall at the east end of the grounds, now a Business Park. The last of these Thanes was Patrick de Calentyre (or Callendar), who lost his lands in 1346, having failed to support King David II in a renewed war with England. The Leving family acquired the estate and eventually changed their name to Livingston. They abandoned the old Thane Hall soon after, having built themselves a new stone tower house on the site of the mansion you see today. The 8ft (2.4 m) thick walls are lined with lime mortar made from the oyster shells dug out of the nearby Neolithic middens.

During its 600-year history, Callendar House has hosted many prominent historical figures, including Mary, Queen of Scots, Oliver Cromwell, Bonnie Prince Charlie and Queen Victoria. After it was destroyed by Cromwell's troops, James Livingston, with his newly honoured title of Earl of Callendar, returned in 1660 to start the rebuilding process, restoring and extending much of the house in a Continental Classical style.

The illustrious Livingston family fought alongside many of Scotland's great kings, gaining them tremendous power and influence. Sir Alexander Livingston became the guardian of King James II after the murder of his father, King James I, in 1436. Alexander's son James was appointed the Great Chamberlain or Master of the Royal Household and became the first Lord Livingston of Callendar.

When King James V died in 1542, King Henry VIII of England saw an opportunity of winning the Scottish crown for England by attempting to arrange a marriage between James' infant daughter Mary, Queen of Scots and his son Prince Edward. However, at the time, Mary was entrusted to the care of a group of powerful nobles, including Sir Alexander Livingston, who bitterly opposed the match. As a result of this slight, Henry invaded Scotland and at Pinkie, on 10 September 1547, thousands of Scots fell in battle, among them Lord Livingston's son and heir. Mary was promptly shipped off to France accompanied by Lord Alexander and the 'four Maries', one of whom was his daughter.

Mary, Queen of Scots, married Francis, the young Dauphin of France and briefly ascended the French throne as King and Queen in 1559. After Francis' premature death a year later, the widowed Mary at the age of nineteen was escorted back to Scotland by Alexander's son, Lord William Livingston. Four years later, she entered the fateful union with her first cousin, Henry Stuart, Lord Darnley. During Mary's rule as Queen of Scotland, she regularly visited the house, and the Livingstons continued to support her throughout her troubled life.

James, 4th Earl of Callendar and 5th Earl of Linlithgow fought a battle at Sherrifmuir for the Jacobite cause with Falkirk men by his side, but the lack of a clear-cut victory brought the Jacobite challenge to a swift end. Afterwards, he returned to Callendar, where Government troops caught up with him. However, tradition says that 'his "loyal bairns" came to his rescue by delaying the soldiers at the Mercat cross, with sticks and stones, thus allowing Earl James to escape into exile.' Consequently, his estates were forfeited and the Earldoms of the Linlithgow and Callendar dynasties became extinct.[4]

In 1783, William Forbes, a wealthy London coppersmith, bought the Callendar estate. His family were originally from Aberdeen, and William, a self-made entrepreneur and businessman, purchased land to become part of the landed gentry. He remodelled and added to the house in the Scottish Baronial style, although subsequent generations renovated it as the French Chateau you see today. William Forbes's influence in the area enabled him to stop the construction of the Union Canal passing through his estate to avoid spoiling the view.

The Forbes family sold the estate to Falkirk Burgh Council in 1962, who abandoned it for over twenty years. A restoration scheme commenced during the 1980s bringing life back to this historic building and parkland.

As we followed a path towards the house, we soon felt the presence of Bride as she swept through Callendar Park from the southeast. From the house, she crosses the boating lake called Callendar Loch and disappears into woodland to the south of the house. This area, full of Scots pines, European larch, oaks, beeches, firs and spruces, is renowned for its walking trails. We ascended a path under a thick canopy of trees along the 'The Blue Trail', taking us high up onto a ridge. As we proceeded further, our dowsing rods started to move to the right, but at that point we could see little point in going through the dense bank of trees and scrubs. We consulted our plan of the woods to find that we had just missed a path called Mausoleum Road, leading to a majestic tomb. We retraced our steps to see that this road was an unmarked narrow dirt track easy to miss. It led us to a set of imposing stone pillars that formed the entrance to an extensive classical domed-shaped Greek-style stone temple with twelve fluted Doric columns on a drum podium half hidden amongst the trees.

Construction of a mausoleum began in 1816 for the first William Forbes, which continued to be used by subsequent members of the Forbes family. A small enclosure surrounding the building is the graveyard for the estate workers. It is incredible how many tombs lie on

Mausoleum of William Forbes, Callendar Park

dragon currents worldwide, no doubt sited deliberately to aid the soul's journey along the paths of the dead to the afterlife or to glorify their ancestral line and perpetuate a successful future lineage.

However, Caroline immediately sensed that the energy was out of balance, and the dowsing confirmed that she was not allowed to enter. The relatively still and stuffy atmosphere surrounding this isolated spot was made all the more sinister by the gate posts scrawled with obscene graffiti and the words 'KEEP OUT' in large bold lettering. I then dowsed that the site guardian had permitted me to enter, so walked towards the entrance. I found the female current flowing through the main body of a now very dilapidated building long forgotten, with its main entrance concreted over, no doubt to put off any further violation of the temple.

Occasionally, we must decide whether performing healing at a sacred place is appropriate, particularly if the dowsing says no. If we ignore the dowsing results and permission from the guardian spirit, we risk experiencing a negative backlash such as flu symptoms.

Returning to Callendar House, we detected Bride travelling northwest towards a vast ditch and bank earthwork, one of the best remaining sections of the Antonine Wall, which cuts through the northern edge of the grounds roughly east–west. Most writers say it symbolised the Roman Empire's 'power and control' over the Caledonian tribes, but its primary purpose was to defend the Legions against the Britons and the Picts.

Section of the Antonine Wall, Callendar Park

Many sources state that Roman historians were the first to record the history of Scotland. Tacitus wrote that the Caledonians lived *'on their flocks, wild game and certain fruits ....'* and were *'.....aggressive, awkward, and difficult to subdue, many with red hair and large limbs'*, reminding him of the barbarians they fought against in the Rhine.[5]

Without having ever set foot in Scotland, Roman writer Dio Cassius wrote *'... they dwell in tents, naked and unshod, possess their woman in common and rear all the offspring. Their form of rule is democratic for the most part, and they are fond of plundering; consequently, they choose their best men as rulers. They go into battle in chariots and have small swift horses; they also have foot-soldiers, very swift in running and firm in standing their ground....'* The Picts and Caledoni continued to attack and harass the Romans throughout their occupation of Scotland, resulting in the construction of the Antonine Wall.[6]

Historians write that the Romans made treaties with the local tribes to protect this vital frontier using a system of scouts to maintain peace and stability in the region. However, excavations showed that defensive pits, the Roman equivalent of a minefield, ran the whole length of the Wall, suggesting they still had much to fear from the Caledonians. Unsurprisingly, relationships with the tribes north of the wall were tenuous. After its abandonment eight years later, the fort buildings were burned or dismantled, with only the rampart and ditch remaining.

However, some sources believe the ditch and bank were there long before the Romans arrived, having been used as a significant trading route by the native tribes. Throughout the post-Roman and medieval periods settlement continued on and around the Antonine Wall, known then as 'Grymisdyke', with the construction of churches, villages, and castles.

Hugh McArthur states that the Antonine Wall follows a land-bridge linking the North Sea with the Atlantic Ocean called the 'Neck of Britain' and that this isthmus or neck is a significant passage for trade between Ireland, Scandinavia, and the east coast ports. He states, *'Whoever held this major strategic route quite literally held the chain that could choke Britain. Moreover, that is why in 142 CE, the Romans began cutting the Wall and why they were not allowed to hold it for very long.'*[7] From 1768–1790, the Forth and Clyde Canal exploited the same land route, bringing the waters of the Forth to the Clyde.

McArthur, the historian of Clan Arthur, also writes that this area was the domain of

Artuir MacAedan of the Manau Gododdin. Although his father was of Irish descent, his grandmother and mother were Britons.

East of Callendar House, the Lugh current crosses another section of the Antonine Wall through the Callendar Business Park, said to be on the site of the 9th century Thane Hall. Excavations showed it contained a central hearth and partly paved floor and would have been the area's central gathering place. At that time, Falkirk was just a small settlement attached to the 7th-century church founded by St Modan 'when wild boar, wolves and aurochs roamed the countryside.'

Here, Lugh connects with a remarkable wooden and metal sculpture located next to the offices of Falkirk Council. Interestingly, the modern artwork has a Celtic carving of a serpent on one of the upright wooden supports rising from the ground. Unfortunately, we could find very little information about this sculpture despite several emails to Falkirk Council. Before entering Falkirk's town centre, Lugh visits the Graeme High School named after Sir John de Graeme, a leader in the army of William Wallace.

The alignment of the Holy Axis, located just under three miles south of Callendar House, is marked by Loch Ellrig that once stood within the vast estates of the Dukes of Hamilton. In Victorian times it was owned by the Ralston family, who left their mansion in ruins until its demolition in 1991 due to the open-cast coal mining operations that engulfed almost the entire area. In 1989, witnesses reported a white light hovering over the loch, one of many unusual UFO sightings within the famous Falkirk Triangle.[8] Plasma lights generally appear over lochs and lakes due to the massive weight of the water on the crystalline geology beneath. Interestingly, many plasma ball sightings worldwide are seen over water.

The 'Speckled' Church of Aidan

Having parked the car in the Howgate Shopping Centre, we made our way to Falkirk's High Street to start our investigation of the Bride and Lugh currents through this busy town, always a challenge at the best of times. We found Lugh entering an alleyway called Kings Court and followed him to see what was attracting his flow. Here we found the old court buildings still occupied by lawyers' chambers, one being Russel and Aitken; James Aitken first practised here in the 1700s. The alley takes its name from the old Kings Arms pub that stood here until the 19th century.

We retraced our steps to the High Street, where we detected Lugh passing through a tower called The Steeple, which at over 140 ft (42 m) high dominates the town's skyline. The squared-sided building you see today was built in 1812 and is now a theatre box office and the third structure to occupy the site. David Hamilton, the famous Glasgow architect, designed the original steeple in the classical style, which included a clock and police cells on the upper floors, still used in 1984. Also, a new bell was added in 1816 bearing the inscription 'May Falkirk Flourish'. On a geomantic level, a steeple acts like an antenna to focus cosmic energy such as orgone to energise the location. Likewise, the bell, resonating a harmonious musical note with such a positive affirmation of success is good feng shui.

The first mention of a steeple was in 1638 when it was used as a Tollbooth. It was later demolished and rebuilt due to severe listing to the right. The steeple is a potent phallic symbol of masculine energy and, therefore, a draw for the male current, perhaps nourished by the orgone that this tall edifice attracts.

Lugh continues to the churchyard of Falkirk's parish 'speckled' church, once the site of St Modan's 7th-century chapel, located on the summit of a low ridge between the High Street and Upper Newmarket Street. Here, he snakes through the grand tombs of William Edmondstoune of Cambuswallace, who fell at the Battle of Falkirk in 1746, and Sir John de Graeme, who died at the earlier Battle of Falkirk when the English defeated Sir William Wallace in 1298. Graeme High School, also on the male current, is named after him.

Blind Harry (c. 1440–1492), also known as Harry the Minstrel, author of *The Actes and Deidis of the Illustre and Vallyeant Campioun Schir William Wallace*, wrote of William Wallace: *'They carried him with worship and dolour into Fawkyrk graith'd him in sepulture'.*[9] Lugh also led us to the grave of Sir John Stewart of Bonkyill, who died at the same battle, an ancestor of the Marquis of Bute. These knights were much revered – even Robert Burns came to kneel at the original stone effigy of Sir John de Graeme in 1787.

As the male current disappears through the southeast corner of the church, Bride meanwhile meanders south of here to an attractive octagonal building just off Cow Wynd, known as the Tattie Kirk. It was built in 1806 by members of the Anti-Burgher movement but abandoned in 1879 when the congregation moved to a new church on Graham's Road. It has since been a joiner's workshop and an ironmonger's store. We smiled at the explanation on the notice board regarding the octagonal shape: '... so there was no corner for the Devil to hide.' The source of the name 'Tattie Kirk' has created much debate, with one suggestion being that it was built over the site of a potato field, 'tattie' being a Scottish word for potato. In many cultures, the octagonal shape is a sacred and religious symbol of rebirth and resurrection.

The feminine serpent continues on a northerly course to Falkirk's oldest pub, the Wheatsheaf Inn established in 1797, although some say an inn has been on this site since the early 1600s. She then travels along the High Street towards the 'speckled' church from the location of the old Mercat Cross, now very close to Lugh at the town steeple. The cross was a focal point for fairs, markets, public proclamations, floggings and hangings, the last of which occurred in 1828. Just to the west of this site is the Cross Well, which Bride also visits. This circular sandstone structure with a domed-shaped top is surmounted by a crowned lion holding the coat of arms of Alexander Livingston, 2nd Earl of Callendar. It was constructed in 1682 when the Earl arranged for a new water supply to be piped to the High Street from his Callendar lands following a drought when both tributaries of the River Carron, the East and West Burns, dried up. In 1871 due to the well's deteriorating condition, it was rebuilt but retained the crowned lion holding the Livingston coat of arms. When the 2nd Earl drank the first waters from his newly built well, he made a toast to 'the wives and bairns o' Fa'kirk giving them the well and all its fountains in a present forever.'[10]

Interestingly, the original medieval walled town was centred on Manor Street and Bank Street, just west of the church. Later as Falkirk grew and developed in the 17th century, the centre shifted to High Street and the new Mercat Cross and Cross Well. The Cross Well, even though it is a conduit from Callendar, is a perfect representation of an *omphalos,* marking the geomantic centre of the new town of Falkirk.

The word 'omphalos', from the Greek word meaning 'navel', embodies harmonious placement beneficial to the landscape, man and the cosmos, usually defined on the Earth's surface by a well, or a marker stone or *gnomon*, which links heaven to earth, invoking a cosmic axis. Finding the omphalos, or the geographical centre of a kingdom, was essential to the Ancient Greeks, Etruscans, Romans and early Celts when establishing their territory.

Centre points are located in every culture, landscape, city, town, and even the smallest village. The ancient Greeks determined the centre of the world to be at Delphi, and the Incas of South America believed it was Cuzco. In the creation myths of the Ancient Egyptians, the 'primordial mound' or 'island of creation' that rose from the floodwaters was the centre of the world at Heliopolis. The Etruscans were an advanced culture developed in Central Italy from 900 BC. Their priest geomancer or *augur* would first survey the land, determined by the position of the stars and planets, and then consecrate a spot, perhaps using visible signs in nature and portents or omens such as lightning strikes. Then a north–south axis would be marked out called a *cardo,* and an east–west line called a *decumanus.* Next, they dug a deep shaft called a *mundus* at the centre point of the new town to connect the surface world of the living to the powers of the 'underworld'. Offerings were dropped into the well, including soil from the native land of the new settlers. The Romans later adopted this ritual from the Etruscans and probably used it to build their many towns and cities in England.

Finding the centre is vital for humanity, for it is from the centre or navel that we receive nourishment. In the womb, the umbilical cord feeds us through the centre of our body, the 'navel'. This fundamental experience transfers symbolically to our existence on the earth plane, hence our natural propensity to locate our 'centre'. According to Nigel Pennick in *The Ancient Science of Geomancy, 'The individual's spirit is centralised in the body, and the body has a physical location, so the world's spirit was thought of as centralised at a fixed point'.*[11] In Eastern martial arts such as Tai Chi, one works on the core or navel from which one can radiate balance and harmony. The navel or omphalos is also the source of connection between the upper and lower worlds and a place to link with the nurturing power of the Earth Mother.

Colin Bloy, who founded the Fountain Group in 1981, would locate the 'centre' of a town or city to help heal communities disturbed by such problems as violence and discordance. Using his spiritual healing techniques, a network of groups made a real and positive difference in the lives of inhabitants in these various affected communities. Healers and dowsers would gather to send healing and loving thoughts to a focal point of the town or omphalos, such as a fountain or market cross. This healing would often continue daily, revealing observable results such as a reduced crime rate and a more positive mood among the townspeople.[12] Dowsers also discovered that the area's energy field had increased frequency.

For the many early tribes, a stone pillar represents the centre of their territory, symbolic of a world axis, a link between heaven and earth. These pillars were the forerunners of the Christian cross, erected in towns and villages across Europe, taking the form of a shaft topped by a stone ball representing the sun and a square base fixing it to earth. The design of the dome-shaped top of the Cross Well symbolises the feminine in contrast to the nearby phallic-shaped steeple visited by Lugh.

From here, Bride continues to the parish church, ascending the bank of the churchyard to enter through the south entrance to form a node with Lugh at the high altar. Usually the church is locked, so for our second visit we telephoned ahead to arrange to look inside. It stands on the site of St Modan's 7th-century chapel known as 'the speckled church' or 'Faw Kirk', rebuilt in the late 11th century by King Malcolm Canmore. St Modan was supposedly the son of an Irish chieftain and an abbot of a chapel near Old Melrose that later became the site of Dryburgh Abbey. However, some believe St Modan never existed and the name instead refers to Mo-Aidan or My-Aidan, and that Aidan or one of his followers founded the earliest church here before arriving at Bamburgh.

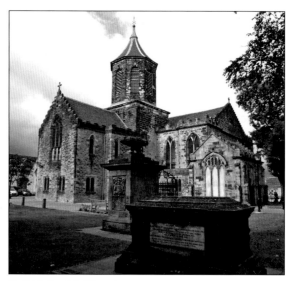

Falkirk Parish Church

George Buchanan, a 16th-century scholar, claimed that the first church at Falkirk used stones in its walls robbed from the Roman fort at Carmuirs – more likely the Roman fort along the Antonine Wall known as *Ad Vallum*. A 13th-century manuscript mentions the existence of a chapel here dedicated to Mary Magdalene and the south transept of the old medieval church included a chapel of the Order of St John of Jerusalem, also known as the Knights Hospitallers, of which Henry Livingston of Callendar was a chaplain in the 15th century. A wood-cut drawing shows a plan of the church before its renovation in 1810-11, with the south transept dedicated at that time to St John the Baptist. The church was extended again in 1892, although its squat squared tower survives from a church built around 1450, and the octagonal bell tower that surmounts it was added in 1733.

When we entered the church, we were surprised to find a modernised and unadorned circular interior fitted only five years ago, which provides space for Christian worship and accommodates local meetings, presentations and concerts. It even became the venue for debate between local politicians during the Scottish referendum campaign in 2014. Interestingly, the altar stands at the church's north end, where we dowse the node of Bride and Lugh. The male enters from the southeast and the female from the south. Set above the main entrance, on the Bride flow, is the supposed foundation stone laid by Malcolm Canmore in 1057. The stone may be a later addition, however, as King Malcolm only succeeded to the throne in 1058, and the carver used Arabic letters and numerals rather than the usual Latin inscription of that period.

In the outer corridors, we find several carved stone remnants of Falkirk's earlier churches, including a Celtic-style crosshead dated to 1200, possibly one of four that marked the church boundary. These crosses would have highlighted this site as a sacred sanctuary for those seeking refuge from persecution, similar to the stones at Torphichen Preceptory. We also encountered the worn grave slab of Alexander Livingston, 5th Lord of Callendar, who accompanied Mary, Queen of Scots as a child to France in 1548 to marry the young Dauphine. The inscription next to the slab reads: 'Alexander, the protector of the young Queen of France, lay in the south aisle of the old church until 1810, and then in the open until 1892'. A roof boss bearing the Livingston coat of arms and stone effigies of various members of the Livingstone family are also on display here, many of them having rested in their family crypt below the present upper hall.

The name 'speckled church' is intriguing, a word that gave rise to Falkirk's original name. However, some sources speculate that its meaning, 'many-coloured stones', refers to stones taken from the Roman Forts of Colania built by the River Carron, said to be a Camelot of Arthur.

In *Kinship, Church and Culture: Collected Essays and Studies*, John W M Bannerman writes that the Brythonic word *brecc* describes decorative metalwork on the famous *Breccbennach Coluim Chille*, which translates as 'the speckled peaked one of Columba'. It refers to a tiny metal casket or house shrine holding a relic of St Columba, which stands about 4 in (9 cm) high. The fabric of the religious relic, made of wood, bronze, gold and silver with highly decorated metalwork, is a fusion of Gaelic and Pictish designs

Celtic-style crosshead, Falkirk Parish Church

probably carved by Ionian monks. It may have had straps attached to carry or wear around the neck. Scholars believe the 'Monymusk Reliquary' in the National Museum of Scotland is the Breccbennach of St Columba.[13] Perhaps this 'speckled' reliquary was kept at St Modan's Church for safety by missionaries from Iona, after which the church acquired the name Egglesbreth or Egglesbrech.

We mentioned earlier that the Tironensian monks held the Breccbennach of St Columba in medieval times, which a 'guardian monk' wore around his neck. King William I awarded them guardianship of this precious relic in 1211, after establishing Arbroath Abbey in 1178, on the proviso that they bore the reliquary in battle. It was also used against the English at Bannockburn in 1314.

Perhaps during its time at St Modan's Church, the Breccbennach was paraded in front of the Scottish army commanded by Sir William Wallace as they marched forth to meet Edward I at the Battle of Falkirk in 1298. Unlike the Battle of Bannockburn, this battle was a decisive English victory, partly due to the betrayal of two of Wallace's 'ignoble peers, jealous of his power', who warned Edward I of the Scottish position and intended tactics. Despite one of the most courageous stands in the history of warfare, Wallace's reputation as a general was crushed, leading him to resign as Guardian of Scotland.

The precise location of the battle has always remained elusive, although Campfield, north of Falkirk's town centre, has long been considered the place, with roads like Wallace Street and Wallace Place marking the spot. Another candidate is just east of Callendar Woods at Mumrills, the site of the most significant Roman fort on the Antonine Wall.

It is well known that William Wallace mustered his troops in Callendar Woods next to Westquarter Burn. To our surprise, we detected Bride here after passing through Wallace's Cave next to the River Avon, also marked by the Holy Axis. We have found this to be a feature on the Belinus Line, where many battle sites or mustering places throughout England and Scotland, including the Isle of Wight, Uffington, Clifton Moor, Arthuret, Killiecrankie and Culloden, are on the serpent flow of both Elen and Belinus.

Many critical battles around Britain took place at sacred places to influence the outcome, the effects reverberating in the local earth energy matrix for years to come. Uffington is an excellent example, featuring Arthur against the Saxons and King Alfred against the Danes. They possibly understood the geographical and energetic significance of the prehistoric Uffington complex, positioned at a point along the Ridgeway, where the telluric and serpent energies of the Belinus alignment and the famous St Michael Line focus together at a cosmic 'Tree of Life'. As we were beginning to discover, the Holy Axis is no exception.

We can only speculate whether St Modan's Church contained a vital relic of St Columba or if Aidan founded a church here. Still, many prominent people throughout history have revered this place, built by Celtic missionaries on a powerful node of the Holy Axis.

North of the church, Bride passes through the old Corn Exchange site and Town Hall that once stood on Market Street, later renamed New Market Street. The Corn Exchange dating from 1857 was Falkirk's most significant venue, hosting lectures, concerts, dances, public exhibitions, auctions and other public entertainments. It was rebuilt and extended in 1879 to incorporate the Town Hall and finally demolished in 1966 when the new office complex for the Town Council opened on West Bridge Street.

Bride visits the Burgh Buildings opposite, built in the Scottish baronial style and established by the town council in 1833. Before that time, the Stentmasters administered the town's affairs and met in the upper rooms of the Steeple on the male current in the High Street. A relief carving on the building depicts the portraits of three of the Nine Worthies. Bride's flow then shifts to gently travel northwest towards a large loop in the River Carron.

Meanwhile, Lugh leaves through the church's northwest corner taking us to the Newmarket Bar in Links Riggs, close to the Masonic temple called Lodge Callendar, which opened in 1906. Crossing Newmarket Street, he continues to a turreted building on the corner of Hope Street and West Bridge Street, formerly the Sheriff's Court House opened in 1868, now funeral directors. We stood looking up at the building's many elaborate carvings including a fleur-de-lys, a rampant lion, a knight's visor and a sword held by a knight's hand pointing upwards into a wolf's throat. We also noticed several law offices in the vicinity. As in many of the towns and cities on the Belinus Line, we often found the male current connecting with law courts and prisons.

Lugh visits Falkirk Town Hall Theatre next to the District Court building just west of Hope Street. We found several theatres on the male and female dragon lines while following the Belinus Line, including the Theatre Royal in Winchester, Swan Theatre in Stratford-upon-Avon, the Opera House Theatre in Manchester and Penrith Theatre. Perhaps the artistry and creative energy of the performers attract the serpent lines to absorb this aspect of human consciousness. Often the design of these buildings is reminiscent of famous Greek temples.

Next to it is Dollar Park, a delightful oasis from the bustling streets, which was bequeathed to the people of Falkirk by locally born Robert Dollar who became the world's wealthiest man. His gift of two white marble Chinese lions still flanks the main entrance on Camelon Road. Here we dowsed the male current flowing to a walled garden and a large standing stone incorporated as a bench. This curious feature surrounded by mature trees, including giant redwoods, is symbolic of a world tree, where you can rest and gently tune into the solar aspect of the Holy Axis. From the outskirts of Falkirk, Lugh flows northwest to Camelon, following the line of Roman forts along the banks of the River Carron and the enigmatic Hills of Dunipace, where Merlin supposedly met his death.

Arthur's O'on

Bride flows north of Lugh crossing a loop of the River Carron to an area of high ground on its northern banks amongst modern houses. We later discovered that at this spot was one of Britain's most historic buildings, one of such importance that if it were standing today, it would be protected as a World Heritage site.

Most historians and antiquarians refer to it as a Roman temple built during the Antonine Wall's occupation, an assumption based on the discovery of a brass finger of a long-lost Roman statue lodged between stones inside the building. Early reports also say a figure of a Roman eagle was visible carved upon the temple floor with other Roman insignia on its walls. However, when Edward I rampaged through Scotland destroying many important Scottish antiquities, he spared the 'temple beside Camelon' after the neighbourhood's inhabitants had already chiselled out all the Roman sculptures and inscriptions.

Sir Robert Sibbald (1641–1722) also recorded the mysterious letters J. A. M. P. M. P. T. engraved on a stone inside under a figure of victory, possibly the Roman Goddess Victoria, that still retained its head and part of the handle of a spear or javelin. According to Gillespie in *Round about Falkirk,* the letters referred to: **J**ulius **A**gricola **M**agnae **P**ictatis **M**onumentum **P**osuit **T**emplum, which translates as 'Julius Agricola built this great painted monument.'

Recorded descriptions say that the O'on was a circular stone-built dome-shaped structure with an east-facing iron door at the base and an aperture in the roof. It measured 22 ft (6.7 m) in height, the external circumference at the base 88 ft (26.8 m) and the depth of the walls 3 ft 7 in (1.1 m). Three or four steps led to the entrance and surrounding the O'on was a ditch and bank earthwork once visible on its northern side. The stone blocks were polished freestones, *'which were not mortised into each other and no mortar was used'*. Each stone had a 'lewis hole' to allow secure lifting with a hinged pair of metal callipers.[14] Another source mentions a tradition that when the Monteiths of Cars removed its iron door, it brought a curse upon the family.

Arthur's O'on is mentioned as far back as the 9th century when Saxon monk Nennius in *Historia Brittonum* described it as a 'round house of polished stone' and attributes it to Carausius.[15] However in 1293, a Newbattle Abbey charter is mystified by the origin of Arthur's O'on, mentioning it as a well-established feature of unknown origin. John of Fordun, a 14th-century historian who wrote *Chronicles of the Scottish Nation*, described it as a *rotundam casulam* or round chamber. He stated that Julius Caesar built it to either mark the northernmost boundary of his military endeavours or to provide a temporary haven from attack, but *'when he was in a hurry to return to Gaul, he left it behind.'*[16] 16th-century royal historian George Buchanan saw it as a memorial to some great Roman victory over the Scots.

William Stukeley, the famous 18th-century antiquarian, published a tract on Arthur's O'on in *Account of a Roman Temple and other antiquities near Graham's Dike in Scotland* (1720), even though he never actually visited the site. Instead, he surmised that it was a temple *'dedicated to Romulus, the parent and primitive Deity of the Romans'* and compared it lavishly to Rome's Pantheon, which he had also never seen.[17] Sir John Clerk of Penicuik House, writing in 1790, counted it among Britain's most important 'wonders' and considered it *'the best and most entire old building in Britain.'*[18]

An illustration of Arthur's O'on was discovered at Blair Castle in 1969 by Catherine Cruft in an unpublished first-hand description. It was bound in a booklet of eight pages sewn together, the cover bearing the title 'Arthur' Oven'. Unfortunately, the manuscript was never signed or dated.

In 1688, the O'on was enclosed within the grounds of a fortification called Stenhouse Castle. Stenhouse derives from 'stone house' referring

Arthur's O'on from Alexander Gordon's 'Itinerarium Septeptrionale' 1726

to Arthur's O'on, marked on Sir William Roy's map of Scotland (1745–1746). In the mid-18th century, this attractive turreted house became part of the land owned by the Carron Ironworks. Another name assigned to this structure is Julius' Hoff, Hoff or Huif, perhaps deriving from the Norse word *hov*, meaning throne or the Gaelic word for a house or hall.[19] Gordon argued it was not a Roman Temple for public worship but rather a *'place of holding the Roman Insignia'* or legionary standards. There is also the suggestion that the name Arthur derives from the old Gaelic word *Art*, meaning house, and *Om*, a retired dwelling or hermitage. The term 'oven' possibly relates to the similarity in shape to the clay bread ovens and old kilns of the 18th century.[20]

In 1743 the O'on served as a folly on the grounds of Stenhouse Castle, later demolished by its owner Sir Michael Bruce, having removed its stones to line a mill dam on the River Carron to save his fortunes. This act of vandalism was reported to the Society of Antiquaries in London, causing outrage among leading antiquarians. According to one contemporary account, the demolition was so complete that even *'the very foundation stones were raised.'*

Unfortunately, during the summer of 1748, a flood destroyed any further evidence of it. Some sources believe that the building of the dam altered the course of the Carron River and any buried archaeology was lost forever. Sir Walter Scott remarked on the O'on's destruction, this *'great glory of the Roman remains in Scotland,'* and *'had not the worthy proprietor thought fit to demolish it, it would have turned the heads of half the antiquaries in Scotland.'*[21] American researcher Robert Mitchell claimed the stones of the O'on survived and lay beneath the grounds of the former Carron Iron Works. Unfortunately, the Scottish antiquities authorities were not interested in uncovering them because a buried mill dam was not considered a scheduled site. The old site of the temple now stands within the back gardens of a housing estate, developed soon after Sir Michael Bruce's Stenhouse Castle was demolished in the 1960s. Sir James Clerk, son of Sir John Clerk, decided in 1760 to have a replica made of the temple to use as a dovecot, which they erected on top of the stable block at Penicuik House.

Standing close to the site of Arthur's O'on, which we dowsed was just west of a road called Castle Drive on the site of a modern housing estate, we wondered if the name was linked to the Scottish Artuir MacAedan of the Manau Gododdin. Perhaps the Roman monument was rededicated to this brave warrior when he died in a battle at nearby Camelon. But sadly, we may never know the true purpose of this mysterious building. However, we believe that this ancient temple was constructed next to the Carron River to harness the potent nourishing force of its waters and the divine goddess in the form of the Bride serpent energy.

The description of an east–facing aperture in the roof of the domed temple was also curious and we wondered whether it was to allow sunlight to illuminate the statue of Victoria, the Roman goddess of victory and success. Many lightboxes align due east to the spring and autumn equinox sunrises to capture the light of the planet Venus, the 'morning star' that rises before the sun, like the east-facing aperture at Rosslyn Chapel and passage tomb of Bryn Celli Dhu in Anglesey. Is it also possible that the brass finger found in the wall of Arthur's O'on belonged to a statue of Venus in her later role as the Roman goddess of victory. During the reign of Caesar, Venus was depicted on coins showing her with a spear called Venus Victorix. I believe

Arthur's O'on was a Roman temple to Venus Victorix to serve as a monument in honour of their conquest over the Picts and a ceremonial ritual place linked to the worship of the planet Venus, later usurped by Artuir of the Manau Gododdin.

From here, Bride's northwest flow continues to the remains of a broch next to an old Roman Road in the Forest of Torwood.

1. Reid, J. 2009. *The Place Names of Falkirk and East Stirlingshire*. Falkirk Local History Society.
2. Scott, Iain. 2006. *Falkirk: A History*. Birlinn Ltd, Edinburgh.
3. Defoe, D. 1927. *A tour thro' the whole island of Great Britain, divided into circuits or journies.* JM Dent & Co, London.
4. Taken from the information boards inside Callendar House 2015.
5. http://www.perseus.tufts.edu/hopper/text?doc=Perseus%3Atext%3A1999.02.0081
6. https://penelope.uchicago.edu/Thayer/e/roman/texts/cassius_dio/77*.html
7. http://clanarthur.org/history/arthur-the-chieftain/
8. https://www.abovetopsecret.com/forum/thread539515/pg1;
9. https://d.lib.rochester.edu/teams/publication/mckim-the-wallace-selections
10. https://falkirklocalhistory.club/around-the-area/castles/cross-well-falkirk/
11. Pennick, N. 1979. *The Ancient Science of Geomancy: Man in Harmony with the Earth.* Thames & Hudson, London.
12. Bloy, C. Thomas, S. 2019. *Who'd Have Thought It.* lulu.com
13. Bannerman, J. W. M. 2016. *Kinship, Church and Culture: Collected Essays and Studies.* Berlinn Ltd, Edinburgh.
14. Gibson, J. C. 1908. *Lands and lairds of Larbert and Dunipace parishes.* Hugh Hopkins, Glasgow. https://en.wikipedia.org/wiki/Arthur%27s_O%27on
15. Morris, J. 1980. *'Nennius' British History and the Welsh Annals.* Phillimore, London.
16. Skene, William. 2014. *John of Fordun's Chronicle of the Scottish Nation.* CreateSpace Independent Publishing Platform.
17. Stukeley, W. 1720. *An account of a Roman temple, and other antiquities, near Graham's Dike in Scotland.* Republished 2010 Gale ECCO, Print Editions, USA.
18. Darrell, J. R. 2012. *Arthur's O'on: A Lost 'Wonder' of Britain, Part 1.* Archaeology, Stanford University, USA.
19. 20. Gordon, Alexander.1726. *Itinerarium Septentrionale.* Republished 2010, Gale ECCO, Print Editions USA.
21. Gillespie, Robert. 1879. *Round about Falkirk: with an account of the historical and antiquarian landmarks of the counties of Stirling and Linlithgow.* Glasgow: Dunn & Wright. pp. 117–137. Retrieved 2 December 2017.

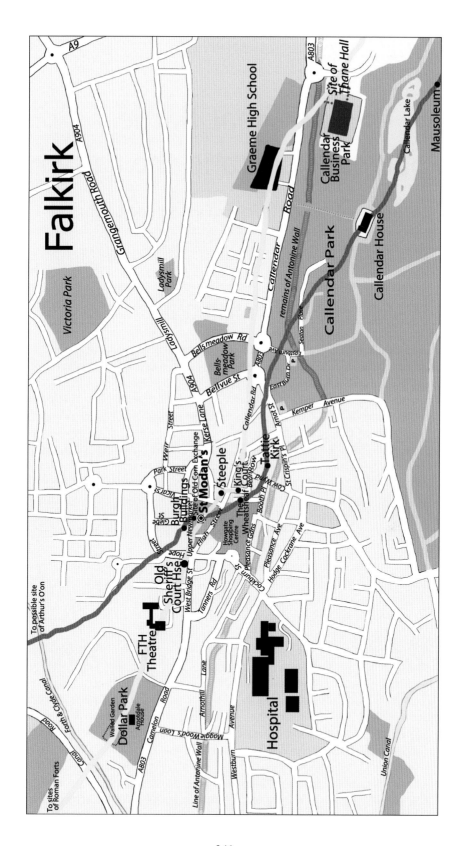

Falkirk

241

Chapter 11

The Great Battle,
a Sacred Island and the Fairy Hill

Bride's Journey from Falkirk to Loch Lomond

The Mystery of the Scottish Brochs

Bride flows northwest through the outskirts of Stenhousemuir and Larbert following an old Roman road that passes through the Forest of Torwood, once the royal hunting ground of Alexander III in the mid-13th century. In medieval times, the forest covered a vast area that stretched from the River Carron to Stirling in the north and inland towards the Campsie Fells. This atmospheric woodland has witnessed many events during Scotland's illustrious history, including the marching armies of William Wallace and an encampment for Sir James Douglas's men before joining the armies of King Robert Bruce at the Battle of Bannockburn.

The owners of this territory were the noble Forresters of Garden, who took their name from their ancient role as guardians of the royal forests around Edinburgh. As a family, the Forresters worked with the land providing timber for the king's artillery, eventually becoming the hereditary keepers of the Forest of Torwood during the reign of King James III (1452–1488).

Within the royal forest, Bride leads us to the Forrester's isolated baronial castle built around 1566 on the site of an earlier fortification. When David MacGibbon and Thomas Ross visited it while researching *The Castellated and Domestic Architecture of Scotland*, published in 1892, it was known then as Torwoodhead Castle.[1] The castle passed to the Baillies in the early 17th century and the Forresters of Corstorphine in 1653. Interestingly, their castle at Corstorphine, on the western outskirts of Edinburgh, was built on the feminine dragon flow associated with the north–south Belinus Line.

In 1957, Glaswegian accountant Gordon Millar acquired the ruin and dedicated over fifty years of his life to restoring it. When he passed away in 1998, his work continued with the foundation of the Torwood Castle Trust. However, in 2015, the Trust ceased to operate, leaving the castle abandoned and neglected, although it still appears remarkably well preserved.[2] There is a wealth of information on the paranormal activity witnessed here, including ghostly apparitions, strange sounds and cold spots.[3]

The atmosphere felt eerie as we followed Bride from the castle through the dense and silent woodland. We were completely alone as we followed a narrow footpath that gently climbed through rows of conifers for what seemed like an age to an isolated clearing at the top of a high ridge. We kept hearing strange sounds and were convinced we saw a spectral figure moving in and out of the pine trees. It reminded us of the scene in J R R Tolkien's *Lord of the Rings*, where Gollum was shadowing the unsuspecting Frodo and Sam.

When we reached the clearing, Bride took us through a mossy entrance supported by an impressive stone lintel, which we soon realised was an ancient monument known as Tappoch or Torwood Broch. Continuing through another door, we descended some steps to the remains of the broch's interior, where we detected Bride exiting the site to the northwest. As we absorbed the Broch's energy, we both felt it had a unique atmosphere, a heady mix of tranquillity, a secret past and otherworldliness.

Interestingly, before excavation, this imposing structure appeared as an earthen mound covering a circular stone-lined chamber built within a natural knoll dating to the Iron Age. According to many accounts, Colonel Dundas of Carronhall first exposed the site in 1864. He removed a mass of boulders and debris, estimated to weigh over 200 tons, uncovering inner walls about 19 ft (6 m) thick, a floor formed by the natural rock and a southeast-facing entrance passage supported by the large lintel. The floor area revealed a central hearth and several relics, including three cup-marked stones, quern stones, stone balls and Iron Age domestic ware, some of which are on display at Falkirk Burgh Museum and the National Museum of Scotland, Edinburgh.

Tappoch Broch, Forest of Torwood

According to Geoff Bailey, Keeper of Archaeology and Local History in Falkirk, *'no attempt was made to find the outer wall-face, which is now almost totally hidden by earth and debris.'* He further writes:

'At ground level, there is an irregular circular chamber/courtyard measuring 10.8m by 9.8m, enclosed by a massive wall some 6.1m thick. This is made of large roughly squared blocks of stone quarried from the immediate locality, with no mortar. There is a narrow entrance passage in the southeast, with some of the lintels still in place. About halfway along the passage is a check for the doorway with a bar hole behind it to secure the door in place. To the southwest, another short passage leads to a stair, which is built within the thickness of the wall. Eleven steps were reported in 1864, but some have been subsequently lost. The side walls of this stair passage slope in towards the top, suggesting that it was originally corbelled. There has been some recent collapse of the walls near the main entrance, but the site is still very impressive. A small internal chamber in the NE sector of the wall appears to be of modern origin and was not reported in either the original excavation of the survey by the RCAHMS in the 1950s. It has been suggested that this was formed by the Home Guard during the war.[4]

Traces of two concentric banks exist today on the site's north, east and south sides. When examined in 1948 by D M Hunter, he found that the ruins of rubble-cored, boulder-faced walls and gaps in both banks appear to align with the broch's entrances.

Interestingly, excavations revealed no Roman remains, which is unusual considering that an old Roman road lies only 196 yds (180 m) to the west. Perhaps they were unaware of its importance and saw the mound as just another burial site of the Picts. However, as we stood pondering the various features of this fascinating site, we began to wonder whether this was a ceremonial chamber rather than the base for a towering broch. Many of the brochs we had previously encountered in Scotland on the Belinus Line lacked a room at its base. The fact that an earthen mound once covered it with signs of a possible ditch and embankment containing cup-marked stones further fed our suspicions that this structure was a sacred sanctuary. Moreover, its entrance aligns with the mid-winter solstice, the most auspicious time for ceremony, honouring the birth of a new solar year.

The purpose and nature of the stone-built broch have puzzled archaeologists for decades. These windowless circular towers are unique to Scotland and, like the round towers of Ireland, are seen as an incredible feat of engineering. The largest stands up to 49 ft (15 m) tall and is built of dry stone with no cement mortar or other binding material to secure the masonry. According to Mike Snowden in *Scotland's Ancient Brochs: A Baffling Mystery on a Colossal Scale,* this was an immense undertaking by the broch builders of the Iron Age, *'comparable to the largest medieval castles (which used mortar to keep their walls together)'.* He also reported that over seven hundred brochs remain across the Highlands, Orkney, Shetland and the Western Isles, some of them appearing to be part of remote settlements.[5]

Dated to the late Iron Age *c.* 400 BCE to 100 CE, the brochs, according to some sources, were used as lookout towers, tribal shelters during local conflicts or grain stores. *Egil's Saga* also mentions the broch as a hideout for eloping lovers. Curiously, building these towers in this style of architecture ended in the 1st century CE, before the Romans invaded Scotland. Although, recent archaeological evidence suggests they continued to be occupied throughout Scotland as late as 900 CE.

In the online article, *Brochs – the Tallest Prehistoric Buildings in Britain,* Ben Johnson writes, *'brochs combine features of fort, fortified house, and status symbol, and could feasibly have served several different purposes in different places and at different times.'* They had a single entrance leading to a circular central courtyard, with small rooms and storage areas and possibly topped with a conical, thatched roof. Johnson also states that brochs *'were never built to deter serious or sustained attack as their defences were simply too weak; the rough stone walls could be climbed by determined attackers and the entranceway lacked external protection and so could easily have been rammed. Lacking external windows and access to the top of the walls, the defenders inside were denied both visibility and the tactical advantage of height, from which missiles could be launched.'*[6]

Brochs were status symbols, according to some authorities, built by tribal chiefs or wealthy landowners to impress. However, pre-Roman remains found within the brochs suggested they belonged to those who enjoyed an opulent lifestyle *'that included imported wines and olives from the Mediterranean.'*

Perhaps one of the finest examples of these mysterious brochs is on the uninhabited island of Mousa in Shetland, which has survived the passage of time virtually intact. The broch, one of a pair built to guard the Mousa Sound, stands 44 ft (13.3 m) high and 49 ft (15 m) in diameter, although the interior only measures 19 ft (6 m) in diameter because of the extremely thick walls. It may have been part of a chain of brochs in this region of Shetland, like beacons.

Mousa Broch, Shetland Isles

Some researchers compare them to Sardinia's Bronze and Iron Age Nuraghi Towers. They have similar dry-stone construction and internal staircases to the Scottish brochs, but their function is unexplained. There is evidence that the Nuraghi sacrificed to the gods, perhaps leading us to believe they had a religious purpose, like the mysterious round towers of Ireland.

The Bannock Burn

'You could have lived in serfdom,
but because you yearned to have freedom,
you are gathered here with me.'
Robert Bruce 24 June 1314

From the woodland at Torwood, Bride continues north to Plean Country Park and the derelict 18th century Plean House, once owned by William Simpson, one of Stirlingshire's wealthiest merchants who made his fortune by trading with the East India Company. A devastating fire almost destroyed the house in the 1970s and after restoration it became a luxury hotel, which also failed to survive.

We followed the current under the busy M9 motorway close to the watery sanctuary of the Bannock Burn and a cairn at the Bannockburn Visitor's Centre and memorial park, just south of the royal town of Stirling. In 1314, Robert the Bruce fought King Edward II's forces here, winning the freedom of the Scots from English domination. However, modern historians believe the genuine site to be just outside the village of Balquhidderock in an area known as the Dryfield, about 0.75 miles (1.21 km) east of Bannockburn.

Interestingly, we found Bride flowing through the grounds of the Battle of Bannockburn Heritage Centre, although her energy was weak and narrow. Here, Robert the Bruce encamped with his army before the battle after moving from his position at Torwood Forest also on the Bride current. The English troops arrived to meet them from the south, crossing the Bannock Burn.

We visited an exhibition at the Heritage Centre to participate in the 'Battle of Bannockburn Experience', which immerses you in the fight's graphic high-tech 3D scenes. For us, though, taking part in the battle experience had another purpose – to find out exactly where the battle took place and whether Bride visits the site.

According to many historians, this significant conflict during midsummer, 23 and 24 June 1314, was part of a long and hard-fought campaign by William Wallace and Robert the Bruce against the notorious English King Edward I and his attempt to conquer Scotland. After Edward died in 1307, his son King Edward II took up his father's mantle, having already accompanied him on previous campaigns against the Scots. In 1314, his objective was to take Stirling Castle with the help of several Scottish nobles, having sided against Robert the Bruce after the killing of Sir John Comyn of Badenoch.

Robert the Bruce statue at Bannockburn Heritage Centre

However, not only had Edward II proved incompetent as a king, but he was also an inept military leader, resulting in divisions and disputes over tactics and the positioning of his senior command. As a result, the English attacked from the south crossing the boggy terrain around the Bannock Burn, disadvantaging Edward's mighty cavalry. When facing Bruce's spearmen, they soon disintegrated and the foot soldiers started to flee, leaving the English infantry to fight the Scots alone. At this point, Edward II fled the battlefield leaving his men to fend for themselves, many slaughtered in the 'great ditch of the Bannockburn'.

Although it is still uncertain where the exact battle site occurred, many believe the English army faced the Scots by the waters of the Bannock Burn. To our dismay, plans at the exhibition centre showed the heart of the battle to be where Bride crosses the river from Torwood.

When we discovered that the Elen current flowed through a holy well at the heart of the battle site of Culloden, mentioned earlier, we both sensed that the violent bloodshed had injured the site's energy and depleted the feminine force and her ability to nourish and heal the land. The molecular structure of water holds memory, so the horrific act of killing and maiming at this sacred watery shrine would profoundly affect the local earth energy matrix and the people's psyche for centuries to come.

A poem by John Barbour called *The Bruce*, written in the 1370s, recalls this pivotal Bannockburn Battle that secured Scotland's future independence and held in the mind of the Scots the tyranny and injustice inflicted upon them by the English.

After the battle, The Declaration of Arbroath, sent to the Pope in 1320, outlined why Scotland should be independent of England with Bruce as their king.

Like Culloden, the memory of Bannockburn endures, perhaps because of the presence of the feminine serpent Bride flowing amid the battle site. The current carries memories and emotions of that historical event, as do the rivers as they radiate out like the spokes of a wheel. Fiona Watson believes the powerful memory of the battle is due to *'the rhetoric of freedom that has chimed throughout the centuries...'* Every year a rally takes place in Bannockburn where the Scots sing Robert Burn's song inspired by Bruce's 'glorious struggle for freedom'.[7]

We felt the feminine current of Bride had experienced the full force of the slaughter and terror facing the men at the Bannock Burn that day, negatively affecting the potency of her power similar to Elen at Culloden, which accounted for her weak and narrow flow. Therefore, we placed our healing stones at strategic places around the grounds of the Bannockburn memorial park to bless and honour the dragon current of Bride, directing healing light through her flow at the various sites of the battle. We removed the stones once we completed the healing.

Bride targets a cairn near the exhibition centre constructed in 1954 to commemorate those who fell in the battle. It stands close to the imposing bronze statue of the battle's hero Robert the Bruce. The cairn, built using stone from the Cambusbarron quarry, stands within a dome of concrete slabs with large boulders at the entrance to replicate a Neolithic henge monument. It has openings to the south and north – the south overlooking the line of advance from Edward II's armies and the north pointing to the bronze statue of King Robert the Bruce, unveiled in 1964. Beyond is Stirling Castle, its takeover being the main objective of Edward II.

Bride is drawn to the 'Borestone' that surmounts the cairn, taken from the battle site, made of blue winstone and incorporated within the modern cairn. According to Derek Alexander, Head of Archaeological Services for the National Trust for Scotland:

'The first memorial to the battle was in fact the Borestone itself: a flat stone with a circular hole four inches in diameter and four inches deep. Tradition has it that the

Borestone was the socket in which Robert Bruce, King of Scots, raised his standard prior to the battle and marks the site of the Scottish camp. The site has been visited by tourists since the 18th century, including Robert Burns, and an engraving of 1826 shows it beside the road in an open rural landscape.' [8]

Cairn with Borestone at Bannockburn Heritage Centre

Some believe Scotland secured its victory with the help of an unknown reserve force, despite their armies being vastly outnumbered. One of the biggest mysteries surrounding the story of this infamous period in Scottish history is whether the enigmatic Knights Templar saved the day for Scotland at the eleventh hour.

According to Christopher Knight and Robert Lomas in *The Hiram Key*, '*these mysterious warriors carried the Beausant (the battle flag of the Templars).*' The year of the battle coincided with the burning at the stake of the last Grand Master of the Knights Templar, Jacques de Molay, upon orders of King Philip IV of France and Pope Clement V. Soon after, the Templars fled France and other parts of Europe to seek refuge in Scotland under the protection of Robert the Bruce who at the time had fallen out with the Pope.[9] As early as 1128, the co-founder and first Grand Master of the Knights Templar, Hugh de Payens, met King David I in Scotland, establishing a seat at Balantrodoch in Midlothian, now known as Temple, next to the River Esk.

However, over the centuries, the Templar's involvement in the battle has been refuted, most recently by Helen Nicholson, Professor of Medieval History at Cardiff University. She claimed that the idea that the Templars helped win the battle for Robert the Bruce was '*hardly more credible than old claims that the kingdom of Scotland was founded by the Egyptian princess Scota*' and had brought an old slur on Bruce's achievements.'[10]

Nevertheless, the fact that the day of the battle was the feast day of John the Baptist, a saint the Templars and Freemasons revered above all others, is thought-provoking. The Templars placed John the Baptist in a higher position than Jesus, and an image of the head of the saint accompanied their initiation rites. Moreover, during the Fourth Crusade to the Holy Land, a group of Templar Knights discovered his skull in the Boukoleon Palace in Constantinople and found it emanating intense energy as if still connected to the body of John, a power they called 'Gnostic consciousness'.[11]

Although many battles have occurred on the Holy Axis, the Battle of Bannockburn seems more powerfully felt. One explanation is a fault line that runs east–west through the area conducive to what is termed a 'thin veil' area. According to local newspaper reports, strange lights in the sky have been witnessed and photographed over Bannockburn and nearby Stirling. One witness said, '*I thought it was an aeroplane at first, but when it tilted forwards, it was a circular shape*', and another stated, '*They were squashed horseshoe shaped with a translucence around the horseshoe shape with yellowish light.*'[12] Perhaps the strange lights are plasma that morphed before the eyes of the witnesses as spaceships. Alternatively, such traumatic events in the area's history may have caused a rip in the space-time continuum that has 'opened a door' or portal to those from other realms. After all, Bannockburn lies within the original Falkirk–Stirling–Bonnybridge Triangle, the hottest UFO spot in the UK.

Whether this was the actual battle site or not, it has become a focus of all the passions and raw emotions towards nationalism and independence for the Scottish nation. However, this site also shares many parallels with Culloden, fought around a watery terrain with a powerful female energy dragon line coursing through the battle site.

The Lost Holy Well

From the mighty bronze statue of the Bruce, Bride continues along the valley of the Bannock Burn as she heads northwest towards the village of Gargunnock. On route, she visits the stately Touch House beneath the northern slopes of the Touch Hills. Touch derives from the Gaelic word *tulach*, meaning hillock, which in medieval times became Tulch.

In 1234, the Frasers held the lands here, which later passed to the Stewart Earls of Buchan, who probably lived in a fortified tower. It commanded an important position overlooking the old road from Stirling to Glasgow, which passed within 200 yards of its doors. At the time, there was no bridge across the Forth, so travellers to Stirling Castle would have had to take this road as it skirted around an impassable swamp.

Alexander, second son of the first Earl of Huntly, acquired the estate in 1408 and built a stone tower to replace the original house, which was later extended and re-fortified. It passed to the Setons in the 15th century, who later developed and improved the tower as a grand mansion. In 1708 the Laird of Touch was one of five lords involved in an unsuccessful attempt to reinstate James VII to the throne. They were the Hereditary Armour Bearers for the Scottish Kings, their loyalty to the Jacobite cause continuing through their support of Bonnie Prince Charlie, who stayed here on his way to the Battle of Prestonpans in 1745. After fleeing the battlefield at Culloden a year later, he found refuge from his Hanoverian pursuers in a cave under a waterfall in Touch Glen.

From the house, the current heads southwest along Touch Burn, where it seeks the old site of St Corbet's Well in Touch Glen, not far from the cave and waterfall called Gilmour's Linn on its western edge. Interestingly, Corbet never existed as a saint and in *Old Nooks of Stirling*, writing after the well had long disappeared, J S Fleming believes the name is a corruption of St Cuthbert. *The Northern Antiquarian* website quotes the various literary remnants that are all that remain to inform us of its former sacred significance.[13]

Much of the folklore surrounding this well refers to its restorative powers. For example, Janet and Colin Bord write in their excellent book *Sacred Waters, Holy Wells and Water Lore in Britain and Ireland*:

> 'St. Corbet's Well on the Touch Hills (Stirling) was said to preserve for a year anyone who drank from it on the first Sunday in May, before sunrise, and it was visited by great crowds at the height of its popularity. But the drinking of spirits became more popular than the drinking of well water, so St. Corbet withdrew the valuable qualities of the water, then eventually the water itself stopped flowing.'[14]

Florence Marian McNeill mentions in her book *The Silver Bough* that locals regularly visited the well in the 19th century on the morning of Beltane:

> 'Husbands, wives, lovers and their sweethearts, young and old, grave and gay, crowded the hill-tops in the vicinity of the well long before dawn, and each party on their arrival took copious draughts of the singularly blessed water. It is reported that St Corbet, after a lapse of years, deprived the well of its life-preserving qualities in consequence of the introduction of "mountain dew" of a less innocent nature into these annual festivals.'[15]

On our travels along the Belinus Line and the Holy Axis, we encounter many holy wells lost to the rigours of modern development, leaving no trace that they had ever existed and giving us no clue of their religious or cultural purpose. In addition, Colin and Janet Bord remind us that some wells suffered violations, either by the curse of a saint, occult practices, or deliberate polluting, *'This theme, of real or imagined insult to the well causing it to lose its power, move its location, or cease flowing altogether, is widespread.'*[16]

From Touch Glen, Bride continues her journey to a grassy knoll close to the southern banks of the River Forth in the village of Gargunnock. Here a church has stood since well before 1500. It was rebuilt and renovated several times, the latest being in 1891. Before the Reformation, Gargunnock came under the Augustinian Canons of Cambuskenneth Abbey, commemorated in the carvings on the ends of the Elders' Benches. Interestingly, in the early 1700s, the 11th Laird of Gargunnock was Sir James Campbell of Ardkinglas House next to Loch Fyne in Argyll, later encountered on Bride's flow.

Gargunnock is associated with tales of witchcraft, relating to wise women tormented by the church, possibly due to their ability to heal. Its old name is *Gargownno*, which derives from the Celtic word *Caer-guineach*, meaning a solid or conical fortress that may refer to a peel tower that once stood next to the banks of the Forth. Before 1800, the village had more significance than today, with the Old Military Road between Stirling and Dumbarton running straight through its centre.

From here, Bride flows across an area known as Flanders Moss, a raised area of bogland now a National Nature Reserve managed by Scottish Natural Heritage. Once an immense and frightening wilderness, it stretched over 10 miles (16 km) to Loch Lomond. During the 18th and early 19th centuries, archaeological finds included a Bronze Age cauldron of beaten bronze found within an earthwork encampment, perhaps thrown into the bog as a votive offering. In the 1970s, the Forestry Commission drained much of Flanders Moss and planted it with a commercial forest. Today much of the plantation is being taken down, restoring the moss to its natural state. Bride focuses on a moated site at Ballangrew, which may have served as a hunting lodge.

Inchmahome Priory

During our early investigations of Bride in this area, some sites were challenging, causing our dowsing results to be unpredictable and confusing, especially when following her through the environs of Bannockburn, as if a trickster spirit was leading us astray. Initially, we believed the flow of Bride from Bannockburn continued westwards towards Loch Lomond, following the Fintry Hills, avoiding Gargunnock and barely connecting with any significant places of power. However, we both felt something was amiss and after a full day of dowsing both the male and female currents, we settled down for the evening in a pub to ponder our findings with a beer or two.

In my relaxed state, I suddenly had the vision of an island within a lake, which I instinctively felt was north of here. Caroline quickly grabbed the map and spread it across the table to locate the place. Sure enough, a lake existed over four miles north of the pub, and it had an island called Inchmahome with the remains of an

Aerial view of Inchmahome Priory, Lake of Menteith (courtesy of Andrew Shiva)

ancient monastery. Caroline remote dowsed over the island on the O.S. map with her pendulum to check for any signs of the Bride current. *'She's not there'*, she announced. But the impression was so strong that I felt we needed to visit the lake to investigate further.

A warm sun greeted us the following day as we headed to the Lake of Menteith, located just off the A81 between Stirling and Aberfoyle. We parked our car by the jetty next to the church at Port of Menteith, where we took a little ferry to Inchmahome. The enchanting scene of the morning mist hanging low over the still waters and cloaking the island filled us with a sense of anticipation as to what we might find. During the ferry trip, one of the Grail stories came to mind. The three Grail questers, Galahad, Percival, and Bors, embarked on a voyage to the mystical island of Sarras, which contained the Holy Grail. The lake was in the old Arthurian realm of *Bannog,* ruled by Lancelot's father, King Ban. After a rival king invaded the kingdom and killed Ban, Lancelot became the ward of the Lady of the Lake. The isle of Inchmahome also epitomises the mystical Isle of Avalon, where a nunnery existed run by the Nine Maidens of legend. Although the island has no history of a nunnery, the area called 'The Nunnery' around Queen Mary's Bower recalls an earlier sanctuary.

The ferry seemed to float across the lake as it transported us to the island, passing silent fishermen in their rowing boats, which only served to amplify the idyllic atmosphere. The lake is one of the finest places for trout fishing in Scotland and is well-stocked, often attracting osprey. William Ballingall, in *Scenes of Scottish Story,* writes of the island, *'the view of it from the water has quite a fairy look, and has been called "an emerald gem in the bosom of the smiling lake."'*[17]

Disembarking from the ferry, we strolled around the picturesque island and tuned into the energy, sensing that it had been highly sacred to the ancient tribes. We were both drawn to a large mound close to the site of the old high altar of the ruined priory, perhaps the remains of an ancient burial site. An information board says that Lochend, on the lake's southern edge, has been inhabited since before the Iron Age, when the Lake of Menteith was home to about eight crannogs. Crannogs are artificial islands that sit right on the lake, usually circular or oval and built as defensive homesteads, possibly as protection from raiding parties and wild animals. Often they were linked to the shore by underwater causeways known only to their inhabitants.

Beyond the lake's western shores are the sites of a Roman fort and two camps at Malling, all revealed through crop marks. Just to the south is the Peace Stone, extensively carved with cup and ring marks, perhaps a place seen as sacred by the earlier cultures.

Inchmahome, from the Gaelic *Innis Mo Cholmaig* meaning 'my-Colmaig's island', is the largest of three islands in the Loch of Inchmahome, later renamed Lake of Menteith in the 1800s. Interestingly there are tentative connections here with Iona and Lindisfarne, for some sources believe 'Cholmaig' refers to St Columba and others to St Colman, a monk from the island of Iona who succeeded St Finan in 661 as Bishop of Lindisfarne. According to early records from Cambuskenneth Abbey near Stirling, there is a reference to an ancient church on the *insula Macholem* or 'isle of my Colman'.[18] Perhaps, Colman and his followers formed a Culdee settlement here in the 7th century, similar to Old Melrose, a perfect place for silent contemplation.

In 1238, Walter Comyn, Earl of Menteith and Lord of Badenoch invited a small community of Augustinian monks, under the auspices of the Bishop of Dunblane, to establish a priory on the island over the site of an earlier church, known then as 'Inchmaquhomok'. The new church's design, with its tall lancet windows, nave piers and arches and elaborately carved west doorway, was said to resemble Dunblane and Glasgow Cathedrals.

Walter Comyn was a member of one of the most powerful families in Scotland and acquired the island through his marriage to Isabella, Countess of Menteith. They lived in an imposing country house on Inch Talla, one of the other islands on the lake.

Over the centuries, Inchmahome Priory received many distinguished guests, including King Robert the Bruce and Mary, Queen of Scots. The ill-fated queen, at the age of four, was hidden here in 1547 following the disastrous defeat of the Scots army at the Battle of Pinkie Cleugh. This conflict was the last pitched battle between the Scots and Henry VIII's armies, having failed to secure the marriage of the infant Mary to his young son, the future Edward VI. When diplomacy failed and Scotland was on the point of an alliance with France, Henry launched a successful war against Scotland, a conflict known as the 'Rough Wooing'. During her three-week stay, Mary would play in the garden with her four companions. In 1874, William Ballingall wrote, *'The pilgrim to Inchmahome in early summer will be delighted with "hosts of golden daffodils" springing up all over the green sward, the descendants of lilies which grew in the infant Mary's garden...'* He also describes the overgrown boxwood trees and orchards that once formed part of the Earl of Menteith's garden, later renamed 'Queen Mary's Bower'.[19]

After the Reformation, when the priory fell into ruin, the Erskine family took possession of the lands and later the Earls of Mar, who sold it in 1922 to the Duke of Montrose. Finally, in 1926 it was handed over to the nation as a site of historical importance.

Amongst the ruins is the old chapter house, which became a mausoleum for the Menteith family. The elegantly recumbent figures of Sir Walter Stewart of Menteith, who died in 1295, and his wife Mary embracing is a pose unique at the time. In the 1800s, it became a tourist attraction thanks mainly to Sir Walter Scott's writings and the arrival of the railway.

Despite its destruction after the Reformation, the priory ruins are still imposing and we imagined how the church might have appeared with its delicate carvings and brightly painted plasterwork. In the south wall of the choir are a group of three canopied stone seats, known as sedilia. After walking through the remains of the cloisters next to a group of sweet chestnut trees thought to date from the 1500s, we decided to find somewhere to sit and attune ourselves to the island's energy.

We found a spot under a tree to connect with the spirit guardians of the island. Soon, we started to receive impressions that the island long ago was the abode of the Bride serpent energy, but occultists had somehow drawn it away. So, we asked the spirit guardians if Bride should return to her rightful place here and received an affirmative answer. So, with their assistance, we visualised Bride's flow and used our crystals and green stones from Iona to imbue the island with pure light and positive energy. Then we waited.

Very soon, we felt the presence of Bride and were surprised at how quickly she had reverted to her original place on the island. We asked the rods to indicate her flow and they moved toward the mound next to the shore that had attracted us earlier. Nearby, a pair of swans nested on a tiny islet on the shoreline. In early traditions, they are associated with the goddess Bride representing the connection between land, sea and sky.

Mound by Inchmahome Priory

From the mound, Bride meanders through the ruins to the site of the high altar and the chapter house, housing the tombs of the Menteith family. Now that she had returned to this magical island, we felt drawn to place our healing stones on her flow to help balance and harmonise her energy.

Swan at Inchmahome Priory

Before leaving, we lingered amongst the fabulous tombs in the atmospheric chapter house. One early 14th-century slab standing upright against the wall caught our eye. It depicted John Drummond as a Grail knight with a spear and a miniature scene of slaying a dragon, perfectly symbolising our Grail journey so far.

When we returned to the jetty at the Port of Menteith, we instantly sensed her presence at the parish church that stands close by. There has been a place of worship on this site since medieval times, and perhaps it is no coincidence that when the church replaced the early chapel on the island of Inchmahome, it was relocated here on its eastern shores, on the flow of Bride.

The Fairy Hill and Aedan's Fort

Like Ireland, Northern England and the Isle of Man, Scotland is full of fairy lore and Doon Hill, just to the south of Aberfoyle's village in the beautiful Trossachs landscape, is featured in one of these tales.

Sometimes called Fairy Knowe or the 'dun-shi', this conical hill shrouded in dense woodland is a place of magic and mystery and is said to be sacred to the elemental realm. It was made famous by the discovery on its summit of the dead body of local clergyman Robert Kirk in the 17th century, minister of Aberfoyle Church from 1685 to 1692, in the old settlement of Kirkton. He was a Gaelic scholar and folklorist who first translated the Bible into his native tongue. He had the ability of second sight and believed in the existence of goblins, fairies and other magical creatures. His book *The Secret Commonwealth of Elves, Fauns & Fairies, Study in Folklore & Psychical Research* [20] created much debate among historians and scholars for centuries. It contained a collection of fairy lore gathered by Revd Kirk from traditional accounts

Aberfoyle Old Parish Kirk, Kirkton, with Doon Hill in the background (Courtesy of Creagmhor)

in the Scottish Highlands between 1691 and 1692, although he died before it was published. It was released more than a century later by Sir Walter Scott in 1815. Folklorist and editor of a later publication of Kirk's book, Stewart Sanderson, described Kirk's collection as *'one of the most important and significant works on the subject of fairies and second sight.'*[21]

While living in Kirkton Manse at the foot of Doon Hill, Kirk was a frequent visitor, and his sudden and unexplained death on the hill has left many questioning the nature of his demise. Sanderson reports that the cleric *'was in the habit of taking a turn in his nightgown on summer evenings on the fairy hill beside his home to get a breath of fresh air before retiring to bed. However, one evening in 1692 – 14 May – his body was found lying, apparently dead, on the hill.'*

Henderson and Cowan, in *Scottish Fairy Belief*, wrote, *'It was thought unwise to speak of one's knowledge of the fairy folk, for revelation of their secrets would incur their displeasure and subsequent infliction of punishment...it was commonly held that those who had been in some way close to fairies would end up in the fairy realm at the termination of their earthly existence.'*[22]

Some say the fairies spirited Kirk away to serve as chaplain to their queen while leaving a changeling body for mortals to bury in the local cemetery. Others believed his spirit became trapped in the large pine tree at the top of the hill, which now acts as a mediator between this world and the fairy realm. Hugh Cheape in *Gaelic Genesis* writes, *'Such was his familiarity with the wee folk, it was said in the district, that he was carried off by them the following year and his headstone stands over an empty tomb.'*[23]

Andrew Lang, who re-published *The Secret Commonwealth of Elves, Fauns & Fairies* in 1893, believed that Revd Kirk had derived his psychic powers from being the seventh son. He also mentions that although there is a tomb in Kirkton churchyard, *'the ashes of Mr Kirk are not there.'* Walter Scott wrote in 1815 that after Revd Kirk's funeral, a ghostly image appeared to his wife and commanded her to speak to Grahame of Duchray:

'Say to Duchray, who is my cousin as well as your own, that I am not dead, but a captive in Fairyland; and only one chance remains for my liberation. When the posthumous child, of which my wife has been delivered since my disappearance, shall be brought to baptism, I will appear in the room, when, if Duchray shall throw over my head the knife or dirk which he holds in his hand, I may be restored to society; but if this is neglected, I am lost for ever.'[24]

True to his word, his ghost appeared at the christening, but Duchray, astonished at seeing the vision, forgot to throw his dirk over its head and Revd Kirk has remained stuck in the fairy world ever since.

After parking in the Aberfoyle information centre car park, we headed for the bridge on Manse Road that spans the River Forth, which eventually took us to Doon Hill. Along the way, we came to the isolated ruins and churchyard of Aberfoyle Old Parish Church, built in 1744, where we found the grave of the Revd Kirk, but perhaps not his bones! Many churches have stood on this holy site where we soon detected Bride flowing through the ruins.

The new settlement of Aberfoyle developed north of the river in 1870 and with the advent of the railway, it soon transformed into a popular tourist destination. Here a new church was constructed, and, as a consequence, Revd Kirk's little church below Doon Hill soon fell into ruin.

Aberfoyle, known in earlier times as Aberphuil or Eperphuil, is strategically positioned on the banks of the River Forth as it surrenders to Loch Ard. Just south of the old church was the supposed site of a stone circle known as the *Clachan*, where gatherings occurred. According to the Canmore website, *The Statistical Account* of 1790 describes it as having ten large stones '*placed circularly with a large one in the middle. They seem to have stood originally on one end but have now fallen and are partly sunk into the earth.*'[25]

Revd Kirk's grave, Aberfoyle Old Parish Churchyard

Gravestone with the carving of an elemental face, Aberfoyle Old Parish Churchyard

We followed Bride from the ruins to the grave of the Revd Kirk, his tombstone carved with his emblem of a sword crossed over a pastoral staff. Here, we had a clear view of the enigmatic Doon Hill looming over us in the distance, the place of Kirk's demise, and we wondered whether the tales were true that his body was not buried here but trapped in the fairy world.

Also in the churchyard on Bride's flow is another elaborately carved gravestone with what looks like the face of an elemental, possibly a pixie with branches coming out of its mouth. Was it alluding to the fey, the fairy energy that you can feel all around you here?

Further along the road, we dowsed Bride flowing through a sizeable pebbly rock conglomerate next to the hedge. We also noticed a carving of a feminine elemental face on the rock's south side. From here, we soon found ourselves at the base of Doon Hill and taking a footpath on our left, we entered the woodland and walked to its summit. Following the winding path, we detected Bride flowing through a tree stump delightfully carved as a fairy house, complete with windows, a tiled roof and steps leading up to the front door incorporating the tree roots. This delightful feature certainly enhances this elemental paradise. Around it, clooties are tied to trees as if

Fairy House, Doon Hill

those who left them there believed it to be a healing place. Perhaps they unconsciously connect with Bride's divine and nourishing dragon energy as she flows through the fairy house.

We met Bride at the summit, where another unexpected sight greeted us. A group of trees encircling a giant pine tree, all adorned with colourful clooties hanging from their branches and bright ribbons wrapped around their trunks. Bride completely encompasses this magical tree circle and its fairy offerings, her width broad and potent.

After descending the hill, we stopped to take in the stunning landscape surrounding it. We wondered why this place attracted such paranormal events. Later research revealed that its proximity to Britain's most significant fault line, the Highland Boundary Fault, may have something to do with it. This massive fissure between two landmasses stretches from the Isle of Arran off the west coast to Stonehaven, just south of Aberdeen. The Highland Boundary Fault separates two different terrains, the Highlands and the Lowlands. Until 410 million years ago, the land we know as Scotland was separated from England by an ocean more extensive than the Atlantic. Over time, the two land masses drifted together, the sea closed up, and the subsequent collision of land pushed up a mountain range as high as the Himalayas. Here the rugged granite mountains of the Highlands meet the gently rolling hills and fertile plains of the softer sandstones and other sedimentary

Fairy Tree on the summit of Doon Hill

rocks of the Lowlands, capable of supporting farming and woodland. The fertile plains include the belt of land between Edinburgh and Glasgow, once coveted by the kings and nobles of Scotland. Perhaps that is why we feel a subtle yet tangible shift in the energies within the landscape as we cross from the Lowlands to the mountainous plains of Northern Scotland.

In *The Enchantment of the Trossachs*, Louis Stott cites Persinger when discussing the mysterious story of Revd Kirk, who suggests that such paranormal events may result from an energy release during an earthquake or some other unexplained earth movement. Stott believes that although earthquakes were not recorded in Scotland until 1789, it might well be the case that the Highland Boundary Fault would have been subject to triboelectricity or rubbing of rock strata and particularly around Doon Hill during the lifetime of Revd Kirk.[26]

The light-ball phenomena witnessed at many places of power around the British Isles tend to manifest in mountainous areas, around fault lines, areas of powerful geology or large bodies of water, like Loch Ness, that weigh down on crystalline rocks creating piezoelectricity from the pressure. Plasma can rearrange its molecular structure to any shape or form, allowing it to connect with our three-dimensional world and, in Doon Hill's case, members of the fairy world.

In ancient times, the dense marshland surrounding Doon Hill was called 'The Moat of Scotland', an impregnatable area that once stretched to Stirling. But for the traveller, the bogs were dangerous to cross and only navigable with the help of an experienced guide, like the character Gollum from Tolkein's *Lord of the Rings* leading Frodo Baggins and Samwise Gamgee through the foul-smelling Dead Marshes, haunted by the slain warriors of a great battle long ago. As ghostly, floating glowing balls surround them on the path, Gollum tells Frodo and Sam not to look at the lights in case they are lured into the realm of the dead.

Marsh lights are called will-o'-the-wisps or jack-o'-lanterns, often seen floating above bogs, swamps or marshes. According to folklore, they mislead travellers believing them to be lanterns showing them the way. Devon and Cornish folklore describe them as 'Pixy-lights', where a Pixie carrying a lantern leads the traveller away from the safe route through the marsh.

Perhaps Revd Kirk was seeing balls of light emitted from the marshland floating up to the summit of Doon Hill to discharge its energy into the hill. Likewise, the lights may originate from the fault line at Doon Hill and then descend into the marshes below. So beware when visiting the 'dun-shi', for you may never return! In reality, plasma loses energy quickly in this dimension, so its life is short. Many encounters say that the lights

Will-o-the-wisp and snake, col lithograph by Hermann Hendrich 1931

soon blink out or disappear into the ground – unless the electromagnetic energy is strong enough to continue the ionisation process, allowing the lights to manifest for longer.

The priest may have experienced a time-slip due to electromagnetic forces built-up within the Highland Boundary Fault, similar to Thomas the Rhymer's fairy adventures at the Eildon Tree near Melrose.

Long ago, local tribes controlled much of the trade coming and going along the 'Neck of Britain' and the old north–south land routes. Perhaps this is why Doon Hill is a candidate for the site of a late 6th-century fort built by Aedan, King of the Dal Riata. Hugh McArthur writes that Aberfoyle's wild mountainous land was a 'Gateway of the Trossachs' and came under the Lordship of Aedan MacGabhran, who became king of the Irish Dal Riata and Pendragon of the Celtic Isle from *c.* 574 until *c.* 608. He was also Prince of Forth and Lord of Aberfoyle and his son Artuir became the Scottish King Arthur. He was a great warrior who fought many famous battles with the Picts and the Angles of Northumbria.

The sources for Aedan's life include *Historia Ecclesiastica Gentis Anglorum* by the Venerable Bede (672–735 CE) and the *Annals of Ulster* and the *Annals of Tigernach.* St Columba crowned Aedan on the island of Iona, but according to Adomnan's *Life of St Columba,* the saint at the time preferred Aedan's older brother Eoganan as king. However, an angel commanded three times that Aedan should be king and Columba only relented when the angel struck him with a scourge (whip).[27]

According to *The Life of St Berach,* Aedan granted the saint his fort at Aberfoyle to build a monastery.[28] Berach was Abbot of Cluain Coirpthe in Connachta in Ireland, and the nearby Fielbarachan Guest House, now the Craigmore B & B, recalls his name. Fielbarachan means Berchán's or Berach's Fair, which took place in mid-October in a field opposite the guest house and local games continued there until the 1930s.

Kirkton Manse at the base of Doon Hill, the former home of Revd Kirk, stands today as a private house on a mound overlooking the old Moat of Scotland. Sir Walter Scott stayed here numerous times between 1790 and 1809, the landscape inspiring his romantic novels and poems. We noticed significant blocks of stones in the wall surrounding the mound, serving as an ancient boundary, and we wondered whether the Manse was the site of Aedan's fort. Looking at the terrain around Aberfoyle, we realised that Aedan's stronghold below Doon Hill would have marked the boundary between the Dal Riata Kingdom and that of the Brythonic-speaking Manau Gododdin, controlling the vital trading routes carrying goods overland to the River Forth. Although there is little sign of this area's fascinating and ancient history today, it still holds powerful magic.

The Oaks and the Well of Balmaha

Bride flows southwest across the vast expanse of Loch Ard Forest to the wild heathlands of Moor Park. The Burn of Achlais leads her to a little-known healing spring called St Maha's Well, surrounded by small stones arranged in a horseshoe. Here in this beautiful but remote setting, you can look down upon the village of Balmaha on the eastern shores of Loch Lomond. The Northern Antiquarian website cites William J

Watson, who states in *The History of the Celtic Place-names of Scotland,* that *maha* derives from the Scottish Gaelic 'Mo-Thatha', *Thatha* having come from the Irish name 'Tua', meaning 'the silent one'.[29]

H G Smith, writing in 1896, stated that St Maha gave Balmaha its name, which probably retains the memory of St Mochai, a companion to St Patrick. He also referred to the well as containing healing properties and visitors would leave clooties tied to a tree that once stood above the well to seek 'the saint's favour'.[30] Most likely, it is the serpent Bride's favour that they sought! Above the well is a standing stone, perhaps a marker or boundary stone or the remains of a hermit's cell.

However, according to the Canmore website, St Maha is the female saint Mocha, or Kentigerna, the patroness of the island of Inchcailloch on Loch Lomond. It also states that the well is still a focus of local cults, frequented by people who leave offerings in the water. A post on the Canmore website dated 2010 mentions a story of a man who died during that year in a local hospital, demanding that he only drink water from St Maha's Well. [31]

From the well, Bride snakes along the lower slopes of Conic Hill to the village of Balmaha, nestling on the picturesque eastern shores of Loch Lomond. Conic Hill marks the Highland Boundary Fault as it crosses Loch Lomond from Doon Hill and offers excellent views for the numerous hill walkers journeying along the West Highland Way. In the summer, Balmaha is a bustling metropolis for tourists visiting the Loch's many islands, for walkers exploring its forest and mountain trails and for those taking their leisure craft out onto the loch.

View of Loch Lomond from the summit of Conic Hill

However, before the 1800s, there was very little here to attract visitors until the advent of the steamers, which used Balmaha as a frequent stopping-off point for tourists. Now, the village offers a shop, café and the popular Oak Tree Inn.

While enjoying a hearty lunch at the pub, we both had a strong sense that Bride was near, so putting down her sandwich, Caroline picked up her rods and went straight to the magnificent oak tree by the outside seating area,

Balmaha Oak

close to where we were sitting, from which we assumed the pub takes its name. *'She's here'*, declared Caroline nodding towards the tree. We quickly finished our lunch and followed her towards Balmaha's famous boatyard, where she connected with another large oak tree with four great limbs branching out from its base. Here we detected a spiral of energy, indicating the presence of a blind spring beneath its roots. We would return the following day to take one of the regular ferries to see if Bride visits Inchcailloch, the home of the winter aspect of Bride.

1. https://electricscotland.com/books/pdf/castellated_architecture.htm
2. https://en.wikipedia.org/wiki/Torwood_Castle
3. https://www.higgypop.com/hauntings/torwood-castle/
4. https://falkirklocalhistory.club/around-the-area/castles/torwood-or-tappoch-broch/
5. https://www.wheelandanchor.ca/2019/08/scotlands-ancient-brochs-a-baffling-mystery-on-a-colossal-scale/
6. https://www.historic-uk.com/HistoryUK/HistoryofScotland/Brochs-the-Tallest-Prehistoric-Buildings-in-Britain/
7. Watson, F. 2018.*Traitor, Outlaw, King: Part One: The Making of Robert Bruce.* Independently Published.
8. https://www.battlefieldstrust.com/media/672.pdf
9. Lomas, R. Knight, C.1997. *The Hiram Key.* Arrow, London.
10. https://www.scotsman.com/news/how-crusading-templars-gave-bruce-edge-bannockburn-2443121
11. Pinkham, M. A. 2005. *Guardians of the Holy Grail: The Knights Templar, John the Baptist and the Water of Life.* Adventures Unlimited Press, USA.
12. https://www.dailyrecord.co.uk/news/local-news/ufo-spotted-over-bannockburn-woman-10629184
13. https://megalithix.wordpress.com/2012/10/29/st-corbets-well/
14. 16. Bord, J. & Bord, C. 1985. *Sacred Waters: Holy Wells and Water Lore in Britain and Ireland.* Harper Collins, London.
15. McNeill, M. F. 1957. *The Silver Bough: Scottish Folklore and Folk-belief.* William Maclellan (Embryo) Ltd.
17. 19. Ballingall, W. 1874. *Scenes of Scottish Story.* Edmonston & Douglas, Edinburgh.
18. McNiven, P. *Place-names and the Medieval Church in Menteith*, University of Glasgow. *The Journal of Scottish Name Studies,* 8, 2014. 51–92.
20. 24. Kirk, R. c 1641-1692. Lang, A. 1844-1912. *The Secret Commonwealth of Elves, Fauns & Fairies: A Study In Folklore & Psychical Research.* David Nutt London (1893).
21. Sanderson, S. 1964. *A Prospect of Fairyland.* Folklore. Taylor & Francis Ltd, Oxford.
22. Henderson, L. Cowan, E. J. 2001. *Scottish Fairy Belief: A History.* Tuckwell Press, East Linton.
23. https://www3.smo.uhi.ac.uk/teagasg/artaigealan/gaelicgenesis.pdf
25. https://canmore.org.uk/site/24072/clachan-of-aberfoyle
26. Stott, L. 2018. *The Enchantment of the Trossachs: The life and mysterious death of Scottish churchman and scholar Robert Kirk and his influential treatise on fairy folklore.* Loch Ard Local History Group.
27. Adomnan of Iona, Richard Sharpe, (Introduction, Translator) 1995. *Life of St Columba.* Penguin Classics, London.
28. Plummer, C. 1968. *Lives of Irish Saints.* Oxford University Press, Oxford.
29. Watson, W. J. 2001. *The Celtic Place-Names of Scotland.* Birlinn Ltd, Edinburgh.
30. Smith, H. G. 1896. *Strathendrick and its Inhabitants from Early Times.* James Maclehose, Glasgow.
31. https://canmore.org.uk/site/43475/moor-park-st-mahas-well

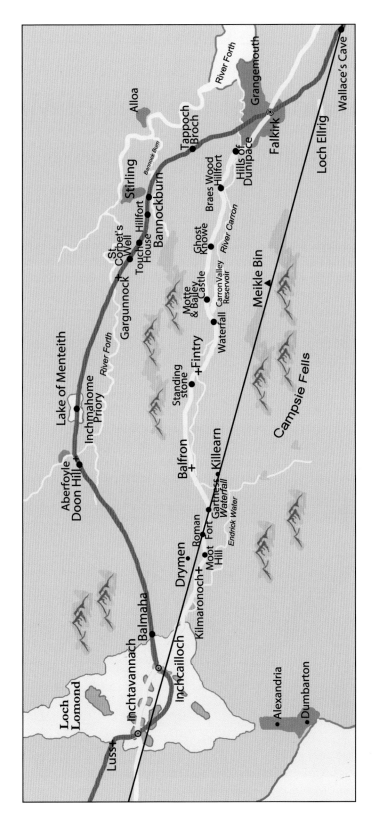

Chapter 12

Camelot and the Trail of Merlin

Lugh from Falkirk to Loch Lomond

After dowsing Lugh across Falkirk Golf Club, close to a loop of the River Carron, we later discovered he was crossing over the site of *Colania*, the name for a group of Roman forts also called 'North Camp' and 'South Camp'. Today the area is called Camelon, from the Gaelic Camalan, just west of the main centre of Falkirk. The name conjures up legends of King Arthur, whose fateful last stand was at Camlann.[1] Historically, Camelon was a strategic port of the River Carron, where land and sea merchants traded. Over two thousand years ago, the river was much broader and deeper to allow ships to sail up to where the golf course is today. *The New Statistical Account of Scotland* states, '*Tradition represents Camelon to have been a seaport, and it is said that fragments of anchors and ancient boats have been found in the soil.*'[2] Perhaps this is why the Romans built a series of forts and camps here to control this vital trade route. Later, the port moved further east to Grangemouth.

In 1522, Hector Boece associated Colania with King Cruthneus' Pictish city, which had 'twelve brass gates'.[3] The city may have been a larger version of Vindobala on Hadrian's Wall with its many gates, which the Picts later usurped. David Nash Ford cites a tradition by Gibson, who wrote in 1695 that the old Roman Fort of Colania at

Reconstruction of Roman Vindobala

Camelon was: '*A little ancient city, where the common people believe there was formerly a road for ships. They call it Camelot. It may be gathered from history that this was the Palace of the Picts.*'[4]

The mention of twelve brass gates around a city of the Picts seems fanciful although too unusual to be a complete invention and may relate to the port taken over after the Romans departed being a place of trade for all types of metals mined in the region, including copper to make brass. *The Statistical Account of Scotland* records that:

'Old Camelon appears to have been formerly a place of consequence. There are now few vestiges of it remaining but not long ago foundations of houses and the direction of some of the streets were visible. Much has been said of the importance of this ancient citadel where the Romans' riches and ornaments of royalty were found there when it was taken by the Romans. But we have no authentic documents by which we can decide whether it was a habitation of some of the ancient tribes of North Britain, or whether it was only a Roman Station.' [5]

Perhaps, the Romans usurped the art of brass-making when they took over the city from the Picts or Britons. Archaeologists working on excavating the Roman fort built 80–83 CE state that it '*would have been one of the most important forts in Scotland*', but alas, a Tesco superstore now stands over the site. However, the developers plan to construct a 'history hut' with help from the archaeologists, Falkirk Council, and Tesco Stores Limited to promote this area's fascinating lost history.

According to David F Carroll in *Arturius: A Quest for Camelot*, Arthur was not a Welsh king but Prince Artuir, son of King Aedan of the Dal Riata. Carroll states that the warrior ruled part of the Brythonic-speaking Manau Gododdin kingdom in the late 500s.[6] Manau Gododdin was an area encompassing the southern shores of the Firth of Forth from the western edge of Edinburgh to Falkirk and Stirling. The *Annals of Ulster* state that Artuir died at the Battle of the Miathi in 582.[7] Many researchers say the battle occurred around the old Roman Forts of Colania within the realm of Manau Gododdin. In *Arthur and the Lost Kingdoms*, Alistair Moffat also places the final battle at Colania and says that Camelon was Arthur's city of Camelot in Manau. The name 'Camlann' in Brittonic may derive from the description of the area's 'twisted land' caused by the many loops in the River Carron.[8]

Carroll also believes that Artuir MacAedan was the true source of the Scottish Arthurian legends and that Camelon was his Camelot. He reasons that '*as Colania was the strongest fortification at the centre of Manau Gododdin, then it is likely to have been his capital, a place called Camelot in the past and still called Camelon today.*'[9]

Moffat mentions that the historic city of Clackmannan, just north of Falkirk on the opposite shores of the Forth, is derived from *Clach na Manan*, meaning the stone of Manau. A rough unhewn stone still survives today, standing next to the medieval tollbooth in the centre of the town, which may be this Clach na Manan stone.[10] Falkirk and its surrounding lands were a frequent battleground for centuries, and witnessed much slaughter between the Romans, Picts, Angles, the Britons of Strathclyde, and later the English and the Scots.

The Hills of Dunipace and Merlin's Tomb

Just west of Camelon, Lugh visits another important historical site associated with the legendary times of King Arthur or Artuir. Close to the north banks of the River Carron, between the towns of Larbert and Denny, are two natural steep-sided conical mounds known as the Hills of Dunipace. They stand next to the site of a 12th-century church dedicated to St Ninian, but only a few of its stones and a graveyard remain. However, the site might be older, as archaeologists found a silver Celtic brooch near the mounds set in amber with a pattern wrought in gold dating from the 6th or 7th century.

The mounds are supposedly natural remnants of a post-glacial beach and stand at the meeting of three ancient and natural land divisions and an old fording place close to where the Bonny Water merges with the River Carron. Here, the English army under Edward I crossed as they headed to the siege of Stirling Castle. There may have been a castle on one of the mounds as correspondence between Pope Alexander III and Geoffrey, Abbot of Dunfermline in 1163, mentions 'the chapel of the castle of Dunipace'. John Hill Burton's *The History of Scotland from Agricola's Invasion to the Revolution of 1688* says a third mound existed at this site with an ancient burial cist on its summit, destroyed for road building materials.[11]

The name Dunipace is an enigma, possibly meaning the 'Hills of Peace', derived from 'dun' being a P Celtic word for hill or mound and 'pace' or *pacis* from the Latin for peace. This translation stems from a Roman document that Dunipace was the location of a peace treaty between the Romans and the Votadini in 210 CE, attended by Emperor Severus and his sons Caracalla and Geta. Carausius, military commander of the Roman Empire in the 3rd century, was also said to have brokered a deal here in 286 CE. Throughout the centuries, the mounds or hills became a notable place of political power and the 16th-century Scottish historian George Buchanan recognised it as a renowned venue for many trials and major negotiations during the reign of Pictish King Domnall I in the 9th century. Furthermore, William Wallace met King Robert the Bruce at the mounds in 1298 to persuade him not to sell the Scottish crown to England through land deals. Here, Edward I of England signed a peace warrant with Scotland in 1301 to appease the French King, who was strongly allied to the Scottish crown.

Another interpretation of *pace* is 'bass', a name often associated with Scottish mounds such as the Bass of Inverurie in its graveyard. Another version of the word is the Welsh P Celtic *din-ya-pas* or 'Hills of the Pass', which may refer to the vital and strategic fording of the Cannon River nearby. Yet another interpretation is 'Hills of Death' from the Q Celtic *duin-na-bais,* which suggests the mounds were used for burial and cremation purposes. In addition, local historian and placename expert John Reid has tentatively proposed that Dunipace might be a rendering of *Dun y Bas*, the 'Hill of the Ford', *bas* being a British word referring to shallow waters. Indeed, the geographical importance of the area is significant, as the mounds lie at a strategic river crossing on the Neck of Britain's trade route between the North Sea and the Atlantic Ocean. Moreover, the many invasions and battles around this river crossing and the surrounding fields suggest that the mounds may mark an important burial ground.

The Hills of Dunipace (courtesy of Nigel J C Turnbull)

Next to the cemetery are the last remaining stones of the 'Place of Dunipace', an old mansion belonging to the Primrose family. Unfortunately, Sir Archibald Primrose was beheaded for supporting Bonnie Prince Charlie in 1745. Curiously, Geoff Bailey's book *Falkirk or Paradise* refers to his ghostly headless body making an annual appearance on 15 November by walking seven times around the Hills of Dunipace.[12]

Our first visit to these intriguing and impressive mounds was on a windy summer's day, adding to the intense atmosphere of this historical and mystical site. The larger of the two hills or mounds, now shrouded in trees, has a flattened top, which appears artificial and possibly created for ceremonial purposes. A slightly smaller mound stands to the southeast in a crop field badly damaged by flooding in the 16th century.

Lugh was detected connecting with both mounds and the old site of Ninian's church, which stands nearby within a circular churchyard surrounded by a stone dyke.

Lancelot, the Arthurian equivalent of Lugh, is said to have crossed the Carron here, where we also find the male current. In his book, *The Road to Avalon*, Arthurian scholar August Hunt theorises that King Ban and his wife left the Stirling area with their son, the infant Lancelot and often forded the Carron close to the Dunipace mounds.[13] A few local sources suggest that Arthur's sixth battle on the River Bassas was here at Dunipace, as in Dun-y-bas.

This area lies within a massive UFO hot spot known as the Falkirk Triangle, where more than three hundred reported sightings of UFO phenomena have been recorded every year since 1992. Falkirk, Stirling and Bonnybridge make up the triangle's three points, and a large proportion of the population within the triangle has spotted a

UFO at some point in their lives. Many of the sightings include flying objects shaped like stars, cigars, and saucers, and some people have experienced flashing lights and even abductions. Over the years, these reports have appeared in the Scottish media, and a local councillor of Falkirk District Council has written several letters voicing his concerns to various Prime Ministers. One of the first documented accounts came in 1992 when local businessman James Walker drove between Falkirk and Bonnybridge.

He spotted a shining, star-shaped object hovering over the road, blocking his path. Then, as

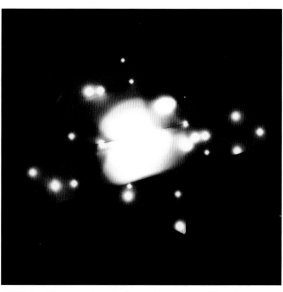

UFO incident at Rendlesham (courtesy of Dimìtar Nàydenov)

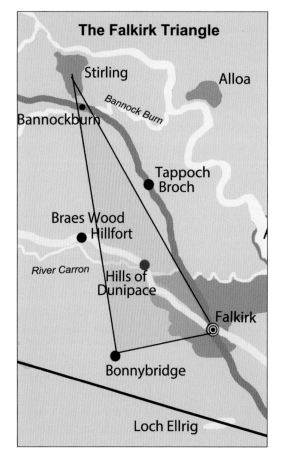

Falkirk UFO Triangle

he sat in his car waiting for it to pass, Walker recalled that it flew away at 'an incredible speed'. Others have reported seeing a 'howling' UFO that 'buzzed' their car, while a cigar-shaped craft was spotted landing on a golf course. In October 1997, Councillor William Buchanan of Falkirk District Council wrote to the then Prime Minister Tony Blair appealing for an investigation into the phenomena, convinced that something strange was happening. The Ministry of Defence, however, declared that they were *'satisfied there is no evidence that the UK's airspace might have been compromised by hostile or unauthorised foreign military activity.'*[14]

However, these sightings are probably plasma lights and a quick look at the geology map of the area gives us a clue as to why there are so many of them within this triangle of towns. Fissures and fault lines between the three towns have seams of iron-rich magnetic stones and carboniferous rocks, crossed by rivers, streams and coal fields. The most significant fault lines are the Highland Boundary Fault to the north and the Southern Upland Fault to the south. It is possible that the effects of tension (piezoelectric), rubbing (triboelectric) or even waves of seismoelectric energy from the faults find their way to the surface as ionised particles in the watery flatlands of this district to become plasma lights. This highly electromagnetic environment helps release electrons and allows the ionisation process to last longer than in other places, permitting plasma to assume self-organisation and adopt the behaviour of any life form it chooses to encounter, whether human, animal or imaginary. Moreover, with the establishment in the minds of the local inhabitants of the area of UFO archetypes, plasma intelligence can take the form of collective cultural expectations, such as spaceships.[15]

Further along the river, we dowsed Lugh at a converted Gothic-style Victorian church opposite the gates of Denovan House, now a private house. The church was initially built to replace St Ninian's at the Hills of Dunipace. After skirting the northern outskirts of Dunipace village, Lugh takes us to an Iron Age vitrified fort in Braes Wood. A little south of here and just over two miles from the Hills of Dunipace is a farmstead called Drumelzier (Fort of Merlin), which reminded us of a small village with the same name next to the Tweed River in an area called Merlindale near Peebles. A local legend states that Merlin was supposedly killed and buried by the Tweed below the church. Here the female dragon current of the Belinus Line flows along the east–west axis of the old Drumelzier Kirk.

After some research, we discovered that Scottish writer Adam Ardrey mentions both sites in *Finding Merlin: The Truth behind the Legend*. The author claims Merlin, also known as Lailoken, was a Scottish Druid, politician and scholar born in 540 CE in Cadzow (now Hamilton, a town located southeast of Glasgow). He died *c.* 618 at Drumelzier near Dunipace, around the time of Arthur or Artuir macAedan, and not at the village near Peebles. Ardrey's research on his burial place rests upon a statement in *Vita Merlini Silvestris*, translated by John and Winifred MacQueen. It consists of a collection of 13th-century Latin prophecies from an earlier Welsh text about Merlin's life. The document mentions that the grave of Merlin lies 30 miles (48 km) from Glasgow near Drumelzier Castle.[16] Interestingly, the remains of a Drumelzier Castle lie about half a mile (1 km) southwest of the hamlet of Drumelzier by the Tweed near Peebles, 37 miles (59 km) to the southeast of Glasgow. However, it only dates from late medieval times.

Other authors have long doubted the legend of Drumelzier by the Tweed being the site of Merlin's grave, including Scottish writer George Chalmers in his book *Caledonia*.[17] Furthermore, Ardrey suggests that the Iron Age vitrified fort in Braes Wood on the Lugh current marks the site of the castle mentioned in *Vita Merlini Silvestris*. Although now just a pile of rubble, excavations show that it had substantial walls and was probably a fortification during the time of Merlin. He also discovered that north of Drumelzier Farm, near the town of Dunipace, a large mound once existed where excavations in 1836 revealed the bones of a man with a vase containing a decayed parchment:

'About two miles to the westward of these hills, [Hills of Dunipace] there was a very beautiful one about forty feet in height, and covering nearly three roods of ground, said

269

also to be artificial. [Rood is an English unit of area equal to one quarter of an acre]. This hill was mutilated, from time to time, for the purpose of repairing roads and other purposes. It was entirely removed about six years ago, to form an embankment on the turnpike road near Denny Bridge. The strata of which this hill was composed, were carefully observed during its removal. These were so regular and as if rising out of and gradually returning again to similar strata in the circumjacent level ground, as to afford conclusive evidence that the hill was not the work of man. On the top of this hill, and about three feet below the surface, was found a coffin or tomb, composed of five large unwrought stones, in which were the bones of a human body, scull and teeth not much decayed. Along with these, was a vase of course unglazed earthenware, containing a small quantity of material resembling the lining of a wasp's nest. Probably decayed paper or parchment, which in the lapse of ages had assumed that appearance. No conjecture could be formed about the individual here interred, tradition being entirely silent on the subject; but this circumstance corroborates the opinion of some writers, that the hills of Dunipace might have been used as burial places for ancient chiefs. For previous to the erection of bridges in this district region the ford was the principal passage over the Carron, and would be the scene of many a bloody conflict between hostile armies. Hence the appropriateness of their name, 'hills of death.' [18]

There is no evidence today of a large mound near Drumelzier Farm, although Ardrey believes the site of Merlin's possible tomb was destroyed and his bones reburied close by. *However, the New Statistical Account of Scotland (NSA) 1834* records a large mound flattened two miles northwest of the Hills of Dunipace. This same mound features on a detailed Lowland map of Scotland (1752–1755) drawn by William Roy, close to where the Avon Burn meets the River Carron.

Could this be the lost mound mentioned by Burton[19] and the burial cist of Merlin's Tomb? The site is also close to the turnpike road at Denny Bridge, said to be made from earth excavated from this sacred hill. Interestingly, in the 1960s, two stone burial cists were uncovered in a field close to the site of the lost mound. The archaeological report mentions the field's name as 'The Roundel', perhaps a suitable description for a sizeable flattened hill. The destruction of the mound occurred around 1836, and it is possible that Merlin's bones and gravestone were recovered and reburied in this field. Unfortunately, there is no trace of the vase and decayed parchment, presumably taken by one of the excavators. Looking across the fence into the field where the mound once stood, we wondered if the legendary Merlin was still entombed beneath the soil.

Mounds of Treasure and Graham's Castle

Lugh continues northwest, passing south of Loch Coulter Reservoir towards Easter Buckieburn and beyond to the farm estate of Craigengelt. Just south of here, by the Buckie Burn, is the site of another lost prehistoric mound called Ghost Knowe. Sadly, like the mound called the Roundel and the possible location of Merlin's tomb, this equally important burial mound was ransacked of its valuables in 1839 and gradually ploughed out over the years. According to records, it measured 12 ft (3.6 m) high and 300 ft (91 m) in circumference at the base, and twelve huge stones surrounded it placed equidistant apart. *NSA 1834* states:

'About six feet from the centre, there stood four upright stones, each about five feet in height, describing an oblong figure like a bed. Within this, a coffin was found, the length of which was about seven feet, three and a half broad, and three and a half deep. The under part or bottom of the coffin was whin-flag, as was the upper part or lid. Within this were found the remains of a human body of ordinary size. The bones, except for a very small part of the skull, were of the consistence of soft chalk and the body had been enveloped in something like a mixture of dyed vegetable matter and tar which when exposed to the atmosphere, emitted a strong odour. Strict orders were given to the labourers that if anything like a coffin was found they should not open it till either the proprietor or tenant was present. But one of them, an old schoolmaster, who knew something of antiquities, went during the night, and carried off a variety of articles, the nature and number of which are not now likely ever to be ascertained. With reluctance, he gave up a stone axe of beautiful workmanship and a gold ring. The ring had a jewel in it, but the jewel was out, and it was what is called 'chased' and must have been worn on a very small finger. A labourer in the neighbourhood sold a variety of things of a rare description to a gentleman in whose possession it is believed they still are. The axe and the ring were the only thing obtained by the proprietor, J. Dick, Esq. of Craigengelt and they are still in his possession.' [20]

A few years later, in 1851, Daniel Wilson visited the site and wrote about the valuable items found there and subsequently sold:

'among which was a golden horn or cup, weighing fourteen ounces, and ornamented with chased or embossed figures. This interesting relic was purchased from one of the labourers by a gentleman in Stirling, and is believed to be still in existence, though I have failed, after repeated applications, in obtaining access to it. The exact nature or value of the whole contents of this cairn is not likely ever to be ascertained. The only articles secured by the proprietor, and now in his possession, are a highly polished stone axe or hammer, eight inches long, rounded at one end and tapering at the other; a knife or dagger of the same material, eighteen inches long, which was broken by one of the stones falling on it when opening the cist; and a small gold finger-ring, chased and apparently originally jewelled, though the settings have fallen out.' [21]

The golden horn or cup with embossed or chased figures seems to describe a Celtic La Tène style *Rhyton*, a conical container from which fluids were to be drunk or poured in some ceremony, such as libation. The La Tène culture supposedly dates from the mid-5th century BCE and originated in Switzerland, where the Celts came into contact with Greek and Etruscan influences from south of the Alps. However, recent controversial research casts doubts on the origins of the Celts and their race. In *The Celts: A Sceptical History*, author Simon Jenkins argues compellingly that the 'Celts' is a misleading concept, bundling together quite distinct peoples.[22]

It seemed a shame that the 'gentleman of Stirling' did not offer this rare and valuable relic to a museum. Nevertheless, the size of the mound with its twelve large stones suggests a high-status burial. Moreover, the Gaelic name *Craigengelt* means 'bloody rocks', which may indicate that this area was the site of a great battle and Ghost Knowe, the burial place of a king that died in combat.

Lugh passes through the site of a further three mounds, next to Earl's Burn two miles west of Ghost Knowe, also recorded by *NSA 1834*:

'Where the lands stretch towards the Earl's burn, there is a very solitary but lovely small valley, in which are three artificial hills, the raising of which must have cost great labour. The entrenchment is the smallest, and is called 'Goodie's knowe.' The middle one, the 'Heart's hill', is by far the finest formed, being nearly circular, and fifty feet high, with a conical top. The third is the largest, of an oblong shape, with terraces on its sides. All of them are covered with the finest grass; and it is evident that the gravel and soil of which they are composed have been taken from the park wherein they stand. There is no tradition when or by whom these works were constructed; but one thing is certain, that the antiquary would be amply repaid for his labour in visiting these interesting remains of times long gone by.' [23]

It is likely that together with the Hills of Dunipace, Merlin's mound and Ghost Knowe, these mounds contributed to one of the most important prehistoric burial sites in Scotland.

Passing over Cairnoch Hill, Lugh enters an unusual square motte and bailey earthwork overlooking the northwestern shores of the Carron Valley Reservoir called Sir John de Graham's Castle. According to the *NSA 1834*, this motte was the residence of Sir John de Graeme of Dundaff, a loyal supporter of Sir William Wallace, killed in 1298 at the Battle of Falkirk. Incidentally, he is also buried on the Lugh current at the Parish Church at Falkirk. The site is one of the best examples of a motte and bailey in the area, with beautiful views across the Carron Valley.

Sir John de Graham's Castle

South of the reservoir, the Holy Axis passes precisely over Meikle Bin, the second-highest peak of the Campsie Fells. According to many Scottish historians, the Campsie Fells was the ancient region of Bannog, a name preserved in Bannockburn, visited by Bride. The Campsie Fells create a mountain fortress between Glasgow and the impassable swamps of the Forth to the north. It was the ancient realm of King Ban of Benoic or Benwick, who, according to the 13th-century *Vulgate Prose Cycle*, ruled during Arthurian times.[24]

Ban's wife, Elaine of Benoic, is from an illustrious bloodline and her lineage can be traced back to the holy bloodline of the biblical King David. After the invasion of her kingdom and her husband's death, Elaine gave her baby son Lancelot to the fairy-like human enchantress 'The Lady of the Lake'. She teaches him to become a knight before sending him to King Arthur's Court. If this was the land of King Ban, then the abode of the Lady of the Lake could either be the Lake of Menteith to the north or Loch Lomond to the west, known anciently as 'The Lake'.

On a high ridge at the base of Meikle Bin's northwestern slopes, above the confluence of the Bin Burn and the River Carron, sit the Machar Stones within the Carron Valley Forest. Despite much speculation about these megaliths, little of their origin or purpose is known.

Fintry and the Knockraich Stone

Lugh continues along the valley of Endrick Water to find nourishment at a waterfall that plunges 94 ft (28 m) into a deep gorge below the Fintry Hills' southern slopes. The Loup of Fintry, as it is known, is one of the most spectacular waterfalls in the Scottish Lowlands and one of the most beautiful. From here, the current flows through a group of almost hidden standing stones on a little hill nearby called the Gowk Stanes.

Gowk means cuckoo, a common name for many standing stones in Scotland. The term suggests a link with spring festivals when the cuckoo arrives, which also relates to fertility. *The Dragon Project,* organised by Paul Devereux in the 1970s at the Rollright Stones in Oxfordshire, recorded ultrasonic emissions from the standing stones at sunrise and sunset at certain times of the year but particularly at the spring and autumn equinoxes. Perhaps these emissions were helpful to the fertility of nature and wildlife, hence why the bird is so revered worldwide.

The chi energy of the waterfall is also absorbed into the stones, amplifying their telluric power needed to reanimate the surrounding landscape. We were unsure whether the stones were natural outcrops or carved into shape by the ancients. Either way, the energy here is tangible and benefits the strong dragon flow of Lugh. Yet another earthen mound attracts Lugh further west of here called the Tinto Myllie Knowe, perhaps another ancient burial place.

The valley of Endrick Water brings us to the little town of Fintry, a Gaelic word for 'fair land'. The name also refers to giants, particularly the legendary Finn or Fionn mac Cumhaill, the Irish or Gaelic Scottish archetype of Arthur who performed incredible feats with his twelve warriors, the Fianna. Perhaps his association with this place originates from tales attached to the area's geology in the form of giant basalt pillars overlooking the town.

Lugh also visits the tower at Fintry's Victorian parish church, in an isolated yet beautiful setting next to a tributary of Endrick Water. People have worshipped here since the 13th century and a church here dedicated to St Modan was granted to the Collegiate Church of St Mary at Dumbarton by Isabel, Duchess of Albany and Countess of Lennox.

The current then diverts northwest to the grounds of Culcreuch Castle Hotel, marked initially on Pont's map of Stirling (1583-1614) as *Kilcroich*, a Gaelic word meaning 'church of creuch or crevice'. Scottish place names with the prefix *kil* generally derive from *cell,* meaning church or holy place. The church of the crevice describes the geology here, where rocky basaltic hills flank the gently narrowing valley. Parts of the castle date back to 1296 when it was the ancestral home of Clan Galbraith, who also owned Inchgalbraith, an island on Loch Lomond near Luss, which we later discovered is visited by the Bride current. Until 2020, it was one of the oldest hotels in Scotland, with a few ghosts to boot. It is now private and no longer accessible to the public. Records give no mention of a religious building on the castle grounds, so we must assume that the church from which the castle takes its name is long gone.

After the modern Fintry Cemetery, Lugh directs us to a standing stone in a field at Knockraich Farm on the outskirts of the village. The Rodger family owns the farm and the quality of their meat and dairy products is renowned throughout the area, which they sell in their prize-winning Courtyard Café. So after a delicious lunch, we approached one of the staff, who directed us to one of the farm's owners to gain permission to visit the stone.

At first, they were reluctant as it would mean us walking through a field of grazing dairy cows. However, they suddenly became intrigued when we explained who we were and the stone's connection to the Holy Axis. To our amazement, they recognised our names, having purchased our book, *The Power of Centre,*[25,] which also refers to many sites in Scotland, so we chatted further about their interest in leys and earth mysteries.

They were happy for us to visit the standing stone when the cows were back in the dairy for their afternoon milking session. Following their instructions on how

Gowk Stone, Knockraich Farm, Fintry

to get there, we soon spotted the solitary megalith, also known locally as the Gowk Stone, standing about 3ft tall in the middle of the field. As we approached, we noticed cup marks on each side of the stone and a circular cavity on top containing a large pebble placed there by one of the family through their knowledge of bullaun stones.

Bullaun stones are megaliths traditionally originating from Ireland, Scotland, and parts of Scandinavia, cut with a series of cup marks. Here, white quartz stones were ground sunwise for luck, wishes or cursing. However, our ancestors would have known that the grinding action would positively and curatively affect the landscape. According to legend, this turning of the rocks was often carried out at Imbolc on 1 February and Beltane at the spring festival on 1 May. Local folklore also alludes to the belief that the rainwater collected in the stone's hollow has healing properties.

In *The Standing Stones of Stirling District*, A F Hutchinson wrote of the Knockraich stone: '*The stone seems to have brought down through the ages a tradition of sanctity in connection with it, as there is a legend to the effect that any attempt to move it is attended by convulsions of nature and evil consequences to the rash disturber.*'[26]

The sun was at a perfect angle to see what appeared to be elemental faces peering out at us from the stone. According to one 16th or 17th-century source, a horse and rider were carved on one of its faces, although no trace of it remains.

As well as marking the Lugh current, we sensed the stone is also integral to the area's prosperity and, therefore, the luck and well-being of the farm and café. The stone seems to function well in this role, as the farm and café are thriving, serving and selling many products made from the high-yield milk the cows produce from the farm's rich grasslands.

The Balfron Oak

Following the westerly flow of Endrick Water, we arrive at a clump of trees near the village of Balfron, marked as a *camp* on old maps and a *motte* on the modern O.S map. However, its history is uncertain and the levelled summit of this site is now featureless and covered with fir trees. From here, the male current takes us to the small village of Balfron and its ancient parish church.

One local legend associated with the area tells that when the men-folk were at a place of sacrifice above the church called Ibert, they heard screams from the settlement below and rushed down only to discover that wolves had taken the children of the village; hence its name Balfron, which is thought to derive from *bail'-a-bhroin* meaning a 'town of mourning.'[27]

The earliest documented church at Balfron belonged to the Order of Augustinian Canons of Inchaffray Abbey in 1303 when the village was known as Buthbren. The local place names Templelea and Spittal allude to a time when the Knights Templar held lands just to the north and west of the church.

The church stands next to Clachan Burn in an area known locally as Clachan, a Gaelic word meaning stone and often given to standing megaliths. In Scotland, the name also applies to a graveyard or a village containing a church.

In the churchyard is a gravestone with a remarkable carving of two entwined serpents with an egg between their mouths. The serpent symbolises rebirth from the mundane to enlightenment and the egg represents the world. The two serpents also represent the kundalini, the *sushumna, ida and pingala*, the body's three principal energy channels. Ida and pingala,

Gravestone carved with entwined serpents with egg, Balfron Church

275

feminine and masculine, interlace around the sushumna creating chakra points as they rise up through the spine to the top of the head. The kundalini starts an awakening within us of divine knowledge represented as an egg, symbolising Creation. This depiction also seemed symbolic of the male and female serpent lines of Lugh and Bride that unite at certain places of power to nurture the birth of the Grail and spiritual illumination within the land as they interlace along the Holy Axis. As we would soon discover, one of these places of Creation is very close to Balfron.

Lugh also passes through an impressive sessile oak located by the church gate, sometimes called the Clachan Oak and the Hanging Tree. It stands next to a fountain, possibly covering the site of an ancient spring. The old oak is now hollowed with age and held together with three iron hoops. According to legend, William Wallace rested here, and later Rob Roy hid beneath its boughs.

The tree, the church and the river feel part of a long-lost enchanted landscape, one of those gateway places to the unseen realms or otherworld. Interestingly, the old oak has been recently treated by pumping compressed air into the soil beneath it and injecting the roots with a seaweed compound, so hopefully, it will continue to enchant for many more years to come.

Balfron Church and oak

The small village of Killearn marks the Holy Axis just over 2 miles to the southwest of Balfron. It was the birthplace of Scottish historian and scholar George Buchanan (1506–1582), who wrote *Rerum Scoticarum Historia* or The History of Scotland, published in 1582. His main claim to fame was tutoring the young Mary, Queen of Scots. During his career, he was a great critic of the vices of the Catholic clergy and openly joined the Protestants Reformed Church. Buchanan's purpose in publishing his History for Scotland was to purge the national history of *'English lies and Scottish vanity'.*[28]

Killearn commemorates Buchanan with a 101 ft (31 m) obelisk, one of the highest in Scotland, made of local white millstone grit, which like granite, is high in crystalline silicate. Such a powerful stone acts as a conductor of cosmic energy, reverberating the memory of Buchanan across the landscape. Furthermore, standing within the aura of the straight alignment of the Holy Axis further amplifies his spirit and earthly deeds.

Further to the southwest, the Holy Axis meets the Lugh serpent at Gartness Bridge that spans Endrick Water, where we find a series of small waterfall pools called the Pots of Gartness. The 'pots' are bubbling cauldrons or bowls formed from a natural cleft in the rock over which river water cascades after a good rainfall. The Scottish poet and broadcaster Maurice Lindsay mentions a mill once existing here: '*The Pots offered a perfect location for a mill and there was an ancient mill on this site before a Woollen mill superseded it. The crumbling remains can still be seen. The old cottages that housed the mill workers are the pretty, hobbit-like, residences overlooking the Endrick, just over the bridge, in the hamlet of Gartness.*'[29]

John Napier of Merchiston (1550–1617), inventor of logarithms, resided in a house here 'when he was making his calculations' but was disturbed by the constant noise of the cascade and the clack of the mill. Napier was an eccentric character sporting a long black beard and cloak and possessed a black pet cockerel. Locals thought him involved with witchcraft due to his strange behaviour. For example, he reputedly identified a thief in his household by bizarrely asking each servant to stroke the cockerel in a dimly lit room. He claimed it would crow when the culprit touched it. Indeed, the thief was soon identified, further fuelling the view that he used magical powers.[30]

Lugh continues to follow the course of Endrick Water as it meanders north of the Campsie Fells towards Loch Lomond. This 30-mile-long river rises in the Fintry Hills and flows through the villages of Fintry, Balfron and Drymen.

Further west, on a minor road between Gartness and Drymen, both Lugh and the alignment meet again at Drumquhassle Roman Fort, located at the end of a natural ridge overlooking the confluence of the Catter Burn and Endrick Water. Today, there is little to see of the old defences, which lie hidden in pastureland. The fort, discovered in 1977, was the last confirmed of a series of 'glen-blocking' garrisons positioned along the Highland Boundary Fault Frontier. They were medium-sized auxiliary forts constructed during the early administration of Sallustius Lucullus, governor of Roman Britain during the late 1st century CE, originally intended as a springboard into the Central Highland Massif. However, they were demolished and abandoned after only a short period of occupation, possibly due to the formation of a tight alliance of the Scots, Picts and Strathclyde Britons, who successfully pushed the Roman force below the Forth-Clyde Neck of Britain. Undoubtedly, the Romans chose this spot on a high plateau because it overlooked a strategic thoroughfare of trade routes that transgressed the Neck of Britain to Loch Lomond and continued to the western coast of Argyll.

Just south of the village of Drymen, close to the eastern shores of Loch Lomond, we dowse the Lugh current at a wooded hill called Catter Law or Moot Hill and a large artificial earthen mound where the administration of justice took place in former times. Although described as a *motte*, it is more likely to be a 'Law Hill' with a ditch around the base commonly used by the Picts, but it may well date back to prehistoric times. Its position at the junction of roads feeding in from three cardinal directions very close to a significant fording of Endrick Water defines this site as historically important. The name *catter* is a British word deriving from *cat* of *cad*, meaning battle, perhaps alluding to a major skirmish between the British, Pictish and Scottish alliance against the Romans while occupying their fort on the Lugh current at nearby Drumquhassle.

A few miles west of Catter Law, the old kirk of Kilmaronock has been an early Christian site since the 6th century dedicated to St Ronan of Iona. Although its history is obscure, records show that in 1324, Robert the Bruce transferred the patronage of the church from the Earls of Lennox to Cambuskenneth Abbey at Stirling. Lugh passes east–west through the present Georgian building into woodland less than half a mile to the west. Here he connects with a holy well, also dedicated to St Ronan, on the northern edge of the woodland, although now very overgrown.

The Venerable Bede (672–735 CE) refers to Ronan of Iona as one of the great protagonists of the Roman custom of celebrating Easter. His feast day, 7 February close to Imbolc, is still celebrated at St Ronan's Healing Wells at Innerleithen in the Borders, where he came to drive out the devil according to local tradition. The wells became a famous spa where people would drink the water from the sulphurous spring in the hope of curing their ailments.

We are approaching the outstanding landscape of Loch Lomond, where the Lugh and Bride currents and the Holy Axis are very close to one another. We find Lugh entering the eastern shores of the lake along a finger of land called Ring Point, almost touching the alignment. Just under a mile to the north is Balmaha, where we last dowsed Bride entering through a large oak tree. According to Scottish author and researcher Hugh McArthur, Ring Point is another possible location of Lancelot's castle, Joyous Garde. McArthur has written extensively about his homeland's history, folklore and traditions and is the historian for the ancient Clan Arthur. We had the pleasure of meeting him in Glasgow, where we had a fascinating discussion about the controversial claim that the legendary King Arthur was the son of King Aedan of the Dal Riata.

In his fascinating book, *The Arthurian Lake: A Secret History of Loch Lomond,* he mentions that his friend Alex Macadam, an ex-officer of the British army and a firm advocate of Arthur's Scottish origin, discovered the site of an ancient tower on Ring Point that he believes was Lancelot's legendary home. King Ban of Benoic or Bannoic, the father of Lancelot, takes his name from the ancient kingdom of Bannog that stretches from Loch Lomond, or 'The Lake' as it was known then, to the Firth of Forth, following a trade route that partly follows Endrick Water.[31] The tower marked the western boundary of this old Kingdom of Bannog. So, as we stood at the edge of the lake looking out towards its sacred islands, we wondered whether these waters were the actual location of the Lady of the Lake legends and, if so, what might lie in store for us on our continuing Grail journey.

1. https://www.ainmean-aite.scot/?id=38828
2. *NSA 1791-1845, Falkirk, VIII, 1845.* https://stataccscot.edina.ac.uk/
3. https://philological.cal.bham.ac.uk/boece/
4. http://www.earlybritishkingdoms.com/archaeology/camelon.html
5. 20. 21. 23. NSA. 1834. https://stataccscot.edina.ac.uk/static/statacc/dist/home
6. 9. Carroll, D. F. 1996. *Arturius - A Quest for Camelot.* Self-published.

7. *Annals of Ulster,* https://celt.ucc.ie/published/T100001A/

8. 10. Moffat, A. 1999. *Arthur and the Lost Kingdoms.* Wiedenfeld & Nicholson, London.

11. 19. Burton, J. H. 2010. *The History of Scotland: From Agricola's Invasion to the Revolution of 1688.* Nabu Press. Also https://www.geograph.org.uk/photo/1748406

12. Bailey, G. B. 2001. *Falkirk or Paradise: The Battle of Falkirk Muir, 1746.* John Donald Publishers Ltd, Edinburgh.

13. http://www.facesofarthur.org.uk/articles/guestdan14.htm

14. https://www.scotsman.com/heritage-and-retro/heritage/five-creepiest-ufo-sightings-scotland-has-ever-seen-636824

15. Collins, A. & Little, G. L. 2022. *Origins of the Gods: Qesem Cave, Skinwalkers, and Contact with Transdimensional Intelligences.* Bear & Company, Rochester, Vermont.

16. 18. Ardrey, Adam. 2010. *Finding Merlin: The Truth Behind the Legend of the Great Arthurian Mage.* Random House, London.

17. Chalmers, G. 2020. *Caledonia; or, A historical and topographical account of North Britain, from the most ancient to the present times.* Alpha Edition, US.

22 Jenkins, S. 2022. *The Celts: A Sceptical History,* Profile Books Ltd, London.

24. Lacy, Norris J. (Ed.). *Lancelot–Grail: The Old French Arthurian Vulgate and Post-Vulgate in Translation,* Vol 1-4. Garland, New York. https://matterofbritain.com/htmlpages/legendliterature3.html

25. Biltcliffe, G. Hoare, C. 2018. *The Power of Centre.* Sacred Lands Publishing, Weymouth.

26. Hutchinson, A.F. 1893. *The Standing Stones of Stirling District.* The Stirling Antiquary, volume 1, 1893.

27. https://balfronheritage.org.uk/balfrons-history/

28. Buchanan, George. 1799. *The History of Scotland from the earliest Accounts of that Nation to the Reign of King James VI.* Chapman and Lang, Glasgow.

29. https://www.scottish-places.info/towns/townhistory814.html

30. https://en.wikipedia.org/wiki/John_Napier#Interest_in_the_occult

31. McArthur, Hugh, D. P. 2010. *The Arthurian Lake: A Secret History of Loch Lomond.* clannarthur.com

Chapter 13

Sacred Islands, Hill of the Grail and the Haunted Church

Lugh and Bride from Loch Lomond to Kilmartin

'What a large part of Loch Lomond's beauty is due to its islands,
those beautiful green tangled islands,
that lie like jewels upon its surface.'
Henry Vollam Morton, English travel writer

*View of Inchcailloch, the 'Lady of the Lake', Loch Lomond
from Duncryne Hill by Grahame Gardner*

The Lady of the Lake

Nestled at the heart of the dramatic and breathtaking mountains and glens of the Trossachs, the vast tranquil beauty of Loch Lomond encapsulates the essence of Scottish scenic splendour. The Loch lies 18 miles (29 km) north of Glasgow and contains the greatest volume of freshwater in the UK, measuring 24 miles (38 km) long and 5 miles (8 km) wide at its southern end. During the Ice Age, it was gouged out by a giant glacier as it moved south. As the ice eventually melted, the sea inundated the area, gradually giving way to freshwater. As a result, the Loch has more fish species than any other loch and a quarter of all UK's flowering plants around its shores.

Known initially as Loch Leven, Loch Lomond has around twenty-two islands, many of which are uninhabited. The 9th-century Welsh monk Nennius wrote:

'The first marvel [first in a series of the wonders of Britain] is Loch Leven [Lomond]. In it are sixty rivers, and men live there, and it is surrounded by sixty rocks, and there is an eagle's nest on each rock, and sixty rivers flow into it, and only one river flows from it to the sea, called Leven.' [1]

Geoffrey of Monmouth mentions that King Arthur and his nephew held the Scots and Picts under siege on the islands of Loch Lomond, where they sought refuge. After Arthur blockaded each river with a fleet of boats, he confined his enemies for fifteen days, forcing them to surrender in their thousands.[2]

Scottish history and folklore researcher Hugh McArthur in *The Arthurian Lake, A Secret History of Loch Lomond,* refers to the Loch as the 'Arthurian Lake' because of the many place names in the area connected with the warrior. Historically, it was known as 'The Lake', and locals still refer to it by this name.[3] Nennius says Arthur fought twelve battles and his second, third, fourth and fifth battles occurred at a river called Dubglas in the region of Linnius.[4] According to local folklore, Arthur had many conflicts overlooking the lake along Glen Douglas (Dubglas) in the Lennox (Linnius) area, possibly those mentioned by Monmouth, leading to the siege on Loch Lomond.

Once a large region of Scotland, Lennox is now confined to a land peninsular between Loch Lomond, Loch Gare and Loch Long as far north as Tarbet. It was a strategically important area that allowed access to the sea from Loch Lomond, avoiding the River Leven and the fortress of Dumbarton in the south.

North of here is Ben Arthur (Arthur's Mountain), now commonly known as The Cobbler and its southwestern crag is called Arthur's Seat. At the top of the loch is a great boulder called *Clach na Briton* meaning the Rock of Britain, which is said to be the northern boundary of the old British Kingdom of Strathclyde, which Arthur helped to protect and defend alongside its king, Ceredig.[5]

Where the River Leven meets the Clyde is the impressive volcanic twin-peaked Dumbarton Rock or Fortress of the Britons. It has been a strategic place since prehistoric times, and a short distance from here is another rock outcrop known as King Arthur's Seat, once owned by Robert the Bruce.

One of the largest and most accessible islands on Loch Lomond is Inchcailloch, and both the male and female currents appear to be flowing towards it as they head westwards from Balmaha.

We were thankful that the day we had chosen for our outing to the island was warm and sunny. As we approached the jetty in Balmaha to board the boats that take visitors regularly to the island, we could feel the strong presence of Bride at the giant oak tree detected previously flowing from its companion tree at the nearby pub. Accompanying us was Scottish dowser and author Grahame Gardner, former chairman of the British Society of Dowsers. The Holy Axis also connects with the island, and we were excited to discover where the alignment and two currents meet, if at all.

Inchcailloch or *Inchcailleach* means 'island of the old women' or, as McArthur states, 'island of the Veiled One or Old Hag'. Legends say that a community of nuns once settled on the island and that Irish saint St Kentigerna died here in 734 CE. She was the daughter of Cellach, King of Leinster and married to Feriacus or Feradach of the Dal Riata, the possible grandson of King Artuir. After the death of her husband, she settled in Scotland, where she worked as a missionary alongside her brother St Comgan and her son St Fillan, eventually settling on Inchcailloch. In the 12th century, a church was built in her memory and later abandoned in 1670. However, the graveyard continued in use until 1947. Many clan members lie here from the MacFarlane and MacGregor families, including ancestors and descendants of the famous Scottish outlaw and folk hero Rob Roy MacGregor.

After disembarking at a small jetty on the island's eastern shores, we followed a path to its highest point. We soon detected the Bride current flowing from the direction of Balmaha crossing a path in Coffin Valley, where mainlanders carried the dead to St Kentigerna's Church.

Continuing along the path, we encountered Lugh at a sharp U-bend, heading for the summit of Endrick viewpoint, the highest point on the island. Here we found him forming a node with Bride at the foot of a Scots pine once sacred to the Celtic Druids, a symbolic 'Tree of Life' or 'World Axis'. Its wood was used to make fires at the winter solstice and its smoke cleansed spaces of negative energy. Interestingly, the Scots pine is said to be a totem tree of the MacGregor clan.

While I was dowsing the node signature of a five-petalled flower on the ground beneath the tree, Grahame spotted a chicken's egg on a homemade nest carefully placed where the boughs meet the trunk. Staring in disbelief, we contemplated the bizarre meaning of this strange offering over the node. Perhaps it was intuitively placed as a symbol of fertility or resurrection, a cosmic egg of creation at the meeting of two great dragon lines. Interestingly, we had encountered an egg on the Lugh current at Balfron the previous day, although carved in stone on a grave between two serpents. Perhaps it was a sign that we had reached the next initiatory level on our pilgrimage of this Holy Axis.

Coffin Valley, Inchcailloch

Inchcailloch, like Doon Hill, is formed from the great Highland Boundary Fault, its physical presence evidenced by the island's sunken central valley. However, this significant fracture is not just a fine line in the ground but a deep fracture or crumple in the Earth's crust from the meeting of two massive continents. Over 450 million years ago, the land we now call Scotland was part of a continent called Laurentia, which included Norway and North America. England, and parts of the east coast of America and Western Europe, formed part of another continent called Avalonia. Over the next 40 million years, the two landmasses moved towards each other, eventually colliding to create the Scottish Alps and the mountains of Cumbria. North of this fault is the magnificent rugged and mountainous

Node Point, Inchcailloch

Highlands with its deep valleys and harsher weather and to the south, the softer and temperate Lowlands more suited to agriculture.

Over the years, there have been many reports of a 'Nessie' or plesiosaur-like creature in Loch Lomond, including one that resembles a giant crocodile. Although Loch Ness is famous for its monster, other strange phenomena have occurred there, including sightings of UFOs, balls of light and time-slips.[6] In his book *Alien Energy*, Andrew Collins refers to an incident dating back to the mid-18th century when a couple, while travelling in a horse and trap near Loch End on the south side of Loch Ness, suddenly disappeared. Local people speculated that they had been kidnapped or attacked by outlaws and thrown into the Loch, but a hundred years later the same couple walked into a local alms house to seek refuge from a storm. The priest who took them in noted that they were wearing old-fashioned clothing and were very confused, unable to explain where they had come from or how they got there. Two days later, they disappeared again. Was it the same couple that disappeared all those years ago? Did they slip forward in time as if the space-time continuum corrected itself, or had they just been temporarily displaced?

Collins refers to the Great Glen Fault that forms Loch Ness and suggests the high magnetism produced by this fault can, under certain conditions, create a 'window' area, a portal or a rupture in time and space.[7] Perhaps it was the combination of the high magnetism of the fault, the storm and, of course, lightning (plasma) which created a surge in the local magnetic field when it struck the ground. Perhaps the Loch Ness and Loch Lomond monsters are past visitors who can manifest in the present briefly and then return without leaving any trace except for the many confused people who witness them.

Often, plasma communicates with us for a specific purpose, a universal consciousness wishing to impart wisdom or knowledge. However, sometimes it is just trickster energy leading us astray. They can appear as 'ascended beings' from other planets or universes here to teach mankind, entering through 'a window' or portal created from the ionised gas released through a fault line or other highly magnetic disturbances. Perhaps the story of the biblical Moses at Mount Sinai is an example of plasma communication. During a storm, with thunder and lightning, the Lord spoke to Moses in a flame of fire and delivered the Ten Commandments.

Inchcailloch is undoubtedly sacred and was once known locally as 'Corpse Island', possibly due to it being the traditional burial place of clan members. The appearance of 'corpse lights' have been seen travelling above ground along Coffin Valley, between the island's cemetery and settlements on the mainland. The otherworldly atmosphere is tangible, further enhanced by its myths and legends as an Avalon and the abode of the Lady of the Lake.

Scottish author Hugh McArthur also refers to the island as a Scottish 'Avalon' and the hill where we find the node point he calls *Tom na Nigheanan* or 'Ridge of the Maidens'. The ridge's name may refer to the Nine Maidens, a pre-Christian goddess cult that frequently appears alongside stories of the Lady of the Lake and the mystical Isle of Avalon.[8] Perhaps Kentigerna knew of this Arthurian tradition and was drawn to establish a nunnery here. The name Inchcailloch or 'isle of the old women', may also be a memory of this goddess cult. Interestingly, Maha, as in Balmaha, is also said to be the pet name of Kentigerna, meaning 'mother'.

The *Caillioch* or *Cailleach* is the winter crone goddess who transforms into the maiden goddess Bride in the summer months. Although there is no evidence of an Irish saint settling here, the notion that the island is associated with maidens, nuns and Kentigerna may indicate that the island was long ago a place to honour the divine feminine.

Interestingly, Sir Walter Scott's most famous poem, *The Lady of the Lake,* includes this isle of the goddess:

'A slender crosslet formed with care
A cubit's length in measure due
The shafts and limbs were rods of yew
Whose parents in Inch Cailliach wave
Their Shadows o'er Clan Alpine's grave,
And, answering Lomond's breezes deep,
Soothe many a chieftain's endless sleep.'

Walking along the eastern shore of Loch Lomond from Balmaha, we noticed the island's shape resembles a reclining goddess. A distant photo of the island, taken by our friend Grahame Gardner from the top of Duncryne Hill, also shows this landscape phenomenon. So perhaps the entire island embodies the legendary Lady of the Lake.

Before arriving at the node, Bride curiously avoids the remains of St Kentigerna's Church. She then exits the island's southwestern shores by a jetty at a finger of land called Port Bawn, meaning white or holy, where she meets the Holy Axis. Here, on

Site of St Kentigerna's Church, Inchcailloch

the edge of a woodland carpeted with bluebells, is a natural spring bubbling out of the ground over which Bride also passes. The area around the spring would have been an ideal spot for St Kentigerna's nunnery, offering a constant supply of fresh and revitalising water. Meanwhile, the Lugh current continues northwest from the node along the MacFarlane Burn before crossing the loch to visit the small islands of Inchfad, Inchcruin and Inchconnachan.

The Isle of the Spear

Bride and the Holy Axis also pass through the privately owned islands of Inchmoan and Inchtavannach. At this point, we decided to continue to the pretty tourist village of Luss on Loch Lomond's western shores. Here we detected Bride at the parish church dedicated to St Kessog, his name meaning 'little spear'. Meanwhile, Lugh crosses the Old Military Road just south of Luss in the hamlet of Aldochlay, in Bantry Bay, which also marks the Holy Axis as it enters the mainland. So having detected Lugh south of Bride meant only one thing, they formed a second node after Inchcailloch. After dowsing over the map, the pendulum identified its location on the island of Inchtavannach. In contrast to Inchcailloch, the name Inchtavannach means 'Monks Island' and is one of the largest islands on Loch Lomond. It is particularly renowned as the Celtic sanctuary of St Kessog, Scotland's patron saint before St Andrew.

Getting permission to visit the island and hiring a boat to take us there was difficult and, due to the COVID-19 lockdown, it was not until April 2022 that we achieved our goal. However, when the day came for our trip, we were thrilled to be greeted by a beautiful warm sunny morning, ideal for walking around a densely wooded island with only vague footpaths to show us the way. Grahame Gardner also joined us on this occasion, already familiar with our various quests along the Holy Axis.

After dropping anchor a few yards from a beach at the island's northwest end, the boat's skipper advised us to wade across to the stony shore. The trip allowed us three hours on the island, which we felt would give us plenty of time to explore and dowse the currents, or so we thought.

Now on firmer ground, we consulted our hand-drawn plan of the island in the hope that we could work out which path to take to start our quest, but as we were to discover, all the tracks were overgrown. We stumbled over thick undergrowth under a dense canopy of trees towards the island's southeast point, where we came to an area of open pastureland with a small farmstead, perhaps the prettiest part of Inchtavannach. The house, built in 1760, is supposedly on the site of an old monastery and graveyard first established by St Kessog. Weaving our way around grazing cows and horses, we detected Bride passing through a group of rocks on a ridge, said to be the location of Kessog's Cave, some 200 yards (180 m) east of the house. The cave was quarried by dynamite blasting in 1860 and now survives as a scoop of rock measuring 14ft (4.2 m) east to west. Although nothing remains of the monastery, a stone incorporated into one of the house's walls is said to be from the time of St Kessog. In the *Ecclesiastical Remains in the Neighbourhood of Luss*, Lacaille writes:

'Vestiges of a structure, said to be the remains of a monastery, stood between the escarpment of rock [Kessog's Cave] and the shore. These turf-covered remains, I was told, had the appearance of great antiquity. As a convenient quarry they provided, when required, a source of easily obtained stones for building, and gradually the ruins disappeared. Several dressed stones were found at this place, and these were built into the wall of a cowshed. My informant showed me a carved one built high up into the east wall, which had formed part of a string of masonry, and which bore a design consisting of running circles and ellipse.'[9]

St Kessog is a remarkable saint whose fame spread far and wide from Keswick in Cumbria to Kessock Bridge near Inverness, although Loch Lomond and the Trossachs have the most place names associated with him. Like many other Celtic saints in Scotland, his story blends half-remembered facts, fiction and propaganda. He was said to have brought Christianity from Ireland and set up a mission on Inchtavannach with his followers. After his death, he was buried at the church at Luss, visited by the Bride current.

He was Bishop of Boine, which according to Dane Sherrard in

Site of St Kessog's Cave, Inchtavannach

Who was Saint Kessog, was not the Irish Boine but a place in Buchanan, in the eastern area of Balmaha. He cites Thomas Dempster and the *Acto Sanctorum* or 'Acts of the Saints', a comprehensive text compiled in Antwerp between 1596–1665 that says Boine was the name of a diocese in the area of Loch Lomond during the time of Kessog and probably included Lennox.[10]

St Kessog (*c*. 460–c 520) had traditionally arrived in the Loch Lomond area before St Columba's missionaries. The pretty town of Luss, situated on the Lennox peninsular, was one of Scotland's most popular places of pilgrimage from pre-Norman times, and travellers came from all over to worship at St Kessog's shrine before his cult declined dramatically after the Reformation.

Born sixty years before Columba, Kessog was the first Christian martyr in Scotland and is considered its true patron saint. Shortly after his death, his name was the rallying battle cry for clan members all over Scotland. Even King Robert the Bruce incited his army with his memory as he led them into battle against the English at Bannockburn. After his success, Bruce made a shrine in honour of the saint at Luss, granting a three-mile sanctuary around his church, like the early shrines at Torphichen and Stowe on the Bride current. This auspicious act reinforced the sacred status of the place, saving it from destruction and bringing thousands more pilgrims to Luss until the Reformation.

Despite his illustrious history, very few people today know of St Kessog and his role as Scotland's first patron saint. In *Walking the Mist: A Practical Guide to Celtic Spirituality*, Donald McKinney writes:

'Perhaps he captured the imagination of the common people in a way that St Andrew failed to do and by working amongst the people they could identify with him as part of their community, unlike St Andrew who was imposed as a political compromise by Kenneth MacAlpin – the Scot who united Dal Riata with the Pictlands.'[11]

One of the enigmas of Kessog is his decision as bishop to create a religious centre on an island, something unheard of at the time, as most religious leaders established themselves at the heart of their ministry. However, Loch Lomond, within the region of Lennox, was at the time the meeting place of three ancient kingdoms – Strathclyde of the Britons, Manau of the Picts and Dal Riata of the Scots. Therefore, deliberately positioning himself on Inchtavannach meant that Kessog's missionary centre could spread the word of Celtic Christianity far and wide. Later in 510 CE, Kessog built a church at Luss, enabling him to preach directly to the locals on the mainland, a short boat trip away. Furthermore, Inchtavannach was a perfect location for his monastery, lying on an ancient trading and pilgrimage route that crossed the Neck of Britain.

The Celtic Church was quite distinct from the Roman Church. The Celtic monks followed a simple life, renouncing personal wealth or comfort and spending much of their time in meditation or worship. In contrast, the Roman Church was more business-like, its followers living a secular life alien to the Celts.

Bride approaches Inchtavannach's southeastern shores from a curious tiny circular island called Inchgalbraith, its only feature being the overgrown ruins of a castle. It was built by the Galbraith clan as a safe refuge, supposedly over an Iron Age crannog. According to the Canmore website, the castle was constructed as a square tower of sandstone boulders and blocks and '*retains a fine entrance and portcullis in its east wall*.'

We encountered Clan Galbraith earlier at Culcreuch Castle, previously visited by Lugh at Fintry. The history of the Galbraiths is fascinating as their Gaelic surname translates as 'British foreigner', deriving from *gall* meaning 'stranger', and *breathnach* meaning 'Briton'. Welsh-speaking Britons of the Kingdom of Strathclyde lived in this area until the 14th century, despite the incoming tide of Irish Gaels and Lowland Angles. According to one source, *'The heraldist Iain Moncreiffe of that Ilk speculated that the Arms of the Galbraiths—which bore three bears' heads—may allude to the British name Arthur that is thought by some to mean "bear."'*[12]

Sir William Galbraith of Buthernock became co-regent of Scotland during the 13th century. His son, Sir Arthur, the fifth chief of the clan, supported Robert the Bruce and married a sister of Sir James Douglas, who accompanied Sir William St Clair with the heart of the Bruce on their fateful journey to the Holy Land. Could the Galbraith Clan be ancestors of the Scottish Artuir, son of Aeden? An ancient verse recalls *'Galbraith of the Red Tower Noblest of the Albannic Race, thy pedigree.'*[13] The Red Tower refers to Dumbarton Castle, the former seat of the Royal House of the Strathclyde Britons, a supposed stronghold of Artuir.

We dowsed the feminine current passing through the site of St Kessog's Cave before flowing north to a large boulder at the base of the island's highest peak in the middle of the island. It rises to 282 ft (85 m) and is known locally as *Tom nan Clag* or 'The Hill of the Bell'.

Lugh enters the island through its northeastern shores to visit an intriguing rock boulder in a delightful little bay called *Clach a' Mhinisteir* or 'the minister's stone'. St Kessog is said to have preached to the locals from this stone as they arrived in their boats. A D Lacaille, in *Ecclesiastical Remains in the Neighbourhood of Luss,* records that:

'Below the escarpment formed by the eastern slopes of Tom nan Clag is a huge flat-topped quadrate boulder of schist. The rock, 30 feet in girth and over 6 feet high, bears no markings; yet that it enjoyed certain importance in the past seems substantiated by its designation "Clach a' Mhinisteir , the minister's stone". Probably the place naturally marked by Clach a' Mhinisteir was one of the "deserts" or retreats of the holy Kessog, but whatever may be conjectured, the name given to the boulder must go back to early times.'[14]

While meditating on the rock, I suddenly had a psychic impression of Kessog standing on the rock, waiting for pilgrims to arrive in small boats, perhaps missionaries. Just then, a boatload of people passed by as I raised my arms to the sky in tribute to the great saint, which caused great amusement to Caroline and Grahame.

Minister's Stone, Inchtavannach

As we followed Lugh up the eastern slopes of Tom nan Clag, we also sensed Bride here and thought at first that they formed a node on the side of the hill. However, we quickly realised they were flowing side by side as if escorting each other to the top. There was no actual footpath to guide us, so getting to the summit was a challenge, with only our dowsing and natural senses to show us the way. At times we became disorientated, but luckily, Grahame's GPS app gave us an exact route to the top. After an almost vertical climb, scrambling through thick layers of vegetation and fallen branches, we were relieved and delighted when we made it to the summit. Standing on a rocky plateau, we gazed at the magnificent view of the Loch.

We dowsed the node point at the centre of an ancient cist or grave unrecorded by archaeology. 'Tom nan Clag' refers to the bell of St Kessog that rang out from the hill to call the faithful from

Node point on the summit of Tom nan Clag, Inchtavannach

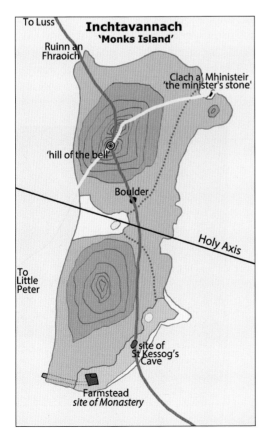

the surrounding areas to prayer. The Earl of Perth purchased the hill in 1675 and acquired the ancient hereditary title Thane of Lennox. Lugh takes a southwesterly course from the node to Loch Lomond's western shores just south of Luss. Bride meanwhile leaves through the island's northwest tip at *Ruinn an Fhraoich* for the parish church at Luss.

Suddenly, Grahame looked at his watch and announced that we had 10 minutes to return to the beach before the boat arrived to take us back to Luss. Luckily, despite a precarious scramble down to the shore, we reached the pick-up point just as the boat arrived.

On our way back to Luss, we marvelled at the delightful features of the island and the wonderful time we had exploring it. However, past and modern antiquarians ignore Inchtavannach and Inchcailloch's spiritual significance and their sacred importance is now long forgotten from the annals of history.

We also felt it significant that they both lie on the Holy Axis alignment and are node points on one of Britain's most famous fault lines. Inchtavannach may have been seen as the isle of the male god or warrior, later adopted by Kessog, or 'little spear' as he was known, symbolic of the spear of the god Lugh.

Luss, the Valley of Light

From St Kessog's Isle, the female current came ashore over the hill called *Tom-na-Paidire* or 'Hill of Prayer' in woodland belonging to the Camstraddan estate before visiting the church at Luss. Naturally, we were eager to investigate inside the Victorian church, but, like many in Scotland, it is only open for services. But fate was on our side, as just at that moment, we met an elderly lady who was able to sell us a book on its history by village historian John McGilp Sinclair. He mentions that the Romans called the lands of Luss *Vallis Lucis* or 'valley of light', perhaps because the teachings of the gospels arrived here with Christian missionaries from very early times.[15]

The author also states that before 510 CE, when Kessog first arrived here, the village was referred to as *clachan-dhu,* meaning 'black hamlet'. It also translates as 'dark stones', possibly alluding to ancient stones that once existed in the vicinity, regarded by early Christians as pagan or evil. Perhaps they were sanctuary stones marking a sacred boundary, like those at Torphichen. St Kessog supposedly met his death at an old Druidic holy site.[16] Was this the site of the 'dark' megaliths?

In *The Lure of Loch Lomond*, Ronald McAllister writes that the Gaelic word 'Lus' describes a plant or herb, believed to be the wild blue iris that grows on the south bank of the Luss River to the south of the church. The plant is a member of the lily family, hence the fleur-de-lys symbols in the church. Other sources claim the name derives from the fragrant herbs growing in the area, used to embalm St Kessog's body.[17]

A church has stood on this site since the 14th century, although two cross-slabs in the churchyard date from the 7th to 9th century. Next to them is an 11th-century hogback tombstone confirming a much earlier religious foundation. We dowsed Bride through a standing stone etched with a crudely carved cross reminiscent of a Christianised megalith. One of the Druidic 'dark stones' perhaps?

Around the back of the church facing the Loch, Bride passes through the tombs of the Colquhoun Clan of Luss, who were said to be guardians of Kessog's relics.

Kessog was born into the royal family of Munster in Southern Ireland in approximately 460 CE. Even as a child, he revealed himself to be very pious and holy. On one occasion, while neighbouring rulers

Ancient stone at Luss Church

visited the King of Cashel, they let their sons play with the young Kessog. When the visiting kings heard that all their sons had drowned during a terrible accident except for Kessog, they became angered, and a war was only averted when Kessog brought the drowned princes back to life after a night of prayer. Such was his holiness that he was sent to a monastery at Nendrum in County Down, where he came under the tutelage of St Machaloi. In due course, Kessog was sent to the great meeting place of three nations at Luss to carry out missionary work.[18]

There is, however, little evidence that Kessog came from Ireland. His name derives from the old British word *Kess*, or *Cess* meaning 'spear' and *og* meaning 'little'. He was known as 'the warrior saint', reminiscent of Lancelot and Lugh and their 'spears of light'. According to *Acta Sanctorum,* Kessog died a martyr on 10 March 520 CE and was interred at Luss.[19] Another legend says brigands or mercenaries murdered him

Statue of a bishop, St Kessog's Church, Luss

at Bantry on the 25 March, the date of the old New Year according to the Gregorian calendar. Bantry Bay is in the hamlet of Aldochlay, just south of Luss, and a cairn here supposedly marked the tragic spot of Kessog's demise. In the 18th century, during local road-building operations, they found the statue of a man dressed in bishop's robes within the cairn. In *By the Banks of Loch Lomond*, Stewart Noble writes, *'Presumably the statue was buried there in a cairn for safekeeping during the Reformation in the 16th century.'*[20] Although nothing remains of his holy relics, Kessog's crozier was in the trust of the Colquhoun clan. The Colquhouns were the hereditary guardians of St Kessog and perhaps his descendants. Interestingly, three artefacts are displayed inside the church rescued from the cairn before demolition. These include a carved stone head, said to be 6th century, a stone font and a statue positioned on Bride's flow. The figure is of a man dressed in bishop's robes, possibly that of St Kessog.

Two miles west of Luss, Bride meanders through Glen Luss to the site of a lost chapel dedicated to St Michael. According to Sinclair, the chapel predates the Reformation by several centuries and mentions a St Bride' Well existing within its bounds. Traces of the chapel exist on a bank above the road just under a mile east of Glenmollochan Farm. Over twenty years ago, Sinclair observed a straight visual alignment of hills from this church, similar to Alfred Watkins' vision, before the trees obstructed the view. These included *Tom-na-Paidire* 'Hill of Prayer' near the church on the Bride current, *Tom-nan-*

Clag on Inchtavannach and Duncryne Hill, known as the 'Dumpling', just east of Loch Lomond overlooking the village of Gartocharn.[21]

The female current then heads northwards across the fells through Glen Striddle to Tullich Farm on the pass of Glen Douglas, the supposed site of several Arthurian battles in the 6th century. The glen was also a vital travel and trade route between Loch Lomond, Loch Long and the North Atlantic Ocean.

Further northwest, at Tighness, we encounter Bride at the parish church of Arrochar on the eastern shores of Loch Long. Set amongst some of the most beautiful scenery on the Cowal Peninsula, this little settlement nestles beneath the high mountains of the Arrochar Alps. The serpent flow passes through the ruins of an older church in the graveyard built in 1659 by the chief of the Colquhoun clan as an alternative place of worship to Luss, which became inadequate for the growing population. It seemed to us that the Colquhouns may have been aware of the female serpent current, using her flow to mark a 'road of the dead'.

The chiefs of Clan MacFarlane also held the lands, descendants of the medieval Earls of Lennox. This little church is the second most important on the Cowal Peninsular, which marks a significant location on the boundary of the three kingdoms of Lennox, Dunbarton and Argyll and a strategic trade route across the Neck of Britain.

After crossing Loch Long, Bride loops south to a large rock called *Clach na h-Eighe* or 'the crying stone' on the loch's western shore just south of the pier. Its name derives from a ringing sound when struck. Although popular with climbers, these ringing rocks are sacred, probably because they emit ultrasound or high-frequency sound waves. Ultrasound heals the human body and the earth, with its gentle acoustic harmonics often detected at megalithic sites.

We continue west to find the current crossing the southern slopes of The Cobbler or, as it was earlier known, Ben Arthur. We next locate her flowing along Glen Croe to Loch Restil near the famous Rest and Be Thankful viewpoint, one of the best in Scotland. From here, she crosses over a Munroe called *Beinn an Lochain* before descending its slopes to the tiny hamlet of Ardkinglas on the shores of Loch Fyne.

The Kilmorich Fonts

Before arriving at Cairndow, a pretty hamlet at the head of Loch Fyne, we turned down a minor road to find Bride crossing the road into Ardkinglas House, where we noticed a large sign at the gate that read 'Tallest tree in Britain'. Knowing that large oaks and chestnuts are a draw for the feminine current, we were curious to see whether Bride might be snaking her way through the grounds. The garden nestles in a beautiful position between Loch Fyne and Kinglas Water and is renowned for having some of the oldest oaks and beeches in the area, said to predate the creation of this ornamental arboretum. Having paid our admission fee, we proceeded along a wooded path. We soon detected Bride flowing through a tall Silver Fir, described as the 'Mightiest Conifer in Europe' with a trunk circumference of over 31 feet (9.4 m). A little further, we encounter a Grand Fir, the renowned 'Tallest tree in Britain', planted in the mid-19th century. Its great boughs encircle you as they loop up towards the sky, almost as if the tree is giving you a massive hug. Its energetic presence reminded us of the 'world tree' in Norse cosmology, a symbolic axis mundi at the centre of the world called Yggdrasill that nourishes gods, humans, animals and nature. It was also the point of communication between heaven and earth and all phases of existence to all living things.

We noticed on the O.S. map that a well once existed on the grounds, although nothing remains of it today – perhaps this was Bride's original focus.

The Campbells of Ardkinglas built a castle here in the 14th century, which remained until 1798. They were a prominent family during the reign of Mary, Queen of Scots, who is said to have visited Ardkinglas in 1563. During the 18th century, the Callander family commissioned the building of a grand mansion at Ardkinglas, described as 'rather dull' and destroyed by fire in 1831. James Callander of Craigforth inherited the estate and introduced new coniferous species to the garden with the help of famous plant hunter William Lobb, who was also responsible for bringing monkey puzzles and giant redwoods to Europe. The house seen today was built in 1907 by Sir Andrew Noble.

We dowsed Bride from the gardens to the remarkable Victorian Kilmorich Church near Cairndow with its impressive octagonal nave, pyramidal roof and tower. We wondered if the name referred to an ancient burial place. The current passes straight through the tower's entrance porch, avoiding the main body of the church, to a medieval granite font with curious carvings. The font has a long history, which became a bit of a saga. It originated from the medieval Kilmorich Church at

Grand Fir, Ardkinglas Gardens

Clachan at the head of Loch Fyne, just over a mile away. From there, it was taken to Inveraray Castle, where it lay in the shrubbery for years before being discovered in the 19th century by Lady Edith Campbell, Duchess of Northumberland, while visiting her father, the 8th Duke. Three remnants of early Celtic crosses, now resting sedately at Cairndow against the church wall, were also taken from the old church at Clachan.

Font at Kilmorich Church, Cairndow

Bride also visits two graves in a section of the churchyard enclosed by a hedge. One has the carving of a sword that reminded us of Arthur's Excalibur of the Grail myths. It bears a curious inscription: '*My sword given to him who shall succeed me in my pilgrimage – my courage and skill to him who can get there.*' The other is the burial place of British Foreign Ambassador Sir Andrew Napier Noble (1904–1987), his father having bought the Ardkinglas estate in 1905.

We continued our journey north along the A83 and at a sharp bend at the head of Loch Fyne the dowsing rods started to twitch. Hidden behind the Oyster Bar, café, and garden centre is the old site of Kilmorich church at Clachan. We parked in the Oyster Bar car park and followed a narrow footpath to the right of the garden centre. A rusty iron gate led us into the old Clachan cemetery, now neglected and overgrown. Nothing remains of this ancient sanctuary except for a ruinous mausoleum and a few gravestones sticking out of the long grass. According to the

Grave carved with Excalibur-style sword, Kilmorich churchyard, Cairndow

excellent online resource *ScotlandsPlaces.gov.uk*, '*The Church of Kilmorich of which we have no early record, is said to mean the Church of Saint Maurice, who is believed to have been sent by Saint Columba about the year 600.*'[22] Although there is no record of a Celtic Christian saint called St Maurice, there is a reference to a Roman St Maurice or Mauritius, who we encountered in Rosslyn Chapel. He supposedly obtained the famous Spear of Destiny or Spear of Lugh.

Despite the site's neglectful state, we felt the energy here enchanting. Standing quietly to soak up the magical atmosphere, we sensed the elemental spirits around us, curious at our presence. We found Bride flowing east–west through what would have been the central axis of the old medieval church, where we believe its font, now at Kilmorich Church at Cairndow, was initially located.

We placed one of our healing green stones from Iona within the old confines of the church, which we felt was a significant sacred sanctuary for the local people long ago, its sanctity enhanced by the presence of the female serpent energy of the Holy Axis. Interestingly, the Gaelic name 'clachan' means 'stones', which may refer to the old stone crosses at Kilmorich Church at Cairndow near Ardkinglas House. Or perhaps Clachan refers to an even older sacred sanctuary, such as a stone circle or cairn.

The female current then loops off to the west, appearing next at Dubh Loch north of Inveraray before ascending a prominent conical hill called *Dun na Cuaiche*, the site of an Iron Age hillfort. The name means 'the hill of the cup, bowl or quaiche', perhaps denoting it as a 'hill of the Grail'. Today Dun na Cuaiche is dominated by a stone tower built as a folly in 1756 by the 3rd Duke of Argyll. However, despite being struck by lightning multiple times, it still stoically stands overlooking the town of Inveraray below.

Inveraray and the Hill of the Cup

Arriving at the attractive county town of Argyll on the western shores of Loch Fyne, we could appreciate why this once royal burgh has been a popular tourist destination for many years. Inveraray is also the ancestral seat of the Duke of Argyll, and fine views of their grand neo-Gothic castle come into view as you enter the town from the north. Crossing the bridge over the River Aray, the old town appears as a vision of grandness with white-walled buildings highlighted with black-mullioned windows and grey slate roofs. The many cafés, pubs, shops and restaurants are a welcome sight to the weary traveller.

Before the 3rd Duke of Argyll redesigned it as a Georgian town around 1750, Inveraray already had the status of a Royal Burgh awarded by Charles I in 1648. However, a settlement here goes back to medieval times known as Kilmalieu.

The Earls and Dukes of Argyll are descendants of the Campbells of Loch Awe, successors of the old Brythonic chiefs of Strathclyde through Clan MacArthur. Historically, they were one of the most significant and influential of the Highland clans and the Campbell chief Cailean Mór was regarded as *'a Charlemagne or King Arthur in their line of chiefs.'*[23]

Sir Colin Campbell became Earl of Argyll and Lord of Lorne in 1457, rising to even greater prominence during the reign of King James III. He moved his seat from Loch Awe to Inveraray in 1474, building a tower house and port where the River Aray meets

Kilmalieu, the old town of Inveraray with Dun na Cuaiche in the background, 18th century drawing by Paul and Thomas Sandby

Loch Fyne. A settlement soon grew around it, creating the Barony of Inveraray. At that time, the town occupied a central position in the mainland kingdom of Argyll, the port giving the Campbells easy trading access to the Firth of Clyde and the sea. Argyll today forms the southern half of the ancient kingdom of Dal Riata, settled by the Scots in the 6th century.

Much to the horror of the townspeople, the 3rd Duke of Argyll (1682–1761) demolished much of the old Royal Burgh, including the medieval Kilmalieu Church, to make way for his new experimental model of enlightened planning. His idea was to create a modern economic and commercial centre with many attractive and architecturally significant buildings, including his castle. One of the residents lamenting the loss of their home cemented his household pots and pans into the Duke's new parkland wall in memory of it.

The inspiration for the new architectural design came from a sketch drawn by the famous 18th-century architect Sir John Vanbrugh, who also designed the great stately homes of Blenheim Palace and Castle Howard. Inverarary Castle is one of Britain's earliest Gothic Revival buildings, combining elements of Baroque and Palladian. However, it is perhaps more reminiscent of Arthur's Camelot, with square castellated walls and turrets at each corner with conical roofs.

The title of Duke of Argyll, created in 1701, elevated the family to one of the most powerful in Scotland. They played a significant role in Scottish history throughout the 16th, 17th and 18th centuries and in 1871, the 9th Duke married Princess Louise, the fourth daughter of Queen Victoria. Moreover, in 1981 aged twelve, the present Duke was appointed to the role of Page of Honour to the HM Queen Elizabeth II.

Inveraray Castle

From the folly on Dun na Cuaiche, Bride meanders to Inveraray Castle passing through the lost site of the old church of Kilmalieu, now in manicured gardens, and enters one of the 'Arthurian' turrets housing the family's private offices. The interior opulence of this grand French-style chateau shows off the lavish designs and furnishings created by some of the best artists and weavers from the Continent.

Interestingly, one of the rooms in the castle is named the MacArthur Room, a reference to their descendants from Loch Awe. The room is renowned for the elaborately carved MacArthur bed, haunted by a young Irish harpist murdered by the Duke of Montrose's men in 1644. The story states that the boy's ghost travelled with the bed from the 15th-century tower house to the 3rd Duke of Argyll's new castle. The ominous sound of harp music is heard from the room whenever a family member is about to die.

Perhaps one of its most famous residents was Margaret, Duchess of Argyll, a Scottish heiress and socialite, married to Ian Campbell, the 11th Duke. She was a renowned beauty and attracted many suitors such as Prince Aly Khan, Prince George, Duke of Kent and the actor David Niven. Ian Campbell divorced his second wife to marry her in 1951. He inherited the titles Duke of Argyll and Chief of Clan Campbell following the death of his first cousin, once removed, in 1949.

When Ian and Margaret first visited Inveraray Castle, they found it in an abysmal state of repair, having been neglected by the eccentric 10th Duke, a bachelor. Margaret immediately fell in love with the castle, perhaps sensing Bride's magical energy and pledged much of her fortune to its restoration. However, their relationship was tumultuous and the marriage fell apart due mainly to Margaret's infidelity and the Duke's addiction to alcohol and gambling. He faced accusations of being physically violent and emotionally abusive, using all three of his wives, including Margaret, for their money to maintain his extravagant lifestyle and the future of Inveraray Castle. Their divorce culminated in one of the worst divorce scandals of the 1960s.

From the castle, we followed Bride south to a field next to the main drive, where to our surprise, she passed through a 9 ft (2.8 m) high standing stone. At first, we thought it had been placed there as a folly, but it was a genuine prehistoric megalith leaning at a slight angle as if marking the serpent's flow to the main town. As we looked north towards the dominant Dun na Cuaiche, visited by Bride, we suddenly sensed that the domed-shaped feminine hill was energetically integral to the town and the surrounding landscape, like the Tor overlooking Glastonbury.

Bride continues into the town to All Saints Scottish Episcopal Church and its impressive separate bell tower standing sentinel like a rocket. The church, built of granite and red brick in 1886, was at the expense of Amelia, Duchess of Argyll, second wife of the 8th Duke. Inside, Bride connects with an old octagonal green epidiorite stone font; epidiorite is an igneous rock made from hornblende and feldspar. According to the guidebook, it was moved here from the former church at Kilmalieu Church, destroyed to make

Standing stone on the grounds of Inveraray Castle

way for the new castle in the 18th century. All that remains of the medieval church is its graveyard, located next to the main road below the castle. Kilmalieu means the church of St Malieu (*c.* 510–592), the patron saint of Argyll, also called Moluag, the pet name for St Lughaidh, an Irish noble of the Dal Riata, his name deriving from the god Lugh. Once again, the Holy Axis dragon currents connect with spiritual warriors associated with this Celtic sun god.

All Saints contains other fascinating items, including a beautiful painting of St George with a slain dragon under his feet and a 12th or 13th-century carved stone column supporting a later stoup from the old Kilmalieu church. Again, we marvelled at how energy lines continue to be attracted to religious objects even if they have been moved to a new site, such as the old fonts from Clachan and Kilmalieu. Another relic from the medieval village is its magnificent stone-carved market cross, standing by the harbour at the junction of Front Street and Main Street.

Interestingly, the minister of Kilmalieu after the Reformation was Niven or Ninian MacVicar, who reputedly had the gift of second sight and prophecy. He is celebrated in local tradition and believed to have conducted baptisms according to Roman Catholic and Reformed rites in this same font.[24] The practice of the seer is integral to Highland life and the Gaelic clergy saw no need to condemn it or associate it with the devil. On the contrary, they regarded the art of foretelling the future as a natural phenomenon and linked it with many prophesy forms in the Old Testament. According to local legend, MacVicar, like Merlin, foresaw his own death through drowning and mentioned it to the Earl of Argyll in conversation. With that, the Earl sent him to Stirling, well away from the sea. But, as fate would have it, a cry of 'fire!' at his new home one day sent the prophet hobbling onto an outside stair. He stumbled and fell head-first into a butt of water, where he drowned.

Font in All Saints Scottish Episcopal Church, Inveraray, from old Kilmalieu Church

The journey of the female current from Ardkinglas to Inveraray is full of Grail or cup symbolism epitomised by the medieval fonts and their present and former locations. Dun na Cuaiche, the hill of the cup, takes its name from the cuaiche or quaich, a two-handled cup used in Druidical sacrifices and later to hold a welcoming drink at clan gatherings. The Grail cup is often considered symbolic of the divine feminine within the land, represented by the Bride serpent, who brings healing and wisdom.

The alignment of the Holy Axis is only 5 miles (8 km) south of here, crossing Loch Fyne near Stuckreoch. The powerful energy radiating from the 'hill of the Grail', the potent presence of the Bride serpent current, and the proximity of the Holy Axis may explain the many tales of strange phenomena witnessed in and around Inveraray over the centuries. For instance, in 1765, a father and son returning from Glen Shira on the east side of Dun na Cuaiche spotted hundreds of soldiers marching in their direction, accompanied by women and children. Fearing for his son's life, they ducked behind a wall out of sight. When they looked up a few seconds later, the entire army had vanished. This phantom army of English red-coats also appeared to the inhabitants of Glen Aray just to the west of Dun na Cuaiche.

A few years later, in 1758, visitors to the castle witnessed a ghostly battle in the skies between the Highlander regiment and garrisoned French troops. More extraordinary still was that the incident mirrored events that happened thousands of miles away in America, where three hundred Highlanders lost their lives assaulting a French fort. The famous physician Sir William Hart was one of the witnesses, along with a friend and servant, who watched a phantom battle unfolding above them in the sky over Dun na Cuaiche while strolling in the grounds of the castle. They could describe vividly soldiers in Highland dress attempting to scale the walls of a fort, foolishly without siege ladders, while being attacked from above by French soldiers. Shortly afterwards, two women arrived breathless from the direction of Kilmalieu at the foot of the sacred hill, having also witnessed the same aerial battle. Research at the time revealed that a British force under General James Abercromby attacked the French fort of Ticonderoga on Lake George in Canada. One of the casualties was Duncan Campbell, a relation of the Earls of Argyll.[25]

Pondering this long-distance vision, I stretched the Holy Axis line beyond Iona around the globe using Google Earth and was amazed to find that the alignment was within 20 miles (32 km) of Ticonderoga, the location of the besieged French Fort. So perhaps the soul energy of the Campbells could somehow send a telepathic message to its thin veil homeland that one of their own was in danger. Maybe the power of the Holy Axis enabled Duncan Campbell to manifest the drama of his death through a psychic window that miraculously appeared over the enigmatic hill of Dun na Cuaiche.

The town has also experienced its fair share of real-life traumatic events. In 1644, the Royalist army under James Graham, the First Marquess of Montrose, attacked the castle and town with fire and sword, killing over eight hundred men, women and children in the streets. The Duke of Argyll escaped in a boat on Loch Fyne whilst the royalist ransacked the town remaining there for three weeks. Such terrible acts would have left their mark within the magnetic field of the local energy matrix and no doubt negatively affect the feminine serpent Bride. Furthermore, high magnetic fields from the piezoelectric pressure build-up in the area's geology could perpetuate trauma in the land. The areas' metamorphosed sedimentary and volcanic rocks, dating to the late Precambrian to the Early Cambrian period, are interspersed with seams of highly paramagnetic granite.

Perhaps this explains why we dowsed Bride's current as unusually narrow and weak as she passed through the castle and All Saints Scottish Episcopal Church. We concluded that some form of earth healing was required to clear the residual energy left by these horrific past events.

As with any healing, its effectiveness is deciding where and when it should occur. The most auspicious times are around the full and new moon and the solar festivals. Sometimes, it may be the feast day of a particular saint connected to the town or a local church. Often our natural senses and the dowsing pendulum help us locate the place to perform the healing using psychic protection. We also consult the spirit guardian of the area to find the answers.

One of the most effective ways of healing a place is through a walking pilgrimage, which we concluded was perfect for Inveraray. The ancient font from Kilmorich Church at Clachan, now in Cairndow Church near Ardkinglas House, and the font from the medieval church of Kilmalieu, now in All Saints Scottish Episcopal Church, are also integral to the healing process. They are highly charged ritual objects that played an essential role in the lives of many of Loch Fyne's former residents, whether during their baptism or Confirmation by the bishop, who draws in the 'holy spirit' from the four directions. Furthermore, both fonts are made of highly paramagnetic igneous rocks with a crystalline matrix that has the ability to record powerful historical events. Sensitives can often receive psychic impressions just by touching them.

On this occasion, 25 June, the feast day of St Malieu or Moluag (*c.* 510–592), the patron saint of Argyll, seemed appropriate, close to the summer solstice and the day after Midsummer 24 June. We began the healing pilgrimage at the Grand Fir or 'tree of life' in Ardkinglas Garden on the Bride serpent current, the closest feature to the site of the lost holy well. Here, for a few moments, we placed a powerful green jade stone from New Zealand called the pounamu. This beautiful green-coloured stone is a hard silica substance called nephrite jade, traditionally regarded as a treasure of immense spiritual power by both the Maori and the more ancient New Zealand race, the Waitaha. They believed it to be a healing stone given by the gods, bringing peace to the land and their people and used to re-open the sacred trails after being desecrated by wars and years of neglect. New Zealand archaeologist Barry Brailsford refers to this stone when walking with the pounamu to restore the old trails of the ancestors as *'carrying the dream of the world we want to see.'*[26]

The pounamu is similar to the green serpentine stone found on Iona, which also holds the highest vibration conducive to healing. St Columba understood this and used them for protection and healing. Serpentine and green jade are revered for their therapeutic powers by indigenous tribes worldwide, including China, New Zealand and Mexico.

After saying a blessing at the tree and calling upon the spirit guardians and elementals, we visualised sending healing light from this point along Bride's serpent flow to the font at the nearby church at Cairndow, the pounamu stone amplifying and reinforcing our intention.

We then carried out the same ceremony at the font at Cairndow and the Celtic church site at Clachan behind the Oyster Bar, before climbing up Dun na Cuaiche, overlooking the castle. Here, we visualised the fonts as Grail cups from which St Malieu pours golden healing energy into the earth at the summit, which then spreads and expands towards the castle and the sites of the old and new churches in Inveraray. Before ending our pilgrimage at the font inside All Saints' Church, we also honoured the ancient cross at the harbour that once stood at the heart of old Kilmalieu village, with the intention of further restoring balance and harmony in the town.

While walking through the pleasant streets of Inveraray, we marvelled at the number of visitors pouring into many of the town's cafés and restaurants. However, despite the jovial hustle and bustle around us, we still felt the atmosphere strange and unsettling. We asked our dowsing rods to point to the town's negative energy source, which immediately took us to the town's former prison and courthouse, now a museum and visitors centre. Here we dowsed a tentacle of detrimental male energy flowing to the Georgian Parish Church at the centre of Inveraray and continuing to All Saints Church tower and font. We both felt a shiver running down our spines with the realisation that this tentacle was damaging Bride's flow, making it weak and narrow. Furthermore, it compromises the overall harmony of the town, including the castle.

We remembered a delightful crystal shop next to the jail on a previous visit to the town. After chatting with the owner, she told us that despite the number of visitors that passed through Inveraray, her business failed to thrive. Sadly it closed soon afterwards. We wondered if her lack of prosperity was due to the dark tentacle of energy from the old jail next door.

We picked one of our many beautiful healing stones and inserted it in a safe position by one of the walls of the old jail. Next, we visualised a glowing healing light surrounding the prison to cleanse, clear and positively transform any harmful energy that may still be lingering there from past traumas. Once done, we returned to the Bride current at All Saints Church and sheltered under a beautiful yew next to the entrance, which we felt would act as a protective guardian while continuing our healing. Here, we saw the tentacle neutralised and releasing its negative hold on Bride's current. We suddenly sensed her flow rejuvenated and reanimated and its width expanding.

Kilneuair and the Devil's Hand

From All Saints Church, the newly invigorated female serpent skirts the northern edges of Inveraray and continues its journey inland over the wild landscape of Eredine Forest. Here she visits a long cairn at Auchindrain with its Folk Museum. Apart from the modern 1970s visitor centre, Auchindrain Folk Museum is a genuine historical site dating back 1000 years, the last of the Highland farming townships preserved in its original landscape.

Bride leads us along a track opposite the museum before crossing a bridge over Leacann Water, marking an ancient route that became a cattle-drove road in the 18th century. The current seems to enjoy this pretty landscape as it passes Loch Gainmheach to reach the southeastern shores of Loch Awe. The Holy Axis alignment also marks the southern waters of Loch Awe, having passed through the hills of Creag Mhor and Beinn Dubh Airigh.

As we drove along the road that hugged Loch Awe's eastern shores, the rods suddenly started to twitch as the road narrowed near the loch's southern tip. Stopping the car, we noticed a little wooden sign indicating a church. We followed an overgrown track for a few yards surrounded by woodland, where we suddenly encountered the isolated ruins of Kilneuair Church within a clearing of the forest plantation. Later research revealed that it is

Kilneuair Church ruins, Loch Awe

dedicated to St Columba and stands next to the route of the old cattle-drove road from Auchindrain.

Loch Awe is the longest stretch of freshwater in Scotland, over 25 miles (40 km). This body of water is a place of mysterious tales and ancient legends, perhaps explained by the fact that it lies on several significant geological faults and fractures of crystalline rock. Old Scottish and Highland myths refer to the ancient goddess Cailleach, who, using her formidable powers, lets the rivers loose to form many of the Scottish lochs. However, Loch Awe was created due to her forgetfulness, the Cailleach having drawn water daily from a well on Ben Cruachan in Argyll, lifting the slab off in the morning and re-covering it at night. But one evening, she forgot to cover the well and the rising waters poured down the mountainside, roaring like a torrent. By the following morning, the valley had filled with water and Loch Awe was born.[27]

The Loch is sacred to the MacArthurs, one of the oldest clans in Scotland, and the ancestors of Clan Campbell, who settled in Inveraray. They were also said to be descendants of King Arthur or, more likely, Artuir, son of King Aedan of the Dal Riata, a group of Irish settlers who came to Argyll sometime in the 5th or 6th century. During the Wars of Independence, the MacArthurs supported Robert the Bruce and fought alongside him at Bannockburn. With Bruce's success, the clan prospered and gained estates from the MacDougalls of Lorne.

The B840 alongside the Loch is one of the most haunted roads in Scotland, with motorists encountering mysterious balls of light, shape-shifting animals and even a hairy Big Foot. Eyewitness encounters also include a mysterious ghost car that terrifies motorists. In John Gregorson Campbell's *Superstitions of the Highlands and Islands of Scotland*, Loch Awe is home to a lake dragon, also known as *Beathach Mòr Loch*, heard in winter breaking the ice as it moves in and out of the frozen loch to hunt and swim. Some eyewitnesses say the beast resembles a giant horse, but others describe it as a colossal eel or a giant centipede with twelve legs.[28] More outrageous are the reports on the loch of a ghost ship resembling a 1900s-style passenger liner appearing in and out of the fog.

The name of the church has taken many forms over the centuries, including Kilnewir, Killenevir and Killenure. The word derives from the Gaelic *Coille-nan-Iubhair* meaning 'Yew Wood'. St Columba founded many monastic cells, and one mentioned by Adomnan on the shores of Loch Awe called *Cella Diuni* was never identified, although many leading authorities now believe it to be the site of Kilneuair.[29] Later, I read that the outline of an earlier circular building could be seen close to the churchyard wall, which may have been an enclosure of a Culdee church contemporary with the time of St Columba.

In the mid-16th Century, Kilneuair became the principal church of the Lordship of Glassary, replacing the old church at Killevin on the western shores of Loch Fyne, founded in the 7th century. According to a local tradition, the stones of Killevin Church were transported to this site to build the new church. They were delivered there by members of the local population by forming a 12-mile human chain over hilly and boggy terrain. A local custom mentioned in the *New Statistical Account* of 1844 states that the church should be founded '*in the manner of the Temple of Jerusalem, without a hammer being laid on a stone at the site of it.*'[30]

A gravestone in the church bears what appears to be a Templar cross, but more likely, it is the tomb of a West Highland knight from the 14th–15th century, carved by the Loch Awe School of stone masons. A village surrounded the church and a market, called *A' Margadh Dubh* or 'the Black Market', was held outside the church gates. Although the congregation abandoned the site when they moved to a new church at Kilmichael Glassary, they continued to use Kilneuair's sacred burial ground until the 19th century.

Kilneuair Church, built on a mound, lies within the supernatural aura of Loch Awe and commands respect when approaching its sacred boundaries. A creaky iron gate leads us into the neglected and overgrown churchyard. As we approached the ruin, we immediately sensed something was wrong, as if we had ventured into a secret forbidden realm. The eerie atmosphere pervading the place made our hair stand on end, and we felt that we had triggered an energy response like an etheric alarm system to keep us mere mortals out.

As we moved further into the ivy-clad ruins, we noticed a recently dug hole, as if someone had been looking for something. As we pondered what this may have been, I sensed the growing presence of an angry spirit. To the east of the nave door, on a sandstone block built into the side of a doorway, are mysterious markings of a five-toed footprint with nails on three of the toes referred to as 'the Devil's hand' now almost invisible. The true origin and significance of this strange impression are unknown. However, legend attributes it to an act of vengeance from the devil upon a local man who dared to doubt its evil power. Challenged to spend a night in the haunted precincts of Kilneuair, he was confronted during his dark and lonely vigil by a huge unearthly hand, which, in attempting to seize him as he fled terror-stricken through the doorway, left its grisly imprint on the portal.

*Devils' handprint at Kilneuair Church ©
Ronald Morris 1977*

We timidly entered the confines of an unusual stone oratory or mausoleum with its white-coloured stone carved with strange symbols, but soon felt the eerie presence again. We suddenly realised that when discovering this enigmatic site, we had failed to request permission from the site's spiritual guardian to enter Kilneuair's sacred sanctuary.

We both looked at each other, knowing that we should leave at once, but not without quickly dowsing the whereabouts of Bride's current first. We soon found her crossing the threshold of the church through the remains of an archway and continuing to an old stone font in the nave of the earlier church. We later discovered that, like the Inveraray fonts, it was made of the powerful green epidiorite rock.

Feeling the dark presence approaching ever closer like a black fog creeping through the ruins, our enthusiasm for the site soon evaporated, and as I shouted, '*We have to leave now!*' Caroline was already heading for the graveyard. Breathless, we sat in the car and looked at each other, wondering whether what we had just experienced was real or imagined.

We remembered the recently dug hole and wondered whether somebody had upset the spirits by treasure hunting. However, we both agreed that before visiting Kilneuair in the future, permission must be sought from the spirit guardian first.

Nevertheless, the dedication to St Columba indicates the importance of this sacred place, with the saint possibly establishing a cell here, mentioned by Adomnan in *Life of St Columba*. The church stands on a significant Highland route through Western Scotland that followed the eastern shore of Loch Awe and the old cattle-drove road to Loch Fyne that eventually led to Loch Lomond and the central interior of Scotland.[31]

Further north, on the opposite shores of Loch Awe, the Holy Axis alignment is marked by the Inverliever Lodge Yoga Retreat. Interestingly, we often find retreat centres on lines of power, its residents perhaps subconsciously drawing from its healing potential.

Bride visits the site of *Clachan Dubh* or 'The Dark Stones', just south of Kilneuair church, now under the waters of Loch Ederline with its floating crannog. Next, she continues to a grand menhir at Creagantairbh Beag, once standing 14ft (4.2 m) tall.

Sadly, the upper part of the stone lies on the ground, broken off long ago during a great storm. The stone would have been one of the tallest in Scotland if it had survived and been a major attraction, but now it is hidden from motorists behind a wall. The current meanders south through a valley to another ancient standing stone at Old Glenan, probably placed there to mark the overland trade route between Kilmartin and Loch Awe. From here, we dowse Bride flowing along the glen of Kilmartin Burn to Laggan Wood waterfall and Kilmartin Castle overlooking the enigmatic Scottish 'valley of the kings'.

Menhir at Creagantairbh Beag near Ford

The Mystery of Crarae and its Sacred Stone

From Inchtavannach, Lugh crossed the loch to Aldochlay, just south of Luss. Here in the bay is a statue of a young boy on a stone plinth called 'Wee Peter', said to be the young son of Laird Colquhoun, who died in a boating accident on the Loch. However, in reality, William Kerr originally designed the statue for a house in London during the 1870s and 80s. He had a fondness for Luss, having spent much of his childhood there, and when the statue was 'surplus to requirements', Kerr decided to install it in Loch Lomond in 1890. Few people, if any, expected it to remain standing for so long, and Wee Peter became known as 'Kerr's Folly'. However, it has stood the test of time and is a testament to Kerr's skills. Interestingly many sensitive people feel depressed when they approach the bay as if the false story of a drowned boy has caused a negative energetic stain on the area. One local stated, *'In spite of the origins of the statue being a happy tale, there is a definite air of melancholy here, perhaps leading to the belief in the drowned child.'* Another recalls:

'As a child, being driven along the western shore of Loch Lomond was always emotionally uncomfortable until the route took us beyond the bay of Luss. This was a memorial to one of the children of the landowning Colquhoun family, who had tragically drowned in this spot, and as we were unfailingly and solemnly reminded of this ghastly event as we passed by, it effectively tainted the Loch's indifferent natural beauty with human sorrow. What was doubly unpleasant was the hierarchy of grief that the statue implied. Many people have lost loved ones, including far too many children, to the dangerous undercurrents of the Loch, but only the rich landowner's child merited remembrance in the spot where they had perished. The Colquhouns took ownership of the landscape to mark their own understandable mourning, ensuring that the beauty spot was remarkable only because of their loss.'[32]

Interestingly, Wee Peter's statue lies close to the supposed lost cairn at Bantry, the place of Kessog's martyrdom. Could the nature of Kessog's death and the eventual destruction of this sacred cairn have also negatively affected the energy here?

Lugh heads west over the Luss Hills above Glen Fruin to a ring-ditched Bronze Age cairn at Auchengaich, once encircled by a kerb of stones declaring its importance as a status burial. In the glen, the MacGregors and Colquhouns of Luss fought each other in a great battle in 1603. The current also passes through a modern cemetery at Faslane, just south of Garelochhead, and a 13th-century ruined church dedicated to St Michael, built to serve the nearby castle of Faslane.

It then crosses Gare Loch, which extends north from the Clyde Estuary into the southern flank of the highlands. Loch Long and Loch Eck also mark Lugh's course as he continues west across the Cowal Peninsular. We soon arrive at the picturesque Lachlan Bay on the eastern shores of Loch Fyne, where he visits the ancient Kilmorie Chapel.

The 7th Century St Maelrubha supposedly founded the chapel, one of the few remaining medieval churches in the west of Scotland. Kilmorie stands within a circular walled graveyard, which gives the impression of a much older sacred sanctuary. A slim shaft of an old Celtic cross and some early Clan Maclachlan tombs may have supplanted the burial ground of the more ancient

Kilmorie Chapel ruins, Lachlan Bay

inhabitants. The Maclachlans trace their ancestry back to Lachlan Mor, a 13th-century chieftain, and through him to Anrothan O'Neill, an Irish prince living in the 11th century. Nearby, Lugh passes through a holy well called *Tobar Cill Moire* or Well of St Mary, its healing properties perhaps attracting considerable devotion in the distant past.

After crossing the Strathlachlan River, Lugh heads northwest through a densely forested plantation to another ruined chapel called Kilbride or 'Church of Bride', once part of an extensive settlement near Castle Lachlan. A footpath from the castle along the shore gives access to this ancient sanctuary now lying under bracken and turf. However, you can still see the circular enclosing wall surrounding its foundations, the Celtic Christians having established a place of worship within an earlier Iron Age enclosure. The old settlement of Kilbride now stands close to a ferry point between Loch Fyne and Crarae on the opposite shore, just south of Furnace. A little west of the chapel is a narrow peninsular jutting out into Loch Fyne that connects the mainland to Kilbride Island, through which Lugh also passes before crossing Loch Fyne's western shores to Crarae Gardens.

The gardens at Crarae are one of the most magical places in Scotland. Its beautiful exotic expanse of trees and shrubs from all corners of the world nestles within a spectacular gorge with numerous waterfalls cascading down the Crarae Burn. From the earliest times, man has revered this hallowed ground, for within these manicured gardens can be found the remains of a Neolithic chambered long barrow or cairn, one of the largest and most important in Scotland. Also here is a Bronze Age burial cairn and a 7th-century Celtic Christian cross, remnants of an early Christian monastic settlement.

Crarae Gardens are open to the public every day and we were fortunate to visit on one of those beautiful warm sunny autumn mornings when the sun dapples the turning leaves and blurs the colours like an impressionist painting. The grand stone house on the banks of Crarae Burn was owned in the early 19th century by the Campbell family of Succoth, and in 1912, Lady Grace Campbell developed the 100-acre woodland. Her son Sir George Campbell and grandson, Sir Ilay Campbell, completed planting many of its exotic trees and shrubs and their descendants still live here today, although the National Trust for Scotland now runs the gardens. Lady Campbell's inspiration probably came from her nephew Reginald Farrer (1880–1920), a famous plant hunter who scoured the world, including the Himalayas, for exotic flora and fauna. The steep-sided Crarae Glen was the perfect habitat to recreate a Himalayan garden with trees and shrubs from China, Nepal and Tibet.

We dowsed the male current flowing through the Bronze Age mound known as the Fairy Knowe and a standing stone erected in 1865. Inside the mound, a stone coffin was discovered complete with ashes and bones. Lugh's flow also passes through the chambered long barrow or cairn nearby, described as the type seen in the Cotswolds. The monument was originally orientated east–west in honour of the equinox sunrises. Its large upright entrance stones reminded us of Wayland Smithy Long Barrow at Uffington and the Bridestones beneath The Cloud in Cheshire, both on the Elen current of the Belinus Line. The inner chamber is still intact and one large and two smaller sarsen stones cover the entrance, albeit slightly dislodged. According to the Canmore website, *'it initially measured 35' long with a paved forecourt, possibly trapezoid in shape and contained inhumed and cremated burials, pottery and a flint arrowhead.'*[33] One of the threshold stones is made of porphyry granite, a volcanic igneous stone quarried locally.

Lugh's flow travels along the chamber's east–west axis and through the entrance facing Loch Fyne. He then meanders through the ornamental garden connecting with a magnificent Tasmanian Eucalyptus tree and an 18th-century mausoleum on a raised mound within

Remains of a long barrow at Crarae Gardens

an ancient burial ground. It is constructed from the local porphyry granite over the site of the old church of Killevin. Also on his flow are the graves of the Carmichael and Campbell family.

Killevin was, according to early sources, the original parish church of an area that included Kilmichael Glassary near Kilmartin. It was later moved to Kilneuair on Loch Awe, previously dowsed on the Bride current. An ancient stone embedded in the churchyard's north wall, incised with the image of an equal-armed cross and a sheela-na-gig, is now in nearby Cumlodden Church at Furnace. Recent excavations at this site identified two large ditches and post holes from an early Christian monastic settlement dating from the 7th century CE.

As already mentioned, the old Killevin church had its stones transported to build the haunted Kilneuair Church at Loch Awe on the Bride current. Later I discovered a book that shed more light on this mystery. *Argyll Curiosities* by Marian Pallister alludes to the stone having supernatural powers and according to one geologist, the rock is unique to this area.[34] The geology of the quarries in Crarae consists of volcanic igneous stones, a form of granite called porphyry. Other ancient churches in Argyll have this unique stone from Crarae within their walls as if it had some sacred importance or power. Interestingly, different cultures revered porphyry, including the ancient Egyptians and the Romans – even the Vatican incorporated significant pieces of this stone into their monuments.

Site of Killevin Church, Crarae Gardens

The quality of the Crarae porphyry granite appealed to the authorities of Glasgow in Victorian times, using it to pave the streets of their city. However, instead of extracting this 'spirit stone' by carving it reverently by hand, they used dynamite to blast it out of the cliffs.

The quantity of dynamite used to extract this precious stone increased as the years went by until one day, on 26 September 1886, they set a considerable charge into the wall of the now horseshoe-shaped quarry. Spectators eagerly filled a hired steamboat along Loch Fyne to witness the colossal blast and to watch the tumbling of thousands of tons of porphyry crashing to the ground. But, unfortunately, what happened next was later recorded as one of the worst-ever disasters in Scottish history. After the blast, a hundred or so excited spectators approached the quarry to have a closer look at the collapsed rock. Soon, some began to choke while others collapsed silently and instantly. Many who rushed to aid the stricken onlookers also fell to the invisible assailant. Over 60 people collapsed unconscious, overcome by the deadly sulphurous hydrogen gas released by the explosion and had to be dragged to the loch. Nine people died, many the day after the blast; more would have succumbed if the brave bystanders had not rescued them.

Crarae quarry

Sulphurous hydrogen gas is naturally occurring in these rocks, but the size of the explosion released considerably more than expected. Most quarry workers know the dangers of being too close to such a blast and had warned the spectators not to approach the quarry. Unfortunately, they were either ignored or their Gaelic accents misunderstood. Some, however, still believe that the spirit of Crarae's sacred porphyry rock struck back at humanity for their lack of respect. The quarry was never used again, but the feet of Glasgow citizens still pound the paving stones of Crarae.

This fascinating area has witnessed every stage of human history, from the earliest Neolithic settlers to the Celtic priests and evangelists who built their religious communities in its vales and on the shores of its lochs. As we stood in Crarae's enchanted garden overlooking the sparkling waters of Loch Fyne, we could feel the magical energy radiating from Crarae Burn as it cascaded down through the deep gorge of porphyry rock.

From here, Lugh continues west across the great expanse of Kilmichael Forest just to the north of Loch Glashan, to the village of Kilmichael Glassary and the church that replaced Kilneuair. Loch Glashan marked an ancient trade route between the Highlands and the west coast of Argyll. Before constructing a dam, workers discovered a large crannog on the loch, revealing craft workshops of some importance from the 1st millennium CE until the 14th century. The workshops may be linked to the great fortress of Dunadd, the capital of the Picts and Dal Riata Scots, further west of here. We wondered if Lugh would visit this hugely significant centre of political and economic power that guards the megalithic complex of Kilmartin.

1. 4. Morris, J, 1980. *'Nennius' British History and the Welsh Annals*. Phillimore, London.

2. Thorpe, L. 1966. *The History of the Kings of Britain*, translated. Introduction to Geoffrey of Monmouth, p.17. Penguin Books, London.

3. 5. 8. McArthur, Hugh, D. P. 2010. *The Arthurian Lake: A Secret History of Loch Lomond*. clannarthur.com

6. Russell, D. 2010. *The Loch Lomond Monster.* Dog Ear Publishing.

7. Collins, C. 2012. *Lightquest.* Eagle Wing Books, USA

9. 14. Lacaille, A. D. 1927-8. *Ecclesiastical remains in the neighbourhood of Luss*. Proc Soc Antiq Scot, vol. 62.

10. 19. https://archive.org/details/actasanctorum01unse

11. McKinney, D. 2005. *Walking the Mist: Celtic Spirituality for the 21st Century.* Hodder Mobius, USA

12. https://en.wikipedia.org/wiki/Clan_Galbraith

13. http://www.clangalbraith.org/

15. 16. 18. 21. Sinclair, John, McGilp. 2010. *Luss: The First Fifteen Hundred Years.* Luss Heritage Group.

17. McAllister, R. 1996. *The Lure of Loch Lomond: A Journey Round the Islands and Environs.* Forth Naturalist & Historian.

20. Noble, S. 2003. *By the Banks of Loch Lomond.* Argyll Publishing.

22. https://scotlandsplaces.gov.uk/digital-volumes/ordnance-survey-name-books/argyll-os-name-books-1868-1878/argyll-volume-54/188

23. https://www.scottish-places.info/parishes/parhistory573.html

24. https://canmore.org.uk/site/23608/inveraray-kilmalieu 26.

25. https://www.paranormaldatabase.com/highlands/

26. Brailsford, B. 1995. *Song of the Stone.* Stoneprint Press, Christchurch, NZ.

27. https://www.mysteriousbritain.co.uk/ancient-sites/wells/loch-awe/

28. Campbell, J. G. 1900. *Superstitions of the highlands & islands of Scotland.* Gyan Books Pvt Ltd, New Delhi.

29. https://canmore.org.uk/site/22788/kilneuair-st-columbas-church-and-churchyard

30. https://stataccscot.edina.ac.uk/static/statacc/dist/exhibition/nsa

31. Adomnan of Iona, Richard Sharpe, (Introduction, Translator) 1995. *Life of St Columba.* Penguin Classics, London.

32. http://www.kintyreforum.com/viewtopic.php?p=50079

33. https://canmore.org.uk/site/40024/crarae-garden

34. Pallister, M. 2007. *Argyll Curiosities.* Birlinn Ltd, Edinburgh.

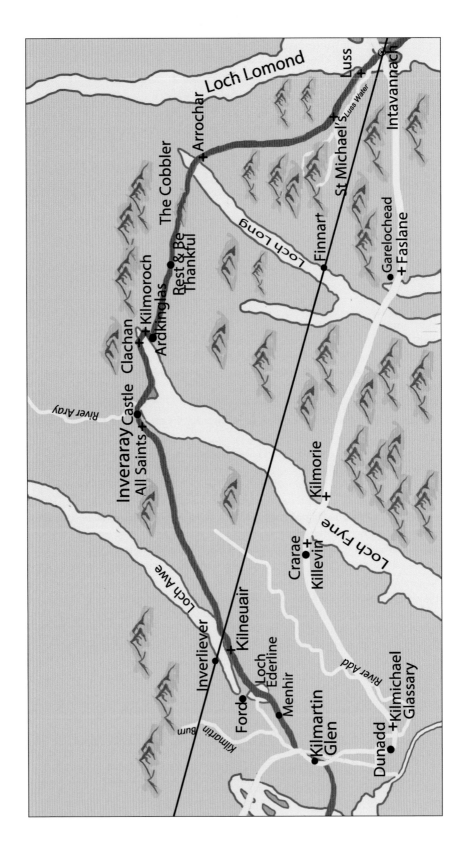

310

Chapter 14

A Royal Citadel, Valley of Kings and Stones of Power

Lugh and Bride at Kilmartin Glen

The church at the small village of Kilmichael Glassary stands silently next to the River Add within a rugged landscape strewn with cup and ring marked rocks and standing stones and overlooked by several old forts of the Celts, their secret past lost to history. Just over a mile away to the west is the mighty hill of Dunadd, the inauguration place of ancient kings.

Lugh passes east–west through the present church, built over the site of a succession of religious houses. In the 18th century, it replaced the mother church at Kilneuair on the Bride flow, which interestingly was built from stone taken from the old church at Crarae, also on Lugh. The earliest church here was possibly settled by Irish missionaries, as indicated by the *kil* in its name, meaning cell. Inside the church is a 9th-century Celtic cross, perhaps a remnant of their presence here. Also, in the churchyard are several worn grave slabs similar to Knights Templar graves dating from medieval times, some of which are on the path of the male serpent.

An ancient cattle fair known as the Kilmichael Tryst, held on a green near the church, was moved here from Kilneuair in the 1400s, where drovers purchased cattle from Islay, Jura, Kintyre and Knapdale. Marion Campbell in *Argyll, The Enduring Heartland*, writes, '*...perhaps the Tryst was returning to an ancient site, a Fair held under Dunadd's protection like the prehistoric fairs in Ireland, Carman or Tailtiu, linked to the Irish kingships.*'[1]

Opposite the church, Lugh passes over a well-preserved natural outcrop of rock carved with the most beautiful examples of cup and ring markings, dating to around 2500 BCE. This massive slab, located within a small enclosed area, is inscribed with up to 170 motifs, including single cups and cup and rings with 'gutters', shaped like 'key holes'. The energy of this decorated rock seemed to be a magnet for the

Cup and ring marked stone, Kilmichael Glassary

311

male current and his flow widened as he passed over the rock. Unfortunately, modern life has encroached upon this unique stone, with local children playing on it, utterly oblivious of its sacred significance.

Dunadd and the Dal Riata

'Turn we now to the other side, and observe that curiously conical hill sticking up alone in the centre of the Crinan moss. This, taking its name from the River which winds round its base, is called Dun-Add, and from time immemorial has been the favourite haunt of the witches and fairies of Glassrie.'

Rusticus' 'The Royal Route' (1858)

On the day of the autumn equinox, when day and night are in perfect harmony, we dowsed Lugh across *A' Mhòine Mhór* or 'the great moss', once known as the lands of Badden, to the fortified rock of Dunadd. During the equinoxes and solstices, dowsers notice a surge of energy through the leys, as if the grid had received a stimulant. So it seemed the perfect time to tune into the Holy Axis and its serpent currents as we followed them towards Kilmartin's highly significant prehistoric complex, with Bride approaching northeast from Loch Awe and Lugh from Kilmichael Glassary in the south.

Walking towards the isolated hill of Dunadd, or 'fort of the Add', the rock stands serene and regal like a recumbent pregnant goddess dominating the surrounding landscape. The terrain was carved and shaped after the end of the Ice Age, the valley having been formed from meltwater rushing down from Loch Awe like a tsunami. The water's force gouged out the valley and created gravel terraces extending all the way to the sea at Loch Crinan. However, the hard quartz rock or volcanic plug that forms Dunadd withstood the flood and remained an isolated feature that eventually became an island. When the meltwater receded, it left behind a large meandering river that we know today as the River Add.

Dunadd

We dowsed Lugh flowing northwest across the hill, his width encompassing a small pear-shaped fort on the summit, where kings were supposedly crowned. He also crosses over a well filled with rubble and covered by a capstone.

Standing at the top of this enigmatic hill, we became mesmerised by the view along the low-lying fertile plain called A' Mhòine Mhór, formed when water levels started to drop in the 6th century. Lugh is magnetised to this supposed inauguration ritual site of the early Picts and Dal Riata kings, just like Elen and Belinus at Forteviot Palace and the Moot Hill at Scone, both having usurped Dunadd as kingship centres of the Picts and the Scots. The early tribes understood the connection between the earth serpents, kingship and sovereignty when establishing their new ruler's dominion over the land.

A footprint in the rock at the summit of the fort is a reminder of an old ceremony of kingship. Also known as the 'Great Rite', this ancient tradition initially took the form of the king 'marrying the land' to exercise sovereignty over the nation while placing their foot in the stone.

The footprint at Dunadd is similar in size and shape to 'King Arthur's footprint' found at Tintagel Castle in Cornwall. Comparable impressions exist at sacred places throughout the British Isles and Ireland where a king, chieftain or overlord placed their feet in stone to take their vows and swear allegiance to the land and its people. The impressions may belong to their ancient predecessors whose use of the stone symbolised a direct link with the earth and the king's role in maintaining his realm so that he could literally 'follow in their footsteps'. Close to the footprint is the carving of a boar and the head of a man smoking a pipe, added by the Picts in 736 CE.[2]

Curiously, the Dunadd footprint is a size seven, smaller than average. Perhaps the old kings had tiny feet? Amazingly, the rock is a replica overlaying the original stone and footprint beneath. I noticed the foot impression points northwest, towards the summer solstice sunrise when the sun is at the height of its power as it reaches its most northern rising. Perhaps inaugurations took place on this auspicious day for the new monarchs to symbolically achieve sun-king status.

Interestingly, the Bride current connects with a footprint of the Virgin Mary at Stowe's holy well near Montrose, sadly destroyed during road widening. Perhaps, the ancient kings at Dunadd symbolically associated the male dragon current, in the form of Lugh, with the solar god/king energy. In contrast, the Celtic Christians at the sacred shrine at Stowe regarded the Virgin Mary as representative of Bride's divine feminine serpent energy.

Both sites also have links to King Arthur, as some authors refer to Dunadd as the Camelot of King Aedan, the father of the Scottish Artuir. However, evidence shows that this supposed ceremonial centre of the Dal Riata Scots, the foundation rock of Scottish power, was first and foremost a place of trade between the indigenous tribes, such as the Picts and the Irish, long before the Dal Riata settled here.

Finds from various excavations of Dunadd's small fort, including those led by Dr David Christison in 1903, J H Craw in 1929, and Dr Alan Lane in 1980, reveal a small settlement during the Neolithic and Bronze ages when the hill stood as an island. A series of protective walls were added in the Iron Age on the west side of the summit that made intelligent use of its natural defensive position. The walls were on different levels, with terraces accessed by gates – but none of this was on a significant scale.[3]

Most of the artefacts unearthed during the various phases of excavation are now in the Royal Museum of Scotland in Edinburgh. They include a Neolithic carved stone ball, Bronze Age vessels and elaborate jewellery dating from the 6th century. Also found were incised stones with Celtic knots, animal and bird motifs, Celtic broaches and ring moulds said to date from the 8th century and many early Christian relics. The act of site continuance here shows how differing cultures regarded Dunadd as a sacred sanctuary throughout history.

The most interesting finds were from metal-working workshops and the number of moulds found there is matched only by the royal site at Lagore in Ireland. However, few Norse artefacts were found here although a coin commemorating the Saxon King Aethelred (978–1016) was unearthed in one of the cairns further up the valley.

During the 6th century CE, when the rock citadel became vulnerable after receding water levels, Dunadd became the capital of the Dal Riata Scots, who fought many conflicts to preserve their precious centre of inauguration. Unfortunately, due to the extensive fortifications by the incoming Scots, little evidence remains of the Iron Age hillfort and its earliest occupants.

Remains of fort on summit of Dunadd

According to the 10th century *Senchus Fer nAlban*, or 'The History of the Men of Scotland', the grandsons of Fergus Mor mac Erc, Comgall and Gábran were the first settlers from Ireland.[4] Other accounts say King Fergus settled Argyll and the Western Isles after losing a significant battle in Ireland around 500 CE. During a major Irish conflict, Fergus took from Tara the *Lia Fáil*, the inauguration stone of Ireland's high kings, also known as the Stone of Destiny, which became the foundation stone for his new Scottish kingdom.

However, there is no evidence that these new settlers fought with Dunadd's local inhabitants, the Picts having established close trading links and marriage settlements with their Irish Celtic neighbours long before. According to some sources, the earliest migration of the Dal Riata occurred sometime in the 3rd century CE, which kept up the vital trade links between the two countries when the Romans closed the doors to England.

Walking around the bare rock citadel just below the pear-shaped summit, we were

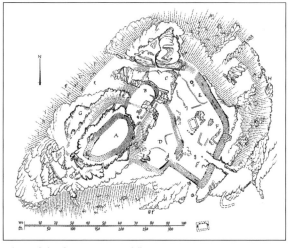

Plan of the fort on Dunadd's summit © Crown Copyright: Historic Environment Scotland

surprised at the moderate size of the terraces and walled enclosures, appearing far too small to be a significant royal centre or court of kings. Furthermore, evidence here of jewellery and glass production and permanent workshops housing smiths working bronze and iron is not proof of a royal fort but an important trade centre of manufacture, producing precious goods for shipping to all parts of Europe. The proximity of such a valuable factory with access to the sea would also attract skilled seafaring artisans, perhaps descended from the Irish Phoenicians, renowned experts in the manufacture of glass and metal. Therefore, Dunadd may have been a factory for goods heading inland towards the Kilmartin Valley and the well-established Neck of Britain trade route towards Inveraray and Loch Lomond, Central Scotland, and beyond.

Although many writers believe Dunadd was a royal centre, there are safer, more prominent locations in the valley for this function with better road links, including Dunardry Hill, close to the ancient port of Crinan. Moreover, although Coppens makes a good point that Dunadd has similarities with other royal centres, such as Dumbarton Rock near Glasgow and Castle Rock in Edinburgh, they are many times larger than the little rock of Dunadd.[5]

The distinguished Celtic scholar W F Skene identified Dunadd as the capital of Dal Riata and the place of inauguration in a lecture at Poltalloch in 1876. He stated, '*F W L Thomas's discussion of the site and the importance of the footprint in ceremonies of inauguration helped to increase the site's status in popular imagination.*' Skene and Thomas also mention an Iron Age hillfort called Dun Monaidh as a possible royal centre of the Dal Riata, now the site of Dunstaffnage Castle at Dunbeg, 25 miles (40 km) to the north of here near Oban.

Some writers inform us that St Columba took part in the inauguration ceremony of King Aedan at Dunadd in 574 CE, although there is no recorded evidence of such an event. In fact, according to Adomnan, who wrote *Life of St Columba*, the saint crowned Aedan on Iona. He mentions that Columba arrived from Ireland with a group of monks in 563, having envisioned crowning a great king, an ambitious and ruthless Irish warrior called Aedan. After his inauguration, Aedan presented the holy island of Iona to Columba, who established a monastery there to spread a new brand of Christianity across the kingdom. Columba became a close advisor to the king and eventually took the role of ambassador to Pictland and Ireland. The Pictish King Brudei or Bruide of Fortrui invited him to his royal hall within a fortified hillfort near Inverness but met him outside, knowing of his reputation as a powerful wizard.[6]

Having made Dunadd their political centre and Iona their holiest sanctuary, the Dal Riata gradually expanded their kingdom eastwards, encroaching on the lands of the Eastern Picts. Kenneth MacAlpin, King of the Dal Riata Scots (842–858), would later usurp the Pictish palace at Forteviot in Strathearn for his royal residence after winning a decisive battle against King Brudei. But, like Lindisfarne, signs and omens in the skies foretold doom before this battle, heralding Brudei's downfall. MacAlpin then moved the Stone of Destiny from Dunadd to Scone and officially ruled over the lands of the Picts. However, researchers have discovered evidence that the Stone of Destiny was kept at Dunstaffnage near Oban and not Dunadd, although the isolated rock with its footprint makes for a better story.

Arthur's Camelot

Dunadd footprint

Another story concerning Dunadd's past comes from Scottish author Adam Ardrey who claims that the rock may be a 'Camelot' of the Scottish King Arthur or Artuir, son of King Aedan of the Dal Riata and descendant of the Ulster Ur-Neill King Fergus. In his book *Finding Arthur, The True Origins of the Once and Future King*, he mentions that the name Arthur is associated with *Ard Airigh*, a common place-name in Argyll. It appears on Timothy Pont's 16th-century map as a fort and hill next to Loch Awe and possibly means 'high pasture', from which the name Ardrey or Ardry derives. However, he also cites John O'Brien, Roman Catholic Bishop of Cork and Cloyne in Ireland, who wrote an Irish-English Dictionary in 1768 compiled from early Irish manuscripts. According to O'Brien, in the 6th century, *Airigh* meant King, Prince or nobleman, and therefore Ard Airigh translates as 'High King', 'High Prince' or 'High Nobleman'.[7]

Just to the southwest of Dunadd, overlooking the Crinan Canal, is Cruach Mòr Dunardry, or 'hillfort of the high prince or king', which Adam Ardrey believes was associated with Artuir. The canal leaves the mainland for the Loch of Crinan and the Sound of Jura at the little port of Crinan, once called Port Righ, meaning King's port. During the time of Artuir, this port would have been a vital trade link across the Neck of Britain as goods travelled along the great waterways between the Atlantic and the North Sea.

Compared to the other Camelot sites, such as Tintagel Castle in Cornwall and South Cadbury Hillfort in Somerset, the summit of Dunadd is too small to accommodate a sizable fort. However, it may well be possible that after Aedan's death, Arthur/Artuir was crowned on Dunadd. Ardrey believes the 'sword in the stone' myth was an actual inauguration ceremony in which Artuir placed his foot in the stone footprint at the summit of Dunadd and received a sword as a token of his new authority. Ardrey also believes the area called Badden, to the southeast of Dunadd, is the possible site of Arthur's twelfth battle, the Battle of Badon. Badden's boundaries stretched north under the shadow of Dunadd and south to where the Badden Burn meats Lochgilphead. However, Badden derives from Baodan, a family closely related to Artuir who may have given their name to this area in the 6th century. He writes:

'Furthermore, unlike so many southern sites, there is no shortage of hills around the lands of Badden, the most prominent being Dunardry. Dunadd was the ceremonial Capital of Argyll, but Dunardry commanded the most important land route in Argyll and was its administrative capital. There is no more likely place for a sixth-century battle than the land about Dunardry, the land of Baodan-Badon-Badden.'[8]

The 9th-century Welsh monk Nennius in his *Historia Brittonum* stated that the warrior Arthur fought his most decisive battle on Badon Hill against the Saxons. If this is indeed the case, then it is unlikely that Arthur fought the Saxons this far north unless, by Saxons, Nennius is referring to the Angles, who eventually settled in Northumbria and became the overlords of Britain in the 7th century. Interestingly, Bede's account of the battle in *Ecclesiastical History of the English People,* written in the 8th century, does not refer to Arthur fighting the Saxons but simply calls them 'these invaders'.[9] Therefore, it is possible that Artuir, son of Aedan, fought the Angles here at Dunadd.

After spending some time on the rock, we believe Dunadd was not a royal palace but a significant ceremonial place for the Picts and the Dal Riata Scots. Furthermore, the Neolithic peoples, who built their monuments just north of here, may also have seen Dunadd as sacred.

The Serpent Temple of Kilmartin Glen

Between the rock of Dunadd and Kilmartin village, 3.5 miles further north, are numerous prehistoric burial cairns, stone circles, henges and standing stones constructed from around 4000 BCE. In addition, many Neolithic stones were reused or remodelled in the Bronze Age and buried in the surrounding fields. '*Old men alive at the beginning of the last century spoke of more than a score of cairns and many standing stones being removed to make way for the plough.*'[10] This level of destruction reminded us of the massive prehistoric complex at Shap in Cumbria on a node of the Spine of Albion.

Philip Coppens, in his online article *Kilmartin: the original Scottish capital* writes, '*Kilmartin seems remote in the 21st century, but in megalithic times, this was as central as Glasgow or London today. It was the site of a capital – the true Scottish capital even.*'[11]

Another feature of Kilmartin Glen is its numerous cup and ring marked stones, perhaps some of the finest examples in Scotland. The concentration of so many sacred monuments from different stages of history suggests that the various cultures considered this particular landscape unique and special, which continued as a hallowed place to perform ceremonies and bury the dead over millennia.

The River Add's inland course from Crinan at the head of the Mull of Kintyre is a vital trade route dating back to Neolithic times leading to Loch Awe, Inveraray and Loch Lomond. Much of the valley at that time was bog but archaeology and pollen analysis indicate that during the Neolithic and Bronze Ages, it was a dryer landscape with crops growing around the stones.

From Dunadd, the male serpent crosses *A' Mhòine Mhór*, the great moss with its 'hummocks, hollows and pools teeming with wildlife, to the Ballymeanoch Stones, a row of four tall standing stones, the tallest standing just over 13 ft (4m) high. Here, he connects with all four standing stones, which are orientated southeast–northwest towards the hill of Dunadd. Two other stones stand a little to the southeast, all possible remnants of a stone avenue. Some researchers believe that the stone northwest of the stone alignment indicates the northerly setting point of the midwinter full moon at the major standstill. To the southeast, the stones indicate the point where sun rises at the winter solstice.

Interestingly, we dowsed another energy line intersecting with Lugh at the most southerly megalith of the four aligned stones, which we determined to be an unidentified female current flowing east–west.

A holed stone once existed here with several cup mark designs, which fell in the 19th century. According to folklore, this was the site of St Colm's market, encircled by a moat, and hands were clasped through the stone's hole each time a deal was struck. When John Barber excavated here in 1977, he found three small deposits of cremated bone in the socket of this fallen stone, the remains of which are now in a ditch at the edge of the field. As we followed the male serpent to each stone, we noticed the two

Ballymeanoch standing stones

Ballymeanoch henge

centre stones carved with numerous cup and ring marks, one recorded as having at least seventy carvings.

Just south of the standing stones, Lugh visits the remains of a small circular earthen henge or cairn about 42 ft (12.8 m) in diameter, surrounded by a single ditch and bank. It supposedly dates from 3000–2500 BCE, and at its centre are the remains of two stone-lined burial cists introduced about 500 years later. In addition, several stones encircle the ditch from what might have been the remains of a stone circle.

During a Geophysical survey of this area published in 2000, Duncan Abernethy discovered a circular anomaly about 63 ft (20 m) northeast of the north entrance of the henge, which he believed might be the traces of a larger enclosed circle almost 65 ft (20 m) in diameter. However, he concludes that without proper excavation, it is impossible to prove that it is not just another of the unusual geological anomalies that run through this area.[12] The size and shape of the Kilmartin henge reminded us of the Neolithic Arthur's Round Table at Penrith, a place of ceremony and celebration that continued until Norman times.

Lugh guided us northwest from the Ballymeanoch Stones towards a group of trees and a large cairn at Dunchraigaig. According to Sharon Webb, it lies upon one of the many gravel terraces formed after the Ice Age overlooking the Glen. It was continually used for burials until the Iron Age, with some cist graves showing evidence of human interment and others with cremated remains and various offerings. Excavations in the 1800s found remains of up to ten individuals in one cist. One of the cists is still visible, covered by a massive capstone. Historic Environment Scotland (HES) claims the cairn is 5000 years old based on the recently discovered images of two carvings depicting red deer with fully grown antlers carved on a rock. They are the oldest known animal carvings in Scotland and the earliest clear examples of deer carvings in the UK from the Neolithic to the Early Bronze Age.[13]

According to archaeologists, Kilmartin's cairns are Clyde Cairns. These are mounds of stones covering slab-built burial chambers used for inhumation and depositing cremated remains, with whole families buried in them *'through the authority validated by their burial ancestors'.* Like Carnac in France, Kilmartin was a prehistoric ritual landscape with a forest of standing stones, timber and stone circles dating from the late Neolithic period. At one time, there were at least thirty barrows and cairns throughout the Kilmartin Glen, including the Ri Cruin cairn, which saw the burial of men and women of noble birth. You could almost describe it as a Scottish 'valley of the kings'.

Although many of the cairns and cist graves were destroyed, particularly during the agricultural improvements of the 19th century, generations of archaeologists have managed to record details of their construction, including their varied sizes and elaborate decorations. Some cist graves inside the cairns contained finely carved grave goods, including jewellery and weapons.

From the cairn, Lugh takes us through a bank of trees consisting of monkey puzzles, oaks and elms to a fenced area in a field near Baluachraig. Here, we find another of these enigmatic stone slabs lying horizontally on the ground decorated with cup and ring marks and spirals, one of several in this area that date from Neolithic times. The reason for carving such varied shapes on so many rocks in the area, some simple whilst others highly elaborate, is still a mystery to archaeologists and anthropologists. However, they believe their location is essential and where you see the most intricate carvings are at entrances to glens or high places overlooking fertile valleys to the sea.

Cup and ring marked stone at Baluachraig, Kilmartin Glen

In his transcript, *Kilmartin Glen*, Professor Richard Bradley says that these carved slabs seem concentrated on the fringes of agricultural land and *'that the most complex motifs are situated in prominent places in the landscape commanding the access routes.'* Furthermore, he observed that in Kilmartin, the various rock art sites found along the sides of the valley are intervisible and increase in complexity the closer they are to the various monuments. Therefore, the most elaborately carved cup and ring marked stones highlight the most sacred places, as if the patterns were for religious purposes or represented some unknown language related to the site.[14] We believe that pecking the stone to create cup marks changes the electromagnetic quality of the rock by attracting energy to it. Also, the powerful symbols on these rocks on either side of this former crop-growing valley promoted fertility by attracting orgone energy, plasma and ultrasound.

However, in *Ley Lines and Earth Energies* by David Cowan and Chris Arnold, Scottish dowser and researcher Cowan discovered that cup-marked rocks produce an energy 'bubble' that projects outwards from the stone and encircles the surrounding area. After pecking a small boulder dowsed with no discernible energy, Cowan found he had created a narrow beam protruding in a particular direction, widening after several yards to create a small telluric circle. He later realised that the focus of the energy was towards the sun at the time of carving. When he turned the rock, the beam obligingly followed, and unhealthy energy lines in its path avoided it. Therefore, the cup mark produced a protective 'bubble' capable of removing negative energy, and additional carvings expanded the bubble. If we relate Cowan's findings to these highly decorated slabs on either side of Kilmartin Glen, it would suggest that their protective 'bubbles' were capable of spanning a considerable area including the whole valley. Perhaps they provided a healthy shield to deter harmful energies from disrupting crop growth in this fertile environment.

Many standing stones were quarried from the cup-marked boulders and decorated rock escarpments along the valley, transferring the protective energetic bubble to the sacred monuments. We wondered if the cup-marked stones predated the Neolithic monuments, perhaps originating at the end of the Mesolithic period during the advent of farming between 6000 and 5000 BCE.

Dr Alison Sheridan, principal curator and head of Early Scottish Prehistory and Archaeology at the National Museum of Scotland, wrote that the Kilmartin farmers led

the way in agriculture as their tools and pottery matched those of the earliest periods in Europe. Did European farming evolve in Kilmartin Glen?

Lugh continued to take us north across the Kilmartin Burn to a group of five megaliths known as the Nether Largie standing stones near the village of Slockavullin. They are the remnants of yet another fascinating complex of monuments leading to Nether Largie South Cairn, which stands a short distance away. In 1970, Alexander Thom toured this site with Magnus Magnusson for a BBC television documentary, *Chronicle: Cracking the Stone Age Code*. He suggested that Kilmartin's monuments '*gave so much information that it must be regarded as one of the most important, if not "the" most important, site in Britain.*' He believed the complex was some lunar observatory for predicting eclipses, although many researchers have since disputed this.[15]

Standing Stone at Nether Largie, Kilmartin Glen

Lugh first connects with two of the tallest standing stones, about 9 ft (2.7 m) in height and set apart from the larger group. Duncan Abernethy's Geophysical survey also picked up interesting anomalies in the Nether Largie complex, including a giant megalith buried below the surface near the central standing stone, which he believed was the fallen upper part of one of the stumps. In addition, the survey showed other buried features, including a ditch and bank formation and sockets belonging to missing standing stones, along with buried stone stumps and other circular anomalies.[16] Abernethy concludes, '*The Nether Largie monuments relate to what would have once probably been a low island at the edge of a flood plain and surrounded by meandering fluvioglacial water channels.*'

Coppens writes:

'The valley is fringed by banks, which create a wide, natural amphitheatre along the length of the Linear Cemetery. Some have therefore speculated that it was indeed an amphitheatre, in which religious ceremonies if not processions, occurred.'[18]

The male current also connects with a small menhir with only the stumps remaining before flowing to another weathered standing stone marking the centre of this group of megaliths. It has magnificent examples of cup markings on its southwest side, with up to twenty-three different impressions. Surrounding its base is a group of smaller stones, perhaps the remains of other megaliths broken up long ago.

Two standing stones further north are the last of this group, one missing its top and having the appearance of a finger pointing to the sky. Lugh creates an S-shaped flow, encompassing all five standing stones and the menhir. An additional standing stone, about 100 yds (90 m) to the northwest of the five megaliths and another 300 yds (270 m) due west, were discovered during 1970s excavations.

My psychic impression was that the Balymeanoch and Nether Largie standing stones were once part of an avenue similar to the West Kennet Avenue leading to the Avebury Stone Circle. It is also reminiscent of a two-mile stone avenue destroyed at Shap in Cumbria. The avenue led to a central stone circle, which we believe formed part of a serpent temple complex similar to Avebury. Perhaps the avenue at Kilmartin also had a central circle, possibly at Nether Largie, where Abernethy's geophysical survey found evidence of other stones.

At Shap, we dowsed Belinus, the male serpent current travelling north along the site of the stone avenue to form a node with his female counterpart at a burial mound at Skellaw Hill. With the help of dowsing, I later discovered that before the central stone circle was destroyed in the 19th century to make way for a railway, it would have been the original location of the node. The currents then diverted to node on Skellaw Hill after the circle's removal.

Dowsing the Nether Largie Cairns

We continued following the male current north to the chambered tomb of Nether Largie South Cairn. This magnificent pile of large, worn pebbles and stones is one of the oldest cairn monuments in the glen, dating back to *c.* 3700 BCE. Originally it was a long and trapezoidal barrow similar to Stoney Littleton in the Cotswolds, with the chambered tomb at its centre measuring almost 19 ft (6 m) long. The interior chamber was divided into four compartments by stone slabs and interspersed with stretches of dry-stone walling, which would have contained numerous burials.[19]

About a thousand years later, the tomb transformed into a round cairn, measuring more than 98 ft (30 m) wide. The alteration accommodated two stone-lined burial cists, each built to house one individual, possibly a local chieftain. It was first excavated in 1864 by archaeologist William Greenwell, Canon of Durham Cathedral and author of *British Barrows*. His finds included flints, cremated and intact human bones, pottery, knives, arrowheads, quartz pebbles and animal remains dating back to the earliest burials.[20]

Lugh disappears inside a cist grave at the southern edge of the cairn covered by a megalith. We clambered on hands and knees inside the cairn, following a stone-roofed passage from its southern entrance to the internal compartment. As we sat at the centre of this womb-shaped chamber, we noticed it still contained features of the original Neolithic barrow, including its large portal stones with faint traces of cup markings.

Nether Largie South Cairn

After meditating inside the cairn, we sensed the familiar power of a node and dowsed the Bride serpent current entering from the north to unite with Lugh inside the cairn.

I returned to the cairn's summit to dowse the two currents in detail while Caroline remained inside, meditating on the node point. She then placed a green pounamu healing stone on the node to help rebalance and revitalise the male and female serpents. Whilst holding the healing stone, the entwined serpents compelled her to etherically rise with them through the stone ceiling of the cairn. Then she saw herself soaring through the air alongside the two serpents heading north along the glen towards the village of Kilmartin. As she looked down, she was aware of passing over several other cairns in alignment with each other and felt Bride and Lugh were showing her the direction of their flow.

Meanwhile, I had a strong sense that I had to connect the cairn with the Nether Largie standing stones and the possible site of a stone circle. Earlier, I picked up a small quartz stone at the base of one of the megaliths, which I held over the cairn. However, I clumsily dropped it and saw it disappearing through a gap in the rocks on top of the cairn. When Caroline returned from her astral spirit journey across the cairns, she shouted to me that a quartz stone had come through the ceiling and landed beside her right on the node.

Walking around the perimeter of Nether Largie South cairn, we dowsed Bride exiting southwest to a nearby enclosure of oak trees known as Temple Wood, where she visits two cairn circle monuments. The name originates from landowner Sir John Malcolm in the late 1800s when he planted trees around the stone rings, presumably believing these monuments to be a Druidic temple site. This place has been assigned many names over the centuries including Half-Moon Wood.

The larger monument of the two, located in the southern part of the enclosure, consists of thirteen stones standing in a circle within a layer of white polished pebbles. At the centre is a cist grave surrounded by a smaller circle of stones, once covered by a massive slab removed before the early 19th century. A sketch of the Temple

Chamber inside Nether Largie South Cairn

Wood circle dated 1818 shows no carpet of pebbles and the capstone missing from the central cairn.

Just to the north is another similar but smaller circle with a long central recumbent megalith and a single smaller stone standing near its circumference. First discovered during excavations in 1929 and further investigated by Jack Scott in the 1970s, these monuments have continued to mystify archaeologists and historians. Many believe the

Temple Wood south circle

site evolved into what you see today over millennia, having been used and reused by several cultures. The first phase of activity began around 3500 BCE, during Neolithic times.

When surveying the site in 1970, Alexander Thom believed Temple Wood was a lunar observatory, with the south circle 'standing in line with a notch in the western mountains where the whole horizon looks as though beavers had chewed it.'[21]

As we strolled through the bluebells in this enchanted copse, we picked up Bride entering the northern circle and connecting with its central stone. We noticed several concrete blocks showing the original positions of many missing standing stones. As we followed Bride into the southern circle, she connected with two of its outer standing stones, one in the north and another in the southwest, before exiting the ring through the cist grave at its centre. Canmore records that two upright stones had faint traces of concentric rings and spirals, 'one bears concentric circles (now very faint); the other has a double spiral spread across two faces of the stone.'[22] Unfortunately, there is no trace of these impressions today.

We wondered whether the white quartz pebbles acted as an energy conductor or light refractor. Similar white quartz pebbles cover many of Ireland's sacred cairns, including Newgrange – one of the world's oldest monuments.

The feminine current then diverts west towards the village of Slockavullin. In the early 19th century, this tiny hamlet became an industrial centre for the Poltalloch Estate and at one time consisted of a smithy, coaching house, brickworks and a mill. As we walked north through the village, our dowsing rods pointed towards a small bridge over a tributary of Kilmartin Burn, where Bride crosses to continue her journey northwest to Loch Craignish.

Returning to Nether Largie South Cairn, we head north, dowsing Lugh and Bride flowing side by side, with the female to the right. We have previously encountered conjoined energy lines on the Spine of Albion at St Catherine's Hill in Winchester. Hamish Miller and Paul Broadhurst describe it as a 'sacred marriage' when dowsing the Michael and Mary currents at Bury St Edmunds Abbey. After visiting the site of a lost cairn, we continued another few hundred yards to Nether Largie Mid Cairn. More dowsing of the side-by-side lines here confirmed they had slightly overlapped, creating a powerful fusion of terrestrial energy. Mid Cairn dates to around 2000 BCE, and when it was excavated in 1929 by James Hewat Craw, he found two burial cists, but any remains were assumed to have dissolved away due to the acidic soil. One of the cists has axe-head carvings that were once visible on the cairn's south side. Metal rails now support the massive capstone to reveal the cist inside.

The cairn appears to stand on a raised platform, perhaps caused by the reduction of the surrounding land from centuries of ploughing. Several kerbstones lined its southern arc, which once stood about 10 ft (3 m) high, sadly removed for road building after excavations. To the right, the Kilmartin Burn meanders close by, which archaeologists believe would have once flowed around the base of the cairns, the water perhaps amplifying the power of these sites.

During the cairn-building period, the climate was much warmer than today, and the valley was rich in fertile soil, with crops growing around the monuments as if they positively affected the harvest.

Just over 500 ft (150 m) away to the north, the serpent currents form a second node inside the impressive Nether Largie North Cairn, which dates between 2000–

1500 BCE. The two currents shrink to a point inside an internal chamber next to a large capstone carved with numerous cup marks. Despite extensive excavation and centuries of locals pilfering its stones for building materials, the cairn is still an imposing monument.

James Craw first excavated North Cairn in 1930, discovering a central cist grave within a chamber surrounded by a circular bank of stones. Next to it were two standing stones decorated with concentric circles, believed to be from the nearby stone circle in Temple Wood. Although we believe they may have originated from a lost central circle near the Nether Largie standing stones. A semi-circular earthen bank found nearby was perhaps the remains of an earlier henge monument. Craw rebuilt and modified North Cairn exposing a chamber to allow visitors easy access, which would have been impossible if left in its original form. The capstone slab inside the cist, next to the node, is carved with at least forty cup marks and various axe head-shaped motifs. Some believe the slab is earlier than the cairn and was moved here and re-shaped into a cist

Nether Largie North Cairn node

slab from another of the missing standing stones. Axe head carvings, similar to those found at Stonehenge, are thought to date back to the Bronze Age and have long been associated with burials and funeral practices.

Like Nether Largie Mid Cairn, any burials at North Cairn had dissolved before the 1930 excavation, and only a single tooth, some bits of charcoal, and ochre remained. Whoever occupied this impressive chamber was highly important, perhaps a king, queen or tribal leader. [23]

Once inside the cairn, we instantly felt the energy out of balance and the atmosphere strange and unsettling. We both sensed that we had to leave after dowsing the node and quickly clambered out of the chamber. This experience was in total contrast to Nether Largie South Cairn, where the energies felt gentle and nurturing. We believe the opening of North Cairn's chamber during excavations somehow disrupted the site's power, perhaps breaking up the many precise layers of earth and stone that originally covered this hidden chamber. After exiting Nether Largie North Cairn, the currents separate, with Lugh heading northeast and Bride northwest to target the largest of Kilmartin's monuments.

Glebe Cairn, Carr's Ley and the Samhain Mountain

Glebe Cairn, just over half a mile to the north of Nether Largie North Cairn, is the most prominent cairn of the linear cemetery, so called because of its situation on the glebe land of Kilmartin Parish Church. Bride and Lugh form the third and final node here, the female current entering the complex's southwest edge and Lugh arriving from the southeast.

Like Nether Largie Mid Cairn, Glebe Cairn lies on a slightly raised ridge, which may represent another of the many gravel deposits that litter this area. According to the information board at the site, excavations of this early Bronze Age stone mound by Revd Greenwell in 1864 revealed two cist graves, one positioned at the centre and the other on the southwestern edge. Two concentric rings of standing stones surrounded the latter, measuring about 3 ft (0.9 m) high and 2 ft (0.6 m) wide. According to another excavator, Canon William Greenwell from Durham Cathedral, the stone circles would have had a sacred significance, possibly to protect the spirit.[24]

The grave at the cairn's southwestern edge contained the burial of a woman. Here, they discovered the partial remains of a jet necklace and a pottery vessel that supposedly contained food offerings to sustain the spirit while travelling to the underworld. The jet necklace is a rare find and most likely belonged to a woman of high status. At the centre of the cairn is a second cist, incorporated later after the mound was enlarged to accommodate it. It contained the burial of a man, possibly a chieftain and the woman's husband. Since these early burials, the mound was used for interment until the Iron Age.

Interestingly, we dowsed the node of Lugh and Bride at the grave of the male. However, judging from a diagram on the information board showing the positions of each grave, the female serpent also connects with the cist containing the woman as she flows southwest–northeast through the cairn.

Glebe Cairn

We found a footpath that took us back to the village and to the excellent museum and café, which served the most delicious tea and cake, much needed after such an intense dowsing session. We marvelled at how lucky the nation is to have such a unique, relatively intact prehistoric complex. So many important sites in Scotland were destroyed by modern development, such as Huly Hill on the Lugh and Belinus currents near Edinburgh, of which only one tumulus and a handful of standing stones remain.

However, we also realised that the Lugh and Bride serpent lines create a node, not once but three times, which constitutes a vital element of this site. Lugh and Bride, however, are only one layer of many that contribute to the history and mystery of this fascinating ceremonial complex.

Another important layer to consider is the orientation of the cairns that all mark a straight ley between Glebe Cairn and Ri Cruin Cairn, another significant mound situated just under a mile to the south of Temple Wood. The impressive Ri Cruin Cairn, said to be the burial of a king, stands within a copse surrounded by other ancient burials. Its original construction dates back to 4000 BCE and contains three cists, of which two are visible, one carved with axe heads.

In 1998, Ian Carr wrote in an article for *The Society of Ley Hunters* that this cairn alignment points to a pyramidal hill in the north called *Dun Chonallaich*, which has a stone citadel on its summit. Its name supposedly derives from *Conallach*, meaning the 'kindred of Conall', referring to a branch of the Northern Uí Néill, who claim descent from Conall Gulban, son of Niall of the Nine Hostages, a former 5th century High King of Ireland. His descendant, Conall macComgaill, was a Scottish King of the Dal Riata from about 558 until 574. However, the true origins of this ancient fort stretch further back in time; its original Celtic name is now lost to the Gaelic language.

Carr's ley then continues to the hill behind called Dun Dubh or the Black Fort, dating to the Iron Age with a flattened summit. According to local folklore, Samhain fires were lit on the more prominent ridge above this ruined fort until recent years. These Halloween fires were stopped by the new owner of the land, using the excuse that they were a fire hazard. However, in reality the owner was a devout Christian who took exception to 'the local pagan goings-on.' Interestingly the previous landlord not only allowed the Samhain festival to continue but also took part in it.[25]

Carr states:

'The Scottish Valley of the Kings alignment, in pointing north to the "black fort", avers to a tradition, a Way, which our culture has avoided for 2000 years, but in shamanic and magickal traditions, north is equated with transformation.'

Because the peak of Dun Dubh is higher than that of Dun Chonallaich and there is no site of historical interest immediately beyond the hill, I believe the actual target of Kilmartin's ley is the levelled summit of the Black Fort. Samhain marks the end of the harvest season, and the tradition of lighting fires on the hill on 31 October is a clue to understanding the sacred origins of the entire Kilmartin complex. Samhain fires welcomed the ancestral spirits to Earth at a time when the veils were thin. The deceased could return to communicate with their descendants, and evil spirits, fairies and gods could come out searching for mischief. The Neolithic peoples in Ireland also celebrated this event, with many of their passage tombs aligned with the Samhain sunrise.

Kilmartin's stone and earthen mounds or cairns were presumably associated with fertility and harvest because of the many crops that grew around them. A fire lit on the top of Dun Dubh would be seen throughout the Kilmartin Valley to signal the day when their ancient ancestors returned to the cairns to fulfil another cycle. Aligning the cairns to this hilltop and the Samhain fires ensures a connection between the spirit world and the land.

Over another cup of tea, it dawned on us that the valley's name Kilmartin, meaning church of St Martin, was also significant. St Martin's feast day is 11 November in the modern calendar, but in the old calendar, it corresponds with the Samhain festival. The hills of Dun Chonallaich and Dun Dubh stand together overlooking the southern base of Loch Awe, a lake long associated with spirits and the dead.

Furthermore, if you are heading from the port of Crinan to journey along the ancient trade routes across the Neck of Britain, the pyramid-shaped hill of Dun Chonallaich and the ceremonial summit of Dun Dubh would have been the perfect landmark.

Carr's linear cemetery alignment continues 2 miles beyond Dun Dubh to the highest peak along this northwest-aligned chain of hills to Cruach an Eachlaich at 1141 ft (348 m), where it meets with the Holy Axis alignment. Cruach an Eachlaich means horseshoe, perhaps because the summit resembles this crescent shape. Though looking down on the peak from Google Earth, it looks like a series of squares with a spiral summit. Although there is nothing written about this hill, we feel there is something magical there.

The serpent currents were also drawing the power from this linear cemetery of cairns to form what appeared to be an elongated node. Perhaps the area's geology plays a part in this curious interaction. Two types of geology meet within the Glen, diamictite (sandstone and mudstone) and mafic or basalt lava, rich in iron and magnesium. Interspersed within these powerful rocks are seams of diorite, similar to whin sill found on Lindisfarne and at Bamburgh. The valley also stands between the Highland Boundary Fault and the Great Glen Fault to the north. The Great Glen Fault runs along the eastern edge of the Black Isle, through Inverness to Loch Ness, Britain's deepest freshwater loch, and to Fort William at the head of Loch Linnhe. It then slices through the southeasterly edge of the Isle of Mull before continuing towards Ireland.

During our research of the Belinus alignment, we learned that geology was a pivotal factor in the siting of prehistoric monuments. For instance, we found that prehistoric earthen mounds all over the country are close to fault lines, particularly on ridgeways. Many of these mounds act like condensers, storing power released from faults during seismic activity. In addition, we dowsed several node points over geological faults, such as the Devil's Punchbowl on Brading Down on the Isle of Wight and the Rollright Stones on the boundary of Oxfordshire and Warwickshire. The serpent energy seemed to draw upon the fountain of telluric energy produced during movements and stresses in the Earth's crust.

Kilmartin's cairns aligned with Dun Chonallaich and Dun Dubh

The Clava Cairns are a group of seven Bronze Age stone cairns near Inverness that stand upon a ridge formed by a secondary fracture of the Great Glen Fault. Two nodes of the Belinus Line connect with these cairns, which provide nourishment for the earth serpent. Many people have witnessed balls of light, plasma and other paranormal events here.

Kilmartin is one of Scotland's most important prehistoric sites, with many impressive monuments still standing. Interestingly, most of the Nether Largie cairns survived relatively intact, having been covered by a thick layer of peat until the 1800s after a climatic event in the 6th century. Locals took the peat from the valley for fuel and stones from the long-hidden cairns to build field dykes and roads. Aubrey Burl described the area as a 'megalithic paradise' and Philip Coppens wrote:

'Kilmartin Valley is remote, even by Scottish standards, but may have been a forgotten centre of prehistoric activity. However, archaeology is slowly uncovering that this tranquil valley may have been, in the past, one of the most important centres – and the true heart of Scotland.'[26]

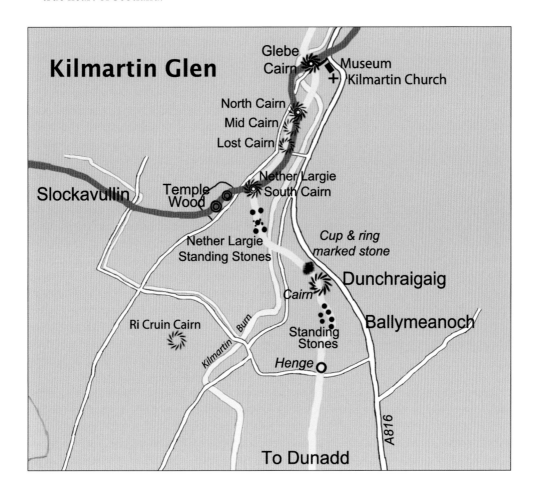

The Church, the Castles and the Rocks of Power

The village of Kilmartin, with its museum and parish church, stands on a high ridge or gravel terrace overlooking Glebe Cairn with stunning views across the sacred valley. Many believe the village and the church were built over another important prehistoric site. Here, early Celtic Christian missionaries established a thriving community possibly from the time of Columba, remnants of which are on display in the churchyard and the nearby museum in the form of exquisitely carved stone crosses. Up to four churches have existed on the site of St Martin's, the present being a Victorian rebuild. Several grave slabs dating back to around 1300 suggest a medieval church replaced a much earlier one, possibly of wood and turf construction. In the late 14th century, this area was part of the barony of Ardskeodnish, held by the Campbells of Loch Awe.

Kilmartin Church with Dun Chonallaich beyond

Two Celtic stone crosses that once stood in the churchyard are displayed inside the church. One has a Celtic knot design and dates to the 8th century. The other shows a crude carving of the Crucifixion dating to the 13th century, described as '*one of the most magnificent medieval stone crosses in the West Highlands*.'[27] It survives in three fragments, and although the right arm of the cross is missing, it still has a powerful presence.

A collection of seven highly decorated medieval slabs are on show inside the Poltalloch Enclosure in the graveyard. Many of them were the tombs of warriors and chieftains, including the Malcolm family, who owned the nearby Poltalloch Estate. Sir Colin Campbell of Glenorchy, founder of Clan Campbell, who died in 1480, is also buried here. Many carved effigies depict knights in armour, their gallant exploits now long forgotten from the annals of history.

From Glebe Cairn, Bride flows northeast towards the restored baronial Kilmartin Castle perched on the side of a hill, now a luxury B & B. It was built in 1550 by the 5th Earl of Argyll for John Carswell, Rector of Kilmartin Church, both wielding significant power over the area. Descended from the Campbells of Wigtownshire, Carswell was Chancellor of the Chapel Royal at Stirling and tutor to the son of the 4th Earl of Argyll, who would later, as the 5th Earl, award him the position of Bishop of Argyll and the Isles, with overall control over the Abbey on Iona. He was a giant, standing over 7 ft (2.1 metres) tall and nicknamed 'the crane' due to his stooping gait.

Carswell was a significant figure in the history of Scottish Gaelic. In 1567 his *Foirm na n-Urrnuidheadh*, the Gaelic translation of the Book of Common Order, became the first work printed in the Goidelic language. In the Introduction, he wrote:

'Some of the literature of the Gaels of Alba and Erin is written in manuscripts of poets and bards, and great is the sin of those who prefer vain lying tales of the People of the goddess Danu, or Milesian heroes and Fionn mac Cuill and his Féinn, and many others I shall not name, to the faithful Word of God and the perfect way of truth.'

He also expressed that the Gaels of Ireland and Scotland *'are terribly discriminated against and have a great lacking, compared to the rest of the world, without our Gaelic language published, as every other race of people throughout the world has their language published.'*[28]

In 1790, the ground floor of the roofless and ruinous castle became a schoolhouse. After its restoration in 2019, it became a B&B offering splendid holiday accommodation with beautiful views across the valley.

After leaving Glebe Cairn, we dowsed the male dragon heading northwest to Carnasserie Castle. The ruin, now managed by Historic Scotland, was John Carswell's last residence, built over the remains of an earlier Keep owned by the Campbells. During the 1560s, French masons from Stirling restored it as a fine mansion befitting a powerful Bishop. Standing high up on a rocky knoll overlooking Kilmartin Burn, it would have appeared as an imposing fortified tower house consisting of five storeys.

Immediately to the castle's northeast is an intriguing earthwork, which *Historic Environment Scotland* describes as the remains of an Iron Age walled enclosure, or dun, dating between the 4th and 1st centuries BCE. Its strategically advantageous position overlooking Kilmartin Glen, where several roads converge, allowed the early cultures to guard the vital trade route to Loch Awe.

Carswell influenced many of the castle's features due to his interest in French architecture and design, which he acquired while serving as chaplain at the Chapel Royal in Stirling Palace. Here, he would have seen first-hand the Renaissance stonework fashioned by James V's French masons. As a result, the castle boasted a level of craftsmanship and detail rarely seen in the West Highlands.

The inscribed heraldic panel above the doorway reads *Dia le ua nduibhne* translated from Gaelic as 'God be with o Duibhne', referring to the race of O'Duibhne, who owned the shores of Loch Awe.[29] The O'Duibhne were the original *Oire Gaidheal*, from which the name Argyll originates, meaning the 'Land of the Gael.' The panel combines the heraldry of the Campbells of Argyll, descendants of the race of O'Duibhne, and the royal arms of Scotland. After Bishop Carswell's death in 1572, the castle passed to the 5th Earl of Argyll but was later destroyed following the 9th Earl's failed uprising against James VII in 1685.

The serpent energy of Lugh passes through the old site of the dun and continues to a deep well carved into bedrock under the tower, the underground water perhaps amplifying its flow. According to the information board, the main hall or audience chamber was on the floor above the well where the bishop conducted his formal business dealings. Here, we found an elaborately carved Renaissance fireplace still in place adorned with interesting carved symbols. An illustration of the 5th Earl of Argyll and the Bishop on the wall caught our attention. They were standing by the fireplace over the flow of Lugh and the potent waters of the well. Accounts from visitors to the castle describe an uneasy feeling, especially around the well. One mentions the sighting of a helmeted rider galloping towards the castle and then vanishing. In the distant past, locals enacted plays here, and more recently, the old walls have seen the production of amateur films – such is the lure of the mysterious atmosphere that permeates this prodigious site.

Carnasserie Castle well

Nearby are standing stones, cairns and cup and ring mark stones, all signs that the earlier Neolithic settlers regarded this area of the glen as sacred. As Lugh continues northwest from the castle, he takes us to the first of these fine monuments.

Standing stones near Carnasserie Castle

Having diverted off its northerly path, the current connects with two tall megaliths on a high shoulder of land close to the scant remains of a cairn. They measure approximately 8 ft (2.5 m) tall and align almost precisely north–south.

From here, a footpath through Forestry Commission land takes us on a two-and-a-half mile hike to a remarkable slab of rock art at Ormaig within a clearing overlooking the islands of Loch Craignish. There are at least eight exposed stone slabs on this ridge, all facing west and all with varying well-defined styles of rock carving, including cups, grooves, cup and ring variants and curious symbols called rosettes. We dowsed Lugh encompassing two of these giant slabs carved with spectacular and well-preserved rock art.

During an archaeological survey by Kilmartin Museum in 2007, Dr Clare Ellis and Dr Sharon Webb found numerous pieces of fragmented white quartz around the cup and marked stones, some unworked and others rounded like hammerstones.[30] The quartz findings support our belief that grinding these white silica pebbles into the stone slabs alters the rock's electromagnetic field, which interacts with the surrounding landscape to increase fertility. The Ormaig site is the finest amongst many dotted around the Kilmartin Valley, as brilliantly outlined in Stan Beckensall's book *The Prehistoric Rock Art of Kilmartin*.[31]

In Ireland, we found many examples of bullaun stones, single stone altars or rock features with significantly deep cup marks containing a smooth rounded or oval quartz pebble. Over centuries, the frequent, almost ritual turning of the pebbles created large hollowed-out cups used for ceremonial purposes at certain times of the year, such as Imbolc and Beltane. According to tradition, grinding the stones sunwise has a positive and curative effect on the health and well-being of the individual and the land.

Cup and ring marked stones, Ormaig

Perhaps the purpose of creating these carvings on the various stone slabs around the glen came after a particular climatic upheaval which resulted in the loss of fertility in the once bountiful lands that these carvings came to overlook. The ancients may have understood that the grinding action helped amplify the stone's magnetic field and, as Cowan discovered, created a fertility bubble around the surrounding areas. Furthermore, the fertilising power contained within Lugh's solar male serpent energy, as he passes over the cup-marked stones at Kilmichael Glassary, Baluachraig and Ormaig, further helps to reanimate the land during its time of need.

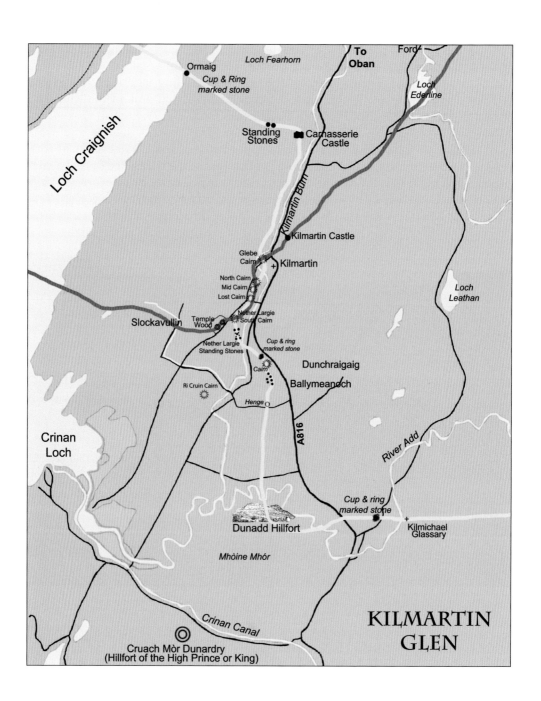

Loch Fearhorn

To
Oban

Ford

Loch
Ederline

Ormaig
*Cup & Ring
marked stone*

Loch Craignish

Standing
Stones

Carnasserie
Castle

Kilmartin Burn

Kilmartin Castle

Glebe
Cairn

Kilmartin

North Cairn
Mid Cairn
Lost Cairn

Loch
Leathan

Slockavullin

Temple
Wood

Nether Largie
South Cairn

Nether Largie
Standing Stones

*Cup & ring
marked stone*

Cairn

Dunchraigaig

Ri Cruin Cairn

Ballymeanoch

Henge

A816

Crinan
Loch

River Add

*Cup & ring
marked stone*

Kilmichael
Glassary

Dunadd Hillfort

Mhòine Mhór

Crinan Canal

Cruach Mòr Dunardry
(Hillfort of the High Prince or King)

KILMARTIN
GLEN

1. Campbell, M. 2001. *Argyll: The Enduring Heartland*. House of Lochar, Isle of Colonsay.
2. https://canmore.org.uk/site/39564/dunadd
3. https://www.gla.ac.uk/schools/humanities/research/archaeologyresearch/
4. http://www.duffus.com/Articles/senchus_fer_n_alban.htm
5. 18. https://www.eyeofthepsychic.com/kilmartin/
6. Adomnan of Iona, *Life of St Columba*. Richard Sharpe (Translator) 1995. Penguin Classics, London.
7. 8. Ardrey, Adam. 2008. *Finding Arthur: The Truth Behind the Legend of the Once and Future King*. Gerald Duckworth & Co Ltd, London.
9. Dumville, D. 2003. *Bede: Ecclesiastical History of the English People*, translated by L. Shirly-Price and D. Farmer. Penguin Classics, London.
10. https://theses.gla.ac.uk/73976/1/10662767.pdf
11. 17. 26. https://www.eyeofthepsychic.com/kilmartin/
12. 16. Abernethy, D. 1993. *Ballymeanoch standing stones and Nether Largie standing stones (Kilmartin and Kilmichael Glassary parish): geophysical survey and possible fallen standing stones,* Discovery Excav Scot, 1993. Page(s): 74-5
13. https://www.historicenvironment.scot/search-results?q=kilmartin+glen+dunchraigaig
14. https://studylib.net/doc/6960763/transcript--professor-richard-bradley--vft-3-kilmartin-glen
15. 21. https://www.youtube.com/watch?v=WafRqdOQK30
19. https://www.historicenvironment.scot/visit-a-place/places/kilmartin-glen-nether-largie-south-cairn/history/
20. https://canmore.org.uk/site/39471/nether-largie
22. https://canmore.org.uk/site/39504/temple-wood
23. https://canmore.org.uk/site/39482/nether-largie-north
24. https://canmore.org.uk/site/39537/kilmartin-glebe
25. https://www.thenorthernantiquarian.org/2009/09/06/dun-dubh-ford/
27. https://canmore.org.uk/site/39532/kilmartin-parish-church
28. Carswell, J. 1970. *Foirm na n-Urrnuidheadh: John Carswell's Gaelic translation of the Book of Common Order*. R. L. Thomson (Editor). Scottish Gaelic Text Society, Edinburgh.
29. https://www.historicenvironment.scot/visit-a-place/places/carnasserie-castle/history/
30. Ellis, Dr. C. & Webb, Dr. S. 2007. *Excavations at Ormaig Cup and Ring Marked Rock Art Site in Argyll*. Historic Scotland. online report https://static1.squarespace.com/ Ormaig-Excavation-DSR.pdf
31. Beckensall, S. 2005. *The Prehistoric Rock Art of Kilmartin*. Kilmartin House Trust.

Chapter 15

The Cauldron, a Holy Isle and the Circle of Buie

Bride and Lugh from Craignish to Mull

'I am the Cailleach,
Goddess of Winter,
Mother of Mountains,
Ageless Lady of Dark Places,
Ancient Crone of Wisdom.
The Winter brings the Spring,
and in death,
I am endlessly renewed.'

Source Unknown

The Corryvreckan Whirlpool

From Slockavullin in Kilmartin Glen, Bride meanders west along the Raslie Burn before crossing Loch Craignish through the little island of Eilean nan Gabhar (Island of Goats) to the beautiful countryside of the Craignish Peninsula. This long north–south finger of land has many Iron Age remains, including forts, cairns and standing stones, many with cup and ring marks. Her primary focus is the ruined chapel at Kirkton, a roofless stone building known over the centuries as Kilmolroy, Kilmory, Kilvaree, Kilmarie or St Mary's Church.

However, *molroy* or *mory* derives from *Maol Rudh* or Maelrubha, an Irish saint (*c.* 642–722) who founded a monastic community at Applecross in Ross. Maol Rudh means red monk referring to his red hair. He became the most revered saint in northwest Scotland after St Columba with over twenty churches dedicated to him, including one at Balnekeil near Durness, the very last node of the Spine of Albion.

The present ruins of Kirkton Chapel date to the 14th century, although its gable end shows traces of its earlier 12th-century foundation. It was abandoned in the late 17th century in favour of a new church at the nearby village of Ardfern.

However, its original dedication to St Maelrubha may indicate the existence of a 7th or 8th-century wooden Celtic church built over a possible pagan ceremonial site.

Grave slabs at Kirkton Chapel

In *Celt, Druid and Culdee*, Isabel Hill Elder revealed that Celtic Christianity flourished in Scotland as early as the 3rd century. It was first established by a religious order known as the Culdees, their name derived from the original word *Culdich* meaning 'distant strangers'. Old church records describe them as *Cele Dei* or *Keledei,* meaning 'Children of God'. This priestly order successfully merged their Christian teachings with Druid lore and adopted the sacred places of the Druids to 'ground' the new Christian message of love and compassion. They often built circular huts within megalithic stone circles, Druid temples, and groves.[1]

The chapel is most famous for its exceptional collection of sculptured stones and ancient tombs, which once stood in the graveyard and are now protected within the ruined remains. According to the Natural History and Antiquarian Society of Mid Argyll, four stone burial cists or tomb chests with broken top slabs are on either side of the chancel. Many of the burials are of the McDougal and Campbell families.

Although this little church is now forgotten and abandoned, the Bride dragon current still recognises its sacred sanctity as it passes east–west through the site. On her flow is a square green-coloured stone faintly incised with a sundial, which may have held an early Christian cross. After some research, we discovered that it is a piece of epidiorite rock, like the old fonts in Argyll.

We braced ourselves against the strong wind and the rain as we accompanied Bride across the road towards the atmospheric Craignish Castle, the old seat of the Campbells of Craignish and Jura. Over the years, it has passed through several hands and in the 20th century, was restored and divided into privately owned apartments. West of the Craignish Peninsula is the island of Scarba, separated from Jura in the south by the Gulf of Corryvreckan with its famous whirlpool, perhaps one of the lesser-known wonders of Britain.

Our instincts told us that the Bride current was heading straight for this unique natural phenomenon, the largest of its kind in Europe and the third largest in the world – but a specially arranged boat trip was the only way we could get there. Local folklore tells us that this great and powerful whirlpool had many associations with the goddess Bride and undoubtedly was held sacred by the ancient inhabitants of this area. The old mariners who first sailed these waters from near and afar were probably well acquainted with its ancient legends.

Several fast-flowing Atlantic tides create this wondrous eddy as the waters cascade into a vast 718 ft-deep (219 m) hole before hitting a rock basalt spike or pinnacle that rises to within 95 ft (29 m) of the surface. The massive upwelling hits the surface in

Corryvreckan Whirlpool (courtesy of Walter Baxter)

pulses, then is swept away westwards by the tidal flow and dissipated into whirlpools. The churning waters resemble a vast boiling vat or froth-filled cauldron, but very few people see its full power as most sail by it in calmer conditions during spring and summer. However, reports from witnesses on the islands say the whirlpool can be 300 ft (91 m) wide at times and 90 ft (27 m) deep. Locals over 20 miles 32 km) away often hear it roaring and witness standing waves reaching up to 15 feet high (4.5 m).

Because of the region's unpredictable weather and sea conditions, it took us three attempts to find a boat that would take us across to the whirlpool to locate the path of Bride. Although the sea seemed relatively calm, we could see the violently churning waters as we approached the Corryvreckan, causing the boat to rock. At that moment, we were offered the wonderful treat of a diving display by a Minke Whale, frequently seen in and around the Hebridean islands from April to October. The skipper managed to manoeuvre the boat to the very edge of the rotating whirlpool so that we were swirling around its outer edge, which was like being on a roller coaster ride. Despite the undulating movement, we focused our minds on the dowsing and, to our amazement, located Bride disappearing into the vortex as she headed for the underwater spike.

Local myths and legends say the spike of basalt at the centre of the whirlpool, over which the female serpent current passes, is traditionally associated with the goddess Cailleach. The Cailleach is the winter aspect of Bride/Brigid, who guards the omphalos at several geographical central locations around the British Isles and Ireland, a theme we explore in our book *The Power of Centre*. Florence McNeill, in *The Silver Bough*, records an old Scottish folktale which links the symbology of the 'Cauldron of the Goddess' with the Corryvreckan whirlpool:

'The Cailleach is the genius of winter and the enemy of growth. Her chief seat is Ben Nevis. She ushers in the winter by washing her great plaid in the whirlpool of the Corryvreckan (Coire Bhreacain – the Cauldron of the Plaid). Before washing, it is said, the roar of a coming tempest is heard by people on the coast for a distance of twenty miles, for a period of three days until the cauldron boils. When the washing is over the plaid of old Scotland is virgin white.'[2]

The Cailleach and her hammer, illustrated by John Duncan in 'Wonder Tales from Scottish Myth and Legend' (1917) by Donald Alexander Mackenzie

The 'Cauldron of the Plaid' refers to legends that describe the goddess washing her plaid of wool (the traditional tartan garment of the Highlands) in the whirlpool. She begins the wash cycle in late autumn, and when the first storms of winter arrive and the tumultuous waters of her 'washtub' spin the pure wool white, it is spread over the mountains to dry.

She is also the death goddess who watches over the culling of old growth, allowing to die what is no longer needed. Yet, in the debris of the passing year, she also finds the gems of nature, new seeds for the coming season. She is the guardian of the otherworld and chooses who will live or die in the whirlpool. The Cailleach transfers the essence of nature's power to the summer goddess Bride, Brig or Brigid, at Imbolc (1 February), then returns to her at Samhain (31 October) to receive it back again. Her oldest totem animal is the deer, which she would herd and milk, often providing them with protection against hunters.

Ancient Gaelic traditions say that the short spell of good weather that often occurs at the beginning of February is called *lathan Bridean* or 'The Days of Bride'. The dual personalities of the goddess in the land – the Cailleach of autumn and winter and Bride of spring and summer – are also recognised in Highland traditions. The Cailleach pounds the ground with her great hammer, thus freezing it and creating frost and snow. During this time, she imprisons Bride, who is kept busy with the impossible task of washing a brown fleece white. She manages to escape her ordeal on the 1 February for three days before being recaptured. During Bride's liberation, far away in the Land of Eternal Youth, Angus Og dreams of the maiden Bride and sets out to rescue her. Eventually, with the help of a mysterious male figure (probably the Green Man), Angus Og liberates her. The Cailleach soon learns of her escape and tries to recapture her, but Bride's release initiates the spring, sapping the hag's power and energy, who quickly gives up the chase, throwing her hammer under a holly bush. Bride and Angus Og are married on 1 May and rule together over the summer months until the winter hag gains her strength and recaptures Bride once more.

The three days of Bride at Imbolc is an allegory of the energetic release of the land's fertility that stirs up the Green Man (power of rebirth). Therefore, the three days from the traditional 1 February to the astrological 3 February is a window of opportunity to send and receive healing from the land at sacred sites.

In Celtic art and myths, the cauldron resurrects warriors slain on the battlefield. In the online article *The Cauldron of Rebirth,* Jennifer Emick writes, '*The gods of water were themselves continuously reborn, and the waters of the cauldron have obvious parallels to the watery environment of the womb, the passageway to new life.*'[3] Resurrected gods and rebirth by watery immersion were integral to Celtic spirituality, later incorporated by Christian missionaries in their baptism rituals.

A related Welsh myth from the *Mabinogion* tells of the Cauldron of Bran, where slain fighters were dipped during a battle. The warriors emerge overnight from the cauldron unharmed, save for the loss of their powers of speech,[4] a possible reference to the reborn soul incapable of speech. Perhaps this tradition is a distant memory of ancient immersion rituals performed at the Corryvreckan Whirlpool.

In the *Life of St Ciaran,* written by the Abbot of Clonmacnoise in Ireland, prayers to St Bridget saved St Columba from the perils of the whirlpool.[5] So why call upon a nun from Kildare for some supernatural intervention? St Bridget is the Christian aspect of the ancient goddess Bride or Brigid, who, in her winter guise, guards the whirlpool.

Under certain conditions, the roar of the Corryvreckan can be heard as far away as Dunadd and Kilmartin. This low rumbling noise must have been noticed and revered by the ancients who built their stone monuments at this important royal ceremonial centre. The Isle of Portland in Dorset bathes in the energies of the powerful collision of several tides off the island's south coast called the Portland Race. The Race is a disruption of underwater currents in the English Channel that collides with a rock ledge 32 ft (10 m) deep off the southern tip of the island at a place where the depth of the Channel is 65–130 ft (20–40 m). At high tide, in windy weather, the Race becomes turbulent like a washing machine, where many boats have sunk over the years. The churning of the sea currents produces a powerful electromagnetic force and beneficial ozone. Ozone is a trioxygen gas with an extra oxygen molecule containing trioxide rather than dioxide. Ozone therapy has proven advantageous for health and healing. Therefore, under the right conditions, the cauldron of the Corryvreckan is a place of healing.

Hugh McArthur believes that the Taliesin poem *Preiddeu Annwn* is an account of an initiation ritual carried out in the Corryvreckan Whirlpool.[6] The verse also mentions King Arthur or Artuir, son of King Aedan, whose ritual centre at Dunadd and central fortress at Dunardry were only 10 miles (16 km) away and, on a clear day, you can see the Gulf of Corryvreckan from the summit of both hills.

Stuart McHardy, in his book *On the Trail of the Holy Grail*, says the Corryvreckan Whirlpool was seen as a 'sacred cauldron' of rebirth and regeneration, representing the creator goddess of the Celts. Moreover, he believes this huge swirling cauldron took the original form of the life-giving Grail rather than a physical cup held by Jesus.[7]

Recent scientific research has shown that whirlpools and eddies fertilise the oceans. Microscopic phytoplankton is a self-feeding component of the plankton family and is a vital part of the ocean's ecosystem. During photosynthesis, phytoplankton removes carbon dioxide from seawater and releases oxygen as a by-product. This process allows the oceans to absorb additional carbon dioxide from the atmosphere. If less phytoplankton existed, atmospheric carbon dioxide or greenhouse gas would increase. Whirlpools distribute surface water rich with phytoplankton carbon and carbon dioxide from humanity's pollution to the ocean floors, where it is locked away and gently dispersed. Moreover, recent discoveries show that giant whirlpools up to 34 miles (55 km) across drive the Earth's climate on an unimagined scale by distributing large volumes of water and heat across the oceans. Therefore, the churning of the cauldron by the primal force of the ocean currents actually gives life to the oceans.

Likewise, the ancient symbol of the cornucopia, representing abundance, nourishment and the Grail, is another expression of the life-giving whirlpool if seen under the water. Like a tornado, its revolving shape diminishing to a point is also reminiscent of a veritable 'horn of plenty'. Abundita or Copia, goddess of abundance and prosperity, carries the cornucopia and empties nourishment into the world like the whirlpools. Yet another aspect of the whirlpool is its swirling power that creates enormous friction, generating a strong electromagnetic field that affects the space-time continuum under certain conditions. Therefore, it was no surprise to discover that the whirlpool symbolises an interdimensional portal to many cultures worldwide and signifies the transition between worlds or a gateway between one reality and another. It is the portal through which the shaman enters from the physical to the spiritual plane.

Florence McNeill also records another piece of folklore concerning a sow that swam out of the Corryvreckan and gave birth to nine piglets near Loch Craignish, which became the progenitors of all the wild boars in Scotland.[8]

The boar or pig is sacred in many religions associated with the moon and the seasonal cycles of life and death and depicted in many carvings and artefacts across Western Europe. McHardy believes the story of the pig is a veiled allegory of the Nine Maidens or priestesses that tend the Grail, and interestingly in Loch Craignish is *Eilean na Nighean* or 'Island of the Maiden'. As mentioned earlier, many scholars believe the magic cauldron in Celtic lore is the origin of the Grail story.

Cornucopia

Therefore, the Corryvreckan Whirlpool embodies the concept of the 'cauldron of plenty' or cornucopia.

The wind that carries the roaring noise of the whirlpool is known locally as 'The Breath of the Goddess'. Perhaps the ozone wind resonating with the sound of the whirlpool drifts into the Kilmartin Valley, energising its stone monuments and fertilising the soil for crops.

We can also interpret spiral Galaxies as life-giving whirlpools of energy and matter, the closest example being the Andromeda Galaxy, seen as a blur near the W-shaped stars of Cassiopeia. Also, in the night sky are the stars of Orion, symbolised by the Hunter, with one foot in a cluster of stars called Zalos, which in Arabic means whirlpool. The stars are clustered in the Eridanus constellation in the southern celestial hemisphere and are said to resemble a river whose earthly counterpart is in 'Northern Europe rich in Amber.'

In *Hamlet's Mill*, Giorgio Santillana and Hertha Von Dechend describe a whirlpool in the sky at Orion's foot:

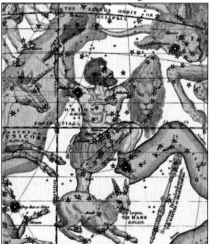

'That there is a whirlpool in the sky is well known; it is most probably the essential one, and it is precisely placed. It is a group of stars so named (Zalos) at the left foot of Orion, close to Rigel (beta Orionis, Rigel being the Arabic word for "foot"'), the degree of which was called "death," according to Hermes Trismegistos, whereas the Maori claim outright that Rigel marked the way to Hades.'[9]

Engraving of Orion the Hunter by Elijah H Burritt, 1835

In modern times, the Holy Axis at 107 degrees points to the rising stars of Orion on the eastern horizon, particularly the stars Rigel and Zalos on his left foot. Therefore, the Holy Axis also orientates to a whirlpool portal in the sky, giving it a magical connection with the upper world.

The boat trip also included another destination, a hidden Culdee sanctuary on one of the Garvellach islands.

Luing and Tir nan Og

From Ormaig, the Lugh current is north of its feminine counterpart as it crosses Loch Craignish to *Eilean Mhic Chrion* or McNivern's Island before arriving close to the marina at the village of Ardfern. The name of this pretty fishing village, located on the south coast of the Craignish Peninsula, means 'headland of alder trees'. It was once a thriving community of farmers and weavers before the Clearances brought about its decline. However, thanks to the present Laird, Ardfern is now a famous centre for those sailing and cruising the Western Isles.

While checking the O.S. map, we noticed that the male serpent was heading towards the remains of an ancient chambered cairn just above the main road. Having turned right by the local school, we followed a lane to a field bordered by a group of houses. One of the residents advised us to go through a small gate where a worn path led us to the ancient monument known as *Clach an T-Sagairt,* meaning 'Stone of the Priest'. The cairn, measuring 5 ft (1.5m) high and 6 ft (1.8 m) wide, has three upright megaliths supporting a capstone. It sits on top of loose stones that originally spanned 42 ft (13 m) in diameter, reminiscent of the cairns at Kilmartin. Sadly, many of these local monuments became quarries for farmers and settlers while building their field walls and roads.

Lugh's trail then targets a high pinnacle rock with the remnants of another cairn on Soroba Hill before crossing the Sound of Jura to the islands of Shuna and Luing in the Firth of Lorn. The current is drawn by a fault line that links the two landmasses. The Isle of Luing, about 16 miles (26 km) south of Oban, has two ruined hill forts, one of which still has traces of its former past, including a flight of stone steps and pillared doorways with cup markings. At the end of the 19th century, excavations of the northern fort unearthed several Bronze Age artefacts, now in the National Museum of Scotland, Edinburgh. Nearby are the picturesque villages of Cullipool and Toberonochy, with quaint whitewashed cottages formerly inhabited by quarrymen who worked the island's slate quarries in the 18th and 19th centuries. The famous Easdale slate has graced the roofs of many grand buildings, including Iona Abbey.

Except for Luing, the Norse Lord of the Isles ruled the Western Isles from the 9th to 13th centuries. Before then, the Dal Riata kings controlled the islands and somehow Luing remained in Scottish control thanks to a treaty signed in 1098 between King Edgar, fourth son of Malcolm III, and King Magnus Barefoot of Norway.

The Holy Axis alignment crosses the island at Kilchattan Church, built in 1934, next to a school and war memorial. It replaced Old Kilchattan Kirk and graveyard, just under a mile south, where we dowsed the male current. The old church was rebuilt several times until its abandonment in 1685, but there are still traces of its

12th-century foundations. The name derives from St Cattan or Cathan, a 6th-century Irish missionary who was a contemporary of St Columba and a member of Dal Riata royalty. He studied under St Patrick and was one of the first missionaries on the Isle of Bute. He supposedly lived as a hermit in a cell at Leccamore on Luing, with many religious settlements in the area dedicated to him, including Ardchatton Priory on Loch Etive.

In the graveyard, we noticed many grave slabs made from locally quarried slate streaked with narrow bands of basalt. Many noble chieftains lie buried here alongside quarriers, sailors and crofters, including the famous Covenanter Alexander Campbell. He led a sect that withdrew from the established Presbyterian Church in 1787 to form a separate congregation known as the Covenanters of Lorn. Masonry in the south wall includes crude carvings of crosses and West Highland galleys or birlinns, some medieval.

Lugh leaves Luing's west coast through a geological feature called the Cobblers of Lorn, formed from a row of 400-million-year-old volcanic rock stacks. The igneous rock

Carvings at Old Kilchattan Kirk, Isle of Luing

high in silica was shaped by the seas during a collision of continents that created the Caledonian mountain chain. As we walked the rocky landscape of Luing, the elementals seemed to be all around us, as if we had crossed the threshold of an enchanted realm. Hugh McArthur tells of a local man on a boat trip along the Luing's west coast from Cullipool, pointing to the island and exclaiming, '*The locals call that Tir nan Og*', the Celtic name of the *otherworld*.'[10]

The male current crosses the Sound of Luing to the small island of Lunga, targeting a well at its northern tip called *Tobar Challuim Chille* or 'Holy Well of St Columba'. He then continues east to the holy island of *Eileach an Naoimh* to meet with Bride.

The Garvellachs and St Brendon's Sacred Isle

The group of islands known as the Garvellachs are located northwest of Scarba in the Firth of Lorne. Legend says they were formed by stones dropped from the goddess Cailleach's basket as she passed by. The islands are also at the centre of a 'sea road' from the Mull of Kintyre, Applecross and Iona, linking Ireland with its Hebridean Culdee communities.

The Garvellachs, meaning 'Isles of the Sea', form a small archipelago in the Inner Hebrides. The smallest and most northerly of the four islands is *Dùn Chonnuill* or 'Conall's Fort'. Conall is also associated with the dun on the summit of the pyramid-shaped Dun Chonallaich, which is the focus of the Kilmartin cairn alignment. The

Eithne's grave, Eileach an Naoimh or St Brendon's Isle, The Garvellachs

Holy Axis passes through the northern tip of the Garvellachs' largest island, *Garbh Eileach* or the 'Rough Rocky Isle', a renowned medieval burial site of kings and queens. The third island is *A'Chùli*, although its older name is *Cùil-i-Breannan* or St Brendan's Retreat. The archipelago's fourth and most southerly island is *Eileach an Naoimh,* meaning 'Rocky Place of the Saints', also known as Holy Isle and St Brendan's Isle. According to Patrick H Gillies in *Netherlorn and its Neighbourhood*, Eileach or Aileach translates as a 'rough stony mound', therefore rocky mound or heap of the saints.[11] Likewise, *Eileacha Naomh* translates as 'holy mounds'.

Early Celtic Christian monks or Culdees retreated here for religious solitude and contemplation, similar to Inner Farne off the coast of Northumberland, the most easterly node of the Holy Axis. Around 542 CE, St Brendan of Clontarf is said to have established the first Scottish monastery on Eileach an Naoimh and later on Tiree. He eventually returned to Ireland to visit St Brigid before she died. His extensive travel, visiting places like Iceland, Greenland and North America, earned him the nickname St Brendan the Navigator.

Some sources believe Eileach an Naoimh is the legendary *Hinba*, where St Columba supposedly first settled before building his monastic community on Iona. According to St Columba's biographer, Adomnan, many miracles and strange incidents occurred at the monastery of Hinba, described as a short sail from Iona. For example, during a Mass there attended by Columba, Kenneth and Comgall, Brendan witnessed a column of fire rising from Columba's head.[12] This story is reminiscent of the column of fire seen over St Brigid's head when she received the veil in Ireland at Croghan Hill.[13] However, Jura, Colonsay, Oronsay and Tiree could also be considered as likely candidates for this mystical isle of Hinba.

Another myth attached to Eileach an Naoimh is that it was the burial site of Columba's mother, Eithne and *Cladh Eithne*, or 'grave of Eithne', still overlooks the remains of the monastic settlement. Here, three upright stone slabs mark a circular grove, one with an incised cross. Once, many highly decorated stones stood around the island, but over time they have been taken to use as gateposts or garden features. On the highest point is *Dun Bhreanain*, or Brendan's Fort, with tremendous views for miles around, including the remaining islands that form the Garvellachs, which are rarely visited.

St Brendan's Celtic Christian settlement consisted of a monastery, the abbot's house, a hospitium, two chapels, a graveyard and three beehive stone huts or cells similar to other Culdee religious settlements found in Scotland, including Old Melrose. Near the jetty is a natural stone-lined spring called *Tobar Challuim-Cille* or St Columba's Well, once the only source of fresh water for the monks.

Most of the 6th-century monastic buildings were destroyed during Norse raids in the 9th century, although the island remained a focus of pilgrimage and burial throughout medieval times. Although the present dwellings date from the 11th century, foundations remain from St Brendan's time. After the Reformation, ownership of the island transferred from Oronsay Priory to the Dukes of Argyll and until the 19th century, tenant farmers used the land for cattle and sheep grazing. The site is now in the care of Historic Environment Scotland.

The island's beehive huts are some of the best preserved in Britain, and although one monk would occupy each cell, they all shared a common 'wall' with a connecting passage. Skellig Michael, off the coast of Kerry in Ireland, also has fine examples of beehive huts. The practice of living in exile in very remote or 'desert-like' places was known as 'white martyrdom' based on an early Egyptian Christian Coptic tradition, which came into Ireland through the abbey of Tours in France with St Martin. From there, it spread to Cornwall, Wales and Scotland. The leaders founded cells, hermitages and monasteries over a wide area, including Glastonbury. The monks would sail to remote islands in curraghs, boats made of skin stretched over a wooden frame. However, the Roman Church threatened their very existence under the guidance of St Augustine when enforced changes to monastic life occurred after the Synod of Whitby in 664 CE.

The island has no jetty, so calm seas are essential for the vessel to dock safely alongside a large rock crag. After a precarious leap from the boat onto the rock, we soon entered the ancient precincts of St Brendan's sacred island. Unfortunately, the boat trip only allowed us one hour to visit the island, so we had to double our efforts to dowse and explore the sites. Luckily, we were the only people dropped off that day, the remaining passengers spending the hour bird-watching further out to sea.

So taking out our dowsing rods, we trooped forward in search of dragons. We located

Bride entering the island near the landing site to connect with the now overgrown remains of St Columba's Well, a stoned-lined natural spring in a gulley that joins the sea at the old harbour jetty. According to the Canmore website, in 1933, Bryce and Knight identified an entrance gate at the mouth of the gully, with fragments of a stone wall believed to be an enclosure.[13]

Bride continues inland, following the gully to a curious subterranean circular cell or souterrain with steps leading down to a little doorway supported by stone lintels. As we crawled inside its atmospheric

St Columba's Well, Eileach an Naoimh

Souterrain node, Eileach an Naoimh

womb-like interior, we noticed a small niche and ledge like an altar with the charred remains of candles. Here, the female current begins to shrink to form a node with Lugh crossing in the middle of the floor. Like other node points associated with the Holy Axis, the cell is within the earth and more conducive to meditation and connecting to the potent telluric force within the land.

Nearby we dowse Bride at an 11th-century roofless chapel with 3-foot-thick walls and a west-facing entrance missing its stone lintel. The underground cell and chapel lie within traces of a pentagonal-shape banked enclosure which seems to be the focal point of the original Culdee monastic site. The pentagram symbolises protection, perhaps a shape deliberately created by the monks around their inner sanctum.

The female serpent continues following the gulley to the island's northern shores before heading for the distant Isle of Mull. The gulley is formed from a fault that runs diagonally through the middle of the island, Bride no doubt benefiting from its rejuvenating and revitalising energy.

We detected the Lugh current entering the island's southeastern shores through two interconnecting beehive cells before continuing to the node point inside the cell. These domed-shaped dry-stoned cells are made of the same locally quarried sandstone as the chapel, each measuring approximately 16 ft (5 m) in diameter and just under 13 ft (4 m) in height. A low passage connects the two chambers, each with an external doorway. The roof is cleverly designed with stone corbelling that perhaps was covered with turf. St Columba and St Brendan may have slept within these cells to commune with cosmic and earthly powers through the solar energy of Lugh. The intense magnetism of the island's geology combined with the presence of a powerful male serpent certainly promotes a potent and heady atmosphere inside the beehive cells, encouraging one to have strong visionary experiences. Perhaps the saints projected their pious thoughts from here to create balance and harmony in the land and its people – a practice learned from their predecessors, the Druids.

Beehive Cells, Eileach an Naoimh

From the node, Lugh heads southwest through the remains of a medieval monastery before continuing to an enclosure, once used to grow medicinal herbs, and a burial ground beyond. He then climbs the hill to a group of ancient engraved cross-slab stones said to mark the grave of St Columba's mother, Eithne. However, some authorities believe it to be the prehistoric remains of a cairn.

The current leaves the island's northwest shores through a 12 ft (3.6 m) high rock column with a natural overhang called St Columba's Pulpit, where local legend says St Columba preached. It is a natural outcrop shaped over millennia by wind and rain to form a canopy resembling a dolmen. It stands at the island's highest point, marked by Dun Bhreanain or Brendan's Fort, where you can just make out Mull's highest peaks beyond the Firth of Lorne.

St Columba's Pulpit, Eileach an Naoimh

350

Sadly, our hour on the island had come to and, and we reluctantly returned to the waiting boat. We marvelled that the island still retains a magical atmosphere, its holiness almost tangible, and felt sure an overnight stay would provoke many revelations and visions.

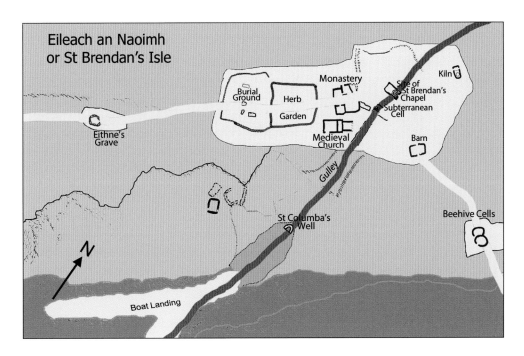

The Isle of Mull and the Druid Stones of Lochbuie

The stunningly beautiful Isle of Mull is the second-largest island of the Inner Hebrides, having a coastline some 300 miles (482 km) long with many tidal lochs and picturesque bays. The island's centre is dominated by the high peak of *Beinn Mhòr*, meaning 'great mountain'. Along with Mull's delightful flora and fauna, one of its main attractions is its wildlife. Thousands of people come each year hoping to glimpse the rare and unusual golden and white-tailed eagles, as well as otters, corncrakes, seals, dolphins and basking sharks. Also, the whooper swan, bar-tailed godwit, greenshank, redshank, snipe and whimbrel are just a few of the many birds that pass through here en route to their summer and winter feeding grounds.

In *Life of St. Columba*, Adomnan calls Mull the isle of Malean, and the Norse and Gaels knew it as *Maleas, Mula, Muile* and *Muileach*, meaning 'brow of a rock', a 'cape' or 'promontory'.[14]

Settlers have been here since around 6000 BCE, its earliest inhabitants leaving behind numerous standing stones, cairns, brochs and a stone circle. Invasions by Norse-Gaelic warlord Somerled in 1156, who ruled from Argyll, took many of the Western Isles away from Scottish control, including Mull. Eventually, Clan MacLean gained ownership, and in 1681 it was the domain of Clan Campbell. By the 18th

Loch Buie, Isle of Mull (courtesy of W L Tarbert)

century, Mull's vibrant and thriving population had vastly reduced due to the infamous Highland Clearances.

Geologically, Mull is fascinating, its oldest rocks having been formed way down in the southern hemisphere, which gradually drifted northwards to its present-day position. Beinn Mhòr is the remnant of a volcano, and the lava pouring out of the fissures formed thick seams of basalt rich in silica, evidence of which can be seen in rocks at Carsaig, Ardtum and near Tobermory on its east coast.

The island is also famed for its folktales of fairies, witches and the Cailleach, so we were not surprised to find the Holy Axis alignment and both the male and female currents passing through Mull before arriving at Iona. Bride starts her journey in the southeast, meandering through Laggan Deer Forest on a peninsular to the isolated *Cailbeal Mheombair* or 'Chapel of Remembrance' near the east shore of Loch Buie. The memorial church, originally dedicated to St Kenneth, stands within a circular churchyard on raised ground. One of its cornerstones has signs of cup and ring marks, alluding to a possible site of a prehistoric ceremonial sanctuary. As we walked in the flow of the female current towards the tiny hamlet of Lochbuie, we were mesmerised by the spectacular views across the bay.

*Cailbeal
Mheombair
or 'Chapel of
Remembrance',
Loch Buie*

The village of Lochbuie and its situation at the head of a remote loch within a natural amphitheatre formed by mountains and forest seemed otherworldly, where one could experience supernatural encounters. We spotted standing stones in a field as we followed Bride's flow just north of the atmospheric Moy Castle, a 15th-century tower house of the MacLaines of Lochbuie.

Lochbuie stone circle, complete with three outliers, stands within a boggy terrain called Druid's Field. We noticed that one or two of the megaliths were etched with mysterious straight lines, reminiscent of the Nazca Lines in Peru, which some researchers believe map the earth's energetic pathways.

As we began to dowse Bride's flow, serenaded by a cuckoo, we detected her passing through a stone in the southeast of the circle to the centre before looping sharply to another stone in the circle's southwest quadrant. We also detected an unknown male energy line crossing with Bride at the centre as it enters from the east. The tallest megalithic outlier stands 129 ft (40 m) from the circle to the southwest, seemingly marking the setting sun on the winter solstice. The smallest and closest of the three outliers, located southeast of the ring, heralds the sun's rising at the winter solstice.

As we rechecked our compass bearings, we were surprised to discover a magnetic anomaly at one of the easternmost stones of the

Lochbuie stone circle

circle that deflected the compass needle 45 degrees. Interestingly, the stone circle sits upon the Great Glen Fault that enters the island's southeastern shores at Duart Point and continues through Loch Spelve and Loch Uisg to Loch Buie. This major fault line was formed by a collision of land masses millions of years ago and runs southwest–northeast, almost precisely in line with the winter solstice sunset and the summer solstice sunrise. The enigmatic Loch Ness is part of this fault, famous for its monster and the many paranormal events occurring there, including floating balls of light.

Undoubtedly, the high energy from the fault creates a haunted atmosphere conducive to plasma encounters, morphing into little people or other creatures from folklore. For example, Lochbuie clan members, who formerly lived in the area, reported the nocturnal sounds of clattering hooves and a jingling bridle from a spectral horse. It bore a headless rider and was a renowned harbinger of death.

Just a few yards from the circle, Bride visits the high altar and font of the tiny St Kilda's Chapel consecrated in 1876 by Lairg MacLaine of Lochbuie. Although there is no historical reference to a saint called Kilda, the name may derive from the old Norse word *Kilda* or *Childa,* meaning 'the source' or spring, as in *Tobar Childe* or Kilda Well on the island of Hirta, the largest of the St Kilda archipelago. Charles Maclean, in *Island on the Edge of the World: the Story of St. Kilda,* speculates that the name may refer to the Culdees.[15] Interestingly, an 800-year-old Celtic stone cross was unearthed at a considerable depth when digging the foundations of the present church here, perhaps a remnant of an earlier Culdee settlement. It was rescued by the priest when French invaders set fire to the earlier church in 1870.

Before leaving Lochbuie, Bride passes through the site of a cairn next to a beach and a local spring called *Tobar Chaluim Chille* or St Columba's Well. We located this long-forgotten spring just under a mile away next to a footpath that follows the shores of Loch Buie towards Carsaig.

Bride continues her journey west through the wild and watery landscape of Brolass that forms part of the Ross of Mull, the island's southernmost peninsula. Here she visits a waterfall called *Eas Mòr* or 'Great Falls', on a tributary of Beach River. The Ross of Mull is a rugged elevated tongue of land formed from layers of lava and seams of Devonian pink granite.

We detect the current again near the hamlet of Mons and the site of an old well, now long gone, just north of the village of Bunessan. She then sweeps across Loch na Láthaich to the tiny island of *Eilean Bán,* or 'White Island', before reaching Creich and the smooth red granite rocks of Tòrr Mòr on Mull's extreme western shores overlooking the holy isle of Iona. A pier once stood here to ship the stone from the Tòrr Mòr quarry to other parts of Europe.

After absorbing the potent and revitalising power of the red rocks, the female serpent heads towards Iona, passing over the Sound to *Eilean nam Ban* or 'women's island'. Its name supposedly derives from a local tradition that *'St Columba suffered no women to stay in Iona',* but compelled all the monks' wives, daughters and sisters to live in this little neighbouring isle, where traces of a building called The Nunnery is still visible. Columba reputedly said, *'Where there was a cow there was a woman; and where there was a woman, there was mischief and trouble'.*[16] Although celibacy was the rule within the community of monks on Iona, marriage existed among the Celtic Christian secular community. Interestingly, Iona itself has also been referred to by the Gaelic name *Ì nam ban bòidheach,* meaning 'the isle of beautiful women', which contradicts this local tradition. We wondered whether Eilean nam Ban refers to the legendary Celtic Isle of the Nine Maidens, mentioned by folklorist Stuart McHardy. As the Bride current crosses the spectacular Sound of Iona towards a world-renowned abbey, we were sad that this fascinating and life-changing journey following the majestic and wise feminine serpent across the idyllic Northumberland landscape and the historic neck of Scotland would soon be ending.

The Cave of the Goddess and Tòrr Mòr

The following day, we returned to the eastern reaches of the Ross of Mull to locate Lugh as he entered Mull from the direction of the Garvellachs. According to our remote dowsing, he appeared to be heading for the rocky basalt cliffs at Carsaig Bay, about 5 miles (8 km) southwest of Bride at Lochbuie. After following the A849 west from Craignure, we turned south at Pennyghael along a narrow road to the little hamlet of Carsaig. After leaving our car near the pier, we arrived at a tiny beach, its dramatic rocks framing the tranquil waters of the Firth of Lorne and the distant islands of Colonsay, Jura and Islay to the south.

The Holy Axis alignment also meets us here as it crosses the Ross of Mull to Carsaig Arches. Muddy and rocky paths lead the walker just under 4 miles west along the bay from Carsaig towards the Nun's Cave and the Carsaig Arches. This stunningly beautiful area of Mull's southern coast is home to golden eagles, buzzards, kestrels and feral goats, a relic of a time past when these animals were among the first to be domesticated on the island. Also, due to the remoteness of the area and the lack of disturbance, otters and the inquisitive common seal often provide amusing entertainment if you are lucky to get close to them.

We located Lugh at the Nun's Cave, with basalt columns forming its V-shaped entrance. It acquired its name after a group of nuns took refuge here, having been driven out of Iona during the Reformation. However, its Gaelic name *Uamh nan Cailleach* means 'The Cave of the (winter) Goddess' and on the cave's west wall are various carvings of holy symbols, some of which are believed to date from the 6th to 9th centuries. Several of them are close to the cave's floor, suggesting it had risen considerably over the years. There are also two masons' marks, supposedly carved by stonemasons in the 18th or 19th century.

The cave emanates a powerful energy due perhaps to the presence of the Lugh current and the geology formed from layers of highly crystalline sandstone and basalt. The atmosphere is further enhanced by the pounding waves below and two waterfalls cascading on either side of the cave's entrance. Under certain conditions, an energetic environment of this kind can induce one to higher states of consciousness, which may explain the reverence attached to so many sea caves around Britain by our ancient ancestors. The shamans and hermits of old regarded these deep caverns as places of initiation.

The Carsaig Arches, marking the alignment just 2 miles further west, take the form of columnar-jointed rock faces formed during prolonged volcanic activity around 60 million years ago. According to one source, '*Successive flows of lava, over at least a 5-million-year period, were extruded from fissures onto Mull's land surface, covering an extensive area of basement rocks. Where the lava has cooled and contracted, pentagonal and hexagonal-sided columns formed*.'[17]

Lugh then heads inland from the cave in a westerly direction across the Ross of Mull to visit Kilvickeon Kirk, a ruined church in a remote yet picturesque setting near Loch Assapool southeast of the village of Bunessan. It was constructed in the 12th century by Benedictine monks from Iona. Its original Gaelic name *Cill Mhic Eòghainn* means 'Church of the son of Ernan' or St Eoghan, a nephew of St Columba. The connection with the Iona saint may indicate an earlier Celtic church or hermitage on this site.

Carsaig Arches

The stone slabs and rounded boulders within its walls are reminiscent of those found in the 9th-century St Oran's Chapel on Iona. A circular stone dyke once surrounded the church and burial ground with a north-facing entrance. Stone pegs in the north wall are all that remain of its original thatch roof, used to secure it with ropes during the frequent gales and storms. However, its most impressive feature is the very weathered carving of a sheela-na-gig, one of only five still in existence in Scotland, also set into the north wall to the left of the main entrance. Sources have described the figure as having hands in its lap and a pointed chin, possibly referring to a beard. However, on closer

Kilvickeon Kirk

inspection, the figure displays what we believe to be hunched shoulders with arms holding open an oval depression, which is most likely a vulva. Sheela-na-gig carvings in many churches around Britain and Ireland are remnants of their pagan past, said to represent the fertility of the Earth Goddess. The exposure of the vulva is perhaps symbolic of the gateway to rebirth through the Yoni of the Goddess, the womb of regeneration.

There were once many finely carved gravestones in the churchyard, of which only a few survive. One has Celtic designs and an image of a rose, the other commemorating a lady called Marieta, the daughter of a nobleman who lived early in the 16th century. At some point, it disappeared, but a replica lies in protective housing inside the entrance to the graveyard.

Marking the alignment just north of here is *An Caisteal Dun,* an Iron Age hillfort located on the summit of a rocky crag projecting from the steep northern slope of *Torr a Bhacain.* It still has traces

Sheela-na-gig, Kilvickeon Kirk

of a dry-stone wall and remnants of two large stone slabs are thought to be its entrance stones. Further west, a standing stone near Tiraghoil also marks the Holy Axis.

We follow Lugh across heather and gorse-strewn moorland to a tiny Victorian church at Aridhglas, also dedicated to St Ernan or Eoghan. Saint Ernan was formerly a prince of Donegal and one of twelve followers who came with Columba to set up and manage the Iona monastery.

Further west, we arrived at the village of Fionnphort, where visitors congregate to take the ferry to Iona. Lugh flows through the southern edge of Tòrr Mòr Quarry and an old burial ground before continuing to a solitary large erratic

Standing stone near Tiraghoil

boulder on the beach deposited during the Ice Age. The boulder, known as 'Fingal's Rock', is a cherished local landmark and has a significant split through its centre. Fingal, in legend, resided in a cave on the nearby Isle of Staffa and built the Giant's Causeway in Ireland, creating a land bridge to Scotland before the sea washed it away. Interestingly, the basalt geology that forms the Giant's Causeway runs under the sea to Staffa. Fingal supposedly rested against this boulder on his journey from Ireland to Staffa and, after waking in a foul temper, picked up the rock and threw it in the air. As a result, it came crashing onto the beach and almost split in two. The locals also call it 'The Swordstone', having the appearance of being cleaved clean in two.

The beautiful smooth red granite rocks of Tòrr Mòr, formed over 400 million years by the constant rubbing of glaciers during the Ice Age, attract both the Lugh and Bride serpent currents, now only half a mile away from each other. Many of the boulders stand as tall stone sentinels, like some lost megalithic city awaiting discovery. The pink granite is formed from molten magma, which crystallised and cooled several miles beneath the Earth's surface. It consists of pink and creamy white feldspar, grey quartz and black mica. When freshly quarried, it is bright pink, which soon fades and erodes due to constant weathering and the acidic peaty water. The Holy Axis alignment passes through the heart of Tòrr Mòr quarry and is very close to Fingal's Rock or the Swordstone, where we last dowsed Lugh. This mighty rock perfectly symbolises the essence of the 'spear-like' Holy Axis, the split in the rock perhaps representing Lugh's magical sword.

A wall of expertly cut pieces of granite in the quarry once formed the abutment of a bridge spanning the trackway that leads down to the pier, reminding us of the ancient walls within Peru's Inca monuments, but on a much smaller scale of course. Hidden in the smooth rocks south of the pier, above the beach, is the 'Cave of the Dead', once used to shelter the coffins of kings and warriors on their final journey to Iona.

As we boarded the little ferry at Fionnphort, we looked wistfully towards the red granite rocks where the Bride and Lugh serpents leave the Isle of Mull. We had a strong

Red granite rocks of Tòrr Mòr

359

sense that these exceptional rocks have helped cleanse and revitalise their flow in readiness for their journey to one of the most sacred isles in the Western World, considered the real Avalon of Britain.

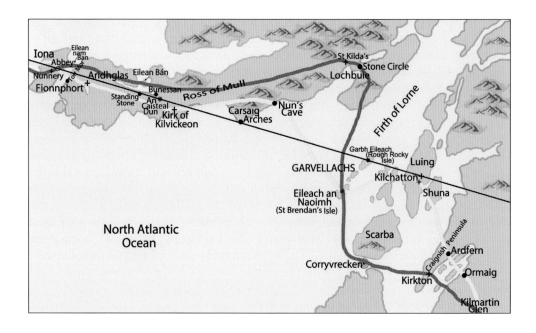

1. Elder, I. H. 1962. *Celt, Druid and Culdee.* Covenant Publishing, London.
2. 8. McNeill, M. F. 1957. *The Silver Bough: Scottish Folklore and Folk-belief.* William Maclellan (Embryo) Ltd, Ash, UK.
3. https://www.scribd.com/author/230366102/Jennifer-Emick
4. Davies, Sioned. 2008. *The Mabinogion.* Oxford World's Classics.
5. 7. McHardy, S. 2006. *On the Trail of the Holy Grail.* Luath Press Ltd, Edinburgh.
6. McArthur, Hugh, D. P. 2010. *Arthur's Battle against the Whirlpool: An Ancient History of the Corryvreckan.* clanarthur.com
9. http://theorionzone.blogspot.com/2009/02/epsilon-eridani-zalos.html
10. McArthur, Hugh. D. P. 2021. *Close Encounters of the Natural Kind.* Independently published.
11. Gillies, P. H. 2019. *Netherlorn, Argyllshire and its Neighbourhood.* Wentworth Press, London.
12. 14. 16. Adomnan of Iona, Richard Sharpe, (Introduction, Translator) 1995. *Life of St Columba.* Penguin Classics, London.
13. Biltcliffe, G. & Hoare, C. 2018. *The Power of Centre.* Sacred Lands Publishing, Weymouth. https://canmore.org.uk/site/22361/garvellachs-eileach-an-naoimh
15. MacLean, C. 2019. *Island on the Edge of the World: The Story of St Kilda.* Canongate Books, Edinburgh.
17. https://www.isle-of-mull.net/things-to-do/geology/carsaig-arches/

Chapter 16

Iona, the Isle of Dreams

'History and legend meet here:
the secular and the holy join forces,
and the fabric and geography conspire.'

Frank Delaney

The Holy Isle of Iona

Ten years have passed since we first set out from Bamburgh Castle to follow the Holy Axis and its male and female serpents across the enchanted lands of Northumberland, the Lothians, the Trossachs and the Western Isles to reach our final destination, Iona. We could relate to the legendary Lancelot, who left his castle Joyous Gard at Bamburgh and witnessed many mysteries of the Grail along the way.

For us, the journey was a fascinating pilgrimage, enthralling and at times frustrating, discovering long-lost sites and renowned places of mystery and power. So many of them have inspired and captivated us, like the eerie moors of Doddington filled with mysterious prehistoric rock art, the lost megaliths of College Valley, the sacred shrine at Stowe and, of course, Scotland's Grail chapel at Roslin Glen and the Neolithic valley of the kings at Kilmartin Glen. The symbolism of the Grail has followed us ever westwards, even when entering the turbulent, dangerous seas of the Corryvreckan whirlpool guarded by the crone goddess Cailleach.

In many ways, the parallels between the holy island sanctuaries of Lindisfarne and Inner Farne, which mark the beginning of our journey, and Eileach an Naoimh and Iona that signal its end, emulated the experience of our east–west pilgrimage of the Holy Axis. For instance, Inner Farne, where we discovered the first node of the serpents Bride and Lugh in the British Isles, is symbolically a place of 'birthing'. Thousands of birds come here each year to breed and raise their young. In contrast, the sanctuaries of Eileach an Naoimh and Iona are places of termination, where many renowned warriors, saints, and kings and queens of old were brought for burial, including Scotland's King Arthur.

In the east, the Holy Axis is marked in the skies by the rising stars of the cosmic deities Orion and Virgo. In the west, the alignment points to where they set into the North Atlantic Ocean beyond Iona. At many sites along this magical pathway, we have connected with Orion's spiritual warrior aspect and Virgo's goddess archetype, Lugh and Bride. Accompanying us were warrior kings and saintly monks of Urien, Edwin, Oswald, Artuir, Aidan, Cuthbert, Kessog and finally, Columba, whose holy island we were about to explore.

Many ancient Celtic myths and legends are associated with this beautiful island, although nowadays Iona is perhaps more famous as the birthplace of Christianity in Scotland. For that reason, it receives thousands of visitors from all over the world every year, who arrive in their droves, day-in-day-out, come rain or shine, from the small ferry at Fionnphort on Mull. However, there is more to its appeal than just its natural splendour and Celtic traditions, for there is hidden in its earth and rocks a magical secret, engendering an atmosphere of enchantment that is veiled and can only be sensed.

For many visitors, a trip to Iona is a short excursion lasting a couple of hours with just enough time to explore the famous abbey and the graveyard of kings, enjoy a walk and cup of tea before heading back to the ferry to catch the last bus back to Craignure. However, for those who can spend a few days here to walk its paths and sample its

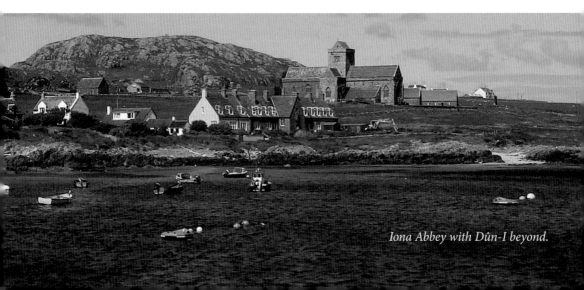

Iona Abbey with Dûn-I beyond.

more remote places, Iona will enchant you. In fact, many visitors and residents have encountered strange happenings here, so we were not surprised to discover that the island, like so many other special places associated with the Holy Axis, is one of those thin veil or etheric 'window' areas, where otherworldly beings might lure you to their secret realms.

Iona is just over three miles long and a mile and a half wide, separated from Mull by the Sound of Iona, a narrow straight of water formed from a geological fault called the Moine Thrust. The immense telluric power of Iona stems from the unique qualities of its ancient metamorphic stone, a type of granite called Lewisian Gneiss. The island is born from a sudden upthrust of this solid rock and remarkably contained not one fossil, forming on the Earth's crust over 2900 million years ago, older even than the rocks of Mull, which only date back 300 million years.

The geology of the island is what makes Iona so unique. Granite under pressure emits high magnetic fields that create an environment conducive to connecting with one's higher consciousness and the Universe. It can also manifest plasma intelligence, which thrives in this highly electromagnetic environment. The power of silica quartz crystal is abundant in Iona's geology and contains different types of marble and serpentine. The more adventurous visitor to the island's fabulous white sandy beaches on its north and west coast will encounter the fruits of this unique geology in the form of spectacular-coloured jewel-like pebbles.

In modern and old Celtic lore, Iona is the 'Island of Dreams' or the 'Isle of Avalon', where Arthur or Artuir, son of Aedan, lies buried. In *The Green Stone*, Graham Philips and Martin Keatman mention an Egyptian green stone or 'Grail stone' taken to the island by a Celtic Iron Age warrior called Gwydion. This small oval-shaped piece of jade remained hidden for centuries until it was retrieved from Iona by John Fitzwarrins, a Knights Templar who received a vision of its whereabouts.[1] He then took it to a preceptory near Biddulph in Staffordshire, which happens to be close to the Elen current and the Belinus Line. In Wolfram von Eschenbach's *Parzival*, the Holy Grail is not a vessel or chalice but a translucent green stone, exactly like the stone retrieved from Iona by Fitzwarrins.

Eo is one of the earliest names for Iona and was still in use in the 9th century when a German monk wrote:

'On the Pictish coast is an isle of the sea,
Floating amidst the waves, Eo is its name,
Where rests the body of the Lord's saint, Columba.'[2]

Eo in Irish Gaelic means 'yew', a tree sacred to the Druids and the dead. Authors Coppens and Moffat conclude that Iona is a modification of *Ioua* or *Iova*, which means 'Yew Island'. However, it was known to be devoid of trees during the Viking raids, and there are no yews on the island today. Perhaps during its prolonged period of settlement, all the trees were felled for building and heating fuel. If so, hardy trees like the yew would struggle to re-establish themselves on such a windswept island. Nevertheless, some of its Celtic place names hint at the existence of yews and pollen analysis shows that a variety of trees grew here when long ago the climate was warmer and the soil more fertile.

In *Iona: A History of the Island,* Florence McNeill wrote that *Ioua* derives from the Pictish *I-shona* or *Ii-shona,* pronounced Ee-hona, meaning 'the isle of saints'.[3] Whereas, others translate it as 'Isle of the Blessed' or 'Fortunate Isles'. Thomas Pennant attributes the name Iona to the Hebrew word *Yonā* or *Jona,* pronounced 'Iona' meaning dove or pigeon.[4] From the air, the island could appear as a dove, a symbolic representation of the spirit or soul. It is also said to resemble a fish, symbolic of the Age of Pisces. We are now edging into the Age of Aquarius, the 'cupbearer', who, like the goddess Bride, brings forth her overflowing cup or cauldron to pour healing, knowledge and change into the Earth's energy matrix.

At one time, the island's name was *Inchcolm* or Columba's Isle. Most people believe St Columba came from Irish nobility and established a monastic Celtic Christian community on Iona in 563 CE. However, there is evidence that the island was a sanctuary for earlier religions, as another name for Iona was *Innis-nam Druidbneach* or 'Isle of the Druids'. The Druids were worshippers of nature, particularly at mounds, wells and springs, and their names and settlements are found all over the island, including its cairns and the hillforts of Dûn'I and Dun Bhuirg.

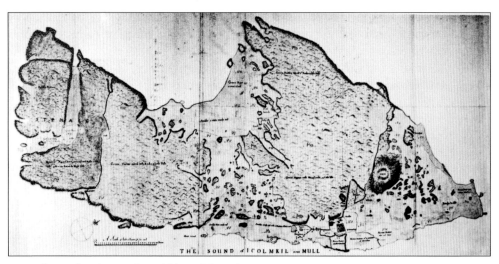

Map of Iona dated 1769 shaped like a fish or dove

In 83 CE, Demetrius of Tarsus sailed through the area to survey the lands for Emperor Domitian. He described a small island used as a retreat for 'holy men' who were considered of pure mind and heart by the area's indigenous people.[5]

Scottish philosopher and historian Hector Boece (1465–1536) discovered an ancient manuscript from the library in Iona.[6] He refers to this lost book in *Historia Gentis Scotorum* (History of the Scottish People), which states that Scottish King Fergus II assisted Alaric the Goth in the sacking of Rome in 412 CE and presented many ancient books to the monastery at Iona. Although little credence is given to this by other historians, if true, a monastery may have existed here before Columba's arrival belonging to the Culdees.[7] Columba himself was an avid book translator, establishing a scriptorium on the island where his monks copied manuscripts from around the world.

Remnants of an old monastic earthwork boundary called the *Vallum* are visible in the abbey precinct and during excavations in 1988, radiocarbon dating of the peaty topsoil beneath it recorded its period of construction as the 1st or 2nd century CE. The earthwork was probably the spiritual boundary of a very early monastery with wooden buildings built by the Culdees, which Columba may have taken for his own. In Manus O'Donnell's *Life of Colom Cille*, Columba expelled two bishops who demanded his submission when first arriving on Iona.[8] The possibility of the existence of a Culdee monastery dating back to the first century may substantiate a story told by a man from the island of Tiree recorded by Fiona McLeod. He stated that Mary Magdalene came to Iona together with a blind woman who was on the run from her jealous husband. He eventually caught up with them and killed his blind wife, and although Mary survived the attack, she died of a broken heart. After her grave was discovered by a monk, Columba, knowing her true identity, had her remains secretly buried in a cave on Iona.[9] Perhaps this story is an allegorical clue relating to Iona being a place of goddess worship, which Columba later banished.

Isabel Hill Elder wrote that many Christians were forced to flee the Holy Land by sea during the Roman persecution, taking the old established trade routes to Europe and Britain. They were referred to as Pythagorean Essenes inspired by Gnosticism, a form of Christianity linked with the Petrine Church of Rome known as Coptic. They also had strong links with the Royal House of David, which would have included Jesus and Mary Magdalene.

The Druids, having foreseen the coming of a future saviour called Hesus, instantly embraced the Gnostic faith brought by these strangers from the Holy Land. They later became known as the Culdees and successfully merged their teachings with Druid lore, corresponding to the original structure of the Celtic Church.

By 156 CE, the Culdees established themselves as the natural successors of Druidism. Many peace-loving Druids, already highly educated in the ancient classics, soon became Culdee priests, building their monastic communities over recognised Druidic shrines.

They honoured the existence of the Supreme Being, the creator of all things, and believed in the evolvement of the soul and life after death. They built circular huts and temples to imitate stone circles and Druid groves, paying heed to the broader cosmic significance of the number twelve, their settlements consisting of twelve monks modelled on the twelve original disciples.[10]

When Celtic Christianity first came to Ireland and Wales, its missionaries incorporated many of their monasteries into existing Druidic colleges. It was in one of these colleges in Ireland that Columba became a student under St Finnian of Clonard and very likely learned of the Essenes and their association with Mary Magdalene. Like Bran and St Patrick before him, Columba attended a Gorsedd of Bards where he pleaded the case for a new form of Druidism, the teaching of Jesus Christ, and declared, '*Christ is my Druid; he is my true miracle worker.*'[11]

At twenty-five, he became a chief advocate for the Celtic Church and climbed the ecclesiastical ladder. Columba was a shrewd politician, and according to historians, he advised warlords how to behave, predicted when they would die and showed an ungodly fascination with the outcome of their battles. Stuart McHardy wrote that he was an unscrupulous manipulator and saw himself as a replacement for the old pagan war gods, a far cry from the true teachings of Jesus, who preached mercy and dissociation from violence.

What followed was his exile from Ulster for provoking a battle between the northern and southern Irish tribes. After a local pagan chieftain violated the sanctity of one of his churches, St Columba pursued him and had him put to death. A conflict between pagans and Christians ensued, which saw the deaths of three thousand pagans for the loss of one Christian. Before the battle, he dreamed that the Archangel Michael appeared to him, promising him victory if, in return, he would make amends

St Columba converting King Brudei of the Picts to Christianity by William Hole c.1899

by 'going out of sight of Ireland' to spread the word of God to the pagans over the sea.

Iona's monastery produced some of the finest illuminated manuscripts, including *The Book of Kells*. However, its actual date and place of origin have been the subject of much debate. Before being ransacked by the Vikings, Iona's workshops were manufacturing some of the finest metalwork and jewellery, and today they are mislabelled in museum showcases worldwide. For example, the Ardagh Chalice found in Ireland has similarities in its designs of items made in the workshops of Iona.

Book of Kells, the Chi Rho page c.800 CE

Many monks died defending their precious sanctuary against the Vikings in 795, and Iona's 'Martyr's Bay' and 'Strand of the Monks' are reminders of that time. Those who survived fled to Kells in Ireland, perhaps taking the Book of Kells and the Ardagh Chalice with them. It also supposedly ended up in the hands of the monks of Lindisfarne

Before the Synod of Whitby in 664, Christianity in Britain existed in two forms distinguished by differing types of service, labelled the 'Ionian' and 'Roman' traditions. They coexisted in the Anglian Kingdom of Northumbria, encouraged by the various ruling monarchs. King Edwin initially established Christianity in his realm after his conversion by Paulinus, a missionary sent from Rome. After his death, however, King Oswald reinstated the Celtic Christian practice through Aidan, having spent time with the monks of Iona during his exile there.

Iona lost its power as a political and spiritual centre when the Pictish and Dal Riata nations became a single kingdom under Kenneth MacAlpin. Having proved himself against the Vikings and carrying Pictish and Gaelic blood, he became known as the 'founding father of Scotland'. The new king moved the Celtic Church from Iona to Dunkeld in the Tay Valley and transferred St Columba's remains to its cathedral. Just as the body of St Cuthbert became a talisman of the Celtic Church, Columba was seen as 'an indispensable talisman of Gaelic success'.[12]

During the reign of King Malcolm Canmore and Queen Margaret (1058–1093), the monastery's survival was assured when Augustinian monks were invited to rebuild the abbey. However, further Viking attacks saw Iona once again in the hands of the Norse rulers. Despite this, the monastic community endured, becoming part of a new 'Kingdom of the Isles' ruled over by a Norse-Gaelic chieftain called Somerled in the mid-12th century. His son Ranald allowed the Benedictine order to establish a grand abbey over the site of the monastery, destroying any archaeological remains from Columba's time. He is also credited with the building of St Oran's Chapel next to the old burial site of ancient kings.

Dowsing at the Abbey

From *Eilean nam Ban* or Isle of the Woman, Bride enters Iona's eastern shore at *Port an Diseirt* or 'Port of the Hermitage'. Perhaps this name refers to a long-lost Culdee cell that existed during or before St Columba's time. She then heads towards Iona Abbey to the ruined remains and earthworks of *Tigh an Easbuig*, the old Bishop's House built in 1499. It was formerly the residence of the bishops of the Isles and was intact in the second half of the 18th century.

Iona Abbey from Abbot's Hill

Within the abbey precincts, the female current enters the northeast corner of the old infirmary, now the museum, displaying some of the finest examples of medieval carved crosses and gravestones in Scotland. We were excited to find her flow inside the museum connecting with a piece of the broken base of an old cross called the *clach-bràth* or 'Judgement Stone', originally located outside St Oran's Chapel. It is also referred to as *Clachan-nan-Druidhean* or Druid's Stone and the 'World's End Stone'. It is possibly one of the island's most important historical relics, and Bride guided us to its precise location. Marian McNeill's *Iona: A History of the Island* (1954) mentions that:

'Near the edge of the path leading to St. Oran's Chapel, there lies a broad, flat stone with a slit and a cavity on its surface. Here there used to lie some small round stones which pilgrims were wont to turn sunwise within the cavity; for it was commonly believed that the "brath", or end of the world, would not arrive until this stone should be worn through.'[13]

Major-General James Forlong's in *Faiths of Men* recalls its mythic origin:

'In Iona, the Druids are said to have made the flat altar stone called Clachan-nan-Druidhean, or Druid's Stone, the stone of fate or of the last day, with round stones fitted into cup hollows on the surface, which the pious pilgrim turns round. The world will end when the stone is worn through. The Culdee monks preserved this monument.'[14]

This remarkable stone records a ritual that began in Celtic times, which survived to the Christian era and continued into the 19th century. The local clergy supposedly threw the original white quartz stones to grind the cavities into the sea.

The practice of grinding stones was somehow integral to initiation at sacred sites performed before entering a Druid grove or perhaps a stone circle and later a Christian church. One wonders if this ancient custom continued from a time when Neolithic or Bronze Age tribes ground quartz stones into rocks to make the mysterious cup and ring marked stones found at many ceremonial sites associated with the Holy Axis.

The Judgement Stone is similar to the Irish bullaun stones that stood near the old churches and round towers. A bullaun, also known as St Brigid's Stones, is a hollowed-out stone that either collected rainwater for healing or held white quartz pebbles turned for divination. Many of these stones survive in Ireland, but have since disappeared in Scotland and are largely overlooked by historians.

The clach-bràth stood at one time near the doorway of St Oran's Chapel, the earliest stone building on the island. This may be significant, for the graveyard of St Oran's Chapel, known as *Reilig Odhráin*, marks the Holy Axis. It was the traditional burial place for the kings of Dal Riata, the Picts and the Lords of the Isles. Furthermore, we believe this stone links to the island's fate, which, according to Iona's folklore, will rise above the waves of a future 'second flood' that will inundate the world.

'Seven years before the judgment,
The sea shall sweep over Erin at one tide,
And over blue-green Isla;
But I of Colum of the Church shall swim.'[15]

From the museum, Bride passes diagonally through the nearby Michael Chapel, initially built in the 1200s as a temporary place of worship for the monks of Iona whilst their new abbey church was under construction. What you see today is modern restoration preserving the original 13th-century structure and still retains its 16th-century windows. Today, it serves as an alternative place of worship to the less intimate abbey church. Its best features are its medieval doorway and the exquisitely carved bishop's chair.

We next locate the current in the chapter house, of which very little of the original layout remains, now used for meetings and workshops. Bride continues through the cloisters, rebuilt in 1938 during a new era of abbey restoration inspired by Revd George

MacLeod, which managed to retain many finely carved medieval features. We noticed various contemporary carvings on the capitals of the arches. One, in particular, caught our eye directly on Bride's flow, that of a female head with flowing hair. The carvings by the Jedburgh-based sculptor Chris Hall were commissioned by the Iona Community in 1967 and completed in 1997. They mainly depict birds, flora and fauna native to the Western Isles and subjects from the Bible. However, one or two are more unusual, including one called 'The offering of Wine', the carving of the wine goblet reminiscent of a Grail cup. Perhaps the sculptor was inspired by the Grail energy of Bride, having spent many years working in the cloisters.

Another beautiful artwork on Bride's serpent flow stands at the centre of the cloister garden. The bronze sculpture by the Lithuanian artist Jacques Lipchitz (1959) is entitled 'Descent of the Spirit', which shows the Virgin Mary descending to earth in a starry cloud carried by the Holy Spirit in the form of a dove supported by animals, birds and humans. At this point, we expected the female flow to divert away from her southwesterly flow and enter the abbey's nave. Instead, her width started to narrow as she approached the southwest corner of the cloisters to a small external building next to the abbey's main west entrance. This shrinkage meant only one thing – we were about to discover a node. At this point, we felt it necessary to reconnect with Lugh, so returned to the eastern shore to pinpoint his arrival.

Carving in Iona Abbey Cloisters called 'The offering of Wine' (courtesy of Holger Uwe Schmitt)

St Columba's Shrine

We dowsed the male current entering the island just north of the ruined remains of a medieval chapel dedicated to St Mary, hidden amongst long grass in a field between the abbey and the sea. Lugh's main focus is the site of an ancient healing spring called *Tobar a' Cheathain*, or the Well of Ceathan or Kian. Sadly, the well is now concrete-lined and covered over. An old rhyme relating to the well says, '*nor did he wish to drink anything, but the good water of Ceathan.*'[16] In an online article entitled *In Search of the*

Lost Wells of Iona, Mike Small identified the existence of eighteen wells on Iona, many having since disappeared, dried up, or like Ceathan's Well, concreted over.[17]

Lugh passes through the abbey's east window and follows the central aisle to the northwest corner of the nave. We noticed his flow is marked by a dragon carving on a capital with foliage coming from its mouth and another of Adam and Eve next to the Tree of Life.

We also notice carvings of two entwined serpents on one of the finely decorated panels of the font near the main entrance and another with the heads of four snakes kissing. Deep pink granite blocks quarried from the Tòrr Mòr on Mull are incorporated into the abbey's walls, giving the building a rosy etheric glow.

King Ranald (1164–1207), son of Norse-Gaelic warlord Somerled, restored many of Iona's monastic buildings, including the abbey and nunnery, when introducing Benedictine monks to the island. Ranald's second son, Donald, established Clan Donald and eventually reclaimed the title of Lord of the Isles in 1354. Iona later passed to Archibald Campbell, 8th Earl and First Marquess of Argyll (1607–1661), who allowed the monastic buildings to slowly fall into ruin and 'dispersed the valuable, irreplaceable library.' Precious grave slabs of the old kings lay scattered about St Oran's burial ground, and many were increasingly damaged or stolen by visitors.

Carvings in Iona Abbey Church, one showing a dragon with foliage coming from its mouth (courtesy of Holger Uwe Schmitt)

It took until 1874 for the 8th Duke of Argyll to finally protect the site and commissioned the architect Robert Rowand Anderson to oversee repairs to the abbey ruins. Then, in 1965, the Iona Cathedral Trust took ownership of Iona's religious buildings, completing the restoration.

The male serpent begins to narrow as it disappears through the northwest corner of the nave to meet with Bride at a node inside a tiny stone chapel called St Columba's Shrine, attached to the west wall of the abbey next to the main entrance.

The 8th or 9th-century chapel that once housed St Columba's Shrine has under the wooden floor two stone coffins – supposedly belonging to Columba and

Old photograph of Iona Abbey and St Oran's Chapel in a ruinous state, 1899

370

one of his successors. Upon the centenary of Columba's death, the monks placed his bones in a silver and gold shrine that attracted pilgrims from all over Europe. An artist's sketch of the shrine depicts it set over the node at the very entrance of the shrine. We often find saint's relics on serpent currents, for example, St Swithun in Winchester Cathedral and St Chad in Birmingham both on the Belinus current.

St Columba's Shrine on node

We were curious by a description in Adomnan's *Life of St Columba*, '..for the place where his bones rest are still visited by the lights of heaven and by numbers of angels.'[18] Was he describing the power of the relic or the node, or the manifestation of plasma intelligence morphing as angels from the archetypal collective consciousness?

When the King of Norway, Magnus Barelegs, raided Iona in 1098, he opened the shrine of Columba but refused to venture inside. Terrified, he locked the door and declared, '*none should be so daring thenceforward to go into that church*.' What did this brave warrior see to make him so alarmed? Was it a ball of plasma hovering over the shrine?

During Viking raids, Iona's monastic buildings suffered severe destruction, with many of its bishops and monks killed by the marauders. However, they must have considered it holy ground as later Norse settles converted to Christianity and several of their kings were buried in Reilig Odhráin.[19]

We wondered what might have marked the node before Columba's time. The Revd George F Macleod, who established the Iona Community in 1938, researched much of Iona's history and traditions and believed a stone circle stood on the site of the abbey and shrine. Some sources say the megaliths were taken away and carved into crosses, and at the Reformation, sixty were thrown into the sea. However, past historians and visitors to the island describe a mystical black stone leaning on one of the outside walls of the shrine used as an oracle or oath stone.

Perhaps this was the famous Lia Fáil or Stone of Destiny, as earlier descriptions say it was a black meteoritic stone. The Lia Fáil was probably used as an inauguration stone on which Columba crowned Artuir's father, Aedan. After the coronation of this new king of the Dal Riata, the black stone was supposedly moved to their stronghold at Dunstaffnage Castle near Oban.

The crowds of visitors made dowsing the node very difficult, but thankfully, we discovered a small room directly above the shrine where we meditated in relative silence. Despite the island's traumatic past and the destruction of the stone circle and abbey, the node point still radiates a vital power. Perhaps the projected pious healing and loving thoughts of the Druids, the Culdees and Columba's followers are still strongly retained within the land here. Likewise, the prayers of modern pilgrims visiting the abbey also contribute to the healing and honouring of this unique site. Through their teachings, the Druids had knowledge of the Earth's subtle energies and how to positively imbue the serpent earth currents with love and light.

From the node point, Lugh passes through a replica cross of St John the Evangelist in front of the abbey entrance; the original dates to around 800 CE and is now in the abbey museum. In medieval times there were many such crosses on the island where pilgrims on their way to Columba's shrine would stop and pray. St Martin's Cross still stands in its original socket to the west of the abbey, carved with vines, ornamental circles, flowers and scenes from the gospels. The crosses were carved by expert stonemasons, having been established on the island from the earliest times. In fact, the Freemasonic Royal Order of Scotland maintains that the earliest lodge formed in Britain was not Kilwinning but Icolmkill, an early name for Iona.[20] The Order is one of the most historic in Britain and can trace its royal roots back to Moses.

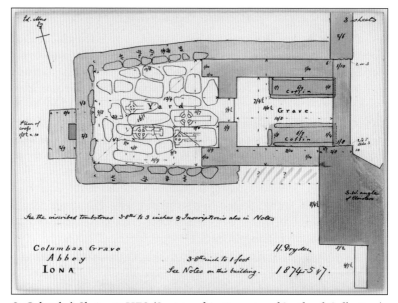

St Columba's Shrine © HES (Society of Antiquaries of Scotland Collection)

Just beyond the cross and opposite the abbey's main entrance, Lugh takes us to a rocky hillock called *Torr an Aba* or 'Abbot's Hill', considered the location of St Columba's Cell and where he later constructed a writing hut. Folklore states that when Columba first arrived, he stood on this rock and pronounced his religious authority over the island. Excavations of the mound showed it to be a natural ridge enhanced by a supporting stone wall to create a conical enclosure. According to the Canmore website, '*on the semi-artificial top of the mound a small, square cell has been built, its low stone walls carefully keyed into irregularities in the rock.*' Carbon dating of organic materials from the top of Abbot's Hill confirms a date between 540 and 650 CE, around the time of St Columba.[21]

Dûn-I and Netta's Story

From Columba's old cell, Lugh heads northwest through the abbey shop to flow across the remains of a causeway known as *Iomaire an Tachair* and through the site of Lochan Mor, a small lake and former abbey fish pond. Beyond is the imposing rock of Dûn'I, the Gaelic name for 'Hill of Iona'; standing at 331 ft (101 m) it is the island's most prominent landmark. After sweeping its southeastern slopes, the male serpent ascends to a beehive cairn on the hill's summit. According to the Canmore website, pilgrims built the cairn over many years bringing stones from other parts of the island. It was a clear sunny day when we climbed the steep slopes, so the views from the top were spectacular, with Mull to the east, Staffa and the islands of the Inner Hebrides in the north and the little island of Colonsay to the south, all clearly visible.

Dûn-I

At the summit, the Lugh serpent swings abruptly to the north, following a narrow turf track to a small peaty pool of water named 'The Well of Eternal Youth', hiding amid the bear rocks and heather. The well is said to have regenerative powers, so sitting next to it, like the many thousands of pilgrims before us, we imbued ourselves with the energy of its precious waters. The wind picked up and caused ripples in the water as we honoured the sacred spring. According to custom, the most auspicious time to drink or wash your face in the water is when the first rays of the morning sun strike the well.

The Well of Eternal Youth, Dûn'I

From the top of Dûn'I, looking southwest, we could see another prominent ridge called *Druim an Aoineidh* with *Carn Cul ri Eirinn* or 'Cairn of the Back to Ireland' on its summit. Below it is *Port a' Churaich* or 'Port of the Coracle' in St Columba's Bay, where the saint first landed.

Lugh then took us west over wet terrain and across many bogs to a hillfort on Iona's western shores called *Dùn Mhanannain* or Fort of Manannán, before heading out to sea. In the *Four Cycles of Irish Mythology*, Manannán mac Lir, meaning 'son of the sea,' was an ancient warrior sea god and king of the otherworld.[22] He is often associated with the Tuatha Dé Danann, an elemental race of elves that brought to Ireland four treasures – the Stone of Destiny or Lia Fáil, an inauguration stone for their kings, the Spear of Lugh, which ensured their victory, the Sword of Nuadha, that spared no one and the Cauldron of Dagda, from which no company ever went away unsatisfied. Furthermore, many romantic accounts of Iona describe it as the abode of the magic cauldron of Celtic myth and legend, said to cure wounds and heal the dead.

Manannan Mac Lir was also a Druid and navigator of the seas who became the High King of the Isle of Man. He wore chainmail armour with a breastplate and cloak that made him invisible at will. On his helmet were two jewels that 'shone like the sun' and he possessed magical spears, swords, and a boat called 'Wave Sweeper' that could glide by volition.[23] His mighty steed 'Enbarr of the flowing mane' could gallop over land or sea. In folklore, the rolling mists that drop down from the mountain into the valleys are called the 'cloak of Manannan'. To be enveloped by the mist can lead one to be transported into another reality where mythical creatures and the souls of the departed dwell. So it seems apt that Lugh's last connection to this sacred isle is through a sanctuary of yet another male-warrior god.

Otta F Swire in *The Inner Hebrides and their Legends* writes that '*Iona, it would seem, first belonged to the ancient Earth-gods, but the primeval Sea-gods coveted the island and won it from them.*' She also mentions a local legend: '*Once, the bones of some huge and strange monster, obviously a dragon, were dug up in Iona – proof, it was felt, that the Sea-gods sacrificed creatures here that man never knew.*'[24]

To the north of Dûn'I is *Cnoc na Carcuil* or 'Hill of the Cell', the possible site of a Culdee beehive hut, and a sacred rock called 'Columba's Seat', also known as 'Hill of the Seat'. When visiting the stone, we felt it emanated an intense magnetism, creating a potent and heady atmosphere conducive to meditation. The beautiful stretch of white sand north of here, called *Traigh an t-Suidhe* or 'Strand of the Seat', is where the saint supposedly had many visions. The beach is well known to the islanders as a place where many energy lines converge. Unsurprisingly, visitors to this part of the island have seen many paranormal events, such as ghostly encounters and sightings of strange lights. One man believed he had experienced a time-slip when he witnessed Viking ships sailing towards the island. So realistic was this encounter that he could accurately draw the boat and its symbols, which was later confirmed as being from the 9th century. Locals refer to these time-slip experiences as 'the call of Iona', where people have found themselves lured into a 'fairy realm', which we now know are more likely to be encounters with plasma intelligences.[25]

Again, as with many other sites along the Holy Axis, geology plays an essential role in creating a conduit between dimensions. A fault line that stretches east–west from the Ross of Mull through the northern part of the Island crosses a major north–south fault known as the Moine Thrust (see Fig. 4). The considerable seismic activity of these two faults combined with Iona's powerful high quartzite pink granite and serpentine rocks has the potential to amplify the island's electromagnetic field. This phenomenon often creates an etheric 'doorway' or portal into the past, which allows spirit or light entities to pass through from parallel worlds or other dimensions.

In Reilig Odhráin, or Oran's cemetery, is a simple grave inscribed 'N.F.F. Aged 33 19th November 1929.' It is the grave of occultist Netta Emily Fornario, who was found dead on the island under mysterious circumstances, which has become a legendary tale amongst the islanders. Having travelled from London, Netta arrived on Iona the

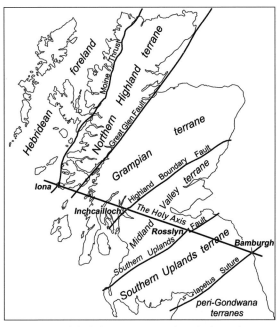

Fig. 4 Map of fault lines associated with the Holy Axis and Iona

previous August with a female companion with enough money and luggage to stay for an indefinite period. She was a member of 'Alpha et Omega', a splinter group of the famous Hermetic Order of the Golden Dawn, a secret society devoted to occult ritual magic, tarot cards, mysticism, telepathy and a strong belief in fairies. The couple found lodgings with a Mrs MacRae, who often took visitors under her roof.

Over the next few months, Netta wandered around the island, visiting sacred sites and places steeped in mysterious folklore and legend, where she engaged in supernatural practices. Until the morning of Sunday 17 November, when Mrs MacRae arose to find her hurriedly packing her luggage, saying she had to return to London immediately. She explained that several people on the island were attacking her by psychic means forcing her to leave.

Many islanders who befriended Netta over the months thought she was an eccentric, especially after hearing of her visions and contact with spirit lights. However, there was nothing odd about Netta's appearance that morning except that her silver jewellery had suddenly tarnished overnight. After quickly leaving her lodgings, she walked down to the jetty even though there was no ferry that day. Later she returned, saying she had received a message to stay and went back to her room and unpacked her things. She then sent a very cryptic message to her London housekeeper saying that she would not be home anytime soon as she had 'a terrible case of healing to deal with' and left for a late afternoon walk.

The following morning she was nowhere to be seen, her bed had not been slept in and all her belongings were neatly folded. A day later, two local men found her lifeless body beside a fairy mound in a hollow area called the Slopes, between A' Mhachair and Loch Staoineig. She was naked except for a black cloak and her feet were covered in scratches, a knife also lay nearby and a cross cut into the grass. However, on the night before her discovery, people witnessed strange blue lights hovering over the area of Loch Staoineig, and a mysterious cloaked stranger was seen accompanying her days before her death.[26]

This story is reminiscent of clergyman Robert Kirk, who was found dead on a fairy knowe called Doon Hill on the Bride flow, who famously claimed to have communed with elementals there. Doon Hill near Aberfoyle is situated next to the Highland Boundary Fault and surrounded by a marshy expanse

Grave of Netta Emily Fornario

known as 'The Moat of Scotland'. The mighty peaks of the Eildon Hills near Melrose in the Scottish Borders, close to the Bride current, are associated with the 13th-century bard Thomas the Rhymer. Having been seduced by a fairy queen at the Eildon Tree at Halloween, he follows her to Elfland where he stays for a year, only to find upon his return that seven years had elapsed.

The Graveyard of Kings and the Willing Sacrifice

Returning to St Columba's Shrine, we tracked the Bride serpent leaving the abbey precinct through a circular stone well located in front of the main door that supposedly dates from the 16th century. Next to it are the remains of other bullaun stones, one made of red granite with two hollowed-out cavities, similar to the clach-bràth in the museum, perhaps used by the ancient inhabitants of Iona to enhance fertility within the land.

Well at Iona Abbey with the remains of a bullaun stone

We noticed a wonderful carving of a dragon above the main entrance, which seemed to point the way to St Oran's Chapel, as if alerting us to something significant. Perhaps it was no coincidence that Bride continues to the chapel along the 'Road of the Dead', the finest medieval paved road in Europe. It was an old Christian processional way along which the coffins of kings and clan chiefs were carried from Martyrs' Bay just south of the main jetty.

Set within a walled graveyard with a finely carved chevron doorway is the tiny St Oran's Chapel, the oldest ecclesiastical building on Iona. However, there is no firm evidence as to its date of construction.

A curious story attached to the chapel's foundation mentions a statement made by Columba to his monks, '*It is well for us that our roots should go underground here… It is permitted to you that one of you go under the earth of the island to consecrate it.*' The monk Oran replies, '*If thou wouldst accept me, I am ready for that.*' And so Oran was interred alive as a human sacrifice, but after three days, Columba ordered the tomb to be opened to see his dear friend's face for one last time. To the horror of those present, Oran suddenly opened his eyes and said, '*There is no great wonder in death, nor is hell what it has been described.*' Embarrassed at his unchristian revelations, Columba ordered him to be immediately reburied.[27]

Carving of a dragon at the entrance of Iona Abbey

Odhráin, or Oran, was believed to be one of St Columba's closest followers. However, Adomnan, his biographer, fails to mention him, perhaps because of his revelations about 'life after death'. This type of willing sacrifice is not uncommon. Many early cultures, such as the British Druids, Aztecs, Toltecs and the Mayans, regarded these acts as essential to save their people from disaster, disease or famine while in the spirit world. Indeed another version of Oran's story says that he willingly sacrificed himself to heal a blight afflicting the northern parts of Britain on the condition that Columba named the chapel after him. There may be some truth to this story as great plagues swept Ireland and parts of Scotland in the 6th century.

St Oran's Chapel and Reilig Odhráin marking the Holy Axis alignment

George Macleod claims that Oran was the last of the Druids, who may have joined Columba's community, having lived on the island before the saint arrived. However, Irish records say Oran from Latteragh in Ireland founded a Christian community on Iona in 548, fifteen years before Columba. Interestingly, Oran's burial and resurrection after three days seem a common theme amongst god-king heroes, including Jesus.

This story of Oran being buried in the earth under the chapel seemed reminiscent of many of the node points of Lugh and Bride. The very first node lies confined under a tower on Inner Farne by a well, and the second is buried beneath the Keep at Bamburgh Castle under a well, where in legend Lancelot lies entombed in a subterranean cave. The node at Rosslyn Chapel disappears inside an underground vault housing the tombs of the St Clair knights. The node at Castlelaw Hill Fort is deep inside an Earth House, the node at Torphichen connects with an underground circular chamber beneath the Preceptory and the cell at Eileach an Naoimh is also set into the earth. We believe these underground places of power were perfect for connecting to the underworld.

The name of St Oran's graveyard, Reilig Odhráin, refers to the burial place of kings, a site far older than Columba's monastic community. Here the Bride serpent current and the Holy Axis meet, which seems an appropriate place to anchor this spiritual Orion/Virgo line in the west, with its associated cosmic warrior god/goddess energy. Although the island has many tales of male heroes, it is also the spiritual home of Bride, who, in local legend, lived on the slopes of Dûn'I tending her sheep. Another bizarre tale says that angels transported her from Iona to Bethlehem on the night of the nativity, where she became Christ's foster mother.[28]

The royal graveyard also marks the island's spiritual heart. Many myths surround its sanctity, including its soil, considered so hallowed that the sins of whoever lay there would be automatically cleansed. Is this why so many kings and warriors desired to be buried there? A survey conducted in 1549 listed sixty-one royal burials, including forty-eight Scottish kings, eight Norwegian, four Irish and one French king. Ecgfrith, King of Northumbria. Kenneth McAlpin, the infamous King of the Picts and first King of Scotland, King Constantine III, Macbeth, King Malcolm II, Somerled, Lord of the Isles and his son Ranald are all buried here.

The grave of Scottish politician John Smith is also in the royal cemetery. He was the Labour leader from July 1992 until his death from a sudden heart attack in May 1994. At this point, Tony Blair took over the leadership and created New Labour, a key turning point in the history of British politics.

We dowsed the Bride current inside the chapel, crossing with another unidentified female energy line emerging from the ruins of St Mary's Chapel just to the east of here. The atmosphere inside felt serene and beautiful, and like Rosslyn's Grail chapel, we sensed the presence of a spiritual 'doorway'. As we sat on the flow of the two feminine

St Oran's Chapel interior

earth currents, with the node point close by at the abbey and the alignment a few feet away in the royal cemetery, there was no better place to contemplate our amazing journey.

Although our Holy Axis adventure was nearly at an end, we felt this pilgrimage reminiscent of a personal quest for the Grail. We also felt privileged that the spirit of Albion had chosen us all those years ago to rediscover this important spiritual route through Northumberland and the Neck of Scotland. Perhaps it wanted us to recognise the sacred significance of the line and its male and female dragon energies and attend to the healing of the many sites along their path. It certainly felt as if we had uncovered a faulty circuit in the earth energy matrix of Britain that had been damaged and forgotten long ago and needed repairing. Perhaps it is no accident that we have 'reconnected' the Holy Axis with the energy matrix of Albion at this time.

A few yards south of the chapel, Bride passes through MacLean's Cross, erected in 1500, where we noticed the carvings of two serpents fighting. The image of fighting dragons reminded us of the famous legend of two brothers, Lludd and Llefelys, sons of the British Iron Age King Beli the Great, who came to the aid of Britain when plagues befell its lands. According to the tale, a terrible scream arose every night on Mayday over the hearth of every house in the land. Such was the menace of the scream that it pierced the hearts of every man, woman and child and struck them with such terror that it made men weak and women barren and the land and animals sick. A wise and intelligent man told the princes that the cause of the plagues was two dragons fighting.

In order to stop the dragons and heal this sickness, a pit had to be dug by Lludd at the centre of his kingdom, where a tub full of the best mead covered by a piece of linen was placed at the very bottom. Lludd kept watch over the pit on the evening of Mayday, where he soon witnessed two dragons fighting in the air in the shape of hideous creatures. After becoming weary, the dragons dropped into the pit and fell into the vat of mead. The piece of linen dragged them to the bottom whereupon they drank the intoxicating liquor and fell asleep. After transforming into pigs, the dragons were transported by Lludd to the strongest place in the kingdom and buried in a stone coffin. Llefelys assured him that as long as they stayed entombed in that place, no such plague would ever blight the island of Britain again.

The health of the land and its people was positively transformed by the dragons' subjugation, transformation and confinement, which we believe is symbolically portrayed by the many underground nodes of the Lugh and Bride earth dragons/serpents.

Bride then directed us to the organic gardens of the Argyll Hotel, abundant with healthy vegetables and fruit, which we heartily enjoyed while dining there that evening.

The Nunnery and the Hill of Angels

Just west of the Argyll Hotel, the female current is also attracted to the summer blooms in the delightful garden of the Nunnery. As we settled down on one of the benches that overlooked this idyllic scene, we felt the pink granite walls enriched this hallowed place. The substantial ruins include remnants of cloisters, a nave and the chancel, all showing signs of fine stonemasonry, particularly on the surviving columns and capitals.

The Augustinian nunnery built in 1203 was dedicated to St Mary the Virgin, said to be the best preserved in Britain. Its first prioress was Bethoc, daughter of Somerled and sister of Ranald. The female community here, known as the Sisters of St Augustine, led a contemplative and secluded life and followed the teachings of St Augustine of Hippo. They wore black habits like the Nine Maidens of Avalon, perhaps reflecting the local name for their holy abode, *eaglais dhubh* or 'the black church'. In contrast, Iona's Benedictine abbey church was named *eaglais mhor,* 'the great church'. The nunnery was also the favoured place of retirement and burial for women of noble birth from Argyll and the Western Isles.

The Nunnery, Iona

As soon as we set foot inside the nunnery, Bride made her presence known, flowing diagonally through its centre to the little St Ronan's Chapel within the ruins, where islanders worshipped between 1250 and 1560.

Excavations beneath it exposed an earlier 8th-century chapel, with burials of an even earlier date, possibly from around the time of St Columba. The graves found at each excavation level were almost all women and children. On display inside the chapel are memorial stones from these early burials and fragments of masonry from the old nunnery.

Where Bride exits the nunnery's south-facing wall, we find a worn and weathered carving of a sheela-na-gig, similar to one at Kilvickeon Church on Mull on the Lugh current. Many religious houses from the medieval period display these pagan symbols, said to represent the fertility of the Earth Goddess. Here, within the very last building visited by the Bride serpent of the Holy Axis, we felt a deep interconnectedness with the divine feminine and nature.

Reluctantly leaving the idyllic surroundings of the nunnery garden, we followed a track west through the centre of the island, which eventually leads to an area called A' Mhachair, and a beautiful beach in the 'Bay at the Back of the Ocean'. During our stroll, we were lulled by the enchanting landscape with its spring flowers and quietly grazing sheep. Then, suddenly, our senses were rudely awakened by the strange noise of rasping and croaking. We looked around us, but nothing seemed to point to the source of this curious sound. Later we discovered it was an extremely secretive bird called the Corncrake that prefers to hide away in tall vegetation.

As we approached A' Mhachair, we picked up Bride crossing to a large elongated mound on our left called *Cnoc nam Aingeal* or 'Hill of the Angels', another one of Iona's ethereal places. Here, a monk secretly observed Columba communing with angels on its summit after the saint had told the monk not to follow him. The angels were aware of the monk and informed Columba of his presence, but rather than punishing him, he asked the monk to keep silent about what he had witnessed. Only after the saint died was the secret revealed. This area is known

Sheela-na-gig, The Nunnery, Iona

locally as *Sithean Mor*, the abode of the island's fairies. The mound was revered as a special place of sanctity and ceremony long before St Columba came to these shores. Pennant wrote that islanders rode around the hill on horseback on St Michael's Day, a practice that survived when the island's ancient inhabitants worshipped their sun god here.[29]

Just west of the mound is *Camas Cuil an t-Saimh* or 'Bay at the Back of the Ocean', where Bride leaves Iona's shores. Bordered by a stretch of wildflower meadow and common grazing for sheep and cows, this is a beautiful spot to observe the sun setting into the sea at the summer solstice. The beach is a vast expanse of white sand with

Hill of Angels

Camas Cuil an t-Saimh or Bay at the Back of the Ocean, Iona

its green and pink rocks and is our favourite place on the island, where we are often entertained by the antics of the wading birds such as the oyster-catcher, named in Gaelic *gille-brigde*, meaning the servant of Bride.

As we strolled along the beach, we found many of the green serpentine healing stones smoothed into pebbles by the sea. The stones originate from some of the oldest rocks in the world and the seams of serpentine found within the Lewisian Gneiss are made of a highly paramagnetic crystalline structure that creates an aura of balance and peace. Today, the larger pieces of Iona green stone or marble, known by some locals as 'Columba's stones', are crafted into fine jewellery and ornaments. The smaller paler sea-polished pebbles are known as 'Columba's tears'. In medieval times, a large green marble altar slab was discovered abandoned amongst the ruins in the abbey. Over time, local crofters and fishermen chipped small pieces from it, believing the stone had healing properties and could protect against shipwreck, fire and miscarriage.

In her article *Iona, Mystic Island*, Iona Miller says the unique Iona geology emits magnetic energy that thins the veil between planes and causes much of the psychic phenomena experienced here. She writes:

> 'The metamorphic nature of the granitic Lewisian Gneiss, combined with earth fold magnetic fields, creates a crystalline lattice energy that is very dense and acts as a receptor to the charged harmonic projections emitted from Staffa. These energy frequencies that bombard Iona segregate in certain pockets into pristine frequencies that correlate to pure musical notes and accordingly to the chakras.'[30]

Miller cites a story told to a Scottish Freemason by an RAF pilot, who explained that *'every time he flew over Iona, the compass would spin around and be useless.'*

Iona's geology attracts many invisible lines of terrestrial power; some say the whole island is a vortex or energy accumulator. One of the most renowned writers on the occult was Dion Fortune (1890-1946). She explored many of Britain's sacred sites during her lifetime and understood the power of these places and how humans could manipulate them. In *Aspects of Occultism*, published in 1962, she wrote:

> 'Whenever a place has had prayers and concentrated desires directed towards it, it forms an electrical vortex that gathers to itself a force, and it is for a time a coherent body that

can be felt and used by man. It is round these bodies of force that shrines, temples, and in later days churches are built; they are the Cups that receive the Cosmic downpouring focused on each particular place.'[31]

Sitting amongst the dunes in the Bay at the Back of the Ocean, we waved Bride off as she gathered pace to start her journey across the vast Atlantic Ocean to the distant lands of North America. It was hard to believe that this long, eventful and fascinating journey across Northumberland and Scotland following the Holy Axis and the Bride and Lugh serpents had finally ended – although, as we were to discover later, Bride and Lugh have one final connection to the British Isles in the island of Tiree. (See Appendix A)

The island of Iona is both magical and ethereal, the tangibility of other planes or dimensions of existence ever-present, leaving you with a sense that communication between the higher or lower realms is possible. It is a place where the Grail energy of the divine feminine is at its most potent. Many regard the Grail as an object, but it is more likely esoteric knowledge spiritually attained through the trials and tribulations

Path to A' Mhachair

of life's challenges. The Grail quest tests our spiritual resolve to better understand the mysteries of the Universe. Even if the finding of the Grail is never achieved, we can still be elevated and positively changed by the experience of the quest itself. Modern pilgrimage is an excellent opportunity to feel at one with the land, the adventure and the knowledge gained along the way being an essential part of the journey.

As the sun began to set on our Holy Axis quest, we returned to the abbey one last time to contemplate on the final node inside St Columba's Shrine. Here we visualised Bride at the very western point of the Holy Axis, representing the celestial Grail archetype Virgo and Aquarius, holding up the cup or chalice. She then feeds pure golden healing light from the chalice through the spear of the Holy Axis to the wounded spiritual warrior at Bamburgh. He is represented by Lugh, Urien and Oswald, who symbolise the cosmic Orion, receiving Bride's healing. Likewise, as the curative light travels along the male and female serpent lines, it heals and revitalises the scars of the many wounded sites along their path.

By walking these sacred routes, communicating with the Mother Goddess and spirit guardians at holy shrines, stones and mounds and appreciating their mystical relationship with the heavenly or cosmic realms, we will receive healing, wisdom and knowledge to help us with our own spiritual growth. But, more importantly, it will enable us to focus our heart centres towards the nurturing and preservation of Mother Earth. The countryside is alive and intelligent and responds to our emotions and thoughts. By restoring the Grail archetype, we can heal the land.

In some small way, we hope that our pilgrimage succeeded in recovering the 'wastelands' along the Holy Axis as we rekindled its vital force and re-established the dragon power within the lands of Northumberland and Scotland. By doing so, the divine curative powers of Bride and her chalice will continue to reverberate along the spear of this important axis of power and restore the masculine warrior energy of Lugh and that of Albion.

---

1. Phillips, G. & Keatman, M. 1984. *The Green Stone*. Grafton Books, London.
2. Stirling, S. A. 2012. *The King Arthur Conspiracy: How a Scottish Prince Became a Mythical Hero*. The History Press Ltd, Cheltenham.
3.13.15. McNeill, F. M. 1959 *Iona: A History of the Island*. Blackie Publishers, Glasgow.
4. 29. Pennant, T. 1769. *A Tour in Scotland*. (Illustrated, 2019). Origin, Bristol.
5. https://biblioscout.net/article/10.25162/historia-2022-0008
6. https://philological.cal.bham.ac.uk/boece/1e.html
7.16.19.24.26.27. Holder, G. 2007. *The Guide to Mysterious Iona and Staffa*. Tempus Publishing Ltd, Stroud.
8. Lacey, B.1998 *Manus O'Donnell's Life of Colum Cille*. Four Courts Press Ltd, Dublin.
9. Macleod, F. 1982. *Iona*. Floris Books, Edinburgh.
10. Elder I H (1962) Celt, Druid and Culdee. Covenant Publishing, London.
11.18. Adomnan of Iona, Richard Sharpe, (Introduction, Translator) 1995. *Life of St Columba*. Penguin Classics, London.
12. Oram R (2001) The Kings & Queens of Scotland. Tempus Publishing, Stroud.
14. Forlong, J.G.R. 1906. *Faiths of man a cyclopædia of religions*. Gyan Books Pvt. Ltd, Delhi, India.

17. https://iona-placenames.glasgow.ac.uk/in-search-of-the-lost-wells-of-iona-guest-blog-by-mike-small/

20. Knight, C. Lomas, R. 2003. *The Book of Hiram: Freemasonry, Venus and the Secret Key to the Life of Jesus.* Stirling, New York.

21. https://canmore.org.uk/site/21649/iona-early-christian-monastery

22. https://www.yourirish.com/folklore/four-cycles-of-irish-mythology

23. https://www.sacred-texts.com/neu/celt/cml/cml09.htm

25. Swire, Otta. F. 1964. *Inner Hebrides and Their Legends.* Harper Collins, London.

28. McNeill, F. M. 1990. *An Iona Anthology.* New Iona Press, Iona.

30. http://ionamiller2010.iwarp.com/custom3_5.html

31. Fortune, D. 2000. *Aspects of Occultism.* Gareth Knight (Introduction). Red Wheel/Weiser, Newburyport, Massachusetts.

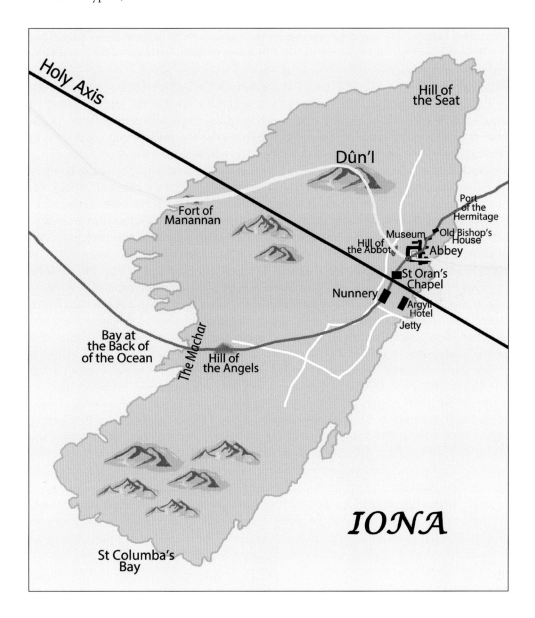

Appendix A

Tiree, the Isle of Healing

Not long after we finished writing and researching the Holy Axis, both Caroline and I received information through dreams and intuition, just as we did at the start of our quest. However, this time it concerned a node that we had missed on the Holy Axis attached to a circular stone feature. After going through all the locations previously visited on the line, we suddenly realised it was a new site yet to be discovered.

At first, I thought it might be another of the Farne Islands beyond Inner Farne, but our dowsing said no. But then we noticed that just to the northwest of Iona, the Holy Axis alignment passes close to the small Outer Hebridean Island of Tiree. When we remote dowsed over a map of Tiree for this elusive node, we received a resounding yes.

Curiously, Bamburgh is where the Holy Axis and the node of the serpent lines first meet in the east, and Iona is the final meeting of the alignment and currents in the west. So, the auxiliary node on Inner Farne beyond the alignment's starting point is in symmetry with the additional node on Tyree beyond the end of the alignment.

A last-minute visit to the island and a preliminary dowse around the southern shore of Tiree indicated that Bride arrives from Iona through *Ceann a Mhara* (Head of the Sea), the most southwesterly headland next to Balephuil Bay. Here, close to the rocky shore, the female serpent visits the scant remains of a medieval chapel dedicated to St Patrick, which lies within an early Celtic Christian monastic site complete with beehive cells, a well, and an enclosing wall. Once called Teampull Phadruig or 'Temple Patrick', the chapel had a square altar that survived until the end of the 18th century. William Reeves recorded in 1854 two small crosses and a nearby mound bearing an oval-walled enclosure, which may have contained a larger cross. Just below the chapel, Reeves also observed a small well in the form of a natural marshy spring near the shore, although there was no trace of it when archaeologists from the Society of Antiquaries of Scotland visited in 1977.[1]

The wild solitude of this site surrounded by the raw elements reminded us of Eileach an Naoimh on the Garvellachs between Craignish and Mull and probably dates to a similar 6th-century period. The well interested us as it is renowned for its healing properties, and indeed Bride passes over what we believe are traces of its curative waters. This is the kind of place we love, for few people know of its history, yet the site seems to have been a significant place for the early Celtic monks. The holy well was probably the focus of the monastery and may have been a renowned healing sanctuary and another candidate for an Avalon in the west of Scotland.

Lugh meanwhile enters 3 miles further east, where we discovered him passing through an old graveyard with an ancient cross just to the north of Balemartine. A notice board here informs us that it was probably the site of Campus Luinge, a monastery founded by Baithene, an associate of St Columba, in 565 CE as a retreat for wayward monks. A parish church dedicated to St Columba existed there from the

13th to the 19th centuries that served the medieval parish of Sorobaidh or Soroby. Iona Abbey, where the currents last formed a node, held this retreat until the Reformation. The graveyard became the burial ground of the chiefs of Clan Maclean, rulers of Tiree from 1390 to 1680. The 7th-century MacLean's Cross on the Lugh flow is now very worn but once showed delicate carvings on both sides including serpents.

Few trees grow on Tiree's flat landscape, and its tallest hill, Beinn Hough, is no more than 390 ft (119 m) above sea level. However, the island, the most westerly of the Inner Hebrides, is renowned for having a warmer, dryer climate than Iona, submerged in the warm Gulf Stream and therefore more fertile. Its name derives from *Tir Iodh*, meaning 'the land of corn' and St Columba is said to have used Tiree as a bread basket for his monastery on Iona. The island's earliest settlers, arriving around 7000 BCE, left behind stone circles, numerous standing stones, cairns and brochs. Bronze Age pottery remains and tools dating from 800 BCE have also been uncovered on the island.

From the graveyard, Lugh meanders northwest to a place enticingly called Ceosabh (Cross), where he passes through a tall standing stone before arriving at the island's Parish Church beside a crossroads. The church has no great pedigree, dating only to the mid-19th century, but it is Tiree's main church and entices the energy of Lugh's current, which taps into the spiritual consciousness of the island. According to the church website, in 1772, the Duke of Argyll instructed his factor on Tiree to convert a house in Scarinish into a church and was later enlarged. However, by the mid-19th century, it was considered too remote for most of the island's parishioners and abandoned for a new site in a more central position.

Lugh then heads towards Beinn Hough and its secondary peak Cnoc Fhithich, which means 'Hill of the Raven', to a ruined stone cairn and two stone circles known as The Hough. One of the stone rings to the northeast measures 131 ft (40 m) across and consists of eleven recumbent stones and the stump of another. The smaller circle has only a couple of megaliths left standing and is closer to the remains of a stone cairn. Here we dowsed Lugh beginning to narrow to the familiar node in the middle of the northeast circle with Bride arriving from the southwest, passing through both stone circles. The site takes its name from a Norse word for a burial and Beinn Hough's other peak refers to the bird of death in the form of the raven. I believe the stone circles and the mound may refer to a sacred place of initiation and burial for the ancient inhabitants of Tiree, a place to connect with the otherworld. The stone circles are similar to those we encountered on the Bride current in College Valley in Northumberland and may have served a similar purpose in drawing down the spirits of the island's mother mountain.

Before meeting Lugh at the Hough circles, the female current took us to a large standing stone called *Creag an Fhoimheir* or the Middleton Stone near Barrapol. The 1.6 m tall stone marks her route between Ceann a Mhara and the node point. From the node, Bride continues north through Kilmoluaig to the eastern shores of Loch Bhasapoll. Her primary focus is Cornaigmore Farm, the site of Kilbride Chapel. According to William Reeves in *The Island of Tiree*, written in 1854, '...*there is a spot on the island still called Kilbride, that is "Brigid's Church." It is on the north side, in the farm of Cornaigmore, and human remains which are found here indicate a cemetery where a small chapel is known to have existed, the walls of which were removed to help in building some adjacent cabins.*'[2] A few gravestones belonging to its cemetery are still visible in the area. A modern chapel, now abandoned, stands just to the east of it.

Here we have the first chapel on the female serpent of the holy Axis dedicated to her namesake and the last before she leaves the British Isles. We honoured her departure at an incredibly long bay of white shelly sand called Tràigh Chornaig, said to be one of the finest beaches in Scotland, a fitting place to wave off our beloved Bride.

Apart from the node, our main highlight here was Temple Patrick, the sanctuary of healing built around a holy spring. Symbolically, the island's curative waters feed into Virgo/Bride's grail cauldron as she pours water along the spear of Lugh/Holy Axis from Iona to heal the wounded king and Albion.

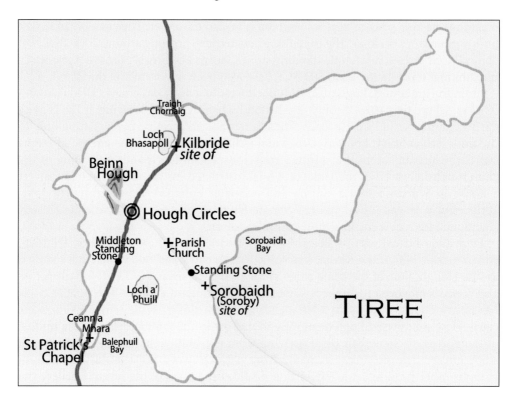

1. https://canmore.org.uk/site/21477/tiree-ceann-a-mhara
2. https://electricscotland.com/books/islandoftiree.pdf

Index

The Power of Centre

Rediscovering Ancient Cosmology and the Celtic Goddess at the Omphalos Sites of the British Isles

Gary Biltcliffe & Caroline Hoare

by Gary Biltcliffe & Caroline Hoare

Priced £17.95 plus p&p
Published March 2018

The spiritual travelogue of Albion and its earth mysteries continues with Gary and Caroline's new book, which explores places of power and forgotten pilgrim routes through the omphalos places of Britain and Ireland. Their research uncovers influential psychic centres linked to the mystery of the axis mundi and royal bloodlines. Also analysed, is their historical association with the oracle and the cult of the goddess.

This book is dedicated to those who love the sacred landscapes of Britain and Ireland, including earth energies, lost knowledge, Celtic cosmology, psychic questing and the mystery of alignments and meridians. As you connect with these old centres of power, it will also help guide you with your own spiritual growth and to experience a reconnection with your god and goddess within.

> *The authors carry forward some of the themes from their Spine of Albion saga - and wind in more than a few memes engendered by Hamish Miller - to produce a radically novel and quite compelling storyline. The premise is that all places have a Centre. Some of these are essentially geopolitical but, as often as not, they are also the critical core location of a community. The Power of Centre will have you scratching around for OS maps you never knew you needed, and trawling the internet for places you've never heard of.*
>
> **Nigel Twinn, author & dowser**

> *Reading this book takes one on a series of pilgrimages that cannot fail to get the travel bug itching.*
>
> **Northern Earth**

> *All-in-all, this is one of the most fascinating and well-researched books of its ilk that is out there.*
>
> **Network of Leyhunters**

Order a signed copy by the authors at www.belinusline.com

Mysterious Portland

Revealing the Sacred Landscape and Legacy of Britain's Masonic Isle

by Gary Biltcliffe

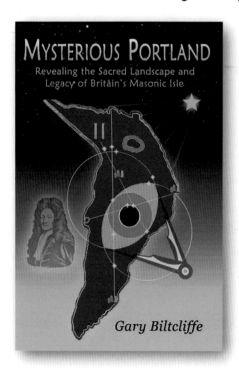

Priced £16.99
Paperback
Published 2022

All over the world, there are islands like Portland in the county of Dorset strategically positioned along the sea coast that were utilised from the earliest periods of human history for religious purposes and trade and yet only legends are left to testify their former glory. It was Portland's missing legacy that set me on a quest to the discovery of a great mystery and the publication of *The Spirit of Portland: Revelations of a Sacred Isle* in 2009 and a new edition in 2016. Recently Portland has revealed more of its enigmas which has stretched my beliefs to the very limits and inspired this new revision with a new title and new pieces of the puzzle. There is a series of five updated walks with maps at the end of this book to help ground the information and connect you to the real Spirit of Portland.

Even the sceptical must acknowledge the thorough research and considerable scholarship that have gone into the book, and it is true that Portland holds more secrets than most outsiders appreciate. **Dorset Life Magazine**

Available from www.belinusline.com.
Kindle Version available from Amazon